# The Psychology of Aging
Theory, Research, and Practice

# The Psychology of Aging
## Theory, Research, and Practice

**Janet Belsky**
*Herbert H. Lehman College*

**Brooks/Cole Publishing Company**
*Monterey, California*

Brooks/Cole Publishing Company
A Division of Wadsworth, Inc.

Printed in the United State of America

10 9 8 7 6 5 4 3

**Library of Congress Cataloging in Publication Data**

Belsky, Janet, [date]
   The psychology of aging.

   Bibliography: p.
   Includes index.
   1. Aging—Psychological aspects. 2. Aged—Psychology.
3. Aged—Mental health services. I. Title.
BF724.55.A35B44   1984      155.67      83-20923
ISBN 0-534-02868-3

Project Development Editor: Marquita Flemming
Production Editor: Candyce Cameron
Manuscript Editor: Rephah Berg
Permissions Editor: Carline Haga
Interior Design: Debbie Wunsch
Cover Design: Vicki Van Deventer
Cover Photo: Courtesy of Fundamental Photographs, New York
Art Coordinator: Judy MacDonald
Interior Illustration: John Foster
Photo Editor: Jude Blamer
Typesetting: Computer Typesetting Services, Burbank, California
Printing and Binding: Halliday Lithograph, West Hanover, Massachusetts

*For David and Thomas Alan, who make the future special.*
*To my grandmother, Lillian Sheerr,*
*for her special example of what the future can be.*

# Preface

The need for this book became apparent when I unsuccessfully looked for a text for my undergraduate course in gerontological psychology. There were many books covering adulthood and aging, but very few were devoted primarily to late life. No existing text seemed broad enough in scope, comprehensively examining both aging research and practice. And, none was both firmly psychological in orientation and also clearly appropriate for students new to the field.

For the past three years I have had the unusual opportunity to work almost full-time designing my ideal book. *The Psychology of Aging: Theory, Research, and Practice* is unique in giving a balanced overview of the field from the dual perspectives of academician and practicing clinician. It covers the classical and current studies in the traditional areas of gerontological psychology. In addition, each topic presented ends with an extensive intervention section illustrating clinical applications of the research findings. My goals throughout are to show how psychological research translates into practice and to offer a full picture of the far-ranging contributions of academic and applied psychology to the understanding of late life.

This is a book written to interest introductory students. I have tried to make it informal and personal in tone, and conversational in flavor. Technical jargon is avoided. Concepts are clearly spelled out. At the same time, I have tried to write an intelligent book, one that is well-grounded scientifically, treats the reader as an equal, and will appeal to readers at a variety of levels of expertise. Rather than just listing results, I carefully describe the procedures, biases, limitations, and implications of the major studies. Whenever possible, I evaluate the accuracy and usefulness of theories, and explore empirical evidence for the effectiveness of clinical interventions. My emphasis is as much on instilling an evaluative attitude as on presenting the facts. I hope this book will offer a realistic portrait of what we do know and will provide readers with the tools and critical framework to question and evaluate future theory, research, and practice in the psychology of aging.

Because I am a clinical psychologist, my aim has also been to write a book that highlights the personal experience of late life, one that gets students to empathize with the aging individual and shows concretely how the research applies to older adults. To make the abstract content of the psychology of aging come alive in an immediate and personal way, the material in each chapter (except the first) is illustrated by an extended clinical vignette that begins the chapter. This clinical case is then referred to repeatedly throughout the subsequent discussion, graphically depicting the impact of the scientific findings on the individual.

The vignettes and the concluding intervention sections give structure and coherent form to each chapter. In addition, the book as a whole is planned to cohere and progress in an orderly way. In contrast to some other texts, I have designed the first chapter to be a true introduction. It spells out themes, principles, and concepts that are then stressed continually throughout the book. In succeeding chapters, the major content areas in the psychology of aging are given equal weight. Two chapters each are devoted to physical processes, cognition, personality, and psychopathology. The characters in a particular vignette are followed in a given two-chapter part. The book concludes with a chapter on death and dying. Behavioral aspects of chronic disease and health care, sensory processes, intelligence, creativity, age-related personality change, sexuality, and the life transitions of retirement, widowhood, and institutionalization are among the topics discussed in particular depth. Because of my clinical background, I give unusually detailed attention to the diagnosis and treatment of late-life psychological disorders.

In addition to the need to critically evaluate theory, research, and practice and to link scientific knowledge with appropriate interventions, another major theme pervades this book—the need to be open-minded, tolerant, and eclectic in approaching the psychological literature and in understanding older adults. Above all, I have tried to write a fair and humanitarian text, one that avoids exclusively championing a single psychological perspective or a particular way to age. I hope this book teaches the value of diversity in theory and practice and conveys to readers an appreciation for the diversity that is the hallmark of late life.

A long series of teachers are indirectly responsible for the ideas expressed in the chapters to come: professors at the University of Pennsylvania and the University of Chicago; psychology supervisors at P&PI; Michael Reese Medical Center; my colleagues and the residents at the Philadelphia Geriatric Center; and students at Lehman College. I am also grateful to the instructors who have directly enriched the following pages by their thoughtful reviews: Helene Ballmer, California State University, Fullerton; Marvin Belsky, New York University Medical Center; Arlene Bronzaft, Lehman College; Alicia Cook, Colorado State University; Stephany Diana, Mott Community College; Allen Fay; Nancy Gonchar, Montefiore Medical Center, New York; Beverley Gounard, State University of New York; Kathy Gribbon, Maricopa County Hospital; Rosalind Hayes; Rosemary Johnson, Arizona State University; Marvin W. Kahn, University of Arizona; Rosalie Kane, Rand Corporation; Regina Kulys, University of Illinois at Chicago Circle; Jeanne C. Mellinger, George Mason University; Paul E. Panek, Eastern Illinois University; Eleanor Simon, California State University, Dominguez Hills; W. Fred Stultz, California Polytechnic State University; Michael G. Walraven, Jackson Community College; and William Whelihan, Philadelphia Geriatric Center. Dr. Rosalie Kane's suggestions appear prominently, as she carefully read the unfinished manuscript three times during its preparation.

It has been a pleasure to know and work with the competent staff members at Brooks/Cole—in particular, Marquita Flemming, C. Deborah Laughton, Candy Cameron, and Rephah Berg—the talented editors, and Vicki Van Deventer, the designer, with whom I have worked most closely. In the end, though, I would never have attempted this undertaking had I not been lucky in life to have a person who always believed I could accomplish what has often seemed an impossibly difficult task. My husband, David, is the one truly responsible for my writing this book.

*Janet Belsky*

# Contents

# PART TWO

# *PHYSICAL PROCESSES*   *35*

**PART THREE**

# *COGNITION*   101

CHAPTER FOUR
## *Intelligence and the IQ Test*   102

CHAPTER FIVE
## *Intellectual Processes: Memory and Creativity*   127

# PART FOUR

# *PERSONALITY*   151

CHAPTER SIX

## *Internal Aspects of the Person: Change, Consistency, and Some Specifics*   152

CHAPTER SEVEN

## *External Aspects of the Person: Life Transitions*   184

**PART FIVE**

# *PSYCHOPATHOLOGY* 223

**PART SIX**

# *DEATH AND DYING*  *293*

CHAPTER TEN

## *At the End of Life*  *294*

# PART ONE

# BASIC CONCEPTS

# CHAPTER ONE

# Stereotypes, Realities: The Psychological Study of Late Life

The following description is a grim characterization of the mythical attributes of old age. It clearly illustrates the unhappy picture often associated with late life.

Older people think and move slowly. They do not think as well as they used to or as creatively. They are bound to themselves and their past and can no longer change or grow. They can learn neither well nor swiftly, and even if they could, they would not wish to. Tied to their personal traditions and growing conservatism, they dislike innovations and are not disposed to favor new ideas. Not only can they not move forward, they often move backward. They enter a second childhood, often caught in increasing egocentricity and demanding more from their environment than they are willing to give to it. Sometimes they become "more like themselves," caricatures of their lifelong personalities. They become irritable and cantankerous, yet shallow and enfeebled. They live in their past. They are behind the times. They are aimless and wandering of mind, reminiscing and garrulous. Indeed, they are studies in decline, pictures of mental and physical failure. They have lost and cannot replace friends, spouse, jobs, status, power, influence, income. They are often stricken by diseases that restrict their movement, their enjoyment of food, the pleasures of well-being. Sexual interest and activity decline. The body shrinks; so does the flow of blood to the brain, which does not utilize oxygen or sugar at the same rate as formerly. Feeble, uninteresting, they await death, a burden to society, to family, and to the self.[1]

If we too bring this initial stereotyped assessment to the psychology of aging (an area of inquiry also called *geropsychology* or *gerontological psychology*), we are far from alone. A variety of surveys show that Americans give old age top billing as the worst time of life (Bennett & Eckman, 1973). People also unite in sharing a well-developed conception about the specific characteristics we label "old" (Rodin & Langer, 1980). Defined negative ideas, like those so starkly spelled out by the set of statements above, are equally held by some medical personnel who must often work with older adults (Solomon & Vickers, 1979).

True, wisdom is one positive attribute that has been associated with old age since ancient times. But the assumption that aging means misfortune also has a history that goes back to ancient Greece (Dangott & Nallia, 1977). Despite a current effort to counter this view in North America, it prevails to the present. A recent survey revealed that Americans feel just as negatively about the elderly and about being old as we did 30 years ago (Solomon & Vickers, 1979). It is a distaste learned early, which then persists. One group of researchers (Jantz, Seefeldt, Galper, & Serock, 1976) found that nearly 90% of a large group of children polled saw older people as passive, unattractive, sick, and weak. The elderly do view themselves less negatively than do children or those under 65. But they participate

[1]Adapted from "Successful Aging and the Role of the Life Review," by R. N. Butler. In *Journal of the American Geriatrics Society*, 1974, *22*. Copyright 1974 by the American Geriatrics Society. Reprinted by permission.

even more vehemently in the shared aversion for the stereotypic, negative traits attributed to their life stage (Rodin & Langer, 1980).

The children questioned by Jantz and associates reacted with horror to the prospect of ever being old. Most were convinced they would never reach that undesired state. Their responses (for example, "Oh no, not me, *I'm* not getting old") have a sad echo at the opposite end of the life span. Older adults too may be reluctant to attribute old age to themselves.

Many people cling to a self-definition of being middle-aged long after the chronological clock makes it clear a reassessment is overdue. In a study of adults 60 and over (Bultena & Powers, 1978), this phenomenon became strikingly apparent. The researchers asked their subjects whether they thought of themselves as middle-aged, elderly, or old. A full 75% checked the first alternative, only 6% the last. When the same group was interviewed ten years later, which made them all at least 70, the figures had changed somewhat, but not as much as we might expect. One-third still called themselves middle-aged. Only one-fourth felt they truly deserved the label "old."

A moment's reflection suggests a possible reason for these statistics. Perhaps it is simply too difficult to face up to the reality of having the negative attributes associated with old age. But another possibility was revealed when the investigators questioned their subjects further at the second test. Those who shifted their identity to *old* over the ten-year span attributed their changed self-definition to negative events, particularly impaired health. Those who maintained a self-perception of middle-aged saw themselves as better than their peers. They simply could not see a similarity between who they were and the image of the typical older person.

The other alternative is that the individuals who view themselves as middle-aged are right. They simply do not deserve the term *old*. But this forces us to reevaluate our assumptions. If only 25% of people over 70 actually fit the old-age characteristics considered universal, then we are misperceiving the vast number of elderly and in the process are doing them a great disservice. Rather than older people being out of touch with reality, we may be oblivious to the truth about them. We may thus be guilty, even though by accident, of a prejudice similar to racism or sexism: *ageism* (Butler, 1974, 1980), or negatively stereotyping those among us over 65.

Ageism, even more than racism or sexism, is personally self-defeating. When we practice this prejudice, we are negating who, with luck, we must become. So for pure self-protection it is imperative to find out the truth. A first step toward this goal is to get a bird's-eye view: a demographic portrait of older people; an insider's picture of their concerns.

## Demographic Realities

*Demography,* the study of populations, gives us a snapshot of the terrain of old age. It also illustrates another reason why our gaining this understanding is such a crucial task: The elderly among us are now an army. The most significant demographic trend in our century is the phenomenal increase in the ranks of older adults. (All statistics in this section are from Allan and Brotman, 1981.)

In 1900 only 4% of Americans were elderly. By 1980 there had been a radical shift. A full 11% of the population had passed 65, the birthday we arbitrarily desig- nate as the entry point of old age. The actual number of older adults had in- creased eightfold (from 3.1 million to 25 million).

As Figures 1-1 and 1-2 show, understanding late life is even more crucial be- cause this demographic shift is far from complete—it is a continuing trend. By the year 2000 some 32 million persons are expected to be over age 65 (12.2% of the total). The proportion will swell rapidly to a high point of 18.3% in 2030 and will then decline somewhat. This peak is due to the bulge in the population called the postwar baby boom. After the Second World War, actually from about 1946 to 1964, the birth rate soared. The baby-boom generation will all have turned 65 by 2030. At that time we will truly be a topheavy society, one dominated by the presence of older adults.

Two major influences are responsible for the phenomenon called "the aging of America." After the baby boom, in the late 1960s and 1970s, the birth rate dropped dramatically, effecting a rise in the proportion of the population 65 and

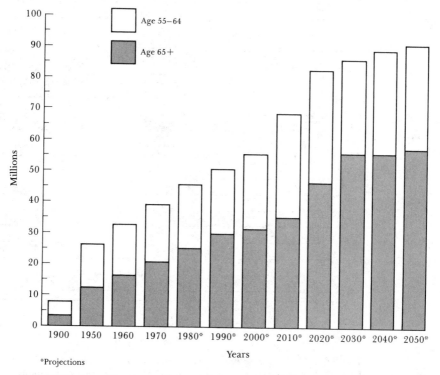

**FIGURE 1-1.** Number of persons aged 55 and over, 1900 and 1950– 2050. *(Source: From* Chartbook on Aging in America *by C. Allan and H. Brotman. Copyright © 1981 by the White House Conference on Aging.)*

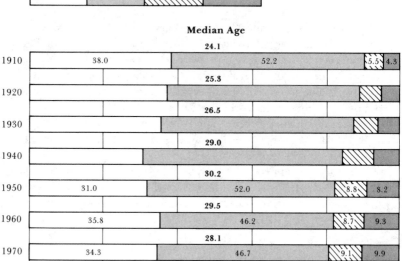

**FIGURE 1-2.** Percentage distribution of the total population by age group, 1910–2050. *(Source: From* Chartbook on Aging in America *by C. Allan and H. Brotman. Copyright © 1981 by the White House Conference on Aging.)*

above. More important, during this century life expectancy has jumped dramatically. Whereas only 40% of babies born in 1900 reached old age, 76% of babies born in 1978 are expected to live to age 65.

Life expectancy information also reveals the two most important statistical realities about the landscape of late life. The elderly population is disproportionately female, and increasingly, it contains more and more of the very old (those 75 and above). The social consequences of each demographic fact are great.

The first phenomenon, many more older women than men, is illustrated in Figure 1-3. Not only do Caucasians outlive people of other races, but now women, no matter what ethnic group, outlive men. Furthermore, although the disparity between non-Whites and Whites is on the wane, the male/female gap has widened steadily. Women can now (as of 1978) expect to survive men their age by an amazing 7.7 years. This difference translates into some startling comparisons: Between ages 65 and 74 there are 1.31 women for every man. Between 74 and 84 the number jumps to 1.66. Over age 85, women outnumber men by 2.24 to 1. Furthermore, by the year 2000 these disparities will increase. For instance, at that time there are expected to be 2½ women aged 85 and above for every man of the same age.

So the reality is that most married women will become widows. Most widows will not remarry. And because there is also a trend away from living with children, many older women now and in the future will probably live alone.

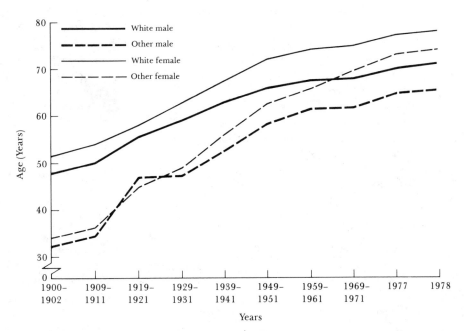

**FIGURE 1-3.** Life expectancy at birth, 1900–1978. *(Source: From Chart-book on Aging in America by C. Allan and H. Brotman. Copyright © 1981 by the White House Conference on Aging.)*

We are not sure exactly why women have outlived men at this accelerating pace, but the second important fact, that there are more people of advanced old age, has a clear-cut cause. Earlier in this century dramatic gains in life expectancy occurred among the young and middle-aged. Since 1950 our strides have been primarily toward extending the expected years of life after age 65. In fact, those who were 65 in 1978 could expect to live, on the average, 16.3 more years. The change is due to a basic difference in the pattern of disease control. During the first half of this century, cures were developed for many acute or infectious diseases (such as diphtheria). These illnesses killed the young and old alike, so their eradication allowed most people to live past youth. We have since become better able to limit (but not cure) diseases that disproportionately strike the relatively old. More of those reaching late life now live the additional years because of inroads in the mortality rate from these late-life illnesses called chronic diseases, such as heart disease and cancer.

But there is a problem along with this plus. We have not wiped out these debilitating diseases but merely helped to better stem their fatal course. So we have added time to the end of the life span, but not necessarily years of high-quality life. The increase in numbers of the quite old means, at least at present, more sick elderly and so an expanding need for medical and nursing care.

In advanced old age, the chance of being physically disabled by illness increases dramatically. In part because of this higher probability, gerontologists often find it useful to make a distinction between two chronological subgroups of older adults: the **young-old** and the **old-old**. The young-old, arbitrarily defined as those aged 65 to 74, are often free from disabling illnesses. The old-old, those age 75 and over, seem to be in a different class. Since they are more likely to have impairing problems, they are more prone to fit at least the physical stereotype of the older adult.

Further facts about today's American elderly, though, suggest we should be cautious in making many additional generalizations. As Figure 1-4 illustrates, despite some variability, older people reside in the 50 states in much the same distribution as the young. The vast majority live in their own homes. Only 5% live in nursing homes. Older people as a group do have fewer years of education and less income than younger adults. However, here too diversity, not uniformity, seems to be the rule. The elderly are represented on all rungs of the economic and educational ladder.

## Personal Realities

Our quite brief demographic account is useful. But these statistics provide only an external snapshot. They may usefully be supplemented by a more experiential view. What are the current problems older Americans face? What are their satisfactions, and what are their major concerns?

Luckily we have this information. A recent nationwide survey was devoted specifically to the issues important to today's American elderly. In 1981 the National Council on Aging, a voluntary organization, commissioned Louis Harris and Asso-

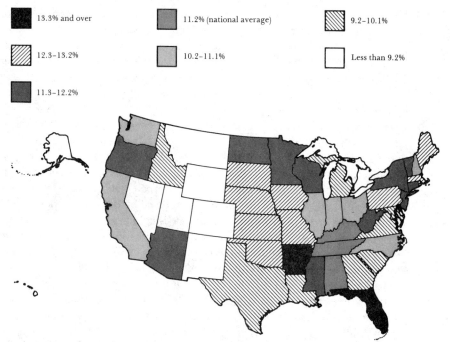

13.3% and over

12.3–13.2%

11.3–12.2%

11.2% (national average)

10.2–11.1%

9.2–10.1%

Less than 9.2%

**FIGURE 1-4.** Percentage of total population 65 and over in each state, in 1979. Note that in most states, the percentage of elderly is within 2 percentage points of the national average. *(Source: From* Chartbook on Aging in America *by C. Allan and H. Brotman. Copyright © 1981 by the White House Conference on Aging.)*

ciates to conduct a second comprehensive survey on aging in America. The public at large was questioned, as was a representative sample of older Americans. Like the first Harris poll, completed seven years before, this survey was an in-depth exploration of attitudes, perceptions, feelings, and facts. It gives a good picture of the experience of late life in America as seen from both an insider's and outsider's view. Here are a few highlights of this most recent nationwide poll (Harris & Associates, 1981).

Americans of all ages, including the elderly, viewed economic concerns—"inflation, high cost of living, high prices"—as the greatest problem generally facing older adults today. But despite this shared perception that financial concerns rank first in importance to the elderly as a group, only two in five older adults polled actually admitted that lack of money was a significant problem in their own lives. In fact, the elderly in the Harris sample were less likely to report being bothered by insufficient income than the younger adults surveyed.

The survey also revealed possible misperceptions of the extent of problems facing the elderly in several other areas. For instance, substantial majorities of the younger Harris sample rated "fear of crime" and "loneliness" as very serious problems for most elderly, but only a minority of the older adults polled cited these as serious personal problems. However, the percentage of the older respondents listing fear of crime as very important personally was substantial (25%) and was slightly higher than the percentage among younger adults (20%). This greater fear, in fact, may be adaptive. Perhaps because older people are more fearful, they are more cautious to avoid high-risk situations. The surprising statistic is that the elderly are less likely than other age groups to be the victims of violent crime (Janson & Ryder, 1983).

Economic anxiety and fear of crime are salient problems for Americans of all ages. But there is one difficulty that clearly is more important to those over 65: poor health. Among the Harris elderly, 21% said their health was "a very serious problem," compared with 8% of respondents age 18 to 54. The older people polled cited the high cost of care as the most problematic aspect of being ill and in need of medical services. They were also troubled by lack of transportation to and from doctors or medical facilities. Only 5% listed quality of care as an issue.

It comes as no surprise that poor health is a more important issue to Americans over 65. But a final highlight of the Harris survey flies in the face of just as certain an assumption we are likely to have about late life—that old age is a generally unhappy time and older people are likely to be dissatisfied with being at this least palatable life stage. Responses of the elderly to a life satisfaction questionnaire yielded surprising evidence to contradict this widely held view. As is apparent from Table 1-1, the Harris elderly reject the idea that, for them personally, the present is the least desirable time. Late life is not generally perceived as a dreary or monotonous period when the past becomes dominant and interests erode. These older adults report being satisfied with who they were and who they are now. A full half report being just as happy in this supposedly "worst" life stage as they were when young.

These rosy responses do need to be qualified somewhat. Overall, life satisfaction scores in the 1981 Harris survey were lower than in the previous poll. Moreover, because older people in America tend to have a bias against complaining (discussed in the next chapter), we may assume these answers are skewed on the positive side. Finally, not all people over 65 share this uplifting view of their present circumstances. Life satisfaction varies greatly from person to person. People in poor health are more likely to have low morale (Larson, 1978). As Box 1-1 illustrates, minorities are another category of elderly whose later years are more in keeping with the accepted gloomy view. Still, the Harris results are testimony against the stereotype. A full one-third of those surveyed refer to their "older years" as their best years.

In summary, then, the demographic truth is that today's elderly defy easy categorization. The experiential truth is that there are some problems but also, at least for many, a present of far from unrelieved gloom. These facts offer a valuable first approach to reality. However, they do not address the prevalent ingrained assumptions, those epitomized by the opening statements of this chapter. Those beliefs largely concern behavior, so it is only by examining behavior in older adults that we can assess their accuracy. The purpose of the psychological study of late life is to provide this comprehensive understanding.

**TABLE 1-1.** Responses of persons 65+ to positive and negative life satisfaction statements.

| | *Percentage Agreeing* | *Percentage Disagreeing* | *Percentage Not Sure* |
|---|---|---|---|
| **Positive Statements** | | | |
| As I look back on my life, I am fairly well satisfied | 87 | 11 | 2 |
| Compared to other people my age, I make a good appearance | 84 | 7 | 8 |
| I've gotten pretty much what I expected out of life | 81 | 14 | 5 |
| The things I do are as interesting to me as they ever were | 69 | 27 | 4 |
| As I grow older, things seem better than I thought they would be | 53 | 38 | 9 |
| I have gotten more of the breaks in life than most people I know | 62 | 31 | 6 |
| I would not change my past life even if I could | 64 | 29 | 6 |
| I expect some interesting and pleasant things to happen to me in the future | 62 | 28 | 11 |
| I am just as happy as when I was younger | 48 | 48 | 4 |
| I have made plans for things I'll be doing a month or year from now | 49 | 47 | 4 |
| These are the best years of my life | 33 | 60 | 7 |
| **Negative Statements** | | | |
| I feel old and somewhat tired | 45 | 51 | 3 |
| My life could be happier than it is now | 55 | 40 | 5 |
| In spite of what some people say, the lot of the average person is getting worse, not better | 48 | 39 | 13 |
| When I think back over my life, I didn't get most of the important things I wanted | 36 | 59 | 4 |
| This is the dreariest time of my life | 27 | 70 | 3 |
| Most of the things I do are boring or monotonous | 21 | 76 | 3 |
| Compared to other people, I get down in the dumps too often | 18 | 78 | 5 |

*(Source: From* Aging in the Eighties: America in Transition, *1981, published by the National Council on the Aging, Inc. Reprinted by permission.)*

## The Focus of This Book: Psychological Reality

At an accelerating pace, mainly since the end of the Second World War (Riegel, 1977), psychology, the study of behavior, has been turning its attention to the elderly (see Figure 1-5). Psychologists study the physical reality of aging, focusing in particular on the behavioral aspects of physical change. They explore in depth how cognitive processes operate in late life. They scrutinize personality and the impact of important age-related life events on older adults. They examine mental disorders—their characteristics, causes, and possible cures. Most recently they have turned to the psychological study of death, the inevitable end of old age. The

---

**BOX 1-1.   The Harris Survey Picture of Minority Aging**

The Harris poll revealed that being minority and elderly means being disad-vantaged in a number of areas, compared with Whites over 65. A primary prob-lem is economic. The older Black and Hispanic respondents had a median income about half that of the Whites ($5000, $5600, and $9000 respectively) and well below the poverty line. More than 1 in 3 had no savings at all, compared with 1 in 4 nonminority older adults. It is no wonder, then, that a large proportion of the Black and Hispanic elderly polled (about 50%) listed not having enough money to live on as a serious personal problem, a much larger percentage than in the group over 65 as a whole (17%).

These economic worries seem compounded by more difficulties in another es-sential area: health. While only 21% of Whites rated poor health as a serious personal problem, for Blacks and Hispanics the figure jumped to 35% and 48%. Older Blacks and Hispanics were also more often troubled by not enough medical care. These respective percentages were 17% and 35%, compared with 6% for Whites.

So, predictably, life satisfaction scores in the poll were somewhat lower for minorities than for Whites. In common with the conditions of life for Blacks and Hispanics under 65, the environment for aging in America seems measurably poorer for those in our major minority groups.

---

succeeding chapters will systematically examine psychological theory, research, and practice in each of these essential areas. The result will be the important perspective those who scientifically study individual behavior are continuing to provide about the reality of the aging process and older adults.

Many psychological theories have been applied in an attempt to better under-stand aging. These often quite circumscribed theories run the gamut from general models of memory to explanations of late-life morale to attempts to account for emotional reactions to the painful event of losing a spouse. Amid this diversity, though, a few theories stand out. Psychologists and others whose interest is behav-ior in late life are more likely to be guided by one of these very few systems of thought. And although many research techniques are used in gerontology, of par-ticular importance are the main ones used to assess developmental change. In the chapters to come, the theoretical perspectives and research strategies described next will be mentioned time and time again.

### Emphasis on Age Irrelevance: Learning Theory and Traditional Psychoanalytic Theory

Behaviorism and Freudian psychoanalytic theory are the two most influential approaches to human behavior. It should come as no surprise, then, that these approaches are often applied to understanding the behavior of older adults. Be-cause these important theories are general accounts of how human beings operate, neither of them has basic precepts describing late life. The same general principles governing psychological functioning at any age also apply to old age.

**Behaviorism.**   Behaviorism (or learning theory) is the premier theoretical system in modern psychology. A single axiom captures the essence of this important world view: the environment is crucial in determining human actions. To understand human behavior, we should look to the reinforcements a person is exposed to in the outside world.

Behaviorists, then, downplay the importance of biology. Our actions are changeable, not a result of fixed biological givens. At least until recently (see Box 1-2), behaviorists have tended to concentrate on what is measurable, preferring overt actions to feelings, needs, and fantasies. They also highlight the present rather than the past. If we understand the current stimuli a person is exposed to, we will understand the way he or she is. Human responses are lawful and are learned through the same fundamental mechanisms. They are acquired directly, through either classical or operant conditioning, or indirectly, through modeling (that is, observational learning).

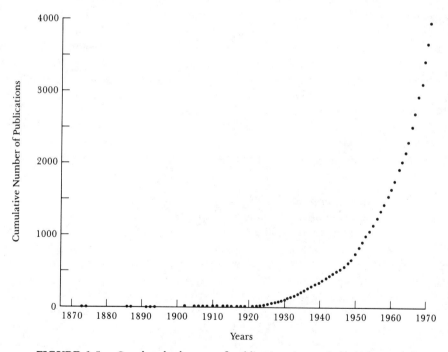

**FIGURE 1-5.**   One hundred years of publications in psychological gerontology. Note the exponential increase in publications, particularly after the 1940s. *(Source: From "History of Psychological Gerontology," by K. Riegel. In Handbook of the Psychology of Aging, by J. E. Birren and K. W. Schaie. Copyright © 1977 by Van Nostrand Reinhold Company. Reprinted by permission of the publisher.)*

**BOX 1-2.    The Cognitive Learning Perspective: Behaviorism's New Approach**

Until the middle to late 1960s, a major tenet of behaviorism was the importance of studying only responses that could be externally measured and quantified. Most people who believed in learning theory felt that internal processes (feelings and thoughts), not being observable and verifiable, were not a legitimate area for a truly scientific study of human beings.

Within the past 15 years this point of view has radically changed. Now understanding thoughts, or cognitions, has become an important focus for most behaviorally oriented researchers and practitioners. Learning theory has a new approach, the cognitive learning point of view (see Mahoney, 1977).

Psychologists and others who embrace the cognitive learning perspective have not abandoned the other tenets of behaviorism. For example, they still firmly adhere to the idea that behavior is lawful and should be scrutinized in a rigorous, scientific way. However, instead of accepting the traditional idea that only overt responses are important, they think it is a person's experiences, thoughts, and beliefs about the world that obey the laws of learning. In fact, for cognitively oriented behaviorists understanding a person's thoughts about his or her environment is more important than understanding the objective characteristics of the environment itself. Human learning is not just a function of a direct mechanical linking of external stimulus and overt response. It is also a product of our cognitions—of how we feel and how we think. Furthermore, just as our thinking affects how we act, the reverse may be equally true. How we actually behave can produce marked cognitive change.

Behaviorism's new cognitive approach is illustrated here in our theoretical discussion of modeling. In Chapter 9 we will describe its application as therapy: a cognitive behavioral treatment for a common late-life problem, depression.

*Classical conditioning,* the most primitive type of learning, involves involuntary responses, actions, or physiological reactions outside conscious control. Here the response innately elicited by one stimulus is paired with another. After a number of pairings or in many cases even one association, a connection is formed, so that the response is now elicited by the new stimulus alone. In actual practice, classical conditioning is most often used to explain the development of emotional reactions, particularly why people feel fearful in inherently neutral situations. For example, a behaviorist would view an older adult's fear of the bath after a fall as due to this type of learning. Falling, a stimulus innately evoking fear, occurred in conjunction with being in the tub. Because of this pairing, the initially neutral stimulus, being in the bath, was classically conditioned to fear. Now fear occurs in association with this intrinsically benign event alone.

The experience of the fall may also involve the second major type of learning, *operant conditioning,* if it then causes avoidance—the older adult refusing to take a bath. There is evidence that physiological or involuntary reactions too can some-times be operantly conditioned (see the short discussion of biofeedback in Chapter 3), but in general, operant, or instrumental, conditioning is the major mechanism explaining our conscious or voluntary actions. Here the principle is simple. Ac-tions that are rewarded, or reinforced, will tend to recur. Those that are not rein-forced will extinguish (that is, disappear). In our example, relief from fear when away from the bath would be a potent reinforcer, one causing and maintaining the operant response of avoiding further encounters with the tub.

Behaviorists view operant conditioning, with its simple explanatory principle of direct reinforcement, as possibly accounting for all voluntary behavior. It can ex-plain responses as diverse as a nursing home resident's angering the institutional staff by refusing to walk or an elderly mathematician's working long hours in his or her field even after being formally retired. Because of the prevalence with which operant conditioning is used to understand elderly behavior, it seems im-portant to go into slightly more detail about this type of learning. For instance, what does one need to know about reinforcement when using the operant ap-proach? Several essentials can be usefully illustrated by using the two very differ-ent responses just described.

First, although some events, such as money or praise, tend to be reinforcing for most people, often what constitutes a reinforcer is variable and person-specific. Each individual has his or her own hierarchy of reinforcement, the events ranked from least to most important in motivating that person. In the case of the nursing home resident, angry attention is likely to be included on that list, as this is what seems to be motivating the response. On the scientist's hierarchy, the same rein-forcer may not appear at all. For the scientist the rewarding event seems to be the possibility of making an important discovery.

But still we cannot be sure. The nursing home occupant might be refusing to walk because this allows him or her to avoid a disliked resident whose room is down the hall—or perhaps because of an altruistic desire to keep a sick roommate company. The scientist's work might have a far from lofty cause: the need to avoid household responsibilities or perhaps an unwanted conflict with a spouse. So a second principle about reinforcement is that the event that is reinforcing can best be determined only by a quite objective criterion: an event is a reinforcer if it increases the probability of the behavior it precedes.

Finally, the frequency or schedule with which reinforcement is administered has a crucial impact on a person's responses. Different schedules of reinforce-ment, such as delivery of reward after every response, at predictable intervals, or irregularly, produce profoundly variable patterns of behavior.

For instance, if the actions of the nursing home resident and scientist were resistant to extinction, continuing for a long time in the absence of a current reward, we would expect a variable-ratio reinforcement schedule as the cause. This is a quite common pattern occurring in daily living. Reward comes at unpre-dictable intervals, and so people learn persistence, the idea that if they keep re-sponding they will eventually get what they want. We would imagine that the nursing home resident had been allowed to use a wheelchair irregularly when a nurse was particularly rushed. We would envision the scientist having a long history with the hit-or-miss quality of scientific discovery. This would teach a lesson of a superficially very different type: only sometimes does my research yield real answers. Only sometimes do my ideas have merit, does my hard work result in tangible rewards.

So these as well as a variety of other principles about reinforcement must be taken into account in an operant analysis of the actions of any older adult. But a behaviorist would be remiss if he or she looked only to direct reinforcement in understanding the responses of the scientist or the nursing home resident. He or she might be wrong to assume that the first older adult had necessarily learned the fear from actually having slipped in the tub. In each case it would be important to look for an alternative route by which these behaviors or any other response might be learned: modeling.

In **modeling,** the third basic type of learning, direct reinforcement is not involved. Responses are learned by observation, by imitating what others do. People will tend to model the behavior of others if they perceive them as being reinforced. Other variables, such as similarity of the model to oneself, enhance the tendency for this type of imitative learning to occur.

For instance, our frightened older person may easily have developed the aversion to the bathtub by learning that an elderly neighbor, so like him- or herself, had broken a hip after falling in the tub. The scientist may have learned to work long hours just by mimicking the behavior of a successful mentor and seeing rewards coming unpredictably to the much-admired person. Finally, the attention given to the nursing home resident's bedridden roommate may really be responsible for the resident's refusal to walk. Acting incapable allows him or her to have this important reinforcer too.

So behaviorists look both to events occurring directly to the person and to indirect experiences, exposure to models, in understanding the older adult. As illustrated in Box 1-3, they then use this same perspective in engineering behavioral change. All the principles just described and others not mentioned in this quite simplified account are used in treatment to help the older person function better.

Before turning from this bare-bones description, it is important to emphasize a crucial final fact about the laws of learning and so the whole learning-theory perspective on late life. The principles of learning are neutral and universal. The same mechanisms account for actions praised as good, derided as bad, or labeled as typical in old age. For instance, those who do not subscribe to learning theory might view the older adult afraid of the bath or the nursing home resident quite negatively: as an excessively timid person or as a person too stubborn to bend. The scientist, as implied earlier, might be admired for maturity and strength of character. Furthermore, an outsider viewing these behaviors might then make another easy inference. The first two older adults' actions could be seen as the typical caution or obstinacy of old age; the scientist's, as the characteristic wisdom of advanced years.

But behaviorists have a very different perspective on responses often viewed as characterological, as a fixed part of the person, or—more important to our discussion—as a natural or intrinsic part of late life. Where others nod knowingly about "the wise older scientist," the "typically stubborn" nursing home resident, or the "predictably too cautious" older person afraid of the bath, behaviorists see merely responses shaped by the universal laws of learning. There are no attributes inherent in people or in aging. It simply *appears* that there is a fixed "wise," "cautious," or "obstinate" elderly way to behave, but that is because older people tend to be exposed to similar environments and so have similar behaviors reinforced.

---

**BOX 1-3.   A Behavioral Treatment Strategy to Promote Walking**

The hypothetical example of our nursing home resident is not unusual. Often the institutional environment permits the development of artificially incompetent, incapable behaviors such as using a wheelchair when one is physically able to walk. Excessive dependency may be accidentally reinforced by the institutional staff. In nursing homes there is plenty of opportunity to model others whose behavior embodies the sick role.

To illustrate the power of operant techniques in reversing excessive helplessness, two investigators (MacDonald & Butler, 1974) chose to modify the very behavior discussed in the text. They wanted to produce walking in two nursing home residents who, though capable, had been insisting on being transported by wheelchair for several months. Until the behavioral treatment was instituted, these residents' actions had seemed incapable of being changed. Both had been repeatedly urged by the staff at the home and their families to walk, with no success.

The first step in the treatment program was to observe the behavior as it normally occurred, so the investigators used the typical procedure followed by the nursing home staff. The residents were transported by wheelchair to the dining room, located on a different floor. During the trip, the researchers talked to the residents. This conversation, it was decided, would be the reinforcer later made contingent on walking alone.

Then the researchers instituted the treatment phase. Each day they told the subjects to walk to the dining room and leaned over to help each older person stand. If the individual did rise, he or she was given praise and conversation. If he or she refused, the refusal was met with a stony silence in transit to the meal. This strategy quite quickly produced a marked change—both residents walked to the dining room.

To illustrate that the new competent behavior could just as easily be reversed, the investigators then applied the same approach to reinstitute the original response. The older adults were praised and talked to only if they rode to the dining room. Walking was met with unyielding silence. Needless to say, within a few days each resident was once again acting incompetent. Reinforcement, the simple mechanism accounting for learning, had had its inevitable effect.

This nonevaluative approach is very different from that of the second major framework used for understanding and helping the elderly: psychoanalytic theory.

**Psychoanalytic Theory.**    The principles of learning theory are succinct, simple, and easily spelled out. This economy of precepts does not apply to the psychoanalytic approach. Freudian psychoanalytic theory is really a diverse amalgam of ideas. It is not a fixed set of basic laws but a continually evolving system that has been steadily added to, modified, and amended over the years, beginning with its originator's own constant efforts at revision.

This means that those who subscribe to this rich theory of human behavior may differ greatly on important specifics. However, psychoanalytically oriented psychologists (and others) do share some crucial beliefs. They view good mothering in early childhood as essential to psychological health. They feel personality is basically formed at a quite early age (5 or before) and then remains relatively stable throughout life. They see personality as having a definite structure. It has conscious and unconscious aspects. The deepest layer of personality, the unconscious, is the most important determinant of human behavior.

In addition to having this layered topography, personality also has three parts: the id, the ego, and the superego. The id is what is present at birth. It is the mass of blind instincts, wishes, and needs the child has when he or she enters the world.

The two other aspects of personality, the ego and superego, evolve during early childhood. First the ego, the largely conscious, reality-oriented part of personality, is formed when the child realizes that immediate gratification of his or her needs must yield to an outside world. Ego functions involve logic, reasoning, thinking and planning, getting what one wants in an ordered, realistic way. Next the superego develops. It is the moral arm of personality, the unconscious internalization of parental and societal prohibitions, norms, and ideals of good behavior. As the child develops, then, he or she learns to conform to the requirements of being a human being. Desires must be adapted to reality. Sometimes they must be abandoned altogether to live a moral, ethically upright life.

Typically, the mother and father are responsible for the adequacy of these accommodations and so for lifelong mental health. If they are empathic and sensitive during the crucial early childhood years, the person will develop a strong ego that will enable him or her to weather and adapt to all the crises of living, including those of late life. If they are insensitive or for some other reason their caretaking ability is impaired, ego formation will not be optimal. The person will be vulnerable, prone to the eruption of the unconscious, and likely to develop problems when encountering the stresses of old age.

For psychoanalysts, events typical in late life, such as illness, death of a spouse, or retirement, are viewed as tests of psychological functioning. These life occurrences are seen as difficult, ones that strain the capacity of the ego to adapt. It is here, if early childhood experiences have not been ideal, that the person is most likely to use defense mechanisms to cope (see Table 1-2), and psychological symptoms arise.

**TABLE 1-2.**  Selected defense mechanisms. (Unconscious distortions of reality that are used to cope with consciously unacceptable feelings.)

---

**Displacement:** The individual transfers a feeling meant for one person or object to a safer, less threatening target.
(Example: The older adult in a nursing home is angry over her treatment by the institutional staff. She becomes furious at her roommate.)

**Projection:** The individual sees an unacceptable feeling or disliked attribute in the self as belonging to another.
(Example: The older adult is angry at his children for not visiting. He comes to feel that his children must be angry at him.)

**Regression:** In a difficult situation, the person reverts to a more primitive (less mature) form of behavior, one that was employed early in life.
(Example: After suffering a mild heart attack, the older adult will not let his wife out of the house and demands round-the-clock nursing care and assistance with eating, dressing, and so on.)

**Denial:** The individual refuses to admit an upsetting situation exists.
(Example: After suffering a stroke, the older adult says her problem moving her arm is caused by arthritis.)

**Reaction formation:** The individual behaves or overreacts in the opposite way to his or her true feelings.
(Example: The middle-aged child calls his difficult, complaining mother constantly, telling her how much he loves her, when he really wants to have nothing to do with her.)

---

So, in the psychoanalytic view, the way a person behaves in old age is consistent with a lifelong behavioral pattern, or personality style (Berezin, 1972). Late life is a time of external difficulty and therefore much potential psychological stress (Cath, 1965; Slater, 1964). To understand behavior, we must look beneath the surface. What unconscious needs, fantasies, and wishes are motivating the older person's surface response? This very different perspective on the elderly is highlighted by looking at how a psychoanalyst would approach the three examples just described.

Both the fear of the bath and the refusal to walk would be viewed as signs of pathology, symptoms having their origin in an unconscious wish. For instance, the prospect of falling in the tub might be seen as stimulating the yearning to be dependent, a desire so foreign to the person's adult self-image that it could not be consciously admitted. Anxiety and avoidance would then be the ideal psychological solutions, both permitting the true need to remain unconscious and also satisfying it by forcing the fearful person to have a companion when taking a bath. For the person who acts incapable of walking, the unconscious wish might be the childhood need to get back at a rejecting parent, a lifelong desire that was then acted out in any situation where others were in control. Here the stress of being institutionalized plus the similarity of the dependent nursing home situation to the dependent one of early life might be seen as producing the symptom.

In both these examples, though, the accuracy of each formulation could be confirmed only by looking to the person's childhood. In the idiosyncratic events, experiences, and themes of the person's long-distant earliest years would lie the key to this manifestation of optimal development gone awry.

Our hypothetical cases also illustrate the general sequence that psychoanalysts feel is responsible for the development of a psychological problem. A stressful event in the present, here the prospect of being dependent, taxes beyond its limit the ability of the adult part of the personality, the ego, to remain firmly in control. Deficiencies in the quality of childhood experiences mean ego formation has not been ideal. So the unconscious childhood desire wins. The sign of its victory over the reality-oriented part of personality is the symptom or psychological problem itself. Furthermore, believing in personality stability, the psychoanalyst would surmise that just such a sequence probably took place more than once in each older person's past. Earlier life stresses too would have had the same tendency to provoke a psychological disorder. In fact, they should have produced the identical symptom being observed now.

The same framework would govern the approach to our third older person: the dedicated scientist. His or her pattern of hard work would likely be seen as a lifelong style, one having its origin in a particular configuration of long-unconscious childhood needs. However, because the scientist's behavior seems appropriate and mature, he or she might be put into a different category than the two other elderly persons. Although the psychoanalyst would caution that we could know for certain only by thoroughly investigating the scientist's life, the scientist's actions do imply an ego in full control, the psychoanalytic criterion of a person in optimum mental health.

**Relative Importance in the Psychology of Aging.**    Behaviorism is by far the dominant theory psychologists use for understanding late life. It clearly outranks the psychoanalytic point of view. A major reason is numerical. More psychologists, particularly those in academic psychology, are likely to subscribe to learning theory. These are the people who tend to do the research, write the papers, and so dictate the direction and determine the advances in the field as a whole. But numbers are only a partial explanation of the disproportion so evident in the chapters to come. Behaviorism's popularity lies in its philosophy, a fact illustrated by a brief summary specifically emphasizing the learning-theory and psychoanalytic perspectives on late life.

*Behaviorism is optimistic.* Its environmental explanation is a refreshing contrast to the widely held negativism of traditional thinking about the elderly (Rebok & Hoyer, 1977; Hoyer, 1973; Labouvie, 1973). Aging does not have to lead to irreversible decline. Older adults are not doomed to behave in preordained, deficient ways. Behavior is not only changeable, but can be modified quite easily. In addition, because current reinforcement alone is important, history, or time spent acting in a certain way, is irrelevant to the ease with which a person can change. This means that older adults are not disadvantaged. They are as capable of modifying their behavior as the young.

*Behaviorism is broad in scope.* The principles of learning account not just for the subset of responses called personality but for any human activity. The theory, then, provides a general framework, one useful for approaching and helping the older person in every area of life.

Psychoanalytic theory has neither of these virtues. It is an explanation of personality and psychological problems alone. More important, it does nothing to dispel, and actually has tended to foster, the negativism about old age. The beginning of the life span, not its end, is crucial. This is the period to which attention should be paid. Behavior is fixed from childhood. It is therefore particularly difficult to change when cemented over many years. Old age is a season of loss, the most difficult time of life.

These fundamental differences in optimism, in acceptance of the elderly as worthy of study, and in ability to study the older person in a complete way have led to a natural self-selection. Psychologists interested in the elderly seem to have an affinity for the learning-theory approach, and in turn, those who follow the learning-theory approach are likely to be more interested in the elderly.

However, we cannot discount the impact of psychoanalytic theory. Many behavioral scientists do use this important theory to understand old age. Their research and clinical insights have provided us with important information about personality stability and change in the middle and later years, about how people adapt to important crises such as loss of a spouse or approaching death, and about psychological problems that tend to be prevalent among older adults. (These contributions will be apparent in following chapters.) In fact, the negativism and neglect in the traditional Freudian point of view have been eliminated and reversed by newer theories within the psychoanalytic tradition. Late life is a time of evolution. It is a period of often positive personality change.

### *Emphasis on Positive Change: Jung's and Erikson's Theories*

Two theorists, Carl Jung and Erik Erikson, have done much to redress the Freudian bias by developing conceptions about personality that take old age into account. Jung's ideas are an explicit rebuke to traditional psychoanalytic theory. He views the last half of the life span as more interesting and more important than the first. Erikson's beliefs are less extreme. Though he doesn't see late life as more important, he still views it as a period to which attention should be paid.

**Jung's Basic Concepts.**   Jung's positive ideas about late life are central to a well-developed theory of what motivates human beings (see Mattoon, 1981). An early, enthusiastic protégé of Freud, Jung abandoned the beginning psychoanalytic movement in 1912 and set up his own very different psychoanalytic school. Jung's major disagreement with the Freudian system centered on just the importance his mentor ascribed to a person's earliest years. Jung rebelled against the retrospective (past-oriented) approach of psychoanalysis, the idea that present psychological functioning is simply a reflection of infantile needs. He believed the present and future to be just as important in explaining behavior as the past. Knowing a person's hopes and goals is as essential to understanding the person as knowing his or her past. As a natural outgrowth of this prospective (future-oriented) view of the person, Jung was interested in specific changes that might take place later in life. In fact, he believed that the most important transition of living occurs during the late thirties and forties. At that time a person has to reverse his or her whole value system and mode of approaching the world.

In Jung's view the young adult is energetic, passionate, self-absorbed, and concerned with aggressively mastering life. In the thirties and forties physical and sexual energy begin to wane. The person knows what it is like to make a mark on the world, so a kind of turning inward naturally occurs. Introspection and contemplation become ascendant. Relationships, understanding the meaning of life, and giving to others become the person's predominant concern.

Jung felt accomplishing this reversal to be a hazardous step. Some people attempt in vain to carry over the values of youth into later life; they stagnate, becoming unhappy, vain, and rigid. However, if development proceeds in an ideal way, a pinnacle is reached. The person can be transformed into a spiritual being.

This transformation signals a state of psychological harmony and differentiation, an integration and acceptance of all the parts of the personality, even ones that the individual had previously denied. So another natural component of this mid-life change is a lack of differentiation between the sexes. Men become more tolerant of the previously repressed feminine component of their personality. Women give more play to their earlier-shunned, de-emphasized masculine side.

Jung also believed this midlife reorientation to have a major function. It occurs in order to prepare the person for impending death, an event he viewed not as the low point but really as the culmination of life. This same assumption about the purpose of late-life personality change, shorn of the positive value attributed to death, is made by our second psychoanalytic observer of old age: Erik Erikson.

**Erikson's Basic Concepts.**   Erikson's ideas about psychological development, unlike Jung's, are not part of a theory that stresses the inherent value of the future, compared with the earlier years. Erikson is a Freudian, who nevertheless departed from traditional psychoanalytic theory to look at psychological growth that might occur throughout the life span. In his view, instead of a single shift at midlife, there are eight critical turning points or steps of development in the life span, each tied to a particular chronological period. The past is still critically important. A person cannot master the issue of a later stage unless, on balance, he or she has successfully traversed the developmental crises of all previous steps. The crucial issue of old age is ego integrity versus despair. Here is how Erikson describes **ego integrity**, the ideal of late-life development.

> It is a post-narcissistic love of the human ego—not of the self—as an experience which conveys some world order and spiritual sense. . . . It is the acceptance of one's one and only life cycle as something that had to be and that, by necessity, permitted of no substitutions. . . . It is a comradeship with the ordering ways of distant times and different pursuits . . . [but] the possessor of integrity is ready to defend the dignity of his own life style against all physical and economic threats. . . . Ego integrity, therefore, implies an emotional integration which permits participation by followership as well as acceptance of the responsibilities of leadership [1963, pp. 268–269].

Erikson, then, sees the developmental goal of old age in terms somewhat similar to Jung's view of the ideal in later life. Like the ideally integrated spiritual person, the individual who has achieved ego integrity accepts who he or she is. In Erikson's view, however, achieving this inner balance and harmony is directly tied to a quite specific process: coming to terms with one's personal past.

Erikson believes that the person who has reached integrity is able to accept death. He envisions a quite different reaction in the individual who regrets how he or she has lived. This unlucky person, desperately afraid of dying, feels frustrated and doomed because it is too late to make amends for his or her allotted years poorly spent. Erikson uses the highly appropriate term *despair* to describe such a person's psychological state.

**Relative Importance in the Psychology of Aging.**   In contrast to Jung's theory, Erikson's formulations about late life are widely known, cited, and accepted by many gerontologists, particularly psychologists and others who provide direct services to the elderly. They have even stimulated another popular theory concerning personality in old age, that the elderly engage in a systematic life review (see Chapter 6). This dominance may result in part from greater accessibility and compatibility. Erikson describes his integrity/despair dimension simply and succinctly within a few pages of one popularly read book (1963; see Recommended Readings). Most important, he does not basically depart from Freudian theory, by far the major psychoanalytic approach to human behavior.

But despite the wider acceptance of Erikson's ideas as truth, there have been few attempts to evaluate them experimentally. Is Erikson right in assuming that the most important task of old age is to make peace with one's past? Is he correct in saying this achievement allows a person to accept death? Finally, how do Jung's more esoteric views fare in the real world, when we examine how personality actually does change in the later part of life? These are some questions that will be considered in succeeding chapters when we look at research evidence for Jung's and Erikson's ideas.

### *Emphasis on Many Perspectives: The Life-Span Developmental View*

A careful reading of our chapter so far clearly shows that a major theme in the psychology of aging concerns change. Three opposing points of view have been offered about development in late life. The first, epitomized by the stereotype presented at the beginning of this chapter, is the widely held assumption that aging equals decline. The next, common to both learning theory and the traditional psychoanalytic view, is that older adults are basically no different from the young. With some qualifications, stability is implicitly seen as predominant in old age. Finally, there is the perspective just mentioned. There may be change for the better, evolution during life's last stage.

Our last psychological orientation, the **life-span developmental approach** (Baltes, Reese, & Lipsett, 1980; Baltes & Willis, 1977) embraces each of these contrasting ideas. This new and important point of view is actually the opposite of an actual theory or assumption about the direction of change. Instead it is in large part a general prescription to be open-minded: pluralism (a variety of points of view) is the best policy to follow in describing and explaining psychological functioning in late life.

Life-span developmentalists, who, as their name implies, are interested in psychological development from birth to death, view development as a life-long process. They are interested in describing its regularities and in spelling out the particular influences responsible for developmental change. But throughout all their writing is a stress on the importance of an all-encompassing approach. Pluralism is important in every area of the psychology of aging. It is crucial with regard to theories. Many models of development and theoretical world views are important in enriching our understanding of older adults. Pluralism also is the watchword of behavior in the real world. Development in late life is multidirectional. Different aspects of behavior change in diverse ways. In addition, individuals can differ greatly; their patterns of aging, too, may follow diverse, individual-specific forms.

So to give some hypothetical examples, wisdom may increase as people age, while physical stamina generally declines. Activities such as reading may remain stable with advancing years, while other interests, such as going to the theater, may change in a curvilinear way. Along each dimension people of a given age will vary greatly. And the way they develop over time in each aspect of psychological functioning may be quite contrary to the way most of their age peers do.

In addition, the causes of any late-life behavioral change are variable. They may be as standard as having experienced some normal biological decline or as idiosyncratic as having to cope with a quite unlikely old-age event such as the death of a child. This means that strategies to help improve behavior in the elderly should not be confined to one or a few techniques. A variety of approaches may be useful in enhancing the quality of life for a given older adult.

Actually, giving practical help is the final major aim of this eclectic world view. Life-span developmentalists want both to describe and explain and also to optimize psychological functioning during a person's later years.

### Developmental Research Methods

Because the scope of the psychology of aging embraces all questions about behavior in the elderly, a variety of research techniques are used in studying the aging process and older adults. But amid this diversity one kind of question stands out. As just noted, in gerontology we often want information specifically about change. What is the truth of the ideas about the direction of development just described? How do older people really differ from the young? How does behavior during old age really change from behavior during other chronological periods— or remain similar to it? Is it true that, as the stereotype says, the older person is a picture of decline? Is it accurate, as Erikson and Jung suggest, that new aspects of personality and different focal interests and concerns emerge during life's later stages? To answer these and other frequently posed questions about development, special research methods are required. The two strategies most often used are cross-sectional and longitudinal studies.

**Cross-Sectional Studies.**  Because cross-sectional research is infinitely easier to carry out, this approach is by far the one most often used to assess developmental change. In *cross-sectional studies* different age groups are compared at the same time on the variable of interest to the investigator—muscle strength, motor speed, mental health, or any of a multitude of possible choices. Often, before the test, the groups are matched or equalized on important parameters, other than age, that are likely to affect their scores. For example, if we were interested in testing the widely held impression that people become more conservative as they age, using the cross-sectional method, our procedure might have the following form. Samples of different-aged subjects (such as twenty 30-year-olds, twenty 40-year-olds, and twenty 70-year-olds) would be picked. The groups would be carefully matched for likely confounding extraneous influences, such as social class or ethnic background. A questionnaire assessing political attitudes would then be administered and the average scores of the three age groups compared. If there were in fact a trend toward less liberal attitudes in successively older groups, we would conclude our hypothesis was supported. With advancing age, people do indeed develop increasingly more conservative views.

However, this easy conclusion would be wrong. Because our strategy does not involve examining people over time, we cannot assume these differences between groups mean that changes actually do occur in individuals as they advance in years. For instance, although a study carried out ten years ago might indeed have shown progressively greater conservatism with age, today or a decade from now the same investigation might show a very different trend. Because of changes in the economy or the need to rebel against the older generation, the youngest subjects might espouse the most conservative views. The most liberal attitudes might be held by the 1960s generation approaching middle age or by the oldest subjects, shaped and molded by the liberalism of the Roosevelt years.

This not unreasonable hypothetical possibility points up the most serious problem with cross-sectional studies. They do permit an accurate assessment of *age differences,* but they do not accurately reveal *age changes.* In this method true changes that occur with advancing age are confounded with differences due to an extraneous variable—being in a different birth group. In gerontology, differences between people born at different times are called "cohort differences."

Cohort is a crucially important term in the psychology of aging. It is a word similar to *generation* but encompasses a less clearly specified time interval. **Cohort** refers to any group of people born within a year or specified short period. For instance, individuals born in 1920, in 1945, and in 1960 constitute distinct cohorts. Snapshots of them at the same age will reveal marked differences not just in externals but in many aspects of psychological functioning. Variation is inevitable because each cohort is exposed to a unique set of cultural and societal experiences as it travels through life.

Not only do cohort factors contaminate the results of cross-sectional studies of attitudes; they are an equally important source of bias affecting the outcome of research in areas seemingly more immune. For example, cohort differences have an important impact on the results of cross-sectional studies of physical performance and of research on the relationship of intelligence to advancing age. In both cases the cross-sectional method (at least in the past) has yielded erroneously gloomy findings. Too much decline appears to occur with age.

As our earlier description of life expectancy increases implies, younger cohorts are exposed to an environment promoting better health than those born in the more distant past. The same, until now at least, has been true of the intellectual environment. For instance, younger cohorts, on the average, have more and more years of schooling. Apart from age, these differences are an advantage promoting better performance by the young; the old are handicapped by having been born at their particular historical time. The true extent of age declines is exaggerated to an unknown degree.

Cross-sectional studies also do not address other issues of interest about development. For example, they do not permit researchers to assess individual patterns of consistency (or change) or how conditions and behaviors in earlier life relate to functioning in old age. Do people who are the most or least physically fit or intelligent when young maintain this relative standing in late life, too? Does having psychological problems in youth mean a person will also be disturbed in old age? How do midlife activities such as exercising, regularly watching the nightly news, and not smoking relate to physical or intellectual capacities when elderly? How do earlier life events affect mental health in the later years? It is possible to get answers of some sort to these questions by asking people who are already older, but by far the best way is to actually follow people over time. This strategy is the all-important longitudinal approach.

**Longitudinal Studies.**   In the longitudinal method, usually one cohort is selected and then periodically tested, using the same measures, over a number of years. This strategy provides a rich source of information about changes that occur with age in the group as a whole and in particular individuals in the sample. However, there also are some problems with this ambitious research technique.

First, conclusions based on longitudinal studies ideally should be restricted to the particular cohort chosen for study. Because each cohort is unique, it is likely to show a different pattern of change as it ages. So our ability to generalize from longitudinal studies is quite limited. We should, in good conscience, be cautious about making statements with regard to aging in the abstract on the basis of data from a single group.

Undertaking a longitudinal study also has considerable practical limitations. It involves a substantial investment of effort and time. The investigator or research team must remain interested in the study and available to continue it over a long span. The topic of the investigation and the measures used to gather information must not become obsolete over the intervening years. Subjects must be recruited who will agree to participate in an extended series of tests. Most important, the sample must be searched out anew each time an evaluation is due. All these problems become more severe the longer the study proceeds. For this reason longitudinal studies that cover a considerable span of time—for instance, following subjects from young adulthood to late life—are very rare.

The last difficulty mentioned, recontacting subjects to return for subsequent tests, is more than just a practical problem. It is an important source of bias in the longitudinal method itself. Participants tend to drop out of the study as it progresses. In later evaluations fewer and fewer of the initial sample remain. But this attrition is not random. The least able subjects are likely to leave. Those who complete the study are an elite group, often unrepresentative of their age peers.

For example, in gerontological research one paramount reason participants give for not completing the full series of evaluations is ill health (see Table 1-3). Subjects who do not return are too ill or have died. Physical illness, however, is related to poor performance in aspects of behavior far afield from just physical skills. The healthiest subjects, then, those who remain in any study, are likely to be high-functioning on a variety of indexes an investigator might choose. Findings based on this select group will probably offer too optimistic a picture by either underestimating declines or by magnifying the extent to which positive changes occur with age in the unselected cohort as a whole.

So longitudinal studies have the opposite tendency from cross-sectional research: their design results in a built-in bias favoring the later years. This favoritism is only exacerbated by another procedural requirement of the longitudinal method: that subjects are repeatedly given the same measures. The more often a person takes a test, the better his or her performance is likely to be, because experience with the measure and the evaluation situation can lower anxiety and increase efficiency. As the longitudinal study proceeds, therefore, its subjects have an increasing advantage along with their advancing years: the beneficial effect of years of practice.

Finally, and perhaps most important, longitudinal studies do not permit us to assess age changes in a pure form. Here also pure age changes, those that result solely from advancing years, are obscured by an important confounding influence: the many life conditions and environmental events that affect the rate of aging at a particular time. For example, because of a lung-cancer scare in a certain year, many in the cohort might give up smoking between two tests. Or because of the widespread acquisition of television sets, most might give up reading within a

**TABLE 1-3.**   Panel attrition during the first four observations of the Duke study.

| Observation | Dates | Subjects with Complete Records | Percentage of 256 Who Returned | Percentage of Non Returnees | | | |
|---|---|---|---|---|---|---|---|
| | | | | Died | Ill | Refused | Other |
| I | 5/55–5/59 | 256 | – | – | – | – | – |
| II | 9/59–5/61 | 192 (10 added) | 71 | 43 | 23 | 20 | 14 |
| III | 1/64–3/65 | 139 (1 added) | 52 | 63 | 26 | 2 | 9 |
| IV | 10/66–7/67 | 110 | 41 | 68 | 18 | 1 | 13 |

*(Source: From "A Physiological, Psychological, and Sociological Study of Aging," by E. Busse. In E. Palmore (Ed.),* Normal Aging. *Copyright © 1970 by Duke University Press (Durham, NC). Reprinted by permission.)*

**BOX 1-4.   Correlation Is Not Causation**

An experiment is the ideal way of determining causes. Here every factor is held constant except the one whose effect is to be determined. If modifying this antecedent element does result in the predicted consequence, then an investigator is able to say the change in the antecedent was the cause.

Making causal statements is vitally important in the psychology of aging. But the experimental approach cannot be used to answer many of gerontologists' most important questions about causes.

For example, researchers cannot conduct a laboratory experiment to test Erikson's hypothesis that reaching integrity makes a person unafraid of death or to determine whether exercising throughout adulthood causes good physical health in old age. Unfortunately, we simply cannot easily manipulate these two important antecedents in the laboratory. So investigators must turn to differences in integrity or exercise that already exist among people and then look at the relation of those differences to a hypothetical consequence either now (that is, less death fear) or, as in the longitudinal strategy, some years hence (that is, good physical health in late life). In both cases they would be using a type of *correlational approach,* determining how one variable relates to one or several others. If indeed a positive association (correlation) were then found, a causal inference might be made: Exercising earlier in life has beneficial consequences for health in the later years. Reaching integrity does indeed enable the older person to be able to accept death.

Particularly by those not familiar with research, this type of conclusion is often reached. Sometimes it is accurate. However, as a closer look at our examples shows, assumptions about causes based on correlations can be fatally wrong. For instance, the association between exercise during adulthood and good health late in life might really be incidental. Both might be caused by a third factor: good genes. People less sickly, more biologically fit, might have more energy during adulthood and so be prone to exercise more. Their same genetic makeup would also result in a healthier late life. A general predisposition toward a calm and accepting approach to living might underlie both integrity (being at peace with one's past) and low death fear (being at peace with one's end). The association between the two qualities in older adults might not really mean the first caused the last, as we initially assumed.

If we could control for all likely competing explanations (that is, the alternatives just mentioned and others), the correlational method could be confidently used to make statements about causes. However, as this is often not possible, we are left with a final caution: When examining this most prevalent research strategy in the chapters to come, be wary. Although we often will be tempted to do so, make assumptions about possible causes with care.

short period. At the next evaluation, then, physical health, which normally might decline, could mysteriously appear to improve, or vocabulary scores, which normally might remain stable (see Chapter 4), could dip in a puzzling way. This important source of error in evaluating real or intrinsic age changes using the longitudinal approach is called **time of measurement effects.**

A methodological strategy has been devised (Schaie, 1965) to separate, or partial out, true age changes from cohort and time-of-measurement effects. This set of procedures, called **sequential strategies,** involves making simultaneous cross-sectional and longitudinal comparisons. As with the pure longitudinal design, sequential methods involve a considerable investment of effort. However, the most ambitious recent developmental research in gerontology is likely to employ this new sophisticated procedure for assessing pure age change.

**An Important Example: The Duke Longitudinal Study.**    Although the longitudinal method has deficiencies and is being replaced by new strategies for determining change, this approach was used in the most important study of the aging process to date, the Duke Longitudinal Study. The landmark Duke study, conceived and begun a full quarter century ago, remains the classic in the field, the most comprehensive single source of information we have today about normal aging.

The Duke Longitudinal Study (see Busse, 1970) was begun in the mid-1950s by a team of researchers at Duke University representing a wide array of theoretical perspectives and areas of expertise. Their purpose was to explore an almost uncharted area of inquiry at the time: the aging process in normal, community-dwelling older adults. The research was to be extremely comprehensive. Extensive medical, psychological, and sociological data were to be collected during each of an extended series of tests.

The subjects were volunteers aged 60 to 94 who lived in Durham, North Carolina, where Duke University is located. They were chosen to reflect the age, sex, ethnic, and socioeconomic distribution of the older population in the area. None was institutionalized. All were required to spend two days at Duke University at regular intervals from the study's inception until their death. The primary inducement offered was a series of free medical examinations.

At the initial round of tests there were 256 participants with complete records, but at successive evaluation periods that number regularly decreased (see Table 1-3). Examinations were repeated every three or four years until 1965, every two years until 1972, and since then once a year.

An amazing 788 or so pieces of information about each subject were coded at each successive test. Medical data included a complete history and extensive physical examination. Particular attention was paid to assessments of vision, hearing, and cardiovascular functioning. Each subject was given a summary rating of overall health and degree of disability. Participants also scored themselves in these areas.

Participants were also examined neurologically. They were evaluated for current psychological disorders and questioned about psychological problems earlier in life. They were given an intelligence test and several comprehensive indexes of personality. Their speed was evaluated in a variety of learning situations. Finally, a full social assessment was conducted. Respondents were questioned about life satisfaction, work and retirement, sexual behavior, family relationships, level of activity, and activities engaged in both then and in the past (see Table 1-4).

The outcome has been manifold and rich. The Duke study has yielded answers to many important questions we might have, not just about age changes in the already elderly but also about how people function and behave in late life. Hundreds of articles in journals and books are devoted to the Duke results. Two full volumes have been compiled to summarize the study's findings. The first, titled *Normal Aging* (Palmore, 1970), is a report of the Duke research through 1969. The second, *Normal Aging II* (Palmore, 1974), is a compilation of data from 1970 to 1973, plus the initial results of a second Duke study of mainly middle-aged adults begun in 1968. Complete references for these highly recommended books are at the end of this chapter.

### The Chapters to Follow

Throughout this book several general themes will organize the discussion. Because of the comprehensive nature of the Duke study, findings from it will be highlighted repeatedly. Because the life-span developmental view stresses the need for comprehensiveness, that view will be the guiding spirit followed in the chapters to come. Most important, though, is the emphasis natural to my being a practicing clinical psychologist. Understanding the personal experience of aging is critical. It is essential to explore psychological avenues for making that experience the best it can be.

To highlight the personal impact of aging, a different case vignette will illustrate the information presented in each succeeding chapter. These vignettes, however, should not be read as though they embodied reactions or experiences universal

**TABLE 1-4.**    Measures used in the Duke Longitudinal Study.

| | |
|---|---|
| Medical history (original and interim) | Psychological data |
| Physical examination | Rorschach (see Chapter 8) |
| Neurological examination | Aspiration level (TAT) (see |
| Mental status (see Chapter 8) | Chapters 6 and 8) |
| Depression and hypochondriasis | Wechsler Adult Intelligence |
| Dermatological examination | Scale (see Chapter 4) |
| Ophthalmological examination | Reaction time (see Chapter 3) |
| (vision) | Social history and information |
| Audiometry (hearing) | Retirement data |
| Electroencephalogram | |
| Chest X ray | |
| Laboratory studies | |
| Medical summary | |

*(Source: Adapted from "A Physiological, Psychological, and Sociological Study of Aging," by E. Busse. In E. Palmore (Ed.),* Normal Aging. *Copyright © 1970 by Duke University Press, Durham, N.C. Reprinted by permission. [Psychological data are included in full.])*

among older adults. It cannot be emphasized strongly enough that diversity and individual differences are the hallmark of life's last stage.

To explore avenues for enriching the experience of old age, psychologically oriented intervention strategies will be described that apply to each topic discussed. Once again, in reading through these existing attempts to help, we must be cautious. Aging should not be thought of as a condition in need of cure. Often what has been done to intervene is quite minimal simply because the elderly have been relatively neglected by psychologists and others whose job it is to provide psychological services.

Then, a final caution seems important. Although occasionally I will present data about biological or social aspects of aging, this book is basically limited to the psychology of late life. But this special orientation should not imply that aging is always approached in a compartmentalized way. As illustrated by the description of the Duke investigation, researchers in a variety of specialties often collaborate in studying older adults. We would see the same phenomenon by glancing through a major gerontological journal or attending a meeting of the Gerontological Society, the national professional organization of researchers and practitioners whose interest is late life. Gerontology is a truly multidisciplinary field!

## Summary

Americans generally view old age in highly negative terms, as a time of unremitting loss and decline, the worst period of the life span. People have definite ideas about the set of behaviors felt to typify the older person, shared conceptions that are learned in early childhood and persist through life. Children reject the idea that they will become old. Older people (even those quite advanced in years) also often resist labeling themselves with this negative term. One reason may be that in fact the attributes popularly associated with being old really do not apply to most elderly persons. These may be stereotypes, examples of a prejudice called "ageism."

Demographic information about today's elderly does suggest that making universal statements about late life is ill advised. Older Americans are a diverse group. The part of our population over 65 (now 11%) has increased rapidly since 1900 and will continue to grow in the future. In 2030, when the baby-boom generation has reached 65, a full 1 in 5 Americans will be older adults. Two generalizations about the older population can be made, however. Because of longevity differences, older women outnumber older men. Because of changes in the pattern of medical advances, the most rapidly growing segment of our older population is that at the upper end (over age 75). These elderly, called the old-old, are more likely to be ill. The young-old, arbitrarily defined as those aged 65–74, are usually much healthier and so seem to warrant being put in a different class.

Information about the issues important to American older adults also belies the typical negative view of old age. A 1981 Harris survey revealed that today's elderly (with the important exception of minorities) report being satisfied with themselves and their current life. They also are less bothered by financial concerns and crime than most of us would expect. However, finances, crime, and health are problems for many Americans over 65.

Because psychology is the scientific study of behavior, psychologists are in a unique position to provide information about the reality of late life. At an increasing rate, particularly since the end of the Second World War, psychologists have been studying the aging process and all facets of behavior in older adults. A small number of theoretical orientations and research strategies have been particularly important in guiding their approach.

Behaviorism is probably the most important of these theoretical world views. This most influential theory in modern psychology emphasizes the importance of the current environment (rather than biology or the past) in behavior. Responses are learned directly, by either classical or operant conditioning, or indirectly, by modeling (observing others). The laws and mechanisms of learning are neutral and universal, so behaviors often called negative or intrinsic to the aging process are not viewed as pathological or basic to old age by learning theorists. How older adults act is a function of their current environment, the particular reinforcement contingencies they are exposed to in daily life.

Psychoanalytic theory is another influential general approach to human behavior used to understand older adults. In this important system of thought, human behavior is motivated by unconscious childhood wishes, fantasies, and needs. The quality of childhood experiences determines lifelong mental health. Because personality is fixed from these earliest years, the way a person acts when elderly is congruent with the way he or she has behaved throughout life. But old age is a time of heightened vulnerability, as it is a period of many losses and much external stress.

Of these two theories, behaviorism is the more widespread approach in the psychology of aging. It has broader applicability, not being just a framework for understanding personality and psychological problems alone. It also is more accepting and optimistic than psychoanalytic theory with its emphasis on early childhood, personality stability, and old age as a season of loss. Learning theorists do not elevate early life at the expense of other ages. How an older adult acts is modifiable, not a lifelong style or a way of behaving that is basic to being at the last life stage. So this perspective tends to be more palatable to those who have chosen to study late life or provide psychological services to older adults.

Two theorists within the psychoanalytic tradition, Erik Erikson and C. G. Jung, have developed positive ideas about personality change in old age, views differing from the Freudian perspective. Jung's belief, part of his own well-developed theory of personality, is that a spiritual transformation begins to occur in midlife. The individual becomes more introspective, less concerned with personal success, and more devoted to philosophical concerns. In addition, a change toward less demarcated sex roles occurs. Erikson departs from traditional Freudian theory mainly in his interest in psychological changes that occur throughout life. He postulates that each chronological period has its own focal issue, or crisis, and that in late life the issue is integrity versus despair. The person who reaches the psychological pinnacle of integrity accepts his or her past and place in the scheme of living and so is also able to accept approaching death. The person who rejects the way he or she has lived feels despair and is frightened at the prospect of dying, Erikson's theory, despite very few efforts to test it empirically, is much more popular and widely accepted than Jung's more arcane formulations about personality.

The life-span developmental perspective is not a specific theory but largely a prescription for an eclectic approach in viewing behavior. Many theories are useful. Change is multidirectional and also often individual-specific. Describing, explaining, and modifying development is the goal of this general orientation used to understand human development at any particular period of life.

Cross-sectional and longitudinal studies are the two major research strategies for assessing developmental change. In cross-sectional research the performance of different age groups at the same time is compared. Such studies confuse cohort differences (differences due to being born at a particular time) with real changes that occur with advancing age and are therefore inferior to longitudinal research, a method that involves following individuals over time.

In longitudinal studies usually one cohort is repeatedly tested over a number of years. This research technique yields information about age changes in that group as well as data on individual patterns of aging and the impact of earlier life experiences on development. However, the longitudinal method also has problems. It is difficult to generalize about the aging process from observing one group. The study must remain relevant, and time and effort must be expended over a period of years. The results are likely to minimize the typical extent of age losses, particularly because only the most able subjects are likely to complete the sequence of tests. Finally, assessing age changes here is problematic too. Time-of-measurement effects or societal events affecting the rate of aging at a particular time may obscure true age changes, using this approach. Sequential strategies, a procedure involving simultaneous cross-sectional and longitudinal comparisons, are now used to disentangle cohort and time-of-measurement effects from pure age changes.

The Duke Longitudinal Study is the most important single investigation in gerontology. This comprehensive study of normal aging was begun at Duke University in the 1950s with over 250 community-dwelling persons aged 60 or over as its subjects. Medical, psychological, and sociological data were collected every several years. The Duke research still remains the landmark in the field—in many psychological areas, the best source of information about the aging process that we have today.

## Key Terms

| | |
|---|---|
| *Geropsychology* | *Behaviorism's cognitive learning approach* |
| *Gerontological psychology* | *Classical conditioning* |
| *Ageism* | *Operant conditioning* |
| *Demography* | *Modeling* |
| *Young-old* | *Ego integrity* |
| *Old-old* | *Life-span developmental perspective* |

*Cross-sectional studies*          *Time of measurement effects*
*Age differences, age changes*     *Sequential strategies*
*Cohort*                           *Duke Longitudinal Study*
*Longitudinal studies*

## Recommended Readings

Baltes, P. B., Reese, H. W., & Lipsett, L. P. Life-span developmental psychology. **Annual Review of Psychology,** 1980, *31*, 65–110.

*Review article summarizing research in this growing area of psychology and the life-span developmental approach to behavior. Difficult.*

Birren, J. E., & Schaie, K. W. (Eds). **Handbook of the psychology of aging.** New York: Van Nostrand Reinhold, 1977.

*The definitive compendium of research in the psychology of aging to 1977. Glance through the chapter headings for an overview of the diverse content of psychological studies. Difficult.*

Erikson, E. H. **Childhood and society** (2nd ed.). New York: Norton, 1963.

*Series of essays by Erikson. Contains chapter describing his eight developmental stages. Moderately difficult.*

Harris, L., and associates. **Aging in the eighties: America in transition.** Washington, D.C.: National Council on the Aging, 1981.

*The comprehensive Harris survey. Information about aging from those over 65 and also about how Americans under 65 see older adults. Not difficult.*

Palmore, E. (Ed.). **Normal Aging.** Durham, N.C.: Duke University Press, 1970.

Palmore, E. (Ed.). **Normal Aging II.** Durham, N.C.: Duke University Press, 1974.

*Two-volume summary of the Duke findings. Moderately difficult.*

# PHYSICAL PROCESSES

CHAPTER TWO

# The Aging Body

Dr. Kennedy, a youthful-looking 71-year-old dentist, has been back at work now for several months since he had to give up his job last year after a fairly serious heart attack. His time in the impersonally run intensive care unit had been frightening enough, but his anxiety about dying was increased by the fact that at exactly the age he had his attack (70) both his father and older brother had died of similar cardiac arrests. In fact, because of this uncanny coincidence, Dr. Kennedy had approached his seventieth birthday with some trepidation. He had felt he too might be predestined (although, being a scientist, he called it "genetically programmed") to suffer their fate at the same age.

Dr. Kennedy's wife had always teased him about being a workaholic, but there was a serious side to her kidding. She intuitively felt that his tendency to pressure himself into working long hours might have precipitated this heart attack as well as the milder one he had suffered at age 55. At that time his cardiologist had told him he should avoid overstressing himself and do something to control his high blood pressure. But Dr. Kennedy was incapable of modifying his work habits and neglected to take the blood pressure pills his physician had prescribed. After this recent scare, though, the idea that he could die hit home with a vengeance. He was only too willing to give up working and to adhere faithfully to any regimen the doctor asked.

Dr. Kennedy had always loved being a dentist, even more so in the past few years because he was so well established professionally. He took particular pride in his continuing success because it was so unexpected. Because a prime requirement of dentistry is a high degree of manual skill, he had always thought he would be too old to practice by his late sixties. In fact, however, the slight loss of dexterity he noticed with patients was more than compensated for by his breadth of experience. He was fond of saying he was probably more adept with his hands than most dentists half his age. Recently, though, he had to admit an upsetting need to refer some particularly tricky cases to a younger colleague.

His wife didn't tell him, but she was somewhat anxious about the emotional effect that stopping work might have on her husband, because his job had always been so important to him. She was right to be worried, because a few months after his retirement Dr. Kennedy seemed even weaker and more disabled than he had been right after leaving the hospital. His physician assured him that his medical tests indicated he should not be feeling as bad as he seemed to be. Dr. Kennedy felt exhausted all the time and on some days could barely walk around the block. He was sure the medical tests had not picked up his true condition, because he had had a similar experience just before his first heart attack. He had been having chest pains and had gone to see his doctor only to be told nothing was wrong. Several days later he was rushed to the emergency room. He had been right then about his actual condition and felt sure he was right now.

His wife felt differently. She could see that her husband's anxiety about his physical state was a constant preoccupation and that he focused on every ache in the vicinity of his chest. She also knew she had been catering to her husband's fears by treating him as an invalid. After talking to the cardiologist, she was referred for a consultation to a psychologist who specialized in behavioral medicine. The psychologist advised her that even if her husband's condition warranted a certain amount of restriction of his activity, it was worth the effort to get him to live a more satisfying, productive life. She suggested that Mrs. Kennedy encourage her husband to return to work and try to reinforce any efforts he made toward being more independent.

Even though it was difficult, Mrs. Kennedy was able to persuade her husband to take a few patients a week by appealing to his pride in taking on challenges. In addition, she refused to do things she had done before, such as opening doors for him or picking him up by car when he was within walking distance of home. These were all suggestions the psychologist had made about not reinforcing dependency and encouraging more self-sufficient behavior.

Initially, she was somewhat frightened about following what she thought might be dangerous instructions. For example, what if this strategy actually increased her husband's chance of having another heart attack? What if he was really incapable physically of having a more active life? Luckily, though, the approach worked to a degree that surprised both Mrs. Kennedy and her husband. A few weeks after returning to work and not being catered to by his wife, Dr. Kennedy had more energy than he had had in months. In fact, he currently hopes to increase the number of patients he sees so that he will be working almost a 30-hour week.

Many psychologists disagree with the idea that age 65 should be the chronological marker that signals a person's entering old age. Although any demarcation is necessarily arbitrary, they argue that if a marker must be picked, 75, the age dividing the young-old from the old-old (see Chapter 1), is a much more appropriate one. At or around age 75 many people begin to have limitations to their ability to function independently; the number who are disabled increases dramatically; and intellectual impairments become more common.

In the biologist's view, however, aging and old age occur much earlier. In addition, in contrast to the psychological theories described earlier that view aging in positive terms, a biological perspective involves the unremitting negatives of the stereotypic view: aging equals decrement. Biologists can sometimes even trace the origins of decremental aging changes to infancy. For example, the development of **atherosclerosis** (fatty deposits on the walls of arteries) is seen as a typical sign of aging. (We would suspect that Dr. Kennedy, for example, would be likely to have a significant amount of atherosclerosis, as this is a primary cause of heart attacks.) However, beginning atherosclerosis has been found in infants, and advanced signs of this condition were found in many Vietnam casualties in their twenties who were autopsied.

Most biological signs of aging, though, begin to set in after growth is complete, in a person's twenties or early thirties (Tobin, 1977). A leading gerontologist has suggested several criteria for whether a particular change qualifies as a true aging phenomenon (Strehler, 1962): It is deleterious—it impairs functioning. It is progressive—it gets worse as a person gets older. It is intrinsic to the person—it is not caused by the environment. It is ubiquitous—it affects every member of our species at least to some degree.

Scientists are still not sure how universal some aging changes are that occur regularly in Western countries. For example, atherosclerosis is a standard accompaniment to aging in industrialized societies. However, in some non-Western countries, it is rare or unknown (Ostfeld, 1975). Atherosclerosis, then, may not be intrinsic to the aging process itself, and it may, therefore, be preventable. So, it is important to understand which signs of aging are universal because it is likely to be easier to learn how to control and possibly eliminate those that are not.

Another important fact about aging is that as people get older, they are increasingly susceptible to disease. When normal aging changes occur to a moderate degree, they are not illnesses, but as described in more detail later, many of these changes at their extreme become what are called chronic diseases. So the chance of developing disease increases with age. In addition, older people are more likely than the young to suffer from multiple illnesses and to get certain characteristic types of diseases. Our clinical example illustrates a common age-related disease. Heart disease of Dr. Kennedy's type typically develops only in the latter part of the life span.

In fact, at least in our society heart disease and the other major killer, cancer, are so closely tied to chronological age that in the very old person who dies at least one of these conditions has a good chance of being present, no matter what the actual cause of death was. In autopsies performed on the very old, it is common to find many pathological changes that would have killed these persons soon if they had not died when they did (Comfort, 1979).

Aging also always has a fixed end. Even though there are reports of long-lived people (see Box 2-2, p. 56), there is little substantiated evidence to suggest that anyone lives past 110. This fixed maximum has not changed since we evolved as a species. What has changed, as mentioned in Chapter 1, is that more of us are reaching the upper half of the theoretical life span (Hayflick, 1976). Figure 2-1 shows life expectancy in different societies and eras, compared with the theoretical ideal.

Our ***maximum life span*** is long in comparison with most animals'. Although some species, such as the Galapagos tortoise, outlive us, the human is the longest-lived mammal. The horse can live about 46 years, the goat 20, and the mouse only 3.3 (Eichorn, 1979). Our long life is intimately related to our large brain, since a mammal's index of cephalization, or ratio of brain to body weight, is positively related to its longevity. The survival advantage of having a large brain in relation to one's body may be that it allows more neurons to function as reserves to replace those lost in the wear and tear of living (Busse, 1977).

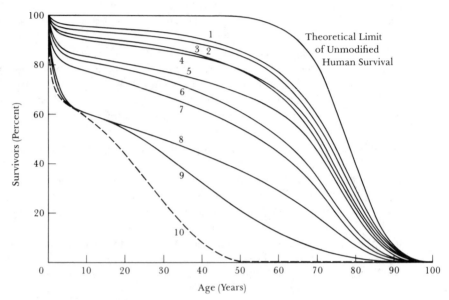

| 1 | New Zealand, 1934–1938 | 6 | U.S. (whites), 1900–1902 |
|---|---|---|---|
| 2 | U.S. (whites), 1939–1941 | 7 | Japan, 1926–1930 |
| 3 | U.S. (whites), 1929–1931 | 8 | Mexico, 1930 |
| 4 | England and Wales, 1930–1932 | 9 | British India, 1921–1930 |
| 5 | Italy, 1930–1932 | 10 | Stone Age People |

**FIGURE 2-1.**   Historical and geographical differences in the human survival curve. *(Source: From* The Biology of Senescence, *by A. Comfort. Copyright 1979 by Alex Comfort. Reprinted by permission of Elsevier Science Publishing Co. and the author.)*

## Biological Theories of Aging

Scientists interested in the biology of aging want to understand what is causing the phenomena just described—the typical characteristics of normal aging; the close association of later life with disease and particularly with certain illnesses; and our maximum life span and its relation to those of other species (Brash & Hart, 1978). To be plausible, any hypothesis these scientists devise should explain, or at least be compatible with, these and other important facts about aging. There are numerous theories of why we age (see Busse, 1977; Busse & Blazer, 1980; Comfort, 1979; Hall, 1976; or Shock, 1977, for a more complete review), but currently most investigators are looking for the key to this all-important process in changes that occur within the basic units of our body—our cells.

The body is composed of two basic constituents: cells, either able to divide or nondividing, and intercellular connective tissue, whose main constituent is a fibrous protein called **collagen**. Most often biologists assume that problems and processes within cells are the root cause of aging. However, some also argue that the collagen-rich extracellular substance may contribute importantly. As we get older, the normally elastic collagen molecules form cross-links and so get stiffer. Collagen cross-linkage is partly responsible for benign aging changes such as wrinkled skin. It also causes potentially life-threatening changes such as ***arteriosclerosis*** (loss of elasticity of artery walls). One theorist (Kohn, 1978) suggests that stiffened collagen may in itself cause our cells—and, therefore, us—to die because it prevents needed nutrients from getting into the cells.

Cellular explanations of why we age have been grouped into two categories: those that suggest random damage to cells is responsible and those that envision aging and death as results of a specific preset biological program (see Marx, 1974a, 1974b, for a review). What complicates the search for a unitary cause of aging is that there may be more than one cause. Each idea examined below may be valid. It is just as likely that the multiple signs of aging have multiple causes as that a single mechanism is responsible for the whole process.

### Random-Damage Theories of Aging

According to the related speculations grouped under the heading of random-damage theories, accumulating faults in the cell's ability to produce proteins are the main cause of aging and death. Protein molecules are essential because they form the basis of all cellular reactions and functions. ***DNA,*** the genetic material in the nucleus of each cell, programs how our bodies develop and work by serving as the blueprint from which these molecules are synthesized. The DNA molecule has the shape of a double helix, which can uncoil to transmit information. It unwinds to synthesize RNA, which, in a complex series of steps, serves as the template for protein formation.

If a part of the DNA molecule essential to forming the protein of a particular cell is changed, and cellular repair processes cannot correct the fault, then it is almost certain that the cell will not be able to function as well as it did. Changes in the DNA molecule are called ***mutations***. Mutations probably occur continually in the course of exposure to environmental insults and in the process of the cell's work. Being responsible for our evolution from one-celled organisms, these changes clearly have a positive function. However, most mutations are deleterious. If their harmful effects are important enough or widespread enough, they will result in production of many defective proteins, and a cell will die.

Some random-damage theorists (for example, Brash & Hart, 1978) view the physical changes that accompany chronological aging as the visible signs of accumulating DNA damage in cells throughout our bodies. As DNA faults accumulate, they reason, more faulty proteins are produced, and more cells malfunction and die. Eventually enough cells or enough critically important ones are lost to cause death.

Other biologists who agree that aging and death are caused by random cellular damage argue that the DNA mutation rate is too slow to cause the basic problem. They believe that the most important changes probably occur further down in the system, at the RNA or protein level. In addition, they argue, environmental substances that cause DNA to mutate, such as radiation, affect the genetic material of dividing cells the most, whereas impaired or destroyed postmitotic (nondividing) cells are responsible for the most important manifestations of physical aging. Critically important structures such as the brain and spinal cord are composed of postmitotic cells. Some gerontologists (Hall, 1976) point out that since deterioration in these structures often causes the most dramatic symptoms of old age, an adequate theory of aging should explain what is most likely to cause specifically postmitotic cells to malfunction and die.

### Programmed-Aging Theories

Random-damage theories assume there is no master plan that causes aging. In contrast to these beliefs is the just as reasonable alternative: old age and death, like growth, are specifically programmed and timed. Ideas differ on where an aging timer is located, what sets it off, and how it operates. Basic to the idea that we are specifically programmed to age, however, is the thought that the orderly quality of many aging changes suggests that the process occurs by a programmed, coordinated plan. And the fact that each species has a fixed life span indicates that some sort of genetic programming must be involved in death (Hayflick, 1976).

An aging and death clock, set to go off at a certain time, might be located in the DNA of each cell. Or the clock could be more centralized, placed in a system responsible for orchestrating many bodily functions. If there were such a central aging clock, two places in particular, because of their widespread influence on the body, seem the most likely candidates to harbor it: the hypothalamus and the immune system.

**The Hypothalamus as an Aging Clock.**  The *hypothalamus* is a tiny structure in the brain that has effects on the body far beyond its size. It is responsible for coordinating many essential functions, such as eating, sexual behavior, temperature control, and emotional expression. It also has a key role in regulating physical growth, sexual development, and reproduction, because it is intimately involved in producing hormones. This structure is centrally responsible for the "death" of at least one bodily system. By shutting off hormone production, it programs the end of female reproductive capacity at menopause. Its far-ranging effects on so many organs make it a likely candidate to regulate other manifestations of aging as well and to serve as the clock or series of clocks that times our death (Comfort, 1979).

**The Immune System as an Aging Clock.**  A crucial system, the *immune system,* is spread out over the body in a diverse collection of tissues. Its function is to protect us against foreign substances. In response to an alien substance such as a microorganism or possibly incipient cancer (cancer cells are also foreign to our body tissues), the immune system responds rapidly. Differentiated "killer" cells are produced and molecules called antibodies are formed specifically tailored to kill the foreign invader. The thymus, a gland involved in the complicated immune response, slowly disappears during adulthood. It has been suggested that this gland may serve as an aging pacemaker, because its disappearance might signal a decline in immune function that has far-reaching effects on our health (Walford, 1969).

---

**BOX 2-1.   Extending the Life Span**

If an impaired immune system is the cause of aging, we may discover ways to slow aging by stimulating flagging immune function. If the problem is a hypothalamic clock, ways of fooling the timer might be found. Even if random cellular damage is the root cause of aging and death, it might be possible to develop substances that make cells more resistant to such damage. Research on the basic cause of aging, then, may have a tremendous impact on all of us. Instead of prolonging the lives of some people to some extent, which is the most that can be hoped for from curing major diseases, the inquiry into why we age has a potentially much larger payoff: it might allow us to retard old age for everyone and lengthen the maximum span of life.

Although many experts may disagree with his point of view, one optimistic gerontologist (Comfort, 1978) believes that the knowledge and tools to accomplish this goal may be available as soon as the last decade of this century. The breakthrough that retards aging and death will have important political, social, and psychological consequences. We can only hope it is the blessing to our species that it should be and does not extend our existence at the price of disrupting our society or destroying our happiness in life.

---

The intact immune system can do two important things: recognize foreign substances and kill them and, at the same time, recognize and so spare the body's own cells. It is thought that when the immune system ages, deficiencies develop in both these areas. Impairments in the aging immune system's ability to stave off foreign attack may explain why older people are more susceptible both to getting and dying from infectious diseases and to developing cancer. Deficiencies in the immune system's recognition of the body's own cells may cause the system to attack the person's own tissues. This phenomenon, called an autoimmune response, is suspected to be instrumental in the development of age-related diseases as diverse as diabetes and senile dementia. In this way, some gerontologists think, a faulty immune system may play a part in many common phenomena of aging and death.

## Normal Aging

Extending the life span—that is, modifying the basic course of aging at its root—may not be such a remote possibility; nevertheless, we are still in the process of understanding some facts about that basic course as it now exists. One important unanswered issue has already been mentioned: how intrinsic to aging itself are some of the typical signs of age that people show in Western countries? In addition, we are currently getting answers to an even more practical question: how do people normally age physically in American society?

### The Baltimore Study: Establishing Norms

The comprehensive Duke Longitudinal Study (see Chapter 1) has given us a wealth of information about the course of physical aging in an already elderly group. In contrast, the ongoing Baltimore Longitudinal Study is examining how the aging process occurs throughout adulthood as a whole (Andres, 1979; Butler, 1977; Tobin, 1977). This ambitious investigation was begun in 1959 under the auspices of the National Institutes of Health. Since then, on a predetermined schedule (usually every two years), male volunteers ranging in age from 20 to their nineties have been thoroughly tested physically and questioned about a variety of health practices thought to affect the rate of physical aging. The investigation is being carried out at the Gerontology Research Center in Baltimore and has now expanded to include women. Its main purpose is to establish norms of physiological functioning for middle-aged and elderly people. It has already had considerable beneficial impact on medical practice.

Until recently, standards for how a person should be performing physically have been based on data derived from young adults (Andres, 1979). This has had some unfortunate consequences for middle-aged and elderly people. Many important diseases such as diabetes were sometimes diagnosed in older adults simply because their biochemistry did not measure up to that of younger people. For example, until the Baltimore study clearly demonstrated that the practice was unreasonable, diabetes had been diagnosed indiscriminately for all age groups when a person's blood sugar level exceeded a certain fixed amount. This criterion had been established by determining what was abnormal for young adults without considering that blood sugar might normally rise with age and that a similar elevation of blood sugar might not have the same pathological significance for the old as for the young. In fact, the Baltimore researchers found that, by the traditional standard, half of their subjects over age 60 were identified as diabetic even though only a few had diabetic symptoms. Concluding that the standard, not the older people, needed changing, the investigators established a more appropriate criterion that took chronological age into account (Tobin & Andres, 1979). The finding with regard to diabetes was a great advance in accurate diagnosis gained from longitudinally studying normally aging adults. (In view of this caution, we would hope that the cardiologist's evaluation that Dr. Kennedy had high blood pressure was based on norms for his age group. Blood pressure, like blood sugar, normally rises with age.)

The Baltimore study, being longitudinal, has the invaluable advantage over cross-sectional studies of being able to accurately capture changes that occur as individuals age. Because it follows people over time (and investigators do not have to rely on a person's memory), it can also examine the impact of poor health practices such as smoking or not exercising on the rate of aging. Conversely, it can help answer the crucial question whether the aging process can be slowed, halted, or even reversed by taking exceptionally good care of one's health. However, the study invariably must fall short of its ideal of developing norms for today's typical American because of the biases inherent in the longitudinal design itself.

Like all longitudinal research, the Baltimore study is confined to an elite group of people and so is likely to present a too optimistic picture of the extent of decremental changes that typically occur as Americans age. In the Baltimore study this is almost certain to occur for several reasons in addition to those mentioned in Chapter 1. The volunteers are mainly college-educated (some with advanced degrees) and relatively affluent (Andres, 1979; Tobin, 1977). This group is therefore likely initially to be healthier than average because socioeconomic status is correlated with longevity (and good health). In addition, we might expect these self-selected subjects to be even more special, for they may have volunteered in part because they were particularly interested in and attuned to precisely what the study is measuring—physical health. Finally, undergoing the extensive tests every few years may accentuate participants' tendencies toward health-promoting behavior between evaluations, making them still healthier than the unselected group of Americans they are supposed to represent. If we add to these factors the other influences favoring the later years intrinsic to the longitudinal method, we can be certain that the Baltimore study will underestimate the extent of deleterious changes that occur normally with age. However, this ambitious effort and other (usually cross-sectional) attempts to assess physical change have allowed us to make some important generalizations about the aging process.

### An Overall Picture of Normal Aging

The first finding of all investigations is something we know just from observing how people of the same age look and act: There is tremendous variability among individuals in the rate of physical aging (Andres, 1979; Kovar, 1977). Some 60-year-olds seem physically more like 40; others appear much older. Differences in appearance are mirrored on specific tests. Capacities as diverse as lung function, grip strength, and sugar metabolism all vary tremendously among people of the same age.

This finding highlights the importance of the pluralistic life-span view. In physical functioning, as in every area of life, individual diversity and individual-specific degrees of change may be the first key to describing older adults. Generalizations about the aging process and older individuals must be made, but it is important to remember that any given person may be very different from the norm.

Even for the individual, making monolithic statements about physical functioning is unwarranted. Different tissues and body systems can vary tremendously in the rate at which they age (Tobin, 1977). Our clinical vignette provides a good example. Dr. Kennedy's manual dexterity appears much above the norm, possibly the equal of a typical 30-year-old's. His heart, in contrast, may be functioning significantly less adequately than would be expected at his age.

In spite of great individual variation, though, we do expect a common phenomenon to occur in successively older age groups: poorer and poorer physical performance. This observably poorer performance is largely the external manifestation of a general deteriorative process that occurs throughout the body. After maturity, the efficiency and maximum capacity at which most bodily functions can work decline progressively (Tobin, 1977). For example, as already mentioned, the older person cannot metabolize sugar as well, so blood sugar may reach a higher level normally than it does in the young. Similar losses of function occur in most physiologic capacities. The older person's heart does not pump as efficiently; the kidneys do not filter wastes as well; the person cannot breathe as deeply as before. Luckily, most organ systems have a built-in extra **reserve capacity,** which is needed and used only in emergency situations, so these losses have little effect under normal conditions. However, they may severely hamper the elderly person when he or she needs to perform at a maximum level—under conditions of stress.

Infection, surgery, emotional upsets, extremes of cold and heat, strenuous exercise—all these are stressors demanding a high level of physical performance. Because the older person's system may not have the reserves to meet these challenges, the individual is more likely to succumb to these insults (Tobin, 1977). More often than for a young person, disease and death can result.

This lessened reserve capacity explains why older people tend to be more vulnerable to abnormal conditions as diverse as running a mile, having the flu, hot summers or cold winters, and moving (as discussed later). Physiologic losses that occur with age are most likely to cause problems whenever a high level of performance is needed. In such situations the older person's system may be incapable of meeting the demand. For example, Dr. Kennedy found that when his work required great dexterity, he could not perform and had to refer the patient to a younger colleague. However, only these extreme work demands led to incapacity and failure, reminding him of his age.

### Some Specific Normal Hallmarks of Age

The limitations just mentioned can be life-threatening when the older person is overtaxed because he or she does not have the necessary reserves. Other physical changes that occur as we age do not have these potentially fatal consequences. However, they may markedly affect how we feel and how we function. Because of their intrinsic interest, I have chosen to focus on just two of the most observable aging signs, gray hair and wrinkled skin, and to describe what causes these classic indicators to appear. Because of their impact on the older person's ability to be independent, two other important nonfatal changes that are likely to occur will also be examined—ones affecting the joints and bones. A complete description of even the most important specific changes that characterize normal physical aging is beyond the scope of this psychologically oriented book. For a more complete understanding of how the body ages, consult the excellent text on aging and health (Kart, Metress, & Metress, 1978) recommended for further reading at the end of this chapter.

Skin changes, hair changes, and to a lesser extent stiffness and loss of mobility due to skeletal changes are reliable hallmarks of advancing age. Interestingly, even though it seems obvious that observing these changes in oneself may affect one psychologically, there is no research on this topic. In an excellent though polemic popular exploration of late life, de Beauvoir (1972) emphasizes that the personal impact of these changes may be far from minimal, as she movingly describes the connection between seeing her new aging image and being aware she has changed: "When I was forty I still could not believe it when I stood in front of the looking glass and said to myself 'I am forty'. . . .Old age is particularly difficult to assume because we have always regarded it as something alien, a foreign species" (p. 283). Our first awareness that we are getting older may overwhelm us in a similar way. All of a sudden we look in the mirror and are shocked (or perhaps pleased) to see the suggestion of wrinkles around our mouth and eyes.

**Graying of Hair.**   Hair begins to turn gray because cells at the base of the hair follicle that produce the pigment for one hair either die or just produce less pigment. As more and more of these pigment cells malfunction and die, a person gets gradually grayer.

The pigmentation in a hair can be interrupted temporarily before that hair becomes permanently gray. In rare cases then, a white hair may again briefly become its youthful color by nature alone, not by artificial means (Selmanowitz, Rizer, & Orentreich, 1977).

**Skin Changes.**   Skin usually begins to wrinkle about the same time as hair begins to get gray, in our twenties and thirties. Wrinkling begins in the areas used the most (Rossman, 1977), so people who are used to laughing may find their personality indelibly fixed in little lines around their eyes and mouth. Those used to frowning unfortunately suffer the same fate; their mood may be permanently imprinted on their face. Our skin, then, is more than just the envelope covering our body. As we get older, it can also be the visible reflection of who we are inside.

In the very old, wrinkles may appear over a person's total skin surface irrespective of use. This type of wrinkling, as well as to a certain extent the use-related type just described, occurs because subcutaneous fat tissue is lost as a person ages, causing the skin to hang slackly (Kart et al., 1978). In addition, as mentioned before, cross-linkages of the most abundant constituent of a person's skin, the protein collagen, contribute to wrinkling by causing skin to lose its elasticity. It then stiffens and forms indelible creases (Selmanowitz et al., 1977).

**Changes in Joints and Bones.**   Age-related changes in joints and bones, like wrinkled skin and gray hair, show us we are getting old. We may not be as agile as we once were and so feel older. These skeletal changes, however, are most important because of their sometimes marked behavioral consequences. If severe, they may significantly limit mobility and so cause radical changes in lifestyle. Like those just mentioned, the following aging signs are probably universal in our society and progressive; however, they usually begin at a later age than skin and hair changes and have their most important effects during the sixties and later.

In middle life the density of a person's bones begins to decrease gradually. This condition is called **osteoporosis.** The degree to which osteoporosis progresses may be affected, among other variables, by exercise and by calcium and vitamin intake during adulthood (Adams, 1977). This loss of bone affects everyone but is most severe in older White women, possibly because their bones are more fragile and less dense to begin with. Osteoporosis may also cause pain and is one reason that people may have lost a few inches in height by old age (Rossman, 1977).

Even though in itself not life-threatening, osteoporosis can indirectly cause disability and hasten death because the bones, being so fragile, are liable to be broken at the slightest fall. Fractures heal much less easily and completely in the elderly, so they may have serious consequences in old age. Because older people may never fully recover from a broken bone, it may signal a permanent loss of independence. Victims of fractures may even be unable to take care of themselves and so must enter nursing homes. Some elderly people, frightened by these possibilities, are overly cautious about avoiding a fall. This fear in itself may cause them to significantly limit their lives, even if a fall has never occurred. So, the psychological ramifications of osteoporosis plus the physical disability it can cause make it a centrally important, even if in itself usually benign, physical change that occurs with advancing age.

The other most prevalent age-related change in the skeletal system, **osteoarthritis,** is also progressive and currently has no cure. It involves a gradual wearing away of the joint cartilage that cushions the bones. In severe cases the resulting exposure of bone on bone without a protective cushion causes pain and stiffness. Although all older people have this deterioration to some degree, only a minority have painful osteoarthritis. However, enough do to make osteoarthritis one of the most common problems of old age (Kart et al., 1978; see Table 2-1).

**TABLE 2-1.**    Prevalence of selected chronic conditions reported in health interviews, persons 65 and over, United States.

| Condition and Year | Number per 1000 Persons 65 + | | |
|---|---|---|---|
| | Total | Male | Female |
| Arthritis, mainly osteoarthritis (1969) | 380.3 | 287.0 | 450.1 |
| Asthma (1970) | 35.8 | 42.3 | 31.1 |
| Chronic bronchitis (1970) | 41.2 | 47.3 | 36.6 |
| Diabetes (1973) | 78.5 | 60.3 | 91.3 |
| Heart conditions (1972) | 198.7 | 199.3 | 198.3 |
| Hernia of abdominal cavity (1968) | 58.8 | 80.9 | 42.2 |
| Hypertension without heart involvement (1972) | 199.4 | 141.2 | 240.9 |
| Ulcer of stomach or duodenum (1968) | 29.0 | 38.4 | 22.0 |
| Impairment of back or spine (1971) | 67.1 | 54.6 | 76.3 |
| Hearing impairment (1971) | 294.3 | 338.2 | 262.1 |
| Vision impairment (1971) | 204.6 | 183.1 | 220.4 |

*(Source: From* Assessment and Evaluation Strategies in Aging: People, Populations and Programs, *report of a conference chaired by G. L. Maddox. Copyright 1978 by the Duke University Center for the Study of Aging and Human Development. Reprinted by permission.)*

# Chronic Disease

Osteoporosis, osteoarthritis, and a host of other age-related changes are also called chronic diseases. So, chronic illnesses are much more common in older people than in the young because they are frequently tied to normal aging. Normal aging changes at their extreme are often labeled chronic conditions. In fact, an important issue in the biology of aging is when this labeling should occur. When should scientists consider normal a deleterious change universally present as people age, and when should they call it an abnormal phenomenon or disease state (see Ostfeld, 1975)?

*Chronic diseases,* in contrast to acute or infectious diseases, have certain characteristics. They are long-term, progressive, and (at least currently) incurable. Their causes are not definitely known. The emphasis in dealing with these conditions is on possible prevention and long-range management, not cure (Kart et al., 1978). Table 2-1 lists some common chronic diseases and their prevalence in older adults. As the table illustrates, Dr. Kennedy's heart condition is a very frequent chronic illness in older people.

Although chronic disease is not limited to late life, it is an extremely important accompaniment of aging. Eighty-five percent of people over 65 suffer from at least one chronic illness. As Table 2-2 shows, chronic disease becomes increasingly prevalent in older age groups.

Chronic disease is also the major category of health problem in the United States. In 1975, for example, over half the money spent on health care went for treatment of chronic conditions (Butler, 1978). A tremendous amount of money is spent each year on research to understand the causes of these illnesses. Chronic diseases frustrate doctor and patient alike.

## Consequences for the Medical Profession: Neglect and the Need to Know More

Because chronic conditions are currently not truly curable, health care experts emphasize, they are a rebuke to the power of medicine. Doctors are trained to eradicate illness. They may be relatively unschooled in how to minimize and man-

**TABLE 2-2.**   Chronic illness and associated disability for various age groups.

| | Age Group | | |
|---|---|---|---|
| *Health Status* | *45–66* | *67–74* | *75+* |
| Number of chronic conditions/person | .41[a] | .65 | .87 |
| Percentage limited in activity because of chronic conditions | .24 | .42 | .56 |
| Bed disability days/year | 9.3 | 10.3 | 17.4 |
| Days of restricted activity/year | 28.0 | 34.0 | 46.0 |

[a]*(Ages 55–59)*
*(Source: Reprinted by permission of the publisher, from* Geriatrics in the United States, *by Robert L. Kane, David H. Solomon, John C. Beck, Emmett B. Keeler, and Rosalie A. Kane. Published by Lexington Books, D.C. Heath and Company, Lexington, Mass.: Copyright 1981, the Rand Corporation.)*

age the effects of illnesses that never totally go away (Kart et al., 1978). Further-more, because the goal of treatment is frequently palliation and symptom control rather than total success, dealing with chronic diseases may not seem as high a priority for doctors as treating conditions that can be cured. True, physicians are deeply interested in illnesses that are defined as chronic (as is clear from the in-tense medical effort focused on treating cancer or heart disease). But still here the basic thrust tends to be cure-oriented, concerned, for example, with the medical or surgical procedure that will have a palpable effect. When, as often happens, no curative intervention is possible, the sufferer (more typically an older person) may be largely ignored.

This disproportionate neglect, long assumed to exist, was graphically demon-strated by the following study (Kane, Solomon, Beck, Keeler, & Kane, 1981). A random sample of physicians in private practice were asked to record the amount of time they spent with each patient on several typical office days. These figures were then looked at as a function of patients' ages. The investigators hypothesized that because patients over 65 were the most likely to be seriously ill, they should be given the greatest amount of attention. We would expect doctors to need more time to examine elderly patients for their likely more complicated conditions and to explain their likely more elaborate treatment.

Instead, to the investigators' surprise, the reverse was true. Looking at three age groups (45–54, 55–64, and 65+), they found relative stability in the average time spent with the younger groups and then a marked drop in the time spent with the oldest. Furthermore, this clear difference for patients over 65 was consistent for office, hospital, and nursing home visits and across all seven medical specialties the researchers examined. Either because elderly patients are seen as more hope-less cases or for some other reason, they are in truth being given short shrift by the medical profession.

However, this very low-priority group, those over 65, are, in proportion to their numbers, the heaviest consumers of medical services (Davidson & Marmor, 1980; see Figure 2-2). Physicians, then, need knowledge that their education may not have given them. Far from being totally refractory to treatment by other than aggressive medical techniques, chronic diseases can often be ameliorated and the disability they cause reduced by less cure-oriented strategies (Bonner, 1974). Fur-thermore, as suggested by the Baltimore findings, the physician who treats an elderly person may need special knowledge of another kind: ideally he or she should know what is normal or abnormal for this age group and so avoid overtreating or undertreating the person.

These are compelling reasons to give medical students some training specifi-cally in geriatrics. Until the past few years, however, American medical schools almost totally neglected this task. As recently as 1976 a national survey revealed that only 15 of 96 United States medical schools offered separate courses on aging as part of their curriculum. Three years later, though, the figure had jumped to 61. It is expected that by 1995 all will offer required training in this important area (Kane et al., 1981). It is hoped that this new interest will stimulate a change in

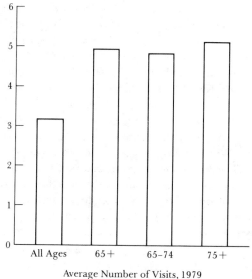

Average Number of Visits, 1979

**FIGURE 2-2.** Physician office and home visits by age group, 1979. Note that older adults make about two visits more per year than the average. *(Source: From* Chartbook on Aging in America *by C. Allan and H. Brotman. Copyright 1981 by The White House Conference on Aging.)*

physicians' attitudes toward the possibility of helping elderly people with chronic problems.

### *Consequences for the Patient: Disease versus Functional Disability*

Chronic illness influences the patient in far-ranging ways. It is often associated with intellectual declines (see Chapter 4), lessened sexual desire and activity (Chapter 6), and depression and other emotional problems (Chapter 8). Negative consequences were apparent in our vignette: Dr. Kennedy's problem clearly had a detrimental impact on the overall quality of his life.

However, a chronic problem, when mild, need have little effect on a person. Much more crucial in our understanding its relevance for the individual is to know another fact—whether the illness limits the person in his or her ability to freely negotiate the world. Table 2-2 illustrates that chronic illnesses only sometimes have this effect. For each age group the percentage of people reporting some activity restriction due to illness is much lower than the percentage reporting an illness itself. It is even rarer to be totally disabled by a chronic condition. So illness should not be equated with disability, and the latter behavioral index of health in the elderly person may be the more important one (Rossman, 1978). This parameter is called the *functional impairment* the disease causes.

Functional impairment is actually so crucial a measure of health in the older person that gerontologists have developed a variety of assessment devices to measure it specifically. Some are quite broad, assessing functional capacities in areas besides physical independence. Some, like the example in Table 2-3, are narrower, designed to evaluate just self-care skills in elderly persons who are significantly disabled. The measure partly reproduced in Table 2-3, the Katz Activities of Daily Living Scale (Katz, Ford, Moskowitz, Jackson, & Jaffee, 1963), was one of the first functional assessment scales and is still the best known. However, as is apparent by inspecting its items, the scale would not be appropriate to use with persons who were only slightly limited in their activities or if it were desirable to know about a more elaborate range of behaviors than simply physical skills. Another important limitation is that this scale makes no attempt to assess the person's environment. As will become abundantly clear later in this chapter and in the next, the external world can work either for or against optimal functioning. Evaluating whether the environment facilitates or impedes the individual is important to understanding that person's potential for behaving more independently.

## How Older People See Their Health

Our stress on the need to go beyond purely medical measures in assessing an older adult's physical capacities brings up the fact that there is yet a third illness dimension that may also be usefully considered: the person's own sense of being healthy or ill. As our vignette shows, the individual's personal perception of being sick can have a marked impact on the degree of functional impairment shown. Dr. Kennedy's ability to work and even to walk around the block, at least initially, was determined not by the severity of his condition as judged by his doctor but by his own idea that he was gravely ill. This leads us to a fascinating area of inquiry: How closely do older persons' evaluations of their own health compare with their physicians' assessments?

### *Self-Assessments and Physicians' Assessments*

We might imagine that the typical doctor would judge how ill an older patient is mainly on the basis of a physical examination and tests. The doctor also might evaluate illness or health from the framework he or she is likely to have been taught—that of a normal younger person. In contrast, when older people evaluate their own health, we might expect them to use very different criteria: the functional limitations their illnesses cause; how sick or well they feel in comparison to peers; and how much of a change they have recently experienced from how they used to feel. Unrelated influences might also enter into their assessments: general satisfaction with their life; level of happiness and fulfillment (Cockerham, Sharp, & Wilcox, 1983; Hickey, 1980); and as in our vignette, intensity of fear about dying. Older adults' own ideas of how healthy they are might therefore differ greatly from their doctors' evaluations, since they may be using these very different criteria.

Several studies done in this country have revealed, however, that physicians and older patients' assessments of health do correlate with each other (Heyman &

**TABLE 2-3.** Katz evaluation form, activities of daily living scale.

*For each area of functioning listed below, check description that applies.*

**Bathing—either sponge bath, tub bath, or shower**

☐ Receives no assistance

☐ Receives assistance in bathing only one part of body

☐ Receives assistance in bathing more than one part of body (or is not bathed)

**Dressing—gets clothes from closets and drawers**

☐ Gets clothes and gets completely dressed without assistance

☐ Gets clothes and gets dressed without assistance except in tying shoes

☐ Receives assistance in getting clothes or getting dressed or stays partly or completely undressed

**Toileting—going to toilet room for elimination; cleaning self after elimination and arranging clothes**

☐ Goes to toilet room, cleans self, and arranges clothes without assistance

☐ Receives assistance in going to toilet room and so on

☐ Does not go to toilet room for the elimination process

**Transfer**

☐ Moves in and out of bed as well as in and out of chair without assistance

☐ Moves in and out of bed or chair with assistance

☐ Does not get out of bed

**Continence**

☐ Controls urination and bowel movement completely by self

☐ Has occasional "accidents"

☐ Supervision helps keep urine or bowel control; catheter is used or is incontinent

**Feeding**

☐ Feeds self without assistance

☐ Feeds self except for assistance in cutting meat or buttering bread

☐ Receives assistance in feeding or is fed partly or completely by using tubes or intravenous fluids

*(Source: Adapted from "Studies of Illness in the Aged: The Index of ADL—a Standardized Measure of Biological and Psychological Function," by S. Katz, A. B. Ford, R. W. Moskowitz, B. A. Jackson and M. W. Jaffee. In* Journal of the American Medical Association, *1963, 185, 914–919. Copyright 1963 by the American Medical Association. Reprinted by permission.)*

Jeffers, 1963; LaRue, Bank, Jarvik, & Hetland, 1979; Maddox & Douglas, 1973; Tissue, 1972). In fact, the degree of agreement when the two are asked specific questions is also high in other Western countries (Shanas, 1974).

When disagreements do occur, some of these studies have revealed that patients are likely to see themselves as healthier than their doctors do (LaRue et al., 1979; Maddox & Douglas, 1973).We would expect this outcome if what was just hypothesized is true. If people judge their health partly by their functional capacity and partly by comparisons with others their own age, they are using a less stringent standard of health than the typical physician.

### Effect of Cultural Norms on Self-Assessments

There may be another reason that older people are likely to rate themselves as less ill than their physicians do. At least for the current cohort of American and Western European elderly, complaining about illness is frowned on. This possibility has been strongly suggested when researchers have compared the results of cross-national surveys that ask older adults in different countries to evaluate their health. In the United States, England, and Denmark, over half of those surveyed rate their health as good. In Poland, Yugoslavia, and Israel, one-quarter or fewer make that claim. The sociologists who have reviewed these studies (Shanas & Maddox, 1976) conclude that these marked differences do not really reflect markedly different rates of illness in the different countries. They are due at least partly to cultural expectations. In Eastern Europe health complaints in old age are tolerated and accepted. In the West they are seen as a sign of weakness and are discouraged.

### Problems in Self-Assessments of Health

The traditional American virtue of suffering in silence (Shanas, 1962), and hence often not going to a physician, may have serious consequences. It may hinder older people from getting needed medical help. In addition, disease may manifest itself differently in old age. Sometimes, for instance, the onset of a serious illness is difficult to differentiate from a previous benign problem the elderly person has. For example, whereas a heart attack in a younger adult is always heralded by excruciating pain, not uncommonly a heart attack in someone of advanced age occurs with slight (Adams, 1977) or unusual (Butler, 1978) symptoms. Moreover, the symptoms of this potentially fatal condition may mimic those of indigestion, a common complaint in old age (Kart et al., 1978). Older people, then, are sometimes especially likely to be unaware that they are really suffering from a life-threatening problem that needs immediate treatment. This misperception can cost them their lives.

So, it may be helpful to educate older people to be attuned to the often subtle cues that their physical condition has changed. In addition, some of this cohort of elderly may need to learn that at least some aches and pains are treatable and should not be minimized or ascribed to "old age" (Kart et al., 1978). Unfortunately, we are only beginning to understand what is normal in late life, and many physicians' lack of training in geriatric medicine prevents them from performing this educative function. Health care professionals themselves may be equally unaware of the signs that indicate illness in an older person.

The need to understand when one is realistically ill or disabled applies not only to elderly who stoically ignore treatable problems but also to those who do the opposite, as in our vignette, individuals who act more disabled than their condition warrants. This latter problem is so important for older adults that gerontologists have given it a special name: ***excess disabilities*** (Kahn, 1977a). Anyone can easily develop excess disabilities, but the elderly are particularly apt to be functioning at a lower level than they can because their environment, both personal and physical (see the next chapter), sometimes reinforces dependence.

It is easy for even the most well-meaning caretaker to engender excess disabilities. For instance, as noted in the last chapter, this often occurs in nursing homes. Nursing home personnel often have no idea of a resident's real potential. It also may be more convenient and less time-consuming to take total care of a person. It may even seem more humane than watching a somewhat disabled individual struggle to care for himself or herself with difficulty. These actions, however, are really doing the person a disservice, as the physical consequences of excess disabilities can be just as bad as the effects of not seeing a doctor in time. Excess disability can become true disability because inactivity weakens people and makes them more vulnerable to disease. It also may depress them because they no longer feel in control of their lives (see Chapter 8). In addition, it is wasteful, depriving the older adult of the chance to live as productively as possible. So, the aim of behaviorally oriented psychologists working with physically impaired older people is often to eradicate excess disabilities. This was the psychologist's goal in our clinical vignette.

### Implications

In conclusion, assessments based on a physical examination and laboratory tests, on a person's level of functional impairment, and on the person's feelings are probably all valid. Each provides us with a useful dimension of health or illness (Hickey, 1980). For instance, our bias is probably to assume a doctor's evaluation is the best. However, this easy inference may not necessarily be correct. The Duke Longitudinal Study provided a most arresting finding about the connection between subjectively rated health and later health (Maddox & Douglas, 1973). Duke volunteers were able to assess their future health better than physicians, even though we would think the latter's judgment, being more objective, should have been more accurate. In fact, it was subjects' own ratings of their health at a given time that were most related to physician-rated health at the next round of tests. Self-evaluations, in other words, were the superior predictor of future physical well-being. There may be several reasons for this result. One strong possibility is that the older person really has access to a very different sort of accurate data— subtle cues about how his or her body is functioning. Here this possibly internal perception of illness seems, in fact, to have been better than the objective, externally verifiable medical one.

At the very least, this Duke finding warns us to be cautious in dismissing an older person's complaints about poor health simply because they are not immediately confirmable medically. A person who has lived for 65 years or more in his or her body may know intimately how it functions. The person's own evaluation of illness may on occasion, as was true of Dr. Kennedy before his first heart attack, be more accurate than we might expect.

## Predicting Longevity

What we are born with—our genes and other influences fixed at birth—and what we are exposed to in the world in the course of development and living are the dual influences determining almost every aspect of who we are. They influence how we think and act, how we look physically and perform physiologically, and the rate at which we age and die.

---

### BOX 2-2.  Long-Lived Populations—a Hoax or a Lesson to Us?

This chapter amply illustrates that as a species we generally are not fulfilling our biological potential. Few if any of us reach the maximum life span we have been allotted. Many of us spend the last few years of life suffering from diseases that, even if not severely disabling, limit our ability to enjoy life to the fullest. Consequently, the discovery of cultures where this supposedly does not happen has generated tremendous excitement. In these societies residents are rumored to live past 100 and to continue living fully active lives till they die. Their existence is hailed as proof that, even without tampering artificially with our biological machinery, we can do better than currently to fulfill our species-specific genetic potential (Leaf, 1973).

Three nonindustrialized or primitive societies are supposed to have an unusually large proportion of healthy, active centenarians: a remote village in Ecuador, a principality in Pakistan, and the highlands of Georgia in the Soviet Caucasus. Certain environmental influences have been reported to account for these residents' long lives.

An anthropologist (Benet, 1977), after spending time living in Soviet Georgia, was struck by the lifestyle differences between this society and our own. She hypothesized that several factors might account for the longevity she observed among the Georgians. The Soviet people ate simple, low-calorie diets composed mainly of fruit, vegetables, and cornmeal; they were expected to do outdoor work until an advanced age; and they were respected by the community for being older. In fact, the more advanced their age, the greater the acclaim bestowed on residents by their peers. Behavioral scientists studying the people in the two other locations have stressed a similar theme. Being respected for one's age, living a healthful, natural life, and being fully integrated into society when old are conditions supposed to characterize all the places where residents are reputed to live a long time.

Eating a low-fat diet, getting physical exercise, and being highly accepted in one's community may truly be good for one's health. However, there is little firm evidence that people in these villages do in fact live longer than people in industrial societies (Medvedev, 1974). For example, when Mazess and Forman (1979) examined actual birth and census records in Ecuador, records that were difficult to obtain, they found that many older people in the village exaggerated their ages by at least a decade and sometimes two. According to the records, none of the supposed centenarians they investigated was really over 100. In all three areas, particularly in Soviet Georgia, much positive publicity has accrued to residents reputed to be long-lived. Because status both within and outside one's village is tied to being old and because there are often few age records, the temptation to fabricate among older residents of these communities may be particularly strong. This tendency may be encouraged by the fact that during adulthood remembering one's exact age becomes less important. As we may know from personal experience as adults, it is easier to forget how old one is when knowing that figure is irrelevant to daily life.

Interestingly, age exaggeration among the very old may be more widespread than we think, not just confined to these remote villages. In institutions, for example, I have noticed people embellishing on an already advanced age to impress listeners. It may be that only as we leave youth and approach our normal life expectancy is our age a liability. Once we reach our eighties or nineties, age becomes an achievement. It is transformed into a badge of a life well lived.

### A General Difficulty

For humans, however, it is difficult to tease out the precise contributions of inborn and environmental influences on many of the aging phenomena just described. Being correlational, most studies that attempt to show a genetic contribution to aging and death neglect to rule out a simultaneously operating environmental influence, and studies supposedly proving how environment affects longevity often inadvertently fail to rule out inborn factors (Palmore, 1971b; Rose & Bell, 1971).

For instance, research evidence that relatives have more similar life spans than unrelated persons and that identical twins have more similar ages at death than fraternal twins is usually used to illustrate the effect of heredity on how long we live. But each phenomenon may have an environmental interpretation, too: Family members, having similar socialization experiences, are likely to have more similar health practices, such as smoking or exercising. These habits, which do affect mortality, may be partly responsible for their more closely correlated deaths. The same is true of identical twins. They may be exposed to more similar illness-producing life experiences because of their very genetic similarity. Once again, in what looks like heredity the environment may be partly to blame.

These complexities are apparent in our clinical vignette. While Dr. Kennedy ascribes his heart condition to genes, his wife attributes his illness to an external cause—too much stress. As her interpretation is more the province of psychology, we now look at empirical evidence for how valid Mrs. Kennedy's assumption may be.

### Effects of Stress

The idea that emotional stress shortens life by increasing one's chance of getting physically ill dates back to antiquity but is just being newly appreciated by scientists. In the past there were always physicians and behavioral scientists who were interested in the idea that emotions could contribute to a person's developing physical diseases, but with a few notable exceptions these professionals confined their attention to conditions that were specifically defined as psychosomatic. It was thought that only a limited group of psychosomatic illnesses (ulcers and headaches are two main examples) could be exacerbated or caused by one's emotional state (Brody, 1983). All other diseases were felt to have purely physical precipitants that could be treated and cured only by physical means, such as drugs.

This idea has been discarded by an increasing number of respectable scientists. A burgeoning specialty called health psychology or **behavioral medicine** (Schwartz & Weiss, 1977) is devoted in part to elucidating psychological precipitants of life-threatening diseases that had always been thought to have purely physical causes—cancer and heart disease, for example. In addition, behavioral medicine adherents have shown the nonspecific role of emotional stress in contributing to a variety of illnesses. In particular, some fascinating research has revealed that one type of stress, significant life change, has this highly general effect on a person's susceptibility to disease.

Two physicians (Holmes & Rahe, 1967) did the first experimental study of a long intuitively felt belief about stress—that marked upsets or changes in a person's life within a short period might increase the chance of getting physically ill. They first developed a life events scale (the **Social Readjustment Rating Scale**) by having a large number of people rate 43 events for the amount of stress that each event would probably cause. These life events included both positive and negative ones (see Table 2-4), as it was thought that any change, good or bad, would constitute a stress that might predispose someone to getting sick.

Holmes and Rahe then showed that more life change did indeed seem to raise the probability of illness, using two techniques: (1) administering the scale to large groups of subjects and then looking at their subsequent rate of disease and (2) asking already ill subjects about life changes they had experienced just before becoming sick (Rahe, 1974). The first type of study, called a **prospective investigation**, is methodologically superior to the second type because, being a type of longitudinal investigation, it eliminates distortions resulting from being asked to remember events.

As we might expect, the correlations between accumulated stress, as measured in Life Change Units, and the incidence of physical problems are far from perfect. This means we cannot use the scale in a specific way to predict a particular person's chances of getting ill. People vary widely in their capacity to adapt to change. In addition, although there is general agreement about the stressful impact of certain life events, people also probably vary in the extent to which individual life happenings will be personally stressful. However, the life-change measure can be used in a general way to predict susceptibility to disease.

The scale has not been standardized on older subjects, but it seems to have much potential relevance to late life. At the very least, the shared view that certain events predictable in old age are highly stressful suggests that some instances of illness among older adults may have an environmental precipitant. For in-

**TABLE 2-4.**   Some items from the Social Readjustment Rating Scale.

| Life Event | Mean Value in Life Change Units |
|---|---|
| Death of spouse | 100 |
| Divorce | 73 |
| Marital separation | 65 |
| Death of close family member | 63 |
| Getting married | 50 |
| Being fired from work | 47 |
| Reconciliation in marriage | 45 |
| Retiring | 45 |
| Pregnancy | 40 |
| Sexual problems | 39 |
| New member in family | 39 |
| Change in finances | 38 |
| Death of close friend | 37 |
| Change in work responsibilities | 29 |
| Outstanding personal achievement | 28 |
| Move to a new residence | 20 |
| Changing schools | 20 |
| Vacation | 13 |
| Christmas holidays | 12 |
| Minor law violation | 11 |

*(Source: Adapted from E. K. Gunderson and R. H. Rahe,* Life Stress and Illness, *copyright 1974. Courtesy of Charles C Thomas, Publisher, Springfield, Illinois.)*

stance, two changes high on the measure, retirement and widowhood, are very probable occurrences for the elderly. Chapter 7 will explore in detail the physical and psychological consequences of these important age-related events. As we will see in this chapter, there is little evidence that retirement and widowhood (for women), at least considered singly, do lead to more illness in old age. Another occurrence listed on the scale, however, has been found to be associated with clear deteriorative changes in the elderly: moving to a new residence. In the gerontological literature, the impact of moving on older adults has been investigated so extensively it has been given a special name, ***the relocation effect.***

The relocation effect was first formally discovered in a group of nursing home patients studied during a two-year period following the announcement of the closing of their institution. The investigators found a marked rise in the death rate, during the first three months after relocation (Aldrich & Mendkoff, 1963). A variety of studies have since examined the impact of moves of varying types—from one community setting to another, from the community to a nursing home, and, as in this first piece of research, from one institution to another.

A general pattern has emerged from these results. With one recent, notable exception (Ferraro, 1983), contrary to what the scale's authors might have predicted, relocation alone does not necessarily have negative consequences for a person's health. For example, relocation when planned by the person and to a more suitable environment may actually result in improvements in health and morale (Yawney & Slover, 1979). However, older people are vulnerable to experiencing negative physical effects when they are moved involuntarily and without adequate preparation. They are also at risk of physical declines when they are moved to a less desirable setting and are already quite physically frail (Brody, 1977; see also our discussion of institutionalization in Chapter 7).

## Interventions

In contrast to inborn influences, environmental precipitants of illness (as in our vignette), such as choosing to work much too hard, can, at least in theory, be changed. However, modifying this behavior or other well-known poor health habits such as smoking or eating the wrong foods is often difficult because many illness-producing practices are immediately reinforcing. An additional principle omitted from our discussion of reinforcement in Chapter 1 is that when a reinforcer is immediate, it has its best effect. The prospect of punishment in a distant future, such as when a young person reaches 65, often lacks the potency in the present to dissuade the person from engaging in currently reinforcing, though clearly life-shortening, activities. For example, in our vignette, Dr. Kennedy developed what a nonbehaviorist would call the willpower to follow his doctor's orders only after the consequences of not doing so became immediately obvious—that is, after his second heart attack.

The same difficulty applies to one's understanding of the role of the relocation effect or of change and stress in general in the genesis of physical disease. It is possible theoretically to minimize the number of life changes we subject ourselves to—or, what is probably better, to develop strategies for dealing with the stressful impact of events that must occur. However, it may be difficult to make these changes in practice without professional help. Knowing about the deleterious effect of emotional stress is very different from having the ability to control our level of tension when a stress actually occurs.

Clinicians trained in behavioral medicine (most often psychologists, psychiatrists, or social workers) provide this professional help (see Davidson & Davidson, 1980). Using psychological principles, particularly behavioral techniques, they try to make it easier for people to change maladaptive, even if immediately pleasurable, health practices. They also work directly to train individuals to voluntarily control their level of tension, usually by employing specific relaxation techniques. In addition, these professionals use psychological techniques to deal with physical illnesses once they have developed. At present they may be most successful in preventing the development of excess disabilities, as the psychologist did in Dr. Kennedy's case. However, in some instances and for some problems they have reported being able to at least ameliorate, if not cure, real physical illnesses by using psychological strategies.

The following two examples from opposite ends of the disability spectrum illustrate how psychological techniques are being used to assist in the prevention and treatment of physical conditions. The two problems selected, though not unique to late life, are more frequent in older people than in young and middle-aged adults. The first illustration is of a training program used with younger people to modify a type of behavior shown to increase the chances of developing heart disease in middle and later life. The program is an instance of what in medicine is called *secondary prevention;* that is, the disease is prevented from developing at all by treating an existing cause. The second example is of a behavioral approach to treat a common problem in the impaired older person, incontinence. This treatment approach would be termed *tertiary prevention:* the disease (or in this case symptom) is cured after it has occurred.

### Modifying Type A Behavior

Type A behavior is a particular stressed way of approaching life that has been shown to increase the probability of developing and dying from a heart attack. Being a behavioral precursor of a major, life-threatening illness, the Type A pattern has been a prime candidate for modification by behavioral medicine techniques.

Since the late 1950s, when two cardiologists (Friedman & Rosenman, 1974) identified the characteristics of what they called the Type A personality and initiated a series of research studies showing that people with this kind of behavior pattern were at risk of cardiac problems, the evidence has mounted that this personality type does in fact get more heart disease (Dembroski, 1977). In contrast to calm, relaxed people, who are called Type B individuals, Type As are exactly the kind of people we might think would get heart attacks. They are competitive, short-tempered, achievement-oriented workaholics. They often act, and put themselves, under tremendous pressure. They cram more and more appointments into an overbooked schedule. They work 25 hours in a 24-hour day. They try to succeed where no one has succeeded before. For example, Dr. Kennedy's tendency to work long hours and to compare his manual skill with that of dentists half his age suggests he is likely to be a Type A person.

In general, the basic problem Type As have is that they are unable to relax. The major purpose of the treatment program described below (Roskies, 1980), accordingly, was to teach these people how to relax and then to train them to use the relaxation response in situations that normally aroused the hypervigilant Type A behavior.

Unfortunately, the first step in initiating the treatment to modify the Type A response, getting subjects to participate, was difficult because this way of behaving, like many other poor health practices, is immediately reinforcing. Our society tends to encourage Type A behavior and reward the Type A person with job success. For instance, Dr. Kennedy probably felt working long hours was a major reason he was so successful in his field. When this immediate reinforcement—for example, professional success—is weighed against the mere possibility of a seemingly distant (though highly aversive) event like a heart attack, it is understandable that unless a treatment program for Type As were made immediately reinforcing, many would drop out of the program.

Roskies (1980) was able to circumvent this problem by treating her subjects in groups. Group members complimented one another for continuing to attend sessions and learning to change their behavior. As Type A people have very easily aroused competitive drives, they found this reinforcing and were more likely to continue attending meetings. In addition, once the relaxed Type B behavior was learned, it became immediately reinforcing in itself, rather than just being a strategy for possibly preventing a heart attack in some hypothetical future. Once the subjects had learned to relax and were able to relax in situations that had previously evoked a Type A response, they found, surprisingly, that far from inhibiting their ability to work, their new way of behaving actually enhanced their productivity. Furthermore, they became more appreciated by coworkers and even found they felt better physically.

Subjects learned relaxation by daily practice at home, using taped instructions. When they had learned to monitor their tension and control it in nonarousing situations, they were told to practice the newly learned responses at work. They were instructed specifically to try out relaxation in job situations where Type A behavior would be most likely to occur—for example, during a business meeting or when having a disagreement with a coworker. In the end, for many participants, Type A behavior was extinguished and replaced by Type B responses. It was hoped that if the new, less stressed pattern was maintained on a long-term basis, these subjects would subsequently develop less heart disease.

### Eradicating Incontinence

Incontinence in the elderly, particularly urinary incontinence because of its much greater frequency, has been called one of the most challenging problems in geriatric medicine. It is estimated to be the cause of more than 20% of admissions to geriatric units in hospitals and nursing homes (Milne, 1976). The suffering this problem may cause older people as well as those around them may be extreme. In fact, incontinence, rather than even severe physical or mental impairment, is often the final indignity that prompts even the most devoted family to seek nursing home placement for a disabled parent (Milne, 1976). So, at the very least, incontinence is indirectly life-shortening. It may add to the disability of an already disabled older person.

Because geriatric medicine has a longer history and is more highly advanced in Great Britain, most of the work on understanding and curing this upsetting problem has been done by English health care professionals. Surveys in Great Britain reveal an alarming amount of incontinence among people over 65. Its total incidence in the elderly population, including mild cases, is estimated to be in excess of 20% (Willington, 1976). Incontinence in institutions and hospitals is even more prevalent. One study revealed that over 45% of the older patients in selected Scottish hospitals were incontinent at some time during their stay (Milne, 1976).

Incontinence is not a disease but a symptom that may have a variety of causes (Adams, 1977). One frequent reason for it is mental impairment, either reversible or chronic (see Chapter 8); a person who is confused or disoriented may be unaware of the signal to urinate or defecate. Other conditions that may engender incontinence are diseases that significantly limit mobility and infections or other problems directly affecting the processes of elimination that prevent the person's having full control (Adams, 1977). In these latter instances in particular, even though the problem is medical, simple environmental manipulations may be help-ful. For example, just making the toilet more accessible to a disabled older person or instructing him or her to go to the lavatory at frequent intervals can sometimes eliminate incontinence or reduce its frequency.

Behavioral interventions are also important in the much rarer cases in which purely emotional precipitants play an important part. For example, one psychia-trist (Sutherland, 1976) lists a number of unconscious factors that he feels may sometimes cause incontinence. Among others, in response to a stress such as hos-pitalization, the older person may use the defense mechanism of regression and, in acting like a child, become incontinent. In response to being ignored, the older person may become incontinent to get attention. In response to being resentful of caretakers, a person may use incontinence as a tool of rebellion.

Reasons are abundant, then, for using psychological knowledge in dealing with this problem. However, the literature contains few studies attempting to scientifi-cally demonstrate the usefulness of psychological techniques in curing inconti-nence. One of the few rigorously controlled investigations (Grosicki, 1968) was unsuccessful. However, even though it did not work, it does illustrate how psycho-logical, in this case operant, methods may be used. Perhaps the treatment failed in this particular instance because the severity of the incontinence and whatever dis-ease was causing it precluded success for any intervention.

The investigator treated incontinent geriatric inpatients using first social and then monetary reinforcement. During the first (14-week) stage of the therapy, ap-propriate behavior was reinforced by positive attention from staff members. Pa-tients were checked for continence at hourly intervals, and if the patient was found to be continent, a staff member would spend a fixed amount of time (three minutes) talking to him or her. During the second stage of the treatment, tokens redeemable for money were either given or taken away depending on appropriate use of the toilet. As a result of the procedure, social adjustment did improve sig-nificantly among the patients. As mentioned, however, continence did not.

We should expect, however, with the growing interest in treating problems of old age using behavioral techniques, that future studies will have a different, more positive theme. Incontinence is only one of a number of previously neglected diffi-culties befalling the very old which psychological strategies should sometimes help.

## Summary

A biological perspective, in contrast to a psychological one, suggests that aging begins relatively early, usually immediately after growth has ceased. Aging changes are internally caused, are deleterious, advance progressively, and occur universally. Aging is also accompanied by an increased incidence of disease and often by multiple age-related illnesses. Our species has a fixed maximum life span that none of us can exceed, at least currently.

Biological theories of aging include both the idea that aging and death occur because of an increasing amount of randomly occurring cellular damage and the idea that the process occurs by an orchestrated master plan. If aging occurs by a master plan, it has been suggested, the clock programming it may be in the hypothalamus or the immune system.

The way physical aging normally occurs in America is being investigated by the ongoing Baltimore Longitudinal Study. A main purpose of the study is to develop norms for a variety of physiological functions for middle-aged and elderly men (and now women). Because the study is longitudinal, it can more accurately measure changes that occur as a person ages, although it unfortunately will minimize the extent to which these deleterious processes normally occur because the Baltimore sample is a physically elite group.

People of the same age vary greatly in their rate of aging. Within the individual, too, aging rates of different tissues and body systems may vary greatly. In general, though, age brings a decline in the efficiency and maximum capacity at which all body functions can work. This is most problematic for the older person under stressful conditions in which the highest level of performance is needed.

Changes in skin, hair, and the skeletal system are not life-threatening but may have an important psychological impact. With age, hair follicles produce less pigment, causing hair to gray; the skin wrinkles because of loss of subcutaneous fat and collagen cross-linkage; and skeletal problems such as osteoporosis and osteoarthritis are likely to develop. These latter conditions may significantly affect a person's life because they can interfere with mobility.

Chronic diseases are common, almost universal, in people over 65, but these conditions only sometimes interfere with a person's functioning. Consequently, in understanding the impact of an illness on a person, it is very important to determine the disability or functional impairment the disease causes. Assessment devices have been developed to measure older adults' functional abilities.

Subjectively rated health is another important parameter of illness that can be assessed. Self-assessments of health correlate with physicians' ratings. When disagreements do occur, self-ratings tend to be more favorable than physicians' ratings. One among several probable reasons that self-ratings are more positive is that complaining is culturally somewhat unacceptable for the current cohort of American and Western European elderly.

Denying true illness may have fatal consequences for the older person. The opposite problem, called "excess disabilities," behaving as if one were more impaired than one is, may also have negative effects. Minimizing excess disabilities is often the aim of behaviorally oriented psychologists who work with older people. In general, though, older people are often good judges of their own health. At least in one study, they were able to predict their future physical condition better than doctors.

Longevity is affected by both inborn and environmental factors. Often studies purporting to prove the importance of one influence alone do not rule out the effect of the other. For instance, similarities in age at death in families and between identical twins are invoked as evidence for heredity, but both findings may be partly due to similarity of environments.

Scientific evidence corroborates the popular belief that emotional stress can increase susceptibility to disease. In particular, marked life changes within a short period have been shown to be related to the subsequent likelihood of getting ill. For older people in particular, relocating to a new environment under certain conditions has been shown to exacerbate or cause physical problems.

Practitioners in the new field of behavioral medicine study psychological precursors of physical diseases as well as attempt to prevent and treat illnesses using psychological techniques. Professional help is often useful, for example, in modifying habits known to cause disease.

Two examples of behavioral medicine techniques come from opposite ends of the disability spectrum. A behavioral program designed to reduce Type A behavior was successful in modifying this pressured way of living, which increases the risk of heart disease. This program involved teaching relaxation techniques. A behavioral program designed to reduce incontinence in severely regressed geriatric patients was, unfortunately, not successful. In principle, however, incontinence should be modifiable using psychological techniques.

## Key Terms

*Atherosclerosis*

*Maximum life span*

*Arteriosclerosis*

*Random damage theories of aging*

*Programmed-aging theories*

*Hypothalamus*

*Immune system*

*Reserve capacity*

*Osteoporosis*

*Osteoarthritis*

*Chronic diseases*

*Functional impairment*

*Excess disabilities*

*Behavioral medicine*

*Prospective investigation*

*The relocation effect*

*Secondary prevention*

*Tertiary prevention*

*Type A personality*

## Recommended Readings

Comfort, A. *The biology of senescence*. (3rd ed.) New York: Elsevier/North Holland, 1979.
*Comprehensive examination of the biology of animal and human longevity and biological theories of aging. Difficult.*

Comfort, A. A biologist laments and exhorts. In L. F. Jarvik (Ed.), *Aging into the 21st century*. New York: Gardner, 1978.
*Noted gerontologist discusses breakthroughs in longevity research, speculates on when we will be able to extend the life span, and considers the implications of our probable success. Readable and not too difficult.*

Kahn, R. L. Excess disabilities in the aged. In S. H. Zarit (Ed.), *Readings in aging and death: Contemporary perspectives*. New York: Harper & Row, 1977.
*Short article describing the concept of excess disabilities. Not difficult.*

Kart, C. S., Metress, E. S., & Metress, J. F. *Aging and health: Biologic and social perspectives*. Menlo Park, Calif.: Addison-Wesley, 1978.

*Lucid exposition of physical changes occurring in different organ systems with age. Also discusses issues in geriatric medicine, institutionalization and its effect on the older person, and death and dying. Beautifully written, excellent, nontechnical overview of physical aging for the nonbiologist. Not difficult.*

Rose, C. L., & Bell, B. **Predicting longevity: Methodology and critique**. Lexington, Mass.: Heath, 1971.

*First three chapters discuss research on factors affecting longevity in humans and problems in isolating the effects of varying influences on the length of life. Somewhat difficult.*

Roskies, E. Considerations in developing a treatment program for the coronary-prone (Type A) behavior pattern. In P. O. Davidson & S. M. Davidson (Eds.), **Behavioral Medicine: Changing health lifestyles**. New York: Brunner/Mazel, 1980.

*Reviews the literature on Type A behavior and heart disease; discusses issues in devising a program to modify the coronary-prone behavior pattern and the author's efforts to set up such a program. (You might want to look through the rest of the book, as each chapter discusses a different behavioral medicine intervention.) Readable and not too difficult.*

# Sensing and Responding to the Environment

Now 79, Dr. Kennedy has been blessed with relatively good health since his heart attack eight years ago. Recently, however, he was forced to retire completely from dentistry. It was not because of lack of stamina; he was able to be on his feet for the long periods required. The problem was lack of speed and agility; he was simply too slow to continue work. Too many times in taking an impression the material would harden before it could be extracted from a patient's mouth; too often, and even more embarrassing, it hardened even before it reached a problem tooth. Vanity alone then dictated it was time to retire. Besides, Dr. Kennedy admitted, retirement was increasingly seeming necessary because it was becoming more difficult to hear.

His hearing problem had long been obvious to everyone else. Dr. Kennedy seemed the last to know, even though he understood intellectually that poor hearing is an occupational hazard of dentistry because of the years spent listening to a high-speed drill. It was difficult to admit he had problems hearing because it was so hard to feel frail and out of control in this way. Besides, it often seemed to Dr. Kennedy that the reason he could not hear was that people spoke too softly and that many places just had too much background noise. Too much noise, in fact, was the reason he asked to change the family's traditional Saturday morning lunch from the popular, crowded pancake house to the quiet delicatessen around the corner.

For years the Kennedys and their daughter and son-in-law had met for lunch every Saturday at the pancake house because of its delicious food. Now they eat at the deli, even though the food is worse, because Dr. Kennedy prefers to. He cannot hear most conversation in the pancake house but can often hear most of what is said in the deli.

The marked change, however, made his family suspicious. They thought he might be exaggerating his problems in the noisier restaurant simply to justify moving the family's lunch place. Dr. Kennedy's daughter, in particular, was suspicious, because she had noticed another variation in her father's hearing that also seemed premeditated: he had particular trouble hearing *her*. Frankly, this selective trouble seemed to suggest that Dr. Kennedy just did not want to listen to what his daughter had to say. It hurt her and made her withdraw emotionally from him even though in the past they had always been unusually close. Besides, she had to admit, avoiding her father became desirable for another reason. It became too exhausting to have to struggle to make herself understood. Consequently, she found herself increasingly drawn to talking to her mother at their weekly lunches.

Her newfound avoidance had a special benefit: for the first time in her married life, she and her mother became very close. In fact, the usually reticent Mrs. Kennedy began to confide in the younger woman about a problem she had—her increasing difficulty seeing.

Mrs. Kennedy said she had been encouraged when the ophthalmologists she visited said her worsening vision at least partly had a curable cause—cataracts.

However, she had been let down when they suggested she put off surgery for a while. The doctors explained that as she was old and had diabetes, her seeing difficulties probably also had a variety of less treatable causes. It was not certain how much a cataract operation would help. In the meantime, though, Mrs. Kennedy confided, her vision was getting worse. It hampered her in most activities and was particularly irksome in the one she enjoyed the most—cooking.

Her daughter was shocked to learn that failing vision had forced the older woman to give up her favorite activity, gourmet French cooking. As Mrs. Kennedy explained, this most demanding cuisine had become just too difficult because she could no longer read the numerals on the stove, the measuring cup, or the food processor. She had finally decided to quit the day her inability to see the color of a soufflé baking in the window of the lit oven caused her to take it out prematurely and dinner to be totally ruined. Even more upsetting, she could see almost nothing in dim light and so felt forced to refuse all invitations that involved going out at night.

This last problem impelled the daughter to action. She asked a psychologist friend who worked with older people to help. The friend suggested the following approach: "See whether you can change the physical environment to make life easier for your mother." Of course, this logically meant starting in the most important place—the older woman's beloved kitchen.

Mrs. Kennedy has now resumed cooking some more complicated dishes because of her daughter's creative efforts. The daughter installed a high-intensity light in the oven and painted large, bold numbers on the stove and other objects in the kitchen. She even found a large-type nouvelle cuisine recipe book for the visually impaired. In addition, because of her talk with the psychologist, the daughter got another special insight. She now knows that what looked like her father's lack of love was in truth lack of hearing and so has resumed her close relationship with him. In fact, next week she is going with him to the audiologist to be fitted with a hearing aid.

Basic to living is our ability to receive information about the environment. Just as crucial is our capacity to respond physically to the data we receive. Limitations in either of these abilities may have far-ranging effects on an older adult. If severe enough or important enough, they will make the person less independent, less able to competently negotiate the tasks of life. They may impair self-confidence and one's sense of security in the world. They may make relationships with others more difficult and cut the person off from pleasures as simple as enjoying a fragrant rose or a beautiful sunset. That is why this chapter is devoted solely to these changes—age-related limitations in sensory and motor abilities.

Our particular focus means this discussion, like much of the preceding one, will deal with negatives, things that go wrong in the latter part of life. Keep in mind that this approach obscures the fact that, as with other age-related physical changes, individuals vary greatly in the extent of sensory and motor limitations.

The typical older person, in fact, does not have impairing problems. Some elderly show no losses at all. Finally, there are many exceptional older individuals whose senses and motor capacities are superior to those of the young.

There are additional pitfalls in comparing the abilities of the elderly in these areas with those of younger adults. Tests measuring performance often have an important built-in bias against the old. Two familiar tests of sensory acuity, those for vision and hearing, are good examples.

The standard hearing test involves a person's saying whether he or she hears each of a series of low-intensity tones. The vision test involves identifying the letters or numbers on the familiar eye chart. Sensitivity or acuity on these measures is judged by the faintest stimulus the individual perceives (for hearing) or is able to identify correctly (for vision).

Older people, however, generally tend to be more cautious than the young (Botwinick, 1966), and this strategy too characterizes their performance on these and similar measures of sensory acuity (Grzegorczyk, Jones, & Mistretta, 1979; Potash & Jones, 1977) and motor ability (Welford, 1977). On tests of sensory acuity, if older people are not sure whether a stimulus has been presented or are uncertain what it is, they are likely to err on the side of caution: they will not guess. On tests of basic motor skills, such as response speed, they have a similar bias. So younger subjects, because they take more risks, are at an advantage. They are likely to be perceived as more capable in comparison with the elderly than they are, simply because their approach is the one that maximizes the chances of doing well.

Finally, in the somewhat negative catalogue that follows, we must keep in mind another optimistic note. Even though some older people tested today seem to manifest significant sensory and motor declines, it is not at all clear that this is inevitable. As we will see, deleterious influences like high levels of noise, leading a sedentary life, and being physically ill in themselves may make impairing problems in old age more likely. So, the extent to which some of these limitations are intrinsic to aging is unclear. Many difficulties today's older people show might possibly be escaped by future cohorts of elderly by the simple strategy of living in healthful environments and taking care of their health.

## Sensory Performance

The sensory data we get from the world are diverse and come from a variety of sources. For example, we can sense pressure, pain, heat, and cold through information provided from special nerve endings (receptors) on our skin. Data originating in our muscles and joints play an essential part in the control of movement by informing us of the position of our limbs. A more poorly understood set of sensors feeds us information about the internal workings of our body. Age-related declines in any of these systems can be important in an older person's life.

Vision and hearing, however, are the sensory modalities most crucial to contact with the outside world. We also have the most complete and detailed information about age-related changes in these senses. For these reasons the discussion below focuses on exploring age changes in these two most primary senses in some depth. We shall also briefly examine limitations in taste and smell. Problems here do not have the dramatic and observable effects on the person that marked losses in sight and hearing do, but the little research that has been done on them is fascinating and has practical potential for increasing the older person's enjoyment of one of life's great pleasures—eating.

### Vision

Many deleterious changes in vision may occur in later adulthood. Some of these impairments are obvious and familiar to all of us. Others are more subtle and are not detected by casual observation. What are some of these apparent and not so obvious difficulties? How common are they in today's elderly? How might our vision be expected to change as we advance in age?

**Overview.**   Of the variety of seeing difficulties that may befall the elderly, the most basic is poor *visual acuity.* A person with limited acuity has problems seeing things distinctly. Acuity is what is being measured when we are asked to identify the numbers and letters on an eye chart.

Older people are more likely to have poor acuity than the young, but there are no firm figures on the differences between age groups (Botwinick, 1978). However, there are estimates of the proportions of people of different ages who have the most severely impaired vision, legal blindness. That this condition is much more likely to affect the old is obvious from a 1966 survey (Fozard, Wolf, Bell, McFarland, & Podolsky, 1977). Only about 250 of every 100,000 Americans aged 40 to 64 were found to be legally blind; among those over 69, the figure jumped to about 1450.

Acuity is thought to decline slightly from early adulthood to the fifties and then fall off increasingly rapidly after age 60 (Ordy & Brizzee, 1979; Pollack & Atkeson, 1978). Being longitudinal, the Duke study was able to capture this accelerated drop directly. When volunteers' vision was tested twice, ten years apart, the incidence of poor visual acuity (corrected vision of 20/50 or worse in the better eye) increased 13% in volunteers initially examined in their sixties. In those first tested in their seventies, the comparable ten-year rise in poor acuity was 32% (Anderson & Palmore, 1974).

Cross-sectional data from the Duke study, however, show that only among the very old was somewhat impaired uncorrectable acuity the rule. More than three-fourths of subjects in their sixties and more than half in their seventies had good corrected vision (20/25 or better) in at least one eye. In the group over age 80, only slightly more than one-third did (Anderson & Palmore, 1974).

As we saw in our vignette, uncorrectable poor acuity is a serious problem because it hampers older people in most of their activities. A second major impairment that affects the elderly has a much more limited impact, although it is actually a more universal aging change. This problem is the familiar inability to see near objects clearly. Its technical name, ***presbyopia*** ("old eyes"), reflects its prevalence in later life. What is not well known is that this classic harbinger of old age does not occur as abruptly as it seems to when a person is apt to notice it suddenly in his or her forties. Ability to focus on close objects begins to lessen gradually as early as childhood (Botwinick, 1978). However, this problem usually becomes severe enough to be perceptible in later midlife (see Vaughan, Schmitz, & Fatt, 1979) and so has been firmly linked, like gray hair or wrinkled skin, to advancing age.

Presbyopia and poor visual acuity are fairly obvious, straightforward problems. Some other age-related difficulties are more specific and may require careful attention to notice. The older person is likely to have particular difficulty seeing well in dim light. Ability to distinguish colors may be deficient, in particular those in the blue-green range. The individual is often more bothered by glare (the sensation of too-bright light) and may have problems shifting focus quickly to objects at different distances. The field of vision is likely to be narrower; that is, the ability to see things at the periphery of one's gaze may decline (Colavita, 1978). Figure 3-1 illustrates the impact some of these difficulties may have on a person's ability to perceive the world.

Age-related limitations in vision are caused by a variety of degenerative influences in the different parts of the eye itself and in the rest of the visual system. Often a combination of deteriorative changes affects a particular aspect of vision. This means, as in Mrs. Kennedy's case, it is often unclear how responsible a given structural change may be for the actual deficit experienced by a particular older adult.

To examine these anatomical alterations, we first need some background: a highly simplified description of the steps (and structures) involved in seeing (see Figure 3-2).

**Steps Involved in Seeing.**    In order for us to see, light enters the eye through the outer part, the cornea, and passes through a clear, viscous fluid called the aqueous humor and then through the pupil, an opening in the next structure, the iris. It then must travel through the lens and a gel-like substance called the vitreous humor to reach the inner part of the eye, the retina, where the visual receptors are located.

A major purpose of the more external parts of the eye is to optimally filter and focus light so the best possible image arrives at the retina. The visual receptors, located on the retina, are the crucial link by which we make contact with the environment. Here light waves are transformed into the nervous impulses carried to the brain.

There are two types of visual receptors. The rods, concentrated at the periphery of the retina, are highly sensitive, but only to gradations in brightness, and are responsible for our seeing in dim light. The cones are responsible for detailed vision, are sensitive to color, and are located in the center of the retina.

**FIGURE 3-1.**   Scenes simulating the vision of typical persons in their twenties and in their late seventies or eighties. Upper panel illustrates increased suscep-tibility to glare; lower, problems of acuity associated with poor contrast. *(Source: From* Handbook of the Psychology of Aging, *by J. E. Birren and K. W. Schaie. Copyright © 1977 by Van Nostrand Reinhold Company. Reprinted by permission of the publisher. Slides prepared by Dr. Leon Pastalan.)*

Impulses originating in the rods and cones travel to the brain via the neurons making up the optic nerve. They arrive at the part of the brain called the visual cortex.

**Age Changes in the Visual System.**   Anywhere along the pathway from the outside world to the visual cortex, changes can occur that may impair the older person's ability to see. As our visual system does not function in a vacuum,

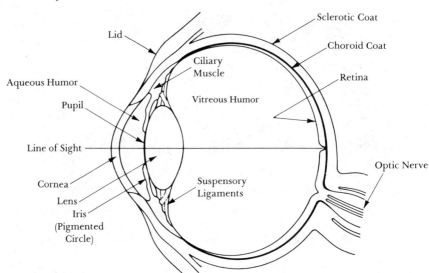

**FIGURE 3-2.**    Anatomy of the human eye in cross-section.

age-related deteriorative changes in other parts of the brain may also affect seeing ability in the older adult (Ordy & Brizzee, 1979). Because the eye is the externally located, or *peripheral part of the visual system,* changes that occur there are called peripheral influences on poor vision. When a visual problem is located higher up, within the central nervous system, the difficulty is said to have a *central* cause.

We begin our catalogue of age changes at the outer cover of the eye, the cornea. (Unless otherwise noted, the information presented below is taken from three reviews: Botwinick, 1978; Fozard et al., 1977; Ordy & Brizzee, 1979.)

Several age changes can occur in the cornea. The most obvious is an easily observed opaque band surrounding the eye, the *arcus senilis,* noticeable in many people by age 50. Often the arcus senilis is not fully completed, however, until the midsixties. The major negative result of the formation of this band is that peripheral vision is reduced because light cannot pass well through this opaque circle (Colavita, 1978).

A change in the next parts of the eye, the iris and pupil, may limit general acuity. However, this negative alteration has its primary impact on ability to see well in dim light. The iris is a pigmented, circular structure (our iris color is our eye color) with a hole, the pupil, in its center. In bright light the iris reflexively expands in width, causing the pupil to become smaller. This enables less light to reach the sensitive retinal receptors and so protects them from damage. In dim light the iris narrows so that the pupil dilates, allowing more illumination to reach the rods and cones. It is these shifts, coupled with chemical changes in the receptors, that help us see in the dark.

As a person ages, the iris becomes less able to change its width. Generally, this loss means that in both dim and bright light older adults, on the average, have smaller pupils than the young. In particular, though, there is a marked difference between the pupil size of young and elderly under conditions of darkness, when the pupil needs to be as large as possible to permit optimal vision (Birren, Casperson, & Botwinick, 1950). So having a smaller pupil means older adults have a kind of fixed internal dimmer. In bright light their deficit is not so problematic. Vision may be only slightly worse. But the elderly may be able to see practically nothing in dim light.

The dimming effect is far from minimal. It is estimated that changes in the pupil and iris and in the transparency of the structure discussed next, the lens, typically permit only about 30% as much light to reach the retina at age 60 as at age 20 (Saxon & Etten, 1978).

Deterioration in the lens is important in a variety of late-life vision problems, as this structure changes in several discrete negative ways as a person ages. One kind of deteriorative change was just mentioned—change in the lens's transparency. As we get older, the previously clear lens gradually gets cloudy. This predictable age-related clouding impairs general visual acuity and also makes the person more sensitive to glare because rays of light are scattered when they hit the partly opaque lens (see Figure 3-1). The pathological end point of the process is a severely clouded or completely blocked lens. This condition is called a **cataract.**

Because no light can reach the retina when the lens is impenetrable, cataracts, at their extreme, result in blindness. However, they do not need to have this devastating effect. Impairments in vision caused by cataracts are often curable. They are treated simply by surgically removing the person's defective lens and either implanting an artificial lens in its place or prescribing special contact lenses or glasses. As Table 3-1 shows, this easy treatability does not extend to the other major conditions causing blindness in older adults.

A second change in the lens's transparency affects color vision. The lens becomes yellowish as a person ages. This yellowing causes a decrease in color sensitivity across the whole visual spectrum. However, in particular it impairs ability to see hues in the blue-green range and causes difficulty in distinguishing these colors.

Our discussion so far implies that the lens may have no other function but to serve as a window. This, however, is far from true. The main purpose of this structure is to bring objects at different distances into clear focus on the retina. It does this by changing shape. When we view near objects, the lens bulges (curves outward). When we view distant objects, it flattens out and becomes elongated.

The lens's image-focusing job is less easily performed as a person gets older, because both it and the ciliary muscle, which control changes in its shape (see Figure 3-2), become less functional. An overall loss in lens elasticity occurs, limiting the ability to shift focus quickly from near to far objects and vice versa. In particular, the lens becomes less able to bulge out. This explains why presbyopia is a natural accompaniment of later life.

There is a controversy over how much degenerative changes in the next part of

**TABLE 3-1.**    Major age-related visual disorders. Note that cataracts are described in the text.

| Problem | Description |
|---|---|
| *Glaucoma* | Excessive fluid buildup in the aqueous humor causes pressure within the eye to gradually increase. Often without warning sight is lost owing to the retinal or optic nerve damage that may result. Can be treated but only if diagnosed early, before structural damage occurs. |
| *Macular degeneration* | Decreased blood supply to the center of the retina, the area containing the highest concentration of cones, may cause central vision to be lost. There is no treatment. |
| *Diabetic retinopathy* | Side effect of long-term diabetes. There are two forms. In background retinopathy, retinal blood vessels hemorrhage or develop abnormalities confined to the retina; central vision may be impaired. In proliferative retinopathy, these vessels grow outward into the vitreous, where they hemorrhage; total blindness may result. Treatment includes controlling diabetes or sealing off leaking blood vessels by laser surgery (which can control the problem but not cure it, as new vessels are apt to form). |

the eye, the crucially important retina, are likely to impair the typical older person's vision. However, one late-life difficulty has, in part, a likely retinal cause—problems adapting to darkness. This is because the process of dark adaptation depends on chemical changes in the rods and cones. The chemical changes involved in dark adaptation occur gradually and are completed only after we spend some time in a dimly lit place. Although there are conflicting studies, it is likely that dark adaptation occurs more slowly for the elderly. It is abundantly clear that older people never reach nearly the completed level of sensitivity of the young. No matter how long they remain in dim light, typical older adults do not see nearly as well as they did when young.

A final type of deterioration, negative changes in the visual system apart from the eye, is inferred from the specific way vision changes beginning in late middle age. As mentioned earlier, dramatic drops in acuity (and other, more specific aspects of vision) occur and continue at an accelerated pace after age 60. The more observable degenerative changes in the external parts of the visual system are insufficient to explain the magnitude of vision losses incurred after middle age. This suggests to researchers that central alterations (that is, neuronal loss and malfunction) must play a large part in these difficulties.

**Consequences.**    Amid our long catalogue of difficulties it may be easy to overlook perhaps the most important point. Although the average older person is likely to have subtle losses in sight, he or she is also unlikely to have marked decrements in this important sense. There are no data, in fact, on whether these usually mild seeing losses affect behavior at all (Ordy & Brizzee, 1979). However, the consequences of severe impairments in vision may be pronounced. In our vignette, Mrs. Kennedy was deprived of her favorite activity, and she was forced to withdraw to some extent from relationships because she did not feel comfortable going out at night.

We might imagine, then, that very poor vision could have some quite global effects. Because of this problem, older people might become more isolated, more limited as individuals because they could no longer do the things they loved. They might feel more vulnerable, less secure, less self-confident. Finally, inability to be in full contact with the world might have another effect, just as ominous: intellectual abilities could decline. What is the evidence that problem vision engenders these negative changes? Several researchers have explored this question using a simple correlational approach. Do people who have severe vision losses perform more poorly on measures of personality and intellect?

In the Duke Longitudinal Study an investigator (Eisdorfer, 1970a, 1970b) used the Rorschach, a widely used test of personality (see Chapter 8), to determine whether severely impaired sight is associated with greater rigidity and immaturity. Contrary to his expectations, there was not a hint of a relationship. The Rorschach performance of volunteers with uncorrectable vision problems and of those with unimpaired corrected vision was identical.

Another Duke investigation, however, had a contradictory result (Anderson & Palmore, 1974). Here when researchers used different indexes of personality, self-ratings and observers' ratings, subjects with poor vision did show deleterious changes. They reported being involved in fewer activities than their peers, and social workers saw them as more isolated and less emotionally secure. These results may be criticized, though, because the personalities of the subjects were not being judged by unaware observers. The social workers, most likely knowing which volunteers had impaired vision, may have rated these respondents less positively simply because they assumed, as many people may (Han & Geha-Mitzel, 1979), that vision problems should lead to isolation or make a person more insecure. The next study, too, has a flaw. Its results at first glance imply a causal link between poor vision and losses in intellect.

In a very low-functioning group (nursing home elderly), Snyder, Pyrek, and Smith (1976) found that respondents who were legally blind received lower scores on the mental status questionnaire, a simple, orally administered test of the most basic cognitive abilities (see Chapter 8), than groups whose vision was better. However, these researchers did not control for general physical health, a variable quite likely to explain the correlations found. Diabetes, for example, impairs health in general as well as being a leading cause of blindness. Poor overall health is related to lower performance on intelligence tests (see the next chapter). So a better causal inference may have to do with possible illness. In the absence of controlling for health, we are on shaky ground in making even the tentative conclusion that impaired vision itself may be implicated in negative cognitive change.

In sum, seeing well is obviously important in a person's life. However, the impact of even severe losses of sight on other aspects of the older adult's behavior has yet to be shown. This uncertainty, as we will see, does not characterize deficits in the other most crucial sensory modality, hearing.

### Hearing

Hearing impairments, unlike vision problems, are clearly tied to other types of negative change in older adults. At first glance this seems puzzling because most of us would think vision was our most important sense. However, losing our hearing in some ways cuts us off even more profoundly from the world than limitations in our ability to see (Saxon & Etten, 1978). It is through our hearing that we make our main contact with other people. We encounter each other through hearing and then understanding speech. It is this perhaps most important aspect of our environment that, as the vignette illustrates, we are limited in fully experiencing when problems occur in our ability to hear. (Unless otherwise noted, the information in the next section is from Maurer and Rupp, 1979.)

**Overview.**   As with problem vision, impairments in hearing are disproportionately the province of the old. It is estimated that more than half the people who have hearing deficits in the United States are over 65. This fact is apparent by comparing the numbers of older and younger people who wear the visible badge of a hearing problem—a hearing aid. Individuals over 65 are 13 times as likely as the rest of the population to own this corrective device. Problem hearing even ranks ahead of problem vision in surveys of chronic impairments suffered by older adults. For instance, in one national poll it was second only to arthritis in frequency of physical problems reported by older people (see also Table 2-1).

Most elderly, however, do not have impairing hearing losses. Like problem vision, significantly limited hearing may not affect a sizable percentage of people until the late seventies. At least this was the finding of a 1970 study. The investigators looked at various sources of data on impaired ability to hear speech sounds in different age groups. By this important criterion of poor hearing, 25% of the old-old had problems, but only about 12% of the young-old did.

The average person's hearing is thought to become gradually less acute beginning in the early thirties for men and the late thirties for women. As is true of vision, hearing losses seem to start to accelerate in late middle age (Ordy, Brizzee, Beavers, & Medart, 1979).

These figures, though, may change radically in the future. There is a clear environmental cause for hearing loss: prolonged exposure to noise. Noisy environments, in fact, cause hearing problems that are so similar to pure age-related deterioration that it is difficult in practice to separate the two (Corso, 1977; Schow, Christensen, Hutchinson, & Nerbonne, 1978). So, many hearing impairments suffered by today's elderly are thought to have dual causes. They are a function both of advancing age and of external, preventable factors such as exposure to too much noise. Unfortunately, in what looks like an increasingly noisy society, the prevalence of poor hearing may be rising. We might expect this problem to become an even more crucial chronic condition in future years.

Even avoiding dire demographic forecasts, we still do not know the exact percentage of older people who have impaired hearing now. The statistics mentioned earlier are estimates and are far from exact. It is also uncertain exactly how many of today's older people have vision difficulties, but estimating the prevalence of problem hearing has particular pitfalls. The elderly tend to be more reluctant to be tested for this particular difficulty. As our vignette illustrates, poor hearing is often a sensitive impairment to admit one has. Not being tested can even seem eminently rational. Hearing problems are relatively easily attributed to the environment rather than to oneself. Finally, it is hard even for experts to agree on the level of difficulty that actually constitutes a problem. One reason is that (as with vision) the adequacy of a person's hearing can vary so radically in different situations. This changeability was evident in our vignette: Dr. Kennedy's hearing was fairly good when there was little background noise or when most family members spoke. When in the pancake house or conversing with his daughter, he could hardly hear at all.

So hearing problems due to aging, like late-life vision difficulties, have some specific characteristics that are far from intuitively obvious. Problem hearing is not, as we might think at first, an unvarying all-or-none affair. Problem hearing due to aging also has a special name—***presbycusis.***

Sufferers from presbycusis have particular trouble distinguishing high-pitched tones. So, they may have more difficulty hearing certain categories of speakers, such as women. They may have problems hearing certain sounds (such as consonants) or certain phrases (such as warnings) that may be fairly loud but are usually delivered in a higher-pitched voice. They may be more impaired by background noise. In a noisy environment it becomes more important to understand the higher-frequency tones in making out the content of a conversation. However, these are the very sounds the presbycusis sufferer has most trouble distinguishing. A general difficulty in being able to filter out irrelevant stimuli as well as one did when young may add to the older person's problems hearing in a noisy place.

Sufferers from presbycusis are also likely to hear less well when someone speaks rapidly (Pickett, Bergman, & Levitt, 1979) or when they cannot see the speaker. This is because, to compensate for their loss, many people with hearing problems read lips. When they cannot use this aid, their hearing seems to be worse.

These selective difficulties can cause misunderstandings when others notice what look like marked peculiarities in the person's ability to hear (Kart et al., 1978; Rosenthal, 1978). As we saw in our vignette, the older adult may be accused of malevolent intentions, of pretending poor hearing at times simply to get his or her way or to avoid having to listen to a particular person.

Another difficulty that some sufferers from presbycusis have, called ***recruitment,*** may only reinforce these negative ideas. Recruitment, a condition whereby a person suddenly experiences an abnormal increase in the perception of loudness as a tone gets progressively louder, is experienced only by elderly having a particular type of presbycusis (Corso, 1977). However, when it does occur in an older person, it can exasperate a speaker who is suddenly told to "stop shouting" when his or her previously normal-voiced communication has not been understood (Oyer, Kapur, & Deal, 1976).

One reason that late-life hearing impairments are so problematic is that they can generate such difficulties in relations with others. But, before looking at this important interpersonal impact in more depth, we need to consider the physical bases for the hearing difficulties that older adults show. As with vision, some background is necessary—an overview of the steps involved in hearing.

**Steps Involved in Hearing.**    Sound waves first reach the outer ear (see Figure 3-3), where the pinna, the external part of the outer ear, helps to collect them. They then travel along the ear canal (external auditory meatus) to the eardrum (tympanic membrane). The waves cause this structure to vibrate. These vibrations are transmitted to the middle ear, an air-filled cavity containing three bones—the malleus, the incus, and the stapes—which amplify the vibrations and transmit them to the inner ear. It is here that the actual hearing receptors, called hair cells, are located (see Figure 3-4).

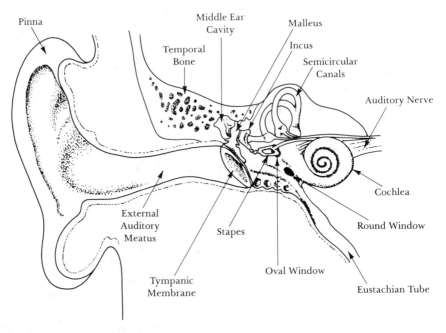

**FIGURE 3-3.**    Anatomy of the human ear, depicting the structures of the outer ear, middle ear, and inner ear.

The cochlea is the part of the inner ear crucial to our hearing. It is shaped like a coil and composed of three fluid-filled compartments—the scala tympani, the scala vestibuli, and the scala media. Vibrations transmitted from the middle ear

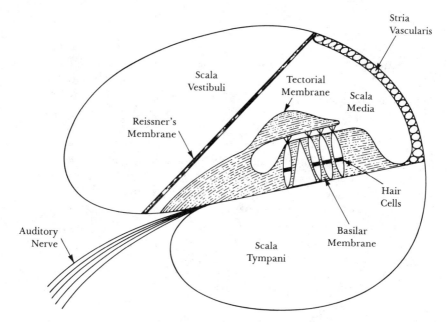

**FIGURE 3-4.**   The human cochlea (cross-section).

set up waves in these compartments. These movements cause the basilar membrane, on which the hair cells sit, to bob up and down. The hair cells then jiggle, shearing against the tectorial membrane, located above them. The resulting bending of the hair cells generates the electrical impulses responsible for our experience of hearing. Impulses generated by the hair cells then leave the peripheral part of the auditory system, the ear, and travel to the cortical centers responsible for hearing via the collection of neurons making up the auditory nerve.

Our perception of the different properties a given sound has, its pitch (highness or lowness), its intensity (loudness or softness), and its timbre (complexity), depends on the way the basilar membrane moves. Different sounds set up differing patterns of motion in the fluid-filled cochlea, which, in turn, cause varying types of displacements of the basilar membrane. This means that for each sound the pattern of hair cells that are stimulated to fire differs. It is through the complex patterning of the nervous impulses generated by the hair cells that we interpret the characteristics of a sound.

Crucial to the anatomical basis of presbycusis is that, except for tones of very low frequencies, the location of the hair cells on the basilar membrane that are stimulated to fire is important to discrimination of pitch. Because of the physical properties of the basilar membrane, high-pitched tones result in maximal stimulation of the hair cells on the portion of the membrane at the base of the cochlea. Lower-frequency tones stimulate hair cells toward the apex of the cochlea most.

Our ability to hear high-pitched sounds thus depends on hair cells at the basal portion of the cochlea being stimulated to fire.

**Age Changes in the Auditory System.**    Presbycusis is due largely to deteriorative changes within the inner ear, the part of the auditory system housing the hearing receptors. This is in marked contrast to age-related impairments in vision, which are often caused by changes in the more external parts of the eye. However, as with vision, there is a growing conviction that central nervous system influences may also play a large part in hearing losses, particularly those incurred specifically in late life (Ordy et al., 1979). Age changes in the outer and middle ear can limit an older person's hearing as well.

Conditions in the outer or middle ear causing hearing problems may be as easily reversible as too much wax in the ear canal. Sometimes, as in a middle ear difficulty called otosclerosis, these problems may be so complicated that they require surgery. When the locus of the difficulty resides in the middle or outer ear, however, an older person is not truly said to have presbycusis. Because the condition involves an impairment in the transmission of sound to the auditory receptors, it is called a ***conductive hearing loss.***

People with a conductive hearing loss are quite unlike the typical sufferer from presbycusis. They do not have special difficulty hearing high-pitched tones; their problem is usually more straightforward and is akin to what most people imagine a hearing difficulty should be. As is true when we wear earplugs, these older adults' ability to hear a sound depends only on its loudness.

But what causes the peculiar high-tone loss so characteristic of presbycusis? To understand this, we must turn to changes in the inner ear.

Four distinct types of deterioration within the inner ear have been linked to presbycusis. Each has been associated with a different form the problem may take (see Corso, 1977). One major cause is loss of the hair cells—and it is hair cells at the base of the cochlea (those involved in the perception of high tones) that tend to atrophy to the greatest extent. As this loss is permanent, late-life hearing disorders most often cannot be cured.

**Consequences.**    What negative psychological consequences might result from Dr. Kennedy's particular difficulty? Dr. Kennedy might easily be hurt by his daughter's rejection. He might also feel misunderstood because of his family's unwarranted distrust. His increasing sense of isolation, coupled with his own frightening perception of not being in control, might then turn to suspicion. He could come to feel that others were against him and that he should always be on guard (see Oyer et al., 1976). In fact, generalizing from this hypothetical scenario, we could envision a particular psychological problem as the pathological extreme of the specific feelings that may be engendered by hearing loss: a paranoid psychosis.

Hearing problems alone do not cause paranoia. However, there is fascinating evidence that among severely disturbed people they are in fact associated with this problem. Cooper and Curry (1976) tested a group of hospitalized older psychiatric patients and discovered a higher-than-expected rate of impaired hearing among patients diagnosed as paranoid but not among those with a comparison problem. Also, in this provocative study, hard-of-hearing paranoid patients were found likely to have had their hearing difficulties for a long time. So deafness, particularly when it develops early, may in truth predispose highly susceptible people to develop paranoid reactions, possibly because of its unique negative impact on interpersonal relationships.

Although not all studies agree (see Thomas, Hunt, Garry, Hood, Goodwin, & Goodwin, 1983), among more normal elderly people, hearing problems are linked to pathological personality signs, but these changes are much less severe. In the same Duke study that found visual problems to be unassociated with any personality changes on the Rorschach, Eisdorfer (1970a, 1970b) also looked at the adequacy of the performance of hard-of-hearing volunteers. These subjects did show signs of personality disorganization. Compared with volunteers with normal hearing, they gave responses that, overall, were less mature and less highly developed. Their responses also were more constricted and rigid.

In addition, even mild hearing losses are clearly linked to the different type of limited performance discussed earlier—poor scores on intelligence tests. Granick, Kleban, and Weiss (1976) established this by correlating hearing acuity with IQ performance among a group of community elderly. In contrast to the investigation exploring this question for vision, though, these researchers took care to test their subjects' health. In fact, they controlled for this important variable by using two groups of subjects, the first very healthy and the second more physically ill. For both of these samples even relatively small hearing losses were associated with poorer overall intelligence-test performance, but the relationships were highly significant for the subtests involving verbal abilities. Here even minimal losses in hearing were tied to clearly worse scores (see also Thomas et al., 1983).

What is particularly interesting about this study is that these subjects had relatively minor impairments, ones we would think should have little effect on their functioning. Are even mild hearing difficulties somehow associated physiologically with more general central nervous system deterioration? Do they relate to less acute intellect because they lower the person's interest in the outside world? Or is the test itself flawed when used with subjects handicapped by possibly not hearing orally presented items? All we can say is that IQ performance seems sensitive specifically to losses in hearing, apart from the possible impact of hearing loss on other aspects of behavior.

### Taste and Smell

Impairments in the more secondary sensory systems of taste and smell do not have such far-ranging effects as hearing problems. However, because taste and smell work together to allow us to enjoy food, limitations in these senses may cause poor nutrition in some older people. In addition, age-related losses in smell sensitivity may be dangerous because smell is an early warning system alerting us to such hazards as fire. Problems here, then, can imperil the older person's safety as well as affecting his or her health (Engen, 1977).

As with vision and hearing, most studies show that the elderly taste and smell less well than the young (Schiffman, 1977, 1979; Schiffman & Pasternak, 1979). However, age differences in taste and smell have been studied less than vision and hearing, and results are more variable. More than with vision and hearing, there are questions about whether the losses observed are due to age itself or to comparisons of often ill elderly people with healthy young adults (Engen, 1977). For whatever reasons, fascinating differences do emerge when older and younger people are asked to use these two senses where they are most important—in identifying and evaluating foods.

In the first of a series of studies on food sensitivity and preferences (Schiffman, 1977), blindfolded college students and elderly adults were asked to identify and rate for pleasantness a variety of blended foods after smelling and tasting them. It was discovered that the older people could not distinguish the vast majority of the foods as well as the students, and the elderly were more likely to rate the foods as weak-tasting.

That impaired smell played a large part in these altered perceptions was shown by the investigator's next study (Schiffman & Pasternak, 1979). Elderly and young adult subjects were asked to discriminate between different food odors compared in pairs. Again, they were asked to rate the pleasantness of the substances they smelled. As in the first study, the elderly were less able than the young to identify most odors. However, their sensitivity was most acute for smells of fruits. Not unexpectedly, the older people were likely to rate the fruit odors as more pleasant.

Taken together, these results show that there is an empirical basis for the frequent complaint some older people have about foods—that they taste too bland and flavorless (Schiffman, 1979). The finding of differential sensitivities to particular odors may also give us insight into food preferences in older adults. We might expect certain foods to be liked better and so eaten more readily at least partly because they are perceived relatively well.

Impaired smell acuity, it has been suggested, may also partly explain another common complaint of older people, that some foods taste bitter or sour. Some foods, such as chocolate and vegetables, are thought to have a bitter taste that is masked by their pleasant odor. If odor sensitivity is impaired, these normally palatable foods taste unpleasant (Schiffman, 1979).

The logical next step from this research and idea was to try to improve the flavor of foods by "amplifying" their smell (see Box 3-1). However, there may be an even easier avenue to enhancing some older adults' enjoyment of food. Eating in late life often loses its appeal because dental problems (for example, ill-fitting dentures) make it difficult or painful to chew. The prescription is then simple: provide high-quality dental care and make visiting a dentist possible for many by expanding government medical coverage to include this service so tied to the quality of life in old age.

**Box 3-1.   Amplifying Food Odors**

The studies cited in the text clearly suggest that one way to increase the older person's enjoyment of foods would be to artificially strengthen their odor. In fact, Schiffman (1979) successfully did just that.

She fortified blended foods with artificial flavoring and then had a group of elderly and young adults taste them and compare them for pleasantness with the same foods in their natural state. As expected, for the older people smell amplification enhanced the palatability of the foods. Young adults had no such reaction; they felt the artificially flavored foods were too strong, criticizing their overpowering odor and taste. For them the more enjoyable foods were clearly the naturally flavored ones. This finding indicates the possibility that amplified foods might be specially marketed to appeal to older people.

## Motor Performance

One of the first generalizations we are likely to make about the behavior of older people concerns their motor capacities. The elderly tend to have less physical strength and stamina than the young. Most important, we are likely to notice a striking fact about motor performance in late life: older adults move or respond more slowly than the young. This loss of response speed is one of the longest-observed (Birren & Renner, 1977) and most highly researched phenomena in the psychology of aging.

Being quick is essential to some very basic activities—crossing a street before the light changes, driving, or even avoiding getting hurt by stepping out of the way of environmental obstacles. The elderly person who is markedly slow is prone to having accidents as well as being out of synchrony with the basic pace that the physical environment seems to demand.

A slower pace can also put the older adult out of step with people and can cause conflict because it is so discrepant from the rate at which most of us like to live. As we are likely to notice when we find ourselves behind a slow driver or must adjust our gait to a slower person's step, our first impulse is to get annoyed. Slowness in itself, then, may be a barrier to good relationships for some elderly people and may be another reason underlying our time-oriented society's negative attitudes toward old age.

### Overview

When psychologists measure response speed in any group, they are looking at one facet of what is called ***psychomotor performance.*** Psychomotor performance is simply a person's ability and dexterity on tasks involving physical actions. A predictable finding is that on tasks testing psychomotor speed older adults, on the average, perform much more slowly than the young. In fact, this slowing is so pervasive and expected that it currently seems to be one of the most certain predictions we can make about how a young person's behavior is likely to differ in later life (Birren & Renner, 1977; Jarvik, 1975).

However, response speed among older adults shows fascinating variability. In addition, the degree to which the elderly are slower depends on what they are asked to do. This is clearly demonstrated in the laboratory, where researchers have systematically investigated what types of psychomotor tasks are particularly difficult for older people. (Unless otherwise noted, the discussion below is derived from a comprehensive review by Welford, 1977.)

Comparisons of the laboratory performance of different-aged people on timed motor tasks almost always show steady and significant declines in speed after young adulthood. However, the response being tested also has an important effect on the magnitude of the losses older age groups show. Performance is slower on complex motor tasks than on those demanding simple actions. For example, older adults do worse on tasks that require aiming at a target than they do when simply asked to strike something as fast as they can. If they are asked to do something involving a sequence of steps, they perform more poorly than if instructed to make a single simple movement.

These more difficult tasks involve not just more complicated action but also more decision making. The person not only has to perform (usually) several discrete moves but also has to prepare and initiate each one. In which part of this sequence the aging person has particular problems is clearly revealed by an experimental procedure measuring what is called reaction time.

**Reaction-time studies** have two basic forms: they may be simple or disjunctive. In the simple reaction-time experiment, a subject is asked to make a predetermined response after a single signal has appeared. For example, the subject may be instructed to press a buzzer or tap his or her foot as soon as he or she can after hearing a tone or seeing a light. In the disjunctive reaction-time experiment, the subject's task is more complicated. He or she is confronted with two or more signals, each (usually) having a different appropriate response. The subject then must tailor the action taken to the signal received, rather than simply making an already prepared response.

In these studies, the time it takes to prepare and initiate the appropriate action is measured separately from the time it takes to make the movement itself so that researchers can isolate the contribution of the decision-making and initiation phase before taking an action to slowed response time. The first period is what is actually called the **reaction time.** It is the time that elapses from the presentation of the signal to act to the beginning of the response. A second measure, called the **movement time,** is the time it takes the person to make the response itself.

Using this procedure, researchers find that movement time may slow somewhat in older age groups. However, it is reaction time that shows the most marked evidence of slowing (Hicks & Birren, 1970). Moreover, in the disjunctive situation, where more decision making is involved, the older person often takes proportionately longer (Botwinick, 1978). This means that the slowed motor performance of the typical older person is a problem primarily in initiating an action. Slowing occurs somewhere in the sequence intervening between the time a signal to respond occurs and the time action is actually carried out. The following hypothetical account describes the steps most likely to constitute this sequence.

### Steps Involved in Taking Action

On the basis of a variety of studies, motor performance has been conceptualized as consisting of the following steps. First, information from the sensory organs, those described in detail earlier as well as other sensors receiving information from the outside world and about the workings of the body, is fed to the brain. Here three discrete central nervous system events are logically thought to occur: the information is perceived, then an action is decided on, and then it is programmed to be carried out. The final result is the response itself performed by the effectors. The effectors comprise both the voluntary muscles and the involuntary reactors of the autonomic nervous system.

This is a simplified account of the actually much more elaborate hypothetical sequence depicted in Figure 3-5. In addition, it is only logical that the identical chain occurs many times in the course of our taking even simple actions. As Welford (1977) states:

> Performance hardly ever consists of a single run through the chain. . . . Even relatively simple actions such as picking up a glass or opening a door involve an iterative process in which an initial action . . . is followed by a series of smaller adjustments each of which depends for its precise form on the outcome of the one before. In other words data from the effector action and its results on the external world are fed back as part of the sensory input for the next run through the chain [pp. 450–451].

So it seems clear that what we probably envision when we think of psychomotor performance, the actual muscular movements a person makes, is only the end point of a more complicated series of events. Now we look at specifically where in this chain the main locus of the typical older person's problem lies.

### Locus of Age Changes in Response Speed

Problems in the last step of the sequence, making the actual movements involved in action, may be highly important in explaining slowed response in some older people. For example, we would expect sufferers from osteoarthritis (see Chapter 2) or other diseases that severely hamper movement to be much slower. Problems at the beginning of the chain, sensory input, could also account for much of the slowness of other elderly people—for instance those whose hearing or vision impairments make it a constant struggle to know whether the environment dictates taking action.

However, reaction-time studies involve clear signals to respond and the reaction-time measure eliminates to a great extent the movement part of the chain.

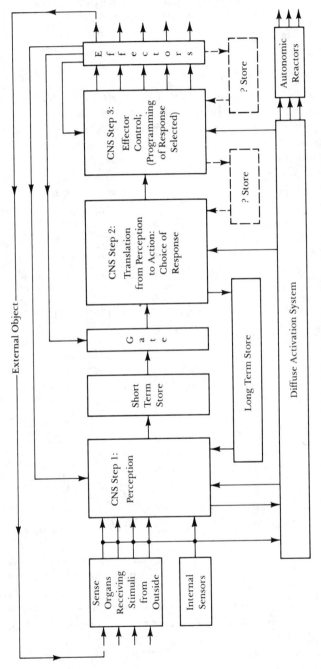

**FIGURE 3-5.** Hypothetical block diagram of the human sensorimotor system. Stores refer to memory functions. (*Source: From "Motor Performance," by A. T. Welford. In Handbook of the Psychology of Aging, by J. E. Birren and K. W. Schaie. Copyright © 1977 by Van Nostrand Reinhold Company. Reprinted by permission of the publisher.*)

The marked reaction-time differences between young and old therefore suggest that as people age, they must have more and more trouble mainly with the middle steps, those involving the central nervous system. Specifically, it is suggested that for most motor tasks the locus of the older person's slowness seems mainly to be the last two hypothetical CNS steps depicted in Figure 3-5—deciding on the appropriate action and then programming its being carried out. In other words, age-related motor deficits are due to impairments in the speed with which the central nervous system can process the information to respond (see also Birren, 1974; Birren & Renner, 1977; Welford, 1969).

### Consequences

But if the older person's slowed motor performance is caused largely by having a generally slower-functioning central nervous system, then we would expect this loss to be far from confined to motor speed. Because all but the simplest behavior requires information processing by the central nervous system, we would imagine that the person might be slower in all activities, not just those involved in taking physical action. This in fact is so. The elderly exhibit a global trait of slowing, which characterizes their performance in situations as diverse as remembering a name or solving a puzzle as well as opening a door (Birren, 1974).

This generalization, though, should not lead us to overlook a very important fact: slowness varies greatly among older individuals. It is relevant to quality only in some activities in life, and the typical older adult's loss of speed is most apparent only in actions involving complex decision making. So before assuming deficiency in an older person, we need to look carefully both at who the person is and at what he or she is being asked to do. This latter condition brings us to the possibility of analyzing what work situations may be particularly problematic in later life.

Our discussion explains, for instance, why Dr. Kennedy seemed to have particular trouble at work with speed. It also suggests that if he could have eliminated the components of his job that involved quickness and the most decision making, he might have been able to practice his profession longer. This analysis could be applied to different jobs to predict the kinds of work for which advanced age might present the most liabilities.

Workers involved in physical labor, when given the chance, seem to perform such an analysis themselves. Several studies in factories have revealed that older workers say they want, and are disproportionately found in, jobs involving relatively heavy work. Heavy work, even though more physically taxing, is less likely to have to be performed at high speed; and as our discussion suggests, quickness, not strength or stamina, is likely to be most difficult for the typical older adult. The reaction-time research, then, explains the preference of older workers for what at first looks like the most difficult work.

In general, though, studies in industry show that even in jobs requiring speed, older laborers do not do as poorly as they do on laboratory tests. The reason seems to be that work involves well-practiced activities, and practice and experi-ence often compensate for the slowing that occurs with age. Selective attrition may also operate here. Older workers whose performance does decline signifi-cantly may be more likely to retire early, so that only the quicker workers remain on the job. But who are these relatively hardy older people likely to be? This question leads us to an examination of the other variation in response speed men-tioned earlier—its variability among people.

### Individual Differences

In one laboratory investigation, when older sportsmen were compared with their more sedentary peers, the athletic older people showed much quicker reac-tion and movement times, response times comparable to those of young adults (Spirduso, 1975). Another reaction-time study had a similar theme. When older adults were at first compared with a group of unselected young people, the typical pattern emerged: the elderly, overall, were slower, However, when their responses were contrasted with those among the younger group who led inactive lives, the surprising outcome was that the older people did just as well (Botwinick & Thomp-son, 1968). This suggests that exercise may affect response speed. Although stud-ies do not all agree (Botwinick & Storandt, 1974), older people who are physically active seem to have quicker reaction times.

Another individual difference that has been tied to reaction time is health, in particular both frank evidence of heart disease and signs of its behavioral precur-sor. In one study (Botwinick & Storandt, 1974) self-reports of cardiovascular symp-toms in a group of elderly people were linked to slower reaction times. In another group of young and middle-aged adults Type A behavior in itself was associated with motor slowing (Abrahams & Birren, 1973).

The first result seems logical. We would expect people who say they have the symptoms of heart disease to be slower not just for possible physiological reasons but for psychological ones, too. A common emotional reaction to the perception that one has this life-threatening problem may be, as we saw in the last chapter's vignette, to try to slow up. However, the link between Type A behavior and slow performance is much less intuitively obvious. These Type A subjects were free from any clinical signs of heart disease. In itself their rushed lifestyle might sug-gest, if anything, that they might have even quicker reaction times than their placid Type B peers.

There are other groups whose symptoms include extremely slow reaction times—for example, patients with brain damage (Hicks & Birren, 1970). The fre-quency of a general measure of brain activity, the EEG alpha rhythm, has also been linked to motor slowing, as it seems to decrease in a parallel fashion with reaction times in successively older age groups. These relationships, as well as those just mentioned, have fueled a variety of hypotheses (see Hicks and Birren, 1970; Spirduso, 1980) about the still unknown physiological cause for the deficits in speed that older people show. They also have promising implications for inter-vening to change the psychomotor performance of older adults (Birren & Renner, 1977).

**BOX 3-2.   Traffic Accidents and the Older Driver**

Essential to being able to drive is the ability to respond quickly to often unpre-dictable signals to act. Just as important is the ability to see and hear well. Age-related vision problems like sensitivity to glare and poor vision in dim light should hinder night driving. To drive in any situation, a person needs good visual acuity, adequate peripheral vision, and the ability to shift focus easily and well. Hearing, too, is important to driving because sound gives us information about the loca-tion of other vehicles. For these reasons we would expect driving to be inherently more dangerous for older people because of their more probable difficulties with seeing, hearing, and response speed. We might expect older drivers to have a higher accident rate than other age groups (except perhaps teenage drivers).

However, there is evidence that the elderly compensate for sensorimotor de-clines by driving less often and avoiding high-risk driving situations. When Planek and Fowler (1971) questioned adults over 65 about their driving patterns and compared their answers with those of respondents aged 50–64, they found this was so. The older drivers operated their cars less frequently. They also drove less at night, on expressways, during rush hour, and in the winter than the middle-aged group.

Possibly because the elderly take this greater care, they are not unequivocally more likely statistically to have auto accidents than younger drivers. However, it is true that older adults are disproportionately involved in accidents of certain kinds. As expected, these types of accidents can be easily tied to their particular difficulties.

Older drivers are more likely to have accidents when they must make a rapid series of judgments and take quick action—for example, when changing lanes (Planek & Fowler, 1971). They also have a higher accident rate due to failing to notice or respond quickly enough to stop signs or traffic lights (McFarland, Tune, & Welford, 1964). In contrast, the most frequent accidents among young drivers have no relation to slowness or sensory declines. They are caused by speeding, traveling on the wrong side of the road, and operating faulty equipment (McFarland et al., 1964).

## Interventions

If cardiovascular disease, a sedentary lifestyle, or a slower alpha rhythm were in fact responsible for slower psychomotor performance, then we might be able to change response speed by somehow modifying these variables themselves. In one study (Woodruff, cited in Birren & Renner, 1977) this was tried. The investigator used biofeedback to teach elderly subjects to speed up their alpha EEG. Biofeed-back is the technique of providing overt feedback to help people modify bodily processes not normally under voluntary control. Woodruff did have some success in speeding up her subjects' reaction times. Her encouraging finding suggests that similar approaches might be tried to improve the capacity of older adults.

For the most part, however, slowness in the elderly, at least for the present, is not reversible. This is also true of the vast majority of late-life sensory impairments that exist today. These difficulties are chronic conditions; they must be adapted to and lived with. Are there still ways of helping the older person with these problems? Are there techniques for minimizing the impact of these limitations that so far cannot be cured?

There are if we develop a different approach, one that views the person not as an isolated unit but as someone whose competence is often largely determined by the environment. This *ecological perspective,* or environmental perspective, on behavior is not new in psychology. It seems, however, to have particular relevance to studying and helping people who have functional impairments like the specific sensory and motor limitations just described. A strategy of this type was the one the psychologist suggested in our vignette.

The contribution of an ecological view of behavior to understanding and helping the specifically disabled elderly has been clearly spelled out by a psychologist (Lawton, 1970, 1975) whose special interest is in planning housing that maximizes competent behavior. He first postulates the following axiom about the importance of the environment: the more disabled a person is, the more crucial the influence of his or her outside world becomes. The ability of impaired older adults to function is highly dependent on the environment they find themselves in. This heightened vulnerability is not true of someone who has no limitations. The person without disabilities is more liberated from the exigencies of the normal environment because he or she is able to perform competently in most typical settings in our society.

Our vignette makes this point very evident. Compare, for example, the differing impact of two environments on Dr. Kennedy and his family. Because of his limitation, Dr. Kennedy could perform competently only when he was in the quiet deli. Other family members suffered no such constraints at all. Having no hearing problem, they were equally at ease in both restaurants; we would expect this to be true of almost any place in which they chose to eat. The obvious reason for our confidence is that restaurants would soon go out of business if their noise level made it too difficult for most of us to hear. In other words, most places in life are tailored to fit, or be congruent with, people's capacities.

However, this fit is specific to people without limitations, not to those who have trouble seeing or hearing or moving quickly. This brings us to our psychologist's important next point. To help these latter individuals function too, we must redesign the world in a different way—to fit their capacities. This strategy is called maximizing *person/environment congruence* (Kahana, 1975).

If the environment any person is in is too undemanding, the person is likely to function at a lower level than he or she is capable of. An example was mentioned in the last chapter: an older adult may develop excess disabilities as a result of experiencing a too supportive interpersonal environment, being treated as an invalid. The opposite extreme, a too complex or too difficult external world, leads to similarly impaired performance. The impact of a too challenging environment is epitomized by Dr. Kennedy's relative incapacity in the pancake house and his wife's in her kitchen. So, Lawton (1970, 1975) suggests that the most appropriate environment may be one that either fits the person's particular capacities or, better yet, slightly exceeds them so the person is pulled to function the best that he or she can.

The ideal of creating person/environment congruence leads us to the exciting topic touched on in our vignette—designing living spaces to encourage competence in people with functional impairments. Here the approach is quite unlike one aimed at cure. The physical environment is seen as capable of functioning, like a pair of glasses or a wheelchair, as a constant support to mitigate the impact of an unchangeable chronic condition. Devices like eyeglasses or wheelchairs that compensate for permanent losses in function are called prostheses. Similarly, the specially planned housing and the suggestions for modifying private homes described below create what gerontological planners call **prosthetic environments** (Lindsley, 1964; McClannahan, 1973).

### Designing Housing for the Elderly

Beginning largely in the last decade, there has been an explosion of interest in how architectural design can help maximize person/environment congruence in housing built specifically for the elderly. Workshops have been held, books written, and actual facilities planned and erected through the collaborative efforts of architects and gerontologists. This elderly housing has the special aim alluded to before: through its physical design (and the services it offers) it seeks to enable the older person with functional limitations to live as independently as he or she is capable of doing for as long as possible ("Introduction: The Age of the Aging, Congregate Living," 1981).

As some background, Table 3-2 gives an idea of the types of facilities that now exist specifically for older adults. These settings encompass those designed for the most impaired elderly to those catering to the relatively independent. Ideally all

**TABLE 3-2.**   Continuum of care for the elderly.

| *Services* | *Type of Setting* | *Brief Description* |
|---|---|---|
| *High* | Acute care hospitals | Diagnosis, medical supervision, surgery (therapy emphasis) |
| *Moderately high* | Hospices (see Chapter 10) | Care for terminally ill |
| | Skilled or intermediate nursing care facilities (see Chapter 7) | RN or LPN, long-term care (intermediate lower level than skilled) |
| *Moderately low* | Homes for the aged | Meals, housekeeping, possibly nursing staff (generally not required) |
| | Congregate care apartments | Apartments with meals available; possibly emergency or coordinating staff |
| *Very low* | Shared housing or specially built elderly apartments | Residential community housing; either tasks shared by occupants or individual apartments |
| | Private homes | |

*(Source: Reprinted from the August 1981 issue of Progressive Architecture, Copyright 1981, Reinhold Publishing. Diagram created by Lorraine G. Hiatt.)*

living arrangements are available in a community and offer what is called a **continuum of care** to fit each older person's needs. The basic thought is that housing at the lower and middle levels of the continuum has a particularly important function to provide. Because it offers some support but less care than a nursing home (see Lawton, Greenbaum, & Liebowitz, 1980), it is hoped that such housing will keep the person with limited disabilities from having to enter this latter type of facility before his or her time (Huttman, 1977; see also the section on institutionalization in Chapter 7). A description follows of how one such housing project was planned and designed ("Introduction: The Age of the Aging, Congregate Living," 1981).

The Captain Clarence Eldridge House, in Hyannis, Massachusetts, is one of 13 congregate care facilities recently built by the state of Massachusetts to serve the needs of the somewhat impaired elderly who do not need the full complement of services provided by a nursing home. To design the building, advice was obtained from a variety of sources—managers of similar housing already in existence, environmental researchers, and older people themselves. The building was planned specifically both to help elderly residents with physical disabilities to be as independent as possible and to serve the residents' psychological and social needs. This intention becomes apparent in looking at the atrium and the communal dining room pictured in Figure 3-6.

**FIGURE 3-6.**    Atrium and dining room of Captain Clarence Eldridge House. *(Source: From "Introduction: The Age of the Aging, Congregate Living,"* Progressive architecture, *August 1981, p. 64-68. A team project of: Donham and Sweeney-Architects of record; Korobkin Jahan Associates-Design Architects; Building Diagnostics, Inc.-Design and Research Coordination. Photo by Steve Rosenthal.)*

The major public spaces, such as the dining room, are located around a central skylighted atrium. This arrangement was used because it admits a good deal of light as well as encouraging socialization. Residents are pulled to enter the communal rooms by their easy accessibility but also can observe public activity before entering it. Specifically to combat the problems discussed earlier, bright colors are used and contrast is employed to help increase visual discrimination. The lack of clutter, which encourages easy mobility, is also a striking feature of the design.

Congregate care facilities provide some meals and other supportive services because their residents need this help. However, this facility was also planned to maximize independence and privacy: each person has his or her own room with a toilet and a small kitchenette, which encourages residents to do some cooking themselves.

Unfortunately, the careful use of design so evident here is still a rarity in elderly housing (Lawton, 1980). Many facilities now in operation, even though built specifically for people with the types of limitations this chapter describes, were erected before it was realized that physical design in itself could promote independence. Besides, it is expensive to plan good housing. As a result, many places today probably still have the flagrant flaws that a random survey of nursing homes revealed in the late 1960s (Proppe, 1968). The institutions Proppe visited were often poorly lit. They had rooms approached by long corridors lacking benches where a frail older person could rest. They were also noisy, having floors and walls that reflected sound rather than absorbing it. They seemed, in sum, designed to maximize person/environment incongruence.

### Adapting Private Homes

Most elderly, even those with disabilities, do not live in special housing. They are likely to live in their own homes, often, as implied in Figure 3-7, in the same place where they have lived for many years (Huttman, 1977; Lawton, 1980). However, there are simple ways of changing these living environments too to encourage competence.

Just from the standpoint of promoting physical independence, one's own home has a single great advantage: it is a familiar setting for negotiating the tasks of life. However, visits to private homes where disabled older people live show that such homes are often deteriorated because of their age and have design features that are unsuited to what their residents now need (Lawton, 1980). This was clearly the case in Mrs. Kennedy's kitchen. To remedy these deficiencies, planners suggest the following.

The impact of vision problems can be mitigated by a well-lit living environment (Bozian & Clark, 1980). Bright, contrasting colors and different textures and shapes of spaces and furniture should be used to increase discrimination (Proppe, 1968; Schwartz, 1975). To prevent accidents caused by poor vision or motor deficits, there should not be too much or too poorly designed furniture (Schwartz, 1975), and there should be no raised floor areas (Huttman, 1977). Large numerals should be used on appliances like ovens and telephones (Bozian & Clark, 1980; Huttman, 1977).

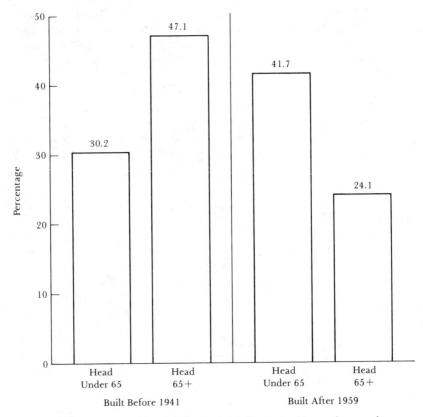

**FIGURE 3-7.**   Age of heads-of-household, for both older and newer homes, 1976. *(Source: From* Chartbook on Aging in America *by C. Allan and H. Brotman. Copyright © 1981 by the White House Conference on Aging.)*

For hearing difficulties devices can be bought that amplify the sound of doorbells or telephones (Huttman, 1977). Carpeting throughout the home should be considered, as it absorbs sound.

For the person who has problems with speed, strength, and agility, doors should open automatically or be light to the touch (Lawton, 1975), shelves and storage places should be easy to reach (Schwartz, 1975), and such devices as grab bars should be installed in places like the bathroom where falls are more likely (Huttman, 1977; McClannahan, 1973). Faucets should be easy to turn on and off, controls should be at the front of the stove (Huttman, 1977), and knobs on all appliances should not be too small or too smooth to be easily grasped by stiff fingers.

With just a moment's thought we could probably add to this brief list. We also might want to extend it to encompass our neighborhood by imagining how we would redesign our street, for example, to fit the capacities of people with sensory and motor problems. Finally, it might be fun to list some specific principles for maximizing person/environment congruence in another essential area—our own behavior with elderly who have the limitations this chapter describes.

## Summary

Older people in general have experienced some sensory and motor declines. However, variability among the elderly, their bias toward caution on tests tapping these abilities, and the likelihood that many deleterious changes observed are not intrinsic to age alone mitigate the negative information we have about sensory and motor performance in late life.

The most obvious vision impairments of old age include uncorrectable poor acuity and presbyopia. Only among the very old is the former problem prevalent. The latter change, poor close vision, is less impairing but more universal in later life. Individuals are likely to notice they have developed this classic indicator of age in their forties.

Other less straightforward vision difficulties older people are likely to have include greater trouble seeing in dim light, particular difficulty distinguishing colors (especially blues from greens), increased sensitivity to glare, difficulty shifting focus to objects located at differing distances, and a narrower visual field. These problems are caused by a variety of deleterious changes in different parts of the visual system.

The major outer parts of the eye—the cornea, the iris and pupil, the lens, and the aqueous and vitreous humor—function to enable the best possible image to reach the visual receptors located on the retina. Nervous impulses travel from the eye to the brain via the optic nerve. The following alterations in the image-focusing structures of the eye are responsible for old-age vision problems: (1) In the cornea, the formation of the arcus senilis limits peripheral vision to some extent. (2) The pupil decreases in diameter, resulting in a loss of acuity, particularly in dim light. (3) The normally transparent lens becomes cloudy, contributing to impaired acuity and increasing sensitivity to glare. The lens also becomes yellowish, limiting color discrimination, particularly for blues and greens. Finally, the lens becomes less flexible, making it difficult for the older person to shift focus quickly. Most important, the lens becomes increasingly less able to bulge out, and presbyopia results.

Changes higher up in the visual system are particularly important in explaining poor vision beginning in late life. Retinal changes are partly responsible for another deficiency an older person may have, impairments in dark adaptation.

Although it is possible that vision losses can lead to negative changes in personality and cognition, there is no clear evidence that they do. The studies that purport to demonstrate these effects do not rule out the possibility that other influences caused the negative relationships found.

Hearing losses, because they cut us off from verbal communication, seem more important in the older person's life than vision losses. Hearing begins to decline slowly after young adulthood, but only among the old-old do a sizable percentage suffer impairing problems in this sensory modality. As a major environmental cause of hearing deficits is exposure to too much noise, impairments may become more common in succeeding cohorts.

Presbycusis, the classic hearing problem that occurs with age, involves a specific loss of sensitivity for high-pitched tones. Presbycusis sufferers are particularly impaired by background noise, by rapid speech, and in situations where they cannot read a speaker's lips to aid comprehension. Because hearing seems sometimes to change so radically under these different conditions, older adults with this condition are sometimes wrongfully accused of purposely pretending not to hear.

In order for us to hear, sound waves cause the tympanic membrane to vibrate. These vibrations are transmitted to the middle ear and finally to the cochlea, where the hair cells, the hearing receptors, are located. The jiggling of the hair cells sets off nervous impulses that travel to the brain. Hair cells at the basal end of the cochlea are responsible for our hearing high-pitched tones.

Deteriorative changes in the outer and middle ear, along the auditory pathway, and in the brain can cause hearing problems. Outer and middle ear problems cause what is called a conductive hearing loss: the person loses sensitivity for tones of all frequencies equally. Central deterioration is also believed to be important in some cases of poor hearing. However, the hearing problems most older people have are caused mainly by deteriorative changes in the inner ear. Specifically, four types of deterioration in the cochlea are responsible for different forms of presbycusis. An important one is atrophy of the hair cells, particularly those at the basal end of the cochlea.

Losses in taste and smell sensitivity in the elderly may be a factor in poor nutrition because they limit pleasure in eating. Older people are less able than young adults to identify foods and are more likely to rate them as bland. Impaired smell seems to play a large role in these altered perceptions, and the palatability of foods to older people can be enhanced by artificially amplifying their smell. Dental problems, too, may diminish an older adult's enjoyment in eating.

Slowed response is a highly predictable, long-researched, and extremely important behavioral change that occurs as people age. Laboratory studies of this phenomenon reveal its universality as well as demonstrating that older adults' speed is poorest on more complicated psychomotor tasks.

To understand more about this loss, in laboratory tests researchers measure separately what is called reaction time, the period elapsing between the time a signal to respond occurs and the beginning of the response. It is reaction time that slows most markedly with age, not movement time, or the time it takes to act. So slow movement in the elderly is primarily a deficit in being able to begin a response quickly.

Taking physical action involves a chain of steps. Stimuli dictating the need to act are first fed to the brain, where three events are thought to occur. The information is perceived, an action is selected, and it is programmed to be carried out. The end point of the sequence is the actual movement. The older person's slowness appears due to problems performing the middle steps: the central nervous system cannot quickly process the information to respond.

This overall loss in information-processing speed means that in any activity an elderly person will perform more slowly, on the average, than a younger person.

Slowness does not affect the quality of many life activities and in the typical older adult is marked only in some situations. But problems with speed explain why older workers prefer jobs involving relatively heavy labor, because here, quickness is not essential. In jobs where rapid performance is important, though, older workers do better than would be predicted in the laboratory, because they are experienced in these tasks and possibly because they are an elite group.

People who lead sedentary lives and/or have heart disease have slower reaction times. Links between slow reaction time and these and other variables point to the possibility of intervening to increase the response speed of older adults as well as hinting at physiological causes for this slowing. At least today, though, the most fruitful way of dealing with motor losses and the sensory deficits described earlier is to try to modify the environment to fit the older person's capacities—to maximize person/environment congruence.

Person/environment congruence permits optimal functioning because the person's environment is neither too simple nor too complex for his or her capacities. Special elderly housing like the Captain Clarence Eldridge House has been designed with this aim in mind. It uses light, color, and lack of clutter to encourage visual discrimination and mobility. This facility is atypical, however, as most special housing for the elderly was not planned to foster person/environment congruence. Similarly, private homes housing disabled elderly people often have design features antithetical to their residents' needs. The physical design of private homes can often be modified to enhance competence, using a similar approach.

## Key Terms

| | |
|---|---|
| *Visual acuity* | *Psychomotor performance* |
| *Presbyopia* | *Reaction-time studies* |
| *Peripheral part of the visual system* | *Reaction time* |
| *Central part of the visual system* | *Movement time* |
| *Arcus senilis* | *Ecological perspective* |
| *Cataract* | *Person/environment congruence* |
| *Presbycusis* | *Prosthetic environments* |
| *Recruitment* | *Continuum of care* |
| *Conductive hearing loss* | |

## Recommended Readings

Birren, J. E., & Schaie, K. W. (Eds.). **Handbook of the psychology of aging**. New York: Van Nostrand Reinhold, 1977. Chapters 19, "Motor Performance"; 20, "Visual Perception and Communication"; 21, "Auditory Perception and Communication"; 22, "Taste and Smell."
*Each of these chapters gives a comprehensive overview of research in the area it covers. In particular, look at the chapter by Welford, "Motor Performance." Difficult.*
Colavita, F. R. **Sensory changes in the elderly**. Springfield, Ill.: Charles C Thomas, 1978.
*This is easier reading than Birren and Schaie (1977). Chapters 2 and 3 give an excellent overview of vision and hearing in the elderly. Not difficult.*

Lawton, M. P. ***Planning and managing housing for the elderly***. New York: Wiley, 1975.

*Instructions on how best to plan housing for the elderly. Also summarizes research on housing and life satisfaction in older people as well as the theoretical rationale for the ecological approach described earlier. Clear and well written. Not difficult.*

Ordy, J. M., & Brizzee, K. R. (Eds.). ***Aging***. *Vol. 10:* ***Sensory systems and communication in the elderly***. New York: Raven Press, 1979.

*Comprehensive technical collection summarizing research and controversy mainly in the area of sensory processes. Some chapters are fairly specific. All assume a good deal of prior knowledge about sensory systems. Very difficult.*

# COGNITION

# Intelligence and the IQ Test

The third year after being widowed, Mrs. Johnson determined to fulfill her lifelong dream of going to college. She had enough income. There were her precious family and friends. Still, something was lacking in her life, a gap that close relationships, her volunteer work at the local nursing home, and the occasional looked-forward-to visit to the symphony or theater had not been able to fill. Her reading was satisfying, but she yearned to discuss the books she read with others. She had to admit that, if pushed, she would even have been willing to open the fruits of her lifelong hobby, writing short stories, to public criticism. In general, she thanked God she had not been burdened with the problems young people faced growing up today. However, she had to admit to a twinge of envy. Now it was accepted, even expected, to get a college education. In her day, for a woman it had been rare; in her family it had been out of the question.

But she was afraid. To some extent she was concerned about feeling foolish among students almost a half century younger than herself. Most important, she was afraid of failure, terrified of not being able to do the work. After all, it had been a good 50 years since she had left school. Besides, everyone knew that as people got older, their intellect began to go. If only there were some way to be reassured she would not suffer the embarrassment and loss of self-esteem of being found incapable, she would enroll at that local state college in a minute. She even noticed in the paper that the college was specially advertising for older adults.

Her closest friend's daughter came up with an ingenious solution for Mrs. Johnson. Recently, concerned for her son, who was doing poorly in school, she had decided on psychological testing. She had noted at the time that the psychologist, whose sensitivity and competence had impressed her, was also qualified to evaluate adults. Her experience was very helpful. It completely allayed her fear that her son was incapable of doing the work. Knowing her mother's friend intimately, she believed it would do the same for Mrs. Johnson.

It took some convincing, but Mrs. Johnson finally agreed. On the day of the evaluation, however, she was more anxious than she had been in a long time. More than anything else, she imagined the testing would reveal what she now knew was an important underlying fear: that she might be going senile or, at the very least, slowly losing some of her quickness of mind. No matter how much she read or was complimented on her intellect, she was well aware of the "facts" about intelligence and age: as a person gets older, memory and reasoning ability inescapably erode.

Luckily, the psychologist understood this particular emotion many older people have in being tested, so she took special care to try to allay her client's anxiety. Because Dr. Sagstad also knew the impact of fatigue on test performance in the elderly, she suggested that they make three rather than the customary two appointments to complete the evaluation. In this instance she had to admit she felt fortunate though, because the purpose of the testing was specifically to determine Mrs. Johnson's potential for doing schoolwork. In general, Dr. Sagstad was reluctant to give the standard intelligence test to older people because of her firm belief that it was inadequate, inappropriate for measuring the types of skills involved in intellectual competence in late life.

The test Mrs. Johnson was given during her first two appointments was the Wechsler Adult Intelligence Scale. To put her at ease, the psychologist explained the general things she would be asked to do during the first session. Dr. Sagstad would be asking questions requiring a verbal response. The test would have different subparts, each of which measured a different type of skill. It was impossible to know the answer to every question. If Mrs. Johnson was unsure, it would pay to guess.

Still, knowing this information did little to defuse her fear. Even though the first few questions were almost foolishly easy, Mrs. Johnson was so agitated she could barely answer.

Soon, though, her anxiety subsided; it was so clear she was doing well. True, the questions on each scale got increasingly difficult, so she eventually knew that some of her guessed-at answers were wrong. However, Mrs. Johnson was pleased to see that her practice of keeping mentally active and interested had paid off. Her reading and knowledge in a variety of areas were amazingly beneficial on several parts of the test.

Unfortunately, her pride evaporated rather early in the second session. Now the types of things she was being asked to do were totally foreign to what she knew and to what she had ever done before. On this nonverbal part of the test she was to perform tasks as ridiculous as putting together puzzles or arranging blocks. Actually, she kidded the psychologist that had she known about this section, she would have crammed by some on-the-job training—time in the playroom with her 4-year-old grandson.

And then there was the anxiety about time. As she carefully explained, it was too difficult to ask older people to work in this way—performing unfamiliar tasks when there was pressure to finish within a specified limit. She wondered aloud what this part of the test could possibly reveal about her thinking both in and outside school. It helped only slightly when the psychologist told her that on this and the other part of the test she was being compared only with people her own age.

Despite her qualms, the final outcome was ideal. The psychologist said she would have no trouble mastering college work. She complimented Mrs. Johnson on her obvious verbal ability. In verbal skills she was superior to the average person her own age and even to the average young adult.

When she asked, somewhat timidly, how she had done in the second part of the test, the psychologist said "As well as the typical person your age." This was amazing in view of what seemed to be, to her mind, an obviously abysmal showing.

Dr. Sagstad ended by expressing just one concern: the only thing that might interfere with Mrs. Johnson's schoolwork was her fear. The psychologist suggested she use the evaluation as a kind of therapy. If she found herself getting anxious when asked for a paper or when taking an exam, she should remember what the test showed about her considerable ability.

The last two chapters described a straightforward, undebatable fact: in spite of some individual variation, there are predictable losses in physical capacities after young adulthood. The task of this chapter is much less neutral or clear-cut: to explore the delicate question whether there are similar decrements in cognition with age. The idea that people get less intelligent as they get older is very far from being a dry academic proposition. Intense debate has surrounded this most sensitive and far from settled topic.

Psychologists argue about every aspect of age changes in intelligence. They question the evidence itself, as different ways of collecting data produce different conclusions about the timing and extent of age declines in intelligence-test scores. They debate its underlying meaning, as there are many likely causes for the IQ losses that are found. Finally, increasingly they are looking askance at the appropriateness of the measures themselves, because it may be that existing tests of intelligence do an inadequate job of tapping cognitive ability in middle-aged and elderly adults.

Each of these interlocking controversies is best understood if we view it within a certain framework: a brief description of the characteristics of the most used IQ test, the ***Wechsler Adult Intelligence Scale,*** or WAIS (Wechsler, 1955). There are many global, or general, measures of intelligence, but the WAIS (and now its successor, the WAIS-R) is almost certain to be the test given when an adult arrives at a psychologist's office for an evaluation. In addition, the facts about age changes in intelligence as well as the controversy surrounding them are clearly shown by centering the following discussion on specifically this most widely used scale. (The newly updated WAIS, the WAIS-R [Wechsler, 1981] has a format and, in most cases, item content virtually identical to that of the 1955 test.)

## The Measure

The WAIS consists of two main parts, a verbal and a performance section. These parts are further broken down into subtests, each of which taps a more specific verbal or nonverbal skill. Items on the scales range from easy to increasingly more difficult, and each scale is discontinued after the person being tested has failed a certain number of questions. As in our vignette, the prescribed way of administering the test is to give the verbal part first, then the performance section. But, the psychologist who tested Mrs. Johnson departed from standard procedure in a sensitive way: rather than insisting the whole WAIS be finished in two sittings she allowed Mrs. Johnson three sessions to complete the test.

As Table 4-1 shows, the verbal and performance scales of this most used test differ in another major way than what their names suggest. The verbal subtests are, in large part, measuring a certain type of intellectual ability—the person's store of knowledge in important areas. This focus on learned knowledge is apparent in four subtests in particular: information, comprehension, arithmetic, and vocabulary. Here what is explicitly being tested is the content of what is known: historical, literary, or biological facts; knowledge of facts important to competently negotiating the environment; knowing mathematics; and familiarity with the meanings of words.

**TABLE 4-1.** WAIS subtests.

| Scale | Description | Sample Simulated Item |
|---|---|---|
| **Verbal scale** | | |
| 1. Information | Fund of knowledge (literature, biology, and so on) | How many wings does a bird have? |
| 2. Comprehension | Knowledge of appropriate behavior, of how to negotiate the environment | What is the advantage of keeping money in the bank? |
| 3. Arithmetic | Arithmetic (time limit) | If two apples cost 15¢, what will a dozen apples cost? |
| 4. Similarities | Verbal analogies (reasoning) | In what way are a saw and a hammer alike? |
| 5. Digit span | Memory (repeat series of digits in same or reverse order) | Say these numbers right after me: 5-2-9-6-6-3. |
| 6. Vocabulary | Word definitions | What does _____ mean? |
| **Performance scale** | | |
| 1. Digit symbol | Copy symbols (time limit) | |
| 2. Picture completion | Pictures; subject asked to identify what is missing (time limit) | |
| 3. Block design | Set of blocks with a different pattern on each side; subject asked to arrange them to conform to design on a card (time limit) | |
| 4. Picture arrangement | Set of pictures; subject asked to arrange in correct sequence so they tell a coherent story (time limit) | |
| 5. Object assembly | Puzzles; subject asked to put them together (each is an object, such as hand; time limit) | |

*(Source: Adapted and reproduced by permission from the* Wechsler Adult Intelligence Scale Manual. *Copyright © 1955 by The Psychological Corporation. All rights reserved. Similar questions from the Wechsler Scales courtesy of The Psychological Corporation.)*

The various performance subtests (with the possible exception of picture completion) have a completely different focus. Here the person is asked to manipulate relatively unfamiliar material, such as blocks, pictures, or puzzles. The emphasis is clearly not on producing what has been learned but on arriving at a new, never previously memorized solution. In addition, the emphasis is much more on speed. Not only are all the performance subtests timed, in contrast to only one of the verbal ones, but on some scales a particular premium is put on rapid responses. A person gets special bonus points for the quickest solution. In fact, speed is really the only or major ability assessed on one performance scale in particular, digit symbol. On this scale the requirement is simply to copy quite easy symbols as fast as possible.

Our vignette illustrates what the psychologist's task is after administering the test: to see how the test taker's score compares with others in his or her age group. The number that expresses this comparative standing is the familiar **IQ** (intelligence quotient).

So the WAIS is like any classroom test that is graded on a curve. A person is assigned a score or IQ based not on absolute performance but on performance compared with that of others in a particular reference group. In this case the reference group consists of people one's own age.

At least for the performance scale, older reference groups are less and less able. This is illustrated in Table 4-2: at successively older ages identical test scores translate into increasingly higher IQs. For instance, looking just at the oldest and youngest groups, the difference is shockingly marked. Older people, on the average, do much more poorly, at least on the nonverbal part of the test. But does this alarmingly poor performance also extend to the verbal scale? Is it confined mainly to particular subtests? Would it also show up if we looked at other than cross-sectional data? These questions bring us to our first area of controversy and fact—age changes on the WAIS, their timing, their extent, and a rationale to explain them.

**TABLE 4-2.**   IQ equivalents of sums of selected performance scores in different age groups.

| | Age group | | | | | | | |
| Score | 20–24 | 25–34 | 35–44 | 45–54 | 55–64 | 65–69 | 70–74 | 75+ |
|---|---|---|---|---|---|---|---|---|
| 90 | 151 | 153 | 157 | 164 | 169 | 173 | 179 | 185 |
| 60 | 112 | 114 | 118 | 125 | 130 | 133 | 140 | 146 |
| 30 | 73 | 74 | 79 | 86 | 91 | 94 | 101 | 107 |
| 1 | 35 | 37 | 41 | 48 | 53 | 56 | 63 | 69 |

*(Source: Adapted and reproduced by permission from the* Wechsler Adult Intelligence Scale Manual. *Copyright © 1955 by The Psychological Corporation. All rights reserved.)*

## Age Changes on the WAIS and Other Intelligence Tests

### *Contradictory and Common Findings of Cross-Sectional and Longitudinal Studies*

Figure 4-1 shows changes on the verbal and performance parts separately for the age groups used to derive the WAIS norms. The patterns of loss on the two scales are very different. After a peak in the early twenties, performance scores steadily decline in each successive age group. In contrast, although there is clearly some negative change in the verbal IQ, it is far less marked. Verbal scores reach a peak somewhat later, and they decline precipitously only in the oldest subjects tested, those in their seventies.

The investigators who determined these norms for adults 64 and older (Doppelt & Wallace, 1955) also examined age differences on each of the verbal and performance subtests. This information gives us a clearer picture of the specific types of cognitive skills that are likely to hold up or decline in older people. Among the six verbal measures, they found that similarities and digit span decreased the most. None of the four subtests described earlier as measuring stored knowledge showed appreciable change. In contrast, no such lack of uniformity characterized the performance subtests: here marked losses occurred on each scale.

These results have been repeatedly replicated. For example, one reviewer (Botwinick, 1967) compared the findings of nine studies examining age differences on the various subtests of the WAIS and its related predecessor. He discovered a

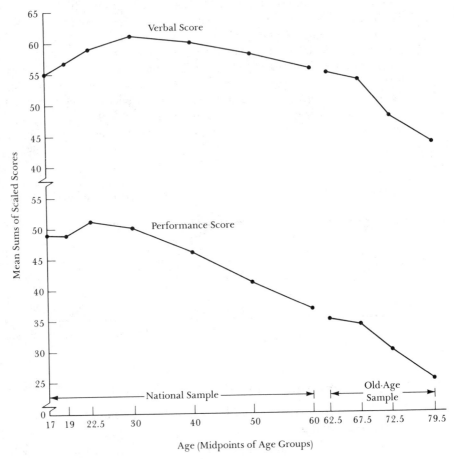

**FIGURE 4-1.**    Verbal and performance scores as a function of age. *(Source: Adapted from Doppelt and Wallace, 1955.)*

remarkably similar pattern in each case: little decline on the verbal measures; pronounced decrement on the performance scales. This phenomenon, in fact— better scores on verbal than performance tests—has been found so universally that it has been given a special title. It is called the ***classic aging pattern*** (Botwinick, 1967, 1977).

No matter how much we stress that the verbal decline revealed in these studies is small, their results clearly offer no cause for celebration over the relationship of intelligence and advancing age. However, we have been examining cross-sectional studies only. By now we should be immediately suspicious of considering this source of data alone. We surely are too sophisticated to assume that these cross-sectional test differences between age groups necessarily mean that real changes occur in cognitive performance as people age. Do longitudinal studies too show this gloomy evidence of unremitting decline? Do they too reveal the classic aging pattern?

As we might expect just from knowing their contrasting bias, longitudinal studies do offer a much more positive view. In fact, most that have followed subjects through middle age show actual gains in IQ. However, even here the classic aging pattern emerges. On verbal measures subjects improve; stability or decline is evident on nonverbal, timed tests (see Botwinick, 1977, for review).

So there is some convergence but also a cause for rejoicing in these results. Now, though, we need to look in more detail at longitudinal research focusing on the group we are really interested in—older adults.

In the Duke study, Eisdorfer and Wilkie (1973) gave the WAIS four times over a ten-year period. Interestingly, they found a slight rise in the full scale scores of their youngest subjects, those initially aged 60 to 69, from the first to the second evaluation (three years later). However, over the full ten-year period their results were not as encouraging. Although these initially young-old volunteers did not do much worse over this span, they did lose some points (see Figure 4-2, p. 110). These declines also conformed to the classic aging pattern—a 2-point decrease on the performance scale, a quite minimal 0.6-point loss on the verbal IQ.

So the results for the young-old Duke volunteers are quite similar to, even if less positive than, those tracing cognition through midlife. However, the Duke findings for the oldest volunteers, those initially aged 70 to 79, were radically different. In this quite old group, IQ declines at each three-year testing were regular and pronounced. By the end of the ten years they averaged a full 7.3 points overall. Also, in these oldest subjects, unlike the young-old, decrements showed no sign of reflecting the classic aging pattern. Losses here were nearly equal on the verbal and performance IQs. This result seems to echo the earlier cross-sectional finding shown in Figure 4-1: the sharp drop in verbal IQ in the WAIS normative sample for the oldest group, subjects in their seventies.

### Conclusions from the Contrasting Methods

Combining information from the two types of studies allows us to conclude that the "truth" about age changes in WAIS performance lies somewhere between the picture of universal decline portrayed by cross-sectional studies and the more positive one painted by longitudinal ones. We know from Chapter 1 that cross-sectional studies are likely to overestimate true age losses in most aspects of functioning. Nowhere, as we will see next, is this bias more evident than when changes in cognitive processes are being assessed. And we also know to be wary of data from longitudinal studies, as they are equally likely to minimize the true extent of declines.

This last eventuality, in fact, is strikingly brought home when we compare the curves in Figure 4-2. (This discussion is taken from a review by Botwinick, 1977; see Recommended Readings.) The figure shows the distorting impact of the longitudinal requirement that analyses be based only on subjects who are available for the whole series of testings. The lower curves depict the results of the 10-year-long

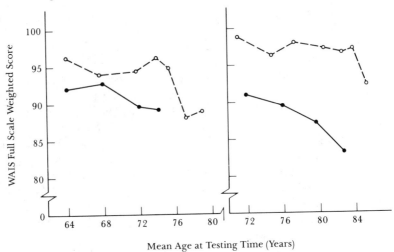

**FIGURE 4-2.** Results of a longitudinal study lasting 10 years and one continuing for 15 years. Subjects aged 60–69 (*N* = 61) and 70–79 (*N* = 37) at the start of the study were tested four times (solid circles) over a 10-year period (Eisdorfer & Wilkie, 1973). The study continued for another 5 years with three additional testings (open circles); 35 subjects from the younger group and 15 from the older group were available for all seven test sessions. *(Source: In "Intellectual Abilities" by J. Botwinick. From* Handbook of the Psychology of Aging *by J. E. Birren and K. W. Schaie. Copyright 1977 by Van Nostrand Reinhold Company. Reprinted by permission of the publisher.)*

Duke study just described and the upper an extension of this same research for an additional 5 years.

Duke investigators not only followed their subjects for 10 years but then also continued the series of testings, examining the cognitive performance of the much smaller group of elderly who were able to participate in three additional test sessions. Figure 4-2 shows the results separately for the subjects who participated in the additional 5 years of testing and those who only continued for the initial 10 years. Not only is the 15-year subgroup more able in general than the 10-year one, but if we considered the performance of only the 15-year participants, we would reach a much more optimistic conclusion about age changes in intelligence. Here no decrement occurs until the late seventies, illuminating by implication how information from the 10-year group too must be positively biased. In other words, the figure illustrates what we already know. In longitudinal studies we generally get an elite, unrepresentative group. This sampling bias means our conclusions about cognitive functioning using this type of data must err on the positive side.

The quantitative differences between longitudinal and cross-sectional studies should not lead us to lose sight of their remarkable qualitative similarities (Botwinick, 1977). Both reveal the classic aging pattern at least until the seventies (see also Jarvik, 1973). Both show the pattern giving way to uniform decline after that. We now look at an explanation that makes sense of these results.

### An Explanation

According to one theory (see Horn, 1970, 1975), there are several distinct types of adult intelligence, of which two are most important. The first, called **crystallized intelligence,** reflects the extent to which an individual has absorbed the content of the culture. It is the store of knowledge or facts the person has accumulated through education. It is this type of cognitive ability that the verbal part of the WAIS seems mainly to be measuring.

The second broad type of intelligence is not dependent on acculturation. It involves an ability tapped more by the performance scale, the capacity to devise a solution when confronted with a new problem, one never before encountered. This capacity is called **fluid intelligence.**

As the person matures, these two initially undifferentiated cognitive abilities become independent of each other. Their very different attributes mean each follows a quite logical separate pattern in relation to age.

Since crystallized intelligence is a person's store of knowledge, it is reasonable to suppose that it remains relatively stable or increases until late in life, because until an advanced age the rate at which new knowledge is gained should equal or exceed the rate at which information is forgotten. However, fluid intelligence, involving problem-solving and reasoning abilities not dependent on learning, is directly tied to physiology: it requires a brain at its neurological peak. As neurons are lost and other decremental changes gradually occur in brain functioning after young adulthood, it makes sense that this type of intelligence should follow a downward path. Fluid intelligence, the capacity mainly reflected in performance scores, should reach its maximum at young adulthood and then steadily decline.

Finally, in the seventies the cumulative effect of losses of job, of health, and of relationships explains the marked decrement in verbal IQ. The reason is that these changes cause withdrawal from the culture (see Chapter 6) and consequently a decline in new learning. At that time forgetting exceeds the rate at which knowledge is acquired, and so verbal scores too fall off.

There is other evidence that crystallized intelligence becomes quite similar, in its pattern of deterioration, to fluid intelligence in old age. When tests specifically tailored to measuring just these two aspects of intelligence in their pure form are given to older adults, the clear differentiation between these skills does not exist. The elderly do not show the same independence between the two classes of ability that younger people do (Baltes, Cornelius, Spiro, Nesselroade, & Willis, 1980).

So the fluid/crystallized distinction gives us a neat explanation both for the classic aging pattern and for its breakdown in advanced old age. However, it far from completes our discussion, as so far we have neglected a most crucial question. In looking just at how test scores change, we have made a possibly unwarranted assumption: that these differences in observed performance really should be equated with differences in intellectual capacity.

## Extraneous Influences in Age Declines

We all know from our own experience that a poor test score does not necessarily mean incapacity—for example, when we bemoan the excessive anxiety or illness that caused us to get a lower grade on an exam than we really deserved. When we realize that these two influences are disproportionately acute for many elderly, we can understand their unfair disadvantage when taking an intelligence test.

In fact, in addition to those just mentioned, several other ***ability-extraneous*** factors conspire to lower the IQs of many in later life. As is true for sensory and motor skills, therefore, judgments about an older adult's lack of capacity based on test scores must be made only with care.

### *Differences in Education*

As in our vignette, older cohorts, on the average, have fewer years of formal schooling. This simple lack of comparable education is one important ability-extraneous variable that may partly underlie the poor performance of the old (Baltes & Schaie, 1974; Granick & Friedman, 1973). For instance, as is apparent by examining Table 4-1, many subtests of the WAIS verbal scale may tap material that is taught in the classroom. This too close tie to school content, in fact, as we will see later, may be an important deficiency of the test itself when used with adults. In addition, a more general skill relevant to performance on tests is honed and refined in school: the knowledge of how to take examinations. Increasing years of education provide more training in this area too, a backlog of experience that unfairly benefits the young.

Education is an ability-extraneous variable that is particularly important in interpreting cross-sectional studies because of the obvious differences in average years of schooling when we compare different cohorts. However, a moment's reflection suggests it may affect the results of longitudinal research too. With any skill, the further a person gets from the specific environment in which it was learned and needed, the less adept his or her performance in that area is apt to be. We would expect, then, that unless an individual's job involved experience taking examinations or using school-related content, his or her score on an IQ test might naturally tend to decline with age.

An implication of this argument is that people in occupations that most closely fit the demands of the measure might show little decline on the WAIS as they age. There is evidence to support this view. In fact, in one study involving just this type of subject the typical cross-sectional finding of decline was actually reversed (Sward, 1945). Professors aged 60 to 80 surpassed their colleagues in their thirties on vocabulary and information tests. There may be a host of reasons for this finding, but one possibility is simple length of experience. The life work of a professor involves skills closely akin to the content of these particular indexes of intelligence (Horn, 1970).

So Mrs. Johnson was probably right in attributing her good verbal performance in part to having kept interested in intellectual activities. Experience with education-related material really does seem to help a person, at least on some verbal subtests of the WAIS. But in the second arena where school experience is an advantage, her behavior was more like the typical older person's: the way she approached the test was poor. For this reason, like many people her age, she may have received a lower score than she ideally should have.

### Differences in Test-Taking Strategy

As was true of Mrs. Johnson, older people are more likely to be anxious than the young when their cognitive abilities are being tested. They also may be more cautious and so less prone to guess even when this would be a good strategy. Being less physically hardy, they may become tired during a long evaluation. Luckily, the psychologist in our vignette was sensitive to these noncognitive influences that may lower performance. She tried to mitigate their impact by sensitive reassurance, special instructions about how to take the test, and allowing more than the typical one or two sessions.

Practicing psychologists have long noticed that older adults, perhaps more than people of other ages, are anxious in situations in which their intellect is being evaluated. One carefully designed study (Whitbourne, 1976) clearly showed both the magnitude of this fear and the extent to which it hurts the older person when he or she is being compared with the young. The results are particularly striking because they involved a group of far from typical elderly. These older adults were a test-taking elite, educationally interested and experienced in taking examinations.

Being anxious during a test is not necessarily bad; because it arouses a person, it may actually help performance. So in looking at the impact of test anxiety, Whitbourne took care to measure facilitating and debilitating types separately, using a scale devised for that purpose (see Table 4-3). Her main hypothesis was that debilitating fear in particular would be more prevalent among the elderly than among young adults. She also checked on the idea that this variety of anxiety

**TABLE 4-3.**   Selected items from the Modified Anxiety Achievement Test, used by Whitbourne.

**Debilitating Subscale**
1. Nervousness while being tested hinders me from doing well.
2. In a test situation in which I am doing poorly, my fear of a low score cuts down my efficiency.
3. The more important the testing situation, the less well I seem to do.
4. I find my mind goes blank at the beginning of any kind of test and it takes me a few minutes before I can function.

**Facilitating Subscale**
1. I work most effectively under pressure, as when the task is very important.
2. When I enter some kind of test situation, nothing is able to distract me.
3. Nervousness while taking a test makes me do better.

*(Source: From "Test Anxiety in Elderly and Young Adults" by S. K. Whitbourne. In* International Journal of Aging and Human Development, *1976, 7, 201–210. Copyright 1976 by Baywood Publishing Co. Reprinted by permission.)*

would indeed be detrimental by seeing whether it correlated with poorer scores. Her subjects were carefully matched for educational experience. The young adults were attending college; the elderly were involved in a continuing education program in which constant evaluations were part of the curriculum.

Using a memory test that involved instructions to remember as much as possible about the content of sentences, Whitbourne did find that the older group had more debilitating anxiety. And, for all subjects a high level of this type of anxiety was indeed impairing: it was associated with lower scores. Furthermore, it was obvious the older adults were more anxious just by observing their behavior. All the college students readily agreed to participate in the study, but more than one-quarter of the elderly refused. Few of the young adults but many of the older subjects were visibly upset during the testing session. In fact, five were so anxious they refused even to complete the experiment.

Our vignette and the first chapter's discussion of ageism show the probable origin of this excessive fear. It is generally assumed by everyone, including older adults, that as a person ages, intelligence declines. Many elderly people, like Mrs. Johnson, may have this idea in mind when they are being tested. Their greater unfamiliarity with the testing situation makes it more stressful. Added to this is the ominous meaning an evaluation has for the old. It is here, older adults may fear, they may come face to face with the fact that their intellectual processes really are impaired.

Anxiety such as this can have a host of negative outcomes. When extreme, it can cause people to block on any answer, because focusing on their fear makes them unable to attend at all to what they know. Or being a potent aversive event, classically conditioned fear (see Chapter 1) can engender total avoidance. As in the study just described, older adults, in response to their anxiety, may simply run away, refusing to be tested at all. Finally, if less excessive, anxiety may simply constrain test takers and make them unwarrantedly cautious. They may not want to risk answering a question unless they are absolutely sure. Because on the WAIS there is no penalty for wrong guesses, this strategy will minimize the chances of doing one's best.

The detrimental impact of excessive caution in answering IQ-test items was revealed in a study in which pretest instructions were first used to encourage elderly subjects either to guess or not to (Birkhill & Schaie, 1975). The subjects then took a general test of intelligence other than the WAIS, a shorter five-part scale.

Under conditions where the person had the option to respond or not respond to items, instructions encouraging guessing did help. Elderly subjects encouraged to risk a response did significantly better on three scales of this five-subtest measure than another group who had been told the opposite, that it was better to leave items they were not sure of blank.

The investigation just mentioned does not actually demonstrate that older adults use a too cautious strategy when taking intelligence tests. However, we might hypothesize this is so because of the research showing that caution is the response style they adopt in other situations (see Chapter 3). So Dr. Sagstad was prudent in instructing Mrs. Johnson to guess. The psychologist's idea of having her complete the WAIS in three sessions rather than the customary two was also wise. As the next study shows, fatigue is another ability-extraneous factor that disproportionately affects the old.

Furry and Baltes (1973) used the same short intelligence test just mentioned but this time compared three age groups: adolescents, adults, and the elderly. They examined the possibly differential impact of a pretest treatment on subsequent performance. Half the subjects in each age group were asked to perform a routine letter-finding task for 20 minutes before taking the IQ test. Exposure to the tiring condition did have different effects for the different-aged subjects. For several of the five subtests, the impact of fatigue was evident, because the pretest treatment magnified cross-sectional differences between the groups.

This means, of course, that fatigue should be taken into account when testing an older person. Just as important, it implies that this problem may explain some of the gloomy evidence of age-related IQ decline. Investigators comparing age groups, particularly on a long and demanding test such as the WAIS, may not have taken into account a simple fact: older people are handicapped at the outset simply because they tire more easily than the young.

Older adults tire more easily for one main reason: they are not as physically hardy or healthy. This brings us to a consideration of probably the most important factor underlying age changes in intelligence—health.

### *Ill Health*

Illness is really an influence best considered ability-extraneous only under certain conditions—when, as is true of an acute disease, it artificially depresses its victim's real IQ score for a limited time. However, if a person has a chronic condition, his or her actual optimum performance may be permanently lowered by the ravages of the disease.

Even if only sometimes extraneous to a person's capacity, ill health is an important reason other than age itself that may account for the gloomy association between declining IQ and advancing years. Older cohorts may do more poorly on IQ tests simply because they are more likely to be ill. A good deal of evidence corroborates this optimistic view.

**IQ Decrements and Illness.**   That health may be crucial in understanding intelligence-test declines is implied by our earlier discussion of the differing results of cross-sectional and longitudinal studies and of longitudinal research of varying lengths. We already know that an important way subjects in longitudinal studies are special has to do with their unusually good health. People usually do not complete these studies for one major reason: they are too ill or have died. So when we see little age decrement in longitudinal studies and even more stability the longer the study goes on, we must suspect good health as a main cause. Conversely, illness seems a good explanation for IQ losses, as progressively more negative changes occur with age when we choose samples that are less and less physically select.

These comparisons, however, do not prove that illness is a main reason for test-score declines. Striking and more direct evidence for its deleterious effect comes from a study conducted almost 25 years ago under the auspices of the National Institutes of Health (Birren, Butler, Greenhouse, Sokoloff, & Yarrow, 1963). The purpose of this research was to study the aging process apart from disease, so the investigators took care to recruit a healthy group of elderly subjects. The 47 male volunteers aged 65–91 who had passed a medical exam participated in a two-week series of studies.

Further medical data compiled during the research period revealed that the carefully selected sample really encompassed two distinct sets of subjects. The first group was totally healthy, showing only the most benign aging changes (for example, evidence of osteoarthritis). The second, comprising somewhat fewer than half the men, did have some signs of subclinical illness. Even though at the time they had no overt symptoms, ten among this group, for instance, had X-ray changes suggestive of heart disease. Overall, this subgroup had higher blood pressure and other laboratory findings showing they were in less than optimal health.

The unexpected finding of a less healthy subsample in the end was not really problematic but became a bonus. It gave the researchers a chance to compare the two groups of elderly men with each other as well as with typical young adults. Among the most interesting of these comparisons occurred when the older groups were given the WAIS (Botwinick & Birren, 1963).

On this test the classic aging pattern emerged for both samples of elderly men. Both subgroups did well on the verbal part of the test and showed marked decrements, in comparison with younger adults, on the performance scale. What was particularly interesting was the difference between the groups. The healthy men did better than their not completely illness-free peers on fully 10 of the 11 subtests of the WAIS. This consistent difference in performance, though admittedly correlational, does seem overwhelming evidence of the deleterious effect of even slight deviations from ideal health on IQ.

If even asymptomatic signs of disease so perceptibly seem to affect intelligence, we can only expect real illnesses to have a more extreme impact. Our first candidate to look at is heart disease because it is such a prevalent and serious condition in late life and because, as we know from the vignette in Chapter 2, it may have twin physiological and psychological consequences, both of which should operate to lower a person's IQ.

Interestingly, however, the connection between heart disease and lower IQ has not been universally found. At least this was true in the Duke study. Here investigators (Thompson, Eisdorfer, & Estes, 1970) correlated medical signs and physician ratings of cardiovascular symptoms with WAIS scores. At first they did find a relationship, disease-free subjects doing better particularly on the performance part of the test. However, an important added control completely erased this association. The ill subjects were disproportionately Black and of lower socioeconomic status. Taking these biasing variables into account, the researchers found no IQ differences at all between the ill and healthy groups. This was true not just at their initial evaluation but at a second testing three years later.

Because it is longitudinal, though, this study excluded the severely ill, those who were too sick to return for a second testing. So it may be that, beyond a critical extreme, heart disease is linked to lower IQ scores. However, the interesting lesson of this research is that we should be cautious in assuming intellectual deficits are unequivocally associated with illness. This is even truer when we assume the same thing of abnormal laboratory-test results.

In addition to examining the effect of heart disease, Duke researchers (Wilkie & Eisdorfer, 1973) looked at the relationship of blood pressure and IQ in their volunteers. As high blood pressure is associated with both heart disease and stroke, they expected that it should correlate with lower scores. Subjects initially 60 to 69 and 70 to 79 were categorized by whether their blood pressure was low, medium, or high; then their current IQ was evaluated and was tested again three years later. Unexpectedly, at the first examination there was no association between blood pressure and IQ for the group in their sixties. For the older volunteers, the predicted relationship did emerge. Those in the high-blood-pressure group did have markedly lower scores on both the verbal and performance parts of the test. For the younger group an association showed up only on the second test. Then they too had significantly lower performance scores.

A more interesting and complex relationship emerged when the researchers followed this younger group for the full ten-year period (see Eisdorfer, 1977; Wilkie & Eisdorfer, 1973). They found that mildly elevated blood pressure was really a plus. Subjects with normal blood pressure had relatively stable scores over this period. Those whose readings were much too high did show the expected IQ declines. Those whose blood pressure was only somewhat too high, however, *improved* in performance over the ten years.

These studies illustrate that although there is considerable evidence implicating ill health as an important factor in intelligence-test declines, there is no automatic or uncomplicated tie between the two. Moreover, the unexpected association between what looks like a sign of pathology and good test performance reinforces the importance of age-specific physical norms (see Chapter 2). Laboratory findings based on what is optimal for young adults may not apply to an older person. In this instance medication given to an older adult whose blood pressure was categorized as slightly too high might have the unexpected effect of lowering his or her IQ.

**IQ Decrements and Death.**    Even if illness only sometimes causes IQ losses, these findings suggest a whole new avenue to pursue. Not only might we use the presence of disease to predict possible intelligence-test declines; we might even envision doing the opposite. Perhaps a drop in a person's IQ might be a clue that he or she is physically ill. In other words, the WAIS might have a whole new purpose as an instrument for physical diagnosis. It could even be a behavioral barometer of a possibly otherwise undiscovered medical problem.

A whole literature actually centers on a fascinating related idea, that IQ losses are an early warning sign of approaching death. This presumption is called the **terminal-drop hypothesis.**

A set of studies begun in Germany in the 1950s firmly established the possibility that an IQ drop might signal approaching death (Riegel & Riegel, 1972; Riegel, Riegel, & Meyer, 1967). In this longitudinal investigation a variety of tests, including the WAIS, were administered three times, at five-year intervals, to a large group of men and women (initially 380 subjects) aged 55 to 75. An interesting pattern emerged. Particularly for subjects under 65, test performance predicted survival. Those who died before completing the testing had lower scores than the survivors. Moreover, subjects who died between the second and third evaluations showed what the researchers called terminal drop—an unusual decline in their scores from the first to the second examination.

On the basis of this and other research, the following quite optimistic hypothesis has been put forth: Terminal drop, rather than age itself, causes IQ declines in later life. The gloomy age decrement that cross-sectional studies reveal is really an artifact resulting from successively older groups containing larger proportions of people in the terminal phase of life. Cognitive loss is caused by something related to but quite different from advancing years—closeness to death (see Siegler, 1975, for review).

Actually, even vocal proponents of this positive idea grant that on nonverbal tests where speed is important losses may indeed be due to age itself. However, they are firm in attributing verbal deficits only to disease and distance from death. In fact, without illness intervening, they assume the verbal IQ remains stable no matter how old a person is (Jarvik, 1973). This assumption may also account for the breakdown of the classic aging pattern in advanced late life; in the very old, death is likely to be universally close and disease is almost invariably found. If the hypothesis is correct, in any search for an IQ index of approaching death, it should be fruitful to focus specifically on the verbal part of the WAIS.

In analyzing data from a longitudinal study of cognition in aging twins, one group of researchers (Blum, Clark, & Jarvik, 1973; Jarvik & Falik, 1963) did just that. First, they found that changes in three verbal scales in particular (similarities, digit span, and vocabulary) discriminated between the survivors and nonsurvivors in their sample. They then developed a formula based on yearly percentage losses in these tests to predict closeness to death. Changes above a certain level they called "critical loss." Critical loss on two or more scales was an ominous harbinger of imminent demise.

Unfortunately, the usefulness of this intriguing procedure is debatable. There is no evidence that the WAIS as a diagnostic tool does a better job than simple medical tests in suggesting who is likely to die soon. Besides, its very accuracy is open to question. There is no consensus that these particular scales are the ones involved in terminal decline (Botwinick, 1977). Even worse, it is not at all certain that terminal drop itself exists. Its reality has been challenged by a well-controlled investigation. In the Duke study (Palmore & Cleveland, 1976) volunteers who died after three or more evaluations did not manifest an accelerated score decline at their last testing.

So we cannot simply explain away declining IQ scores with advancing age as due to distance from death, for this idea is not fully proved. However we can say this with certainty. There are many alternative explanations for the losses observed. The ability-extraneous influences just described may account in good part for these declines. In addition, the age-decrement view of intelligence is currently being challenged by the last point mentioned at the beginning of the chapter. The content of the test itself may be deficient; the WAIS may be an inadequate index of intelligence in late life. This idea is really part of a larger controversy over the validity of IQ tests in general.

## Validity of the Test

Tests such as the WAIS or SAT are increasingly being scrutinized and declared unfair or even banned (Bersoff, 1973). There is some justification for this public concern and action. The names these scales go by strongly imply they measure something more than they actually do. In psychological language this controversy involves questions of *validity.* The WAIS and other standardized intelligence tests may not be accurately measuring what they purport to (see Bersoff, 1973; McClelland, 1973).

The problem is that these scales are not indexing just what their name strongly implies, an immutable ability or fixed attribute called "intelligence." This should be clear from our previous discussion. If the nonintellectual factors enumerated earlier, such as anxiety or years of schooling, do affect IQ scores, then the WAIS is not measuring anything like cognitive capacity in a pure form. Even the lesser assumption that the test accurately measures current intellectual performance has also been criticized. The compelling argument specifically with regard to the elderly proceeds as follows (Birren, 1973; Charles, 1973; Schaie, 1977, 1978).

All intelligence tests are limited, bound by the particular framework from which and reference group for whom they are constructed. There can be no totally transsituational IQ test, as the measure must refer to specific behaviors deemed signs of intelligence in a particular context. The earlier tests on which the WAIS is based were constructed to tap intelligence in a particular area, capacity to perform well in school. For this reason, although the WAIS and related tests may be good indexes of the concept for children and adolescents, there are questions about their validity for middle-aged and older adults. Except in rare cases such as Mrs. Johnson's, the main situation in which intelligent behavior is called for in later life is not the classroom, as it is in life's earlier stages.

So some experts in cognition and aging (Schaie, 1977, 1978, 1980; Willis & Baltes, 1980) are currently stressing the imperative need to develop new, more *age-relevant intelligence tests.* These new measures, they argue, unlike the existing ones, must have real *ecological validity.* By this term they mean the tests must better refer to the actual life situations and skills appropriate to intelligence during most of adulthood.

## Interventions

Not surprisingly, then, the effort to develop an age-relevant IQ test is a major focus of intervention research in cognition and age. Side by side with this attempt is another that is just as important but less revolutionary: to improve the performance of older adults in areas of intelligence as traditionally defined.

### Designing an Age-Relevant IQ Test

As we might imagine because of his vocal convictions about the inadequacy of current measures, Schaie (see Box 4-1) is the person who has given the most attention to devising an age-relevant IQ test. His initial step toward attaining this goal was to suggest a typology of the different skills that might be important to intelligence at particular times of life (1977). He divided the life span into four stages (see Figure 4-3). During the first, childhood and adolescence, he posited, the most important aspect of intelligence is ease of learning. The person's primary aim is to acquire the content of the culture and the skills to be an independent adult. During the next part of life, young adulthood, cognitive competence means how well the person can use what he or she has learned to achieve life goals. This Schaie calls the achieving stage. During middle age, responsibility, good long-range decision making, and for some the ability to integrate complex relationships are the

---

**BOX 4-1.    The Baltes-Schaie / Horn-Donaldson Debate**

As this chapter makes clear, it is not easy to summarize the findings about the relation of intelligence and age. First there are the less-than-positive facts, in particular the discouraging findings of cross-sectional studies. Then there are the mitigating explanations: the impact of influences other than age or ability on IQ scores; questions about the ecological validity of the test; and, as we will see, evidence that IQ in the elderly can be changed. It is not surprising, then, that experts themselves have widely divergent opinions about what the research shows. These differences can explode into public debate when it comes to presenting findings about this emotional topic to those not in the field.

Alarmed by two articles written for a wide audience by their colleagues Baltes and Schaie (1974; Schaie, 1974), which put the most positive cast on the research, Horn and Donaldson (1976) felt compelled to respond. Their rebuttal was followed by a rejoinder (Baltes & Schaie, 1976), which, in turn, evoked an irate response (Horn & Donaldson, 1977), followed by another short, more temperate rebuttal (Schaie & Baltes, 1977). Interestingly, the psychologists involved in this exchange are the top researchers in the area; consequently, the intensity of their disagreement is a revealing sign of the equivocal nature of the "facts" about intelligence and age.

The original articles strongly implied that the assumption of intellectual loss with advancing years is a myth. The basis for this presumption was Schaie and his coworkers' sequential research (Chapter 1 briefly described this method) showing that differences between cohorts, not advancing age, could explain much of the IQ decrement found in cross-sectional studies.

Horn and Donaldson (1976) strongly disagreed. They contended that it was a distortion of the facts to say *no* decline exists at all. All research, including Schaie's, demonstrates losses in an important area of cognition. Even the most optimistic types, longitudinal studies, show evidence of decrements in fluid intelligence.

Schaie and his coworker (Baltes & Schaie, 1976) countered by saying they had been misinterpreted. They had never meant to imply that no specific cognitive ability might fall off; their idea had been merely to stress the inaccuracy of the assumption of universal decline. They pointed to large differences between individuals in IQ stability or change. They also stressed the impact of ability-extraneous influences on the performance of older adults. Most important, they emphasized their misgivings about the validity of current tests, particularly the assumption that they measure intelligence in an adequate way. They concluded that a life-span developmental position should be critical to any summary statement. Intellectual change with age is multidirectional. It occurs to varying degrees in different individuals and also varies in a complex way across specific abilities.

As we might expect, Horn and Donaldson (1977) responded by calling this a distortion, an attempt to obfuscate the clear empirical evidence of decline. In addition, they made another interesting point. By questioning the merits of IQ tests as adequate indexes of intelligence and by adopting the life-span perspective stressing lack of uniform change, Baltes and Schaie were actually giving up; they were saying that it is impossible to describe, measure, and generalize about intelligence in a scientific way.

The final rejoinder was brief (Schaie & Baltes, 1977): The assumption of universal decline is false, and adopting it would have serious social consequences. There is overwhelming contradictory evidence that warrants a more optimistic view. Rather than assuming irreversible deficits, we should explore the modifiability of the IQ. This nonnihilistic approach will have both theoretical and practical importance; it also is more positive and humane.

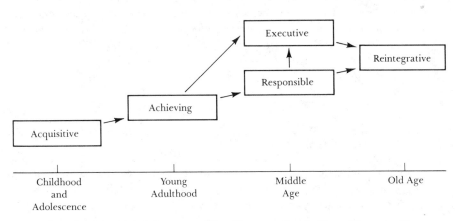

**FIGURE 4-3.** Schaie's stages of intelligence. *(Source: From "Toward a Stage Theory of Adult Cognitive Development," by K. W. Schaie. In* The International Journal of Aging and Human Development, *1977–78, 8, 129–138. Reprinted by permission.)*

hallmarks of intelligence. Finally, in old age, questions of "why should I know" achieve primary importance. Here, in what Schaie calls the reintegrative stage, personality and attitude are much more critical to cognition than before.

This typology, if valid, shows why current tests may not be adequate indexes of intelligence during the last two stages of life. For instance, the WAIS measures problem-solving skills and speed and the mastery of school-related material. During middle and old age good sense, wisdom, and an appreciation of larger meanings may be the most important signs of intelligence. Furthermore, Schaie (1978) feels, in old age a more concrete type of IQ test may be needed than the abstract WAIS—one explicitly tied to the actual life situations older people face that demand intelligent behavior.

This belief dictated Schaie's next step: to go from theory to the field, to develop an actual taxonomy of these intelligence-evoking events. As the best way to do this is to ask those who know, Schaie and his coworkers (Scheidt & Schaie, 1978) directly approached older people. The respondents gave interview and diary reports of daily episodes and events. The researchers classified these situations along different dimensions and then returned to the elderly, who rated the episodes according to their frequency or commonness, the emotion they engendered, and how difficult they were to cope with. The next step in the plan is to identify behavioral strategies that are intelligent—that is, good, or highly effective—and those that are noncompetent, or poor. This will allow the researchers to devise alternatives for actual test questions.

As is apparent, this is a carefully planned, highly ambitious, and well-orchestrated effort. Using a different and much less exhaustive approach, two investigators (Gardner & Monge, 1977) have already developed an actual set of questions for a possible test.

Because Gardner and Monge believed, like Schaie, that current IQ tests are biased against older adults, they attempted to show that cognitive decrement is not universal by devising scales suited to different age groups and then administering them to volunteers from the twenties to the seventies. Tests conceived as most appropriate for the elderly and people in late middle age included scales tapping knowledge of finances, diseases, and death and dying. There were also a vocabulary test geared to different generations and a set of questions involving modes of transportation used in the past.

Not surprisingly, on the scales favoring the old, the classic age IQ pattern was completely reversed. Adults in their fifties and early sixties tended to get the highest scores. Those in their twenties did the worst.

This study succeeded in showing that our ideas about life-span changes in cognition are dependent on the tests we use. However, the particular questions devised, because they refer to knowledge important in later life, might also form the beginnings of an age-relevant IQ test.

### Improving Performance on Current Tests

We know by now that the IQ score an older person receives should be modifiable because it is really an amalgam. It reflects the person's true ability plus a host of potentially changeable external, nonintellectual factors. We also know that these ability-extraneous influences exert a particularly potent negative impact on older adults' performance. The implication of these truths is quite positive: there may be a good deal of plasticity in IQ, particularly in old age. There may be considerable room for improving cognitive competence in late life.

Behaviorists would have taken this optimistic stance all along, as their perspective dictates looking first to the environment as the locus of intellectual deficits. In fact, an operant analysis suggests reasonably that the simple explanatory principle of extinction can be invoked in accounting for some cognitive losses in old age. The life situation of a retired person or someone whose contacts with the outside world are restricted because of functional impairments may simply provide too little reinforcement to prevent atrophy of intellectual skills (Baltes & Labouvie, 1973; Labouvie-Vief, Hoyer, Baltes, & Baltes, 1974). This suggests interventions might be fruitfully made at a societal level—for example, offering special educational programs to older adults (Granick & Friedman, 1973; Schaie, 1974). One effort to do this is described in our discussion of retirement in Chapter 7. Another avenue would be more specific and focused: direct training in the skills measured by the test. Several investigators have tried to improve the IQ of older adults by doing just that.

In one investigation (Hoyer, Labouvie-Vief, & Baltes, 1973) the aspect of intellect researchers chose to modify was response speed. As Chapter 3 makes clear, this was a particularly ambitious selection. Speed of responding is generally believed to be biologically based and so unmodifiable by any type of limited training.

The researchers first divided their subjects into three groups: a control, one given practice on the task but no reinforcement, and one given both practice and reinforcement. The task on which the training and testing were done was a paper-and-pencil measure. However, they also looked at whether improvements here would generalize to other tests on which speed was important.

Unfortunately, the results were not as good as was hoped. Both practice groups did improve, the reinforced group more than the other; but the differences between these subjects and the controls were not statistically significant, and there was little evidence for transfer of the gains found.

Other studies involving training have produced more encouraging findings. For example, one (Plemons, Willis, & Baltes, 1978) demonstrated that fluid intelligence in the elderly could be improved. Training subjects on a task tapping this global aspect of cognition produced results not only on that task but also to some degree on other tests of fluid abilities. Even more impressive, at least for the original training test the beneficial effects of the intervention persisted. At a six-month later testing, the group with practice did better overall than the controls.

In a second study (Labouvie-Vief & Gonda, 1976) elderly subjects were given specific training in monitoring their cognitive performance on a reasoning task by making statements such as "What do I have to do?" or "Think before I give up." Another group was merely given nonspecific practice on the test. The researchers looked for improvement both on the training task itself and on another measure of reasoning. They found some provocative results.

On an immediate test using the original measure, the subjects given specific training were superior both to a control group and to the nonspecific practice subjects. Overall, however, nonspecific practice was more beneficial. The subjects in this group were superior both at a later testing on the original measure and at both testings on the transfer task. So this research too demonstrates clear plasticity of cognitive performance, in particular with training of an unexpected kind—pure (nondirected) practice itself.

## Summary

The idea that intelligence may decline with age has caused much debate. Controversy concerns the timing and extent of age decrements, the causes of losses that do appear, and the adequacy, or validity, of the IQ test itself.

The Wechsler Adult Intelligence Scale (WAIS) is the test most often used to measure intelligence in adults. It has a verbal and a performance (nonverbal) part, each of which is composed of several subtests. Many of the verbal subtests measure a person's fund of knowledge. Many of the performance scales tap the ability to arrive at a new solution when asked to manipulate unfamiliar material. Speed is also important on the performance scale.

The IQ score is based on a person's performance compared with others of the same age. Cross-sectional data on which the WAIS age norms are based reveal that scores peak in young adulthood and continuously decline in successively older age groups. These declines are steadier and more marked and begin at an earlier age for the performance scale; here each subtest shows about the same pattern of decrement. Scores on the verbal part of the test, in particular on subtests measuring stored knowledge, decline little until the seventies and older, and then they too drop precipitously. This picture—marked decrement on the performance scale and little on verbal tests—appears so universally that it is called the classic aging pattern.

The classic aging pattern is also found in longitudinal investigations, but these studies offer a much more positive picture of the age/intelligence relationship. Some show that verbal scores actually increase through midlife and then remain stable until advanced old age. However, the Duke study revealed that the oldest group (volunteers initially in their seventies) showed clear losses of equal magnitude in verbal and performance IQ over a ten-year period.

As cross-sectional and longitudinal studies have contrasting biases, the truth about the timing and extent of age decrements must lie somewhere in between. The two methods concur, however, in showing the classic aging pattern until the seventies and uniform decline after that. An explanation of this result is based on the presumption that the verbal and performance tests tap basically different intellectual abilities.

These broad abilities are called fluid and crystallized intelligence. Fluid intelligence may be largely what is being measured by the performance scale. It consists of creatively devising a new solution to a problem and so is based more directly on biology, requiring that the brain be at its physiological peak. This may be why performance scores steadily decline after maturity. In contrast, the verbal scale may tap largely crystallized intelligence, defined as actual learned knowledge. As a person's fund of knowledge may increase or remain stable until late in life, this accounts for why verbal IQ may decline relatively little until advanced old age.

The WAIS is not a pure measure of intellectual capacity, as noncognitive factors also influence a person's score. Unfortunately, negative ability-extraneous influences may be most important for the old. For example, because today's elderly have fewer years of education, on the average, than young and middle-aged adults, they are at a disadvantage, having less familiarity with the school-related content of IQ tests and less practice taking tests in general.

The older adult's approach to the testing situation may also work against receiving an optimum score. The elderly tend to be excessively anxious when taking tests of intelligence or memory; they may be overly cautious; and they are likely to tire more easily than younger adults.

Illness is another important influence apart from age alone that can affect IQ. In one dramatic finding, even slight deviations from ideal health were associated with lower test scores. However, a relation between poor health and lower IQ is not universally found. In fact, in one study, an abnormal laboratory finding of slightly elevated blood pressure was associated with a rise in test scores over a ten-year period.

The terminal-drop hypothesis states that accelerated IQ losses are an early warning signal of approaching death. For instance, in one study, declines on some subtests of the verbal scale in particular were found to identify elderly people whose death was more likely imminent. Some subsequent research has failed to show that terminal drop exists, so the reality of this interesting phenomenon is in question.

The validity of IQ tests as measures of intelligence in older adults has been questioned because their content measures skills important specifically to doing well in school. These abilities may be quite different from those required for cognitive competence in middle and late life. For this reason efforts are being made to specify the actual attributes of intelligence in the later years in order to develop more age-appropriate IQ tests. Another focus of intervention research is to try to improve older adults' performance on the skills involved in intelligence as currently defined. A variety of such efforts have been successful, demonstrating that IQ in the elderly is plastic—capable of being enhanced.

## Key Terms

*WAIS verbal scale*

*WAIS performance scale*

*Classic aging pattern*

*Crystallized intelligence*

*Fluid intelligence*

*Ability-extraneous influences on IQ*

*Terminal-drop hypothesis*

*Validity*

*Age-relevant intelligence tests*

*Ecological validity*

## Recommended Readings

Baltes, P. B., & Schaie, K. W. On the plasticity of intelligence in adulthood and old age: Where Horn and Donaldson fail. ***American Psychologist***, 1976, *31*, 720-725.*

Botwinick, J. Intellectual abilities. In J. E. Birren & K. W. Schaie (Eds.), ***Handbook of the psychology of aging***. New York: Van Nostrand Reinhold, 1977.
*Comprehensive review article. Moderately difficult.*

Horn, J. L., & Donaldson, G. On the myth of intellectual decline in adulthood. ***American Psychologist***, 1976, *31*, 701-719.*

Horn, J. L., & Donaldson, G. Faith is not enough: A response to the Baltes-Schaie claim that intelligence does not wane. ***American Psychologist***, 1977, *32*, 369-373.*

Schaie, K. W., & Baltes, P. B. Some faith helps to see the forest: A final comment on the Horn and Donaldson myth of the Baltes-Schaie position on adult intelligence. ***American Psychologist***, 1977, *32*, 1118-1120.*

---

*These articles constitute the fascinating and acrimonious debate about how to view the facts on cognition and age. Will give you an excellent idea of the issues as well as the very different points of view of the experts. Highly recommended. Not difficult.

# CHAPTER FIVE

# Intellectual Processes: Memory and Creativity

Mrs. Johnson decided to enroll in two courses the next semester. She carefully chose one in which she knew she would do well, creative writing, and one in which she was not so sure, introductory psychology. The psychology course was difficult because of the voluminous number of facts and concepts to be learned. Besides, she did not relish the idea of having her grade based totally on performance on exams. After all, no matter how positive the evaluation by Dr. Sagstad had been, she could not help remembering that the comparison had been with people her own age. In a classroom full of young adults, her performance might fall short.

Luckily, at least she could be sure about creative writing. The short stories she regularly wrote for her own amusement did not seem to have gotten worse over the years. In fact, her greater life experience may have lent them a maturity and depth absent in her youth. And she had no qualms about being blocked. The urge to write was as strong now as it had been in her twenties. So was the actual amount of work she regularly produced, which was remarkable because she had heard that creativity declines as a person ages.

Her memory was a different matter. Two weeks ago she had forgotten a hairdresser's appointment, and two weeks before that she had had to be reminded by her friend they were meeting for lunch. And then at that party her son had given to celebrate finishing his first novel, she had been astonished at how easily she forgot the name of an occasional guest. Actually, these negative ruminations had to stop. She had to admit that this train of thought was set off by the annoying thought that her soon-to-be-famous child had not called in a week.

When her son finally did call the next day, he laughed off these concerns. In fact, he had been meaning to phone earlier to convey some information in a very different vein. When leaving the party, several of his guests had commented on his mother's marvelous memory. Not only was it personally flattering that after meeting so many new people she could so easily remember them, but it certainly seemed a rebuke to some of those ideas about old age. Several commented that her grace and her remarkable recall of names and faces put their ability to shame.

What her son was really thinking about his mother's complaints, he was too polite to say. They seemed to follow a predictable pattern: she got upset about her memory when she was really upset about other things. Now it was because she was feeling neglected; he had not called for some time. There was also the realistic fear that with his new book would come the inevitable trips to promote it that would take him away from home. He thought, with some malice, that it was easy for his mother to focus on what she felt was an inevitable problem of old age instead of admitting to an obviously selfish emotion: she was not unmitigatedly happy about his success. She half wished it were not happening, because it would leave him less time for her. Thank God, he thought, for her plan to enroll in college. And thank God it would force her to do what he had urged all along: get an appointment book like everyone else.

Actually, her semester in college did erase Mrs. Johnson's complaints. She got praise from her creative writing professor and an A for unusually outstanding work. This obvious success even gave her a perspective on what to tell her son when he voiced fears of not being able to write a second or third book. Although she could not speak for everyone, her experience certainly demonstrated that creative work could be produced at any age.

The only unfortunate event of the semester was that C she got in psychology. This grade was particularly irksome because it so clearly was caused by her anxiety during the three hourly exams. Each time after handing in a test, much of the information she had not remembered had the annoying tendency to miraculously reappear. This experience led her to question the accuracy of a definitive statement the professor had made about memory in people of her very age. Citing evidence from studies in which elderly people had been given memory tests, he had said a marked decline in ability is usual, perhaps universal, in late life.

The last chapter examined age/cognition relationships in a general way. Now we consider age changes in some specific cognitive processes. The two abilities that are the focus of this discussion, memory and creativity, differ to the greatest possible extent. However, perceptions about these aspects of cognition share a common theme: as was clearly illustrated in the "ageism" statement that begins this book, when people get older, we expect their memory to get worse; and we similarly expect that people are likely to be less creative as they age.

Our discussion of memory is limited to changes in normal older adults. Chapter 8 will describe pathological disorders of memory. A very different approach will be used in viewing age and creativity. Here our focus is the atypical person, as we are considering only those whose job it is to produce unique, original work; and here our analysis is not confined to old age. We will be viewing creative achievements throughout adulthood, looking for the particular life periods for different fields when creativity peaks and wanes. Unfortunately, this overly narrow range of subjects and overly wide age range is a necessity rather than a choice. We simply have too little information on late-life creativity or on age changes in this important aspect of thinking in more average adults.

## Memory

More than any other problem, poor memory is the complaint that seems to epitomize old age. Even though we may be too enlightened to equate late life with senility, still we assume all elderly people have suffered some memory loss. As was true in our vignette, older adults share this perception. Most, if asked, would probably say they are more forgetful than they used to be. Some, in just as revealing a way, would brag that their memory is as good as before. What is the basis of this perceived deficiency, one so important it either is naturally taken for granted or must be vigorously denied? The answer to this question has been pursued by experimental psychologists in laboratory research having a particular format.

Laboratory investigations of learning and memory usually compare a group of elderly with young adults on some verbal measure. A list of words, letters, or nonsense syllables is presented orally or visually. Then, after a number of presentations, the person's recall of these items is assessed. A common variation on this procedure is called the ***paired-associate technique.*** Items are presented in pairs, and, given one, the subject is asked to produce the other. Sometimes memory is tested by simply asking the person to reproduce the items without any hints. This is called *free recall.* Sometimes hints are given, such as the first letter of the correct word. This is called ***cued recall.*** Finally, another common technique is the ***recognition*** approach. As in multiple-choice tests, the subject is simply asked to pick out the correct alternative from a number of possibilities.

In general, studies of this type show a clear basis for real-life reports of memory loss. The elderly do significantly worse than the young. As we will see in our discussion of pathological memory in Chapter 8, there are physical changes in the brain that may explain this poorer performance. However, variations in the tasks themselves also produce differences in the degree of decrement found. This leads us to the real purpose of laboratory memory investigations: they are conducted not so much to document the existence of a deficit as to localize it. The question researchers often want to know is in what aspect of remembering the elderly have most difficulty (see Craik, 1977; Poon, Fozard, Cermak, Arenberg, & Thompson, 1980). We can best understand their efforts by briefly outlining the way memory is currently conceptualized—the information-processing model.

### Overview

According to the presently accepted view, memory is an active process involving attention and rehearsal. Material to be remembered passes through three stages, or separate stores.

First, a stimulus arriving from a particular sense is held briefly in a ***sensory store*** specific to that modality. For example, what is seen enters a visual store (iconic memory), what is heard, an auditory store (echoic memory). Material in a sensory store is just a raw image, something like a photocopy, which is lost quite rapidly, from ⅓ to 2 seconds after being presented. Individual features that are attended to, however, are transformed into verbal information and enter the next store, ***primary memory.***

Primary memory is best viewed as a kind of temporary holding process or gate rather than a structured store. Information here is confined to a very limited number of items, the amount that can be maintained at one time in conscious awareness. This fragment is lost if it is displaced by other material. If not, after being rehearsed, it enters the third and last store, ***secondary memory.***

When we speak of memory, we are really talking about the contents of this last system. Secondary memory is the relatively permanent, large-capacity store that is the repository of our past. In order for us to remember something, information in this large store must logically have undergone three steps: it must have been adequately learned, or ***encoded,*** in the first place; it must have been adequately ***stored;*** and finally, it must be capable of being ***retrieved,*** or gotten out.

### The Older Adult's Difficulty

A variety of studies (see Craik, 1977; Smith, 1975) agree on one point. The elderly have little or no deficit in either of the first two systems, sensory or primary memory; their problem resides in secondary memory. Where researchers do not concur at all is in the process in the system that is mainly or solely at fault. What is debated is whether memory deficits in old age are due mainly to an acquisition (encoding) problem, a storage problem, or a retrieval problem (Smith, 1980).

One reasonable approach to testing the question would be to devise studies eliminating a single aspect of memory in particular and then compare the performance of old and young. If age differences are minimized or even significantly reduced, then it would seem reasonable that the older person's problem resides in that step or process that has been omitted. This, in fact, is a main strategy that has implicated retrieval—getting stored information out of secondary memory—as at least part of the older person's difficulty.

Recognition tests and measures of cued recall largely eliminate the retrieval requirement, because the correct information is either totally or partly presented and so does not have to be searched for and retrieved (Smith, 1980). On tests of this type the usual deficit of the elderly is reduced. In fact, in some investigations age differences are actually eliminated by using cues. Evidently, then, impaired retrieval is the main source of the memory deficit often observed in late life.

But does this procedure really prove retrieval is the problem? Some researchers answer no. One study (Harkins, Chapman, & Eisdorfer, 1979) revealed that a better guessing strategy, not better memory itself, could be responsible for the comparatively good performance of the old on recognition tests. Here response strategy was specifically evaluated and was found to differ between a young and an old group. The older adults spontaneously adopted an approach that resulted in an inflated correct recognition rate, which made it appear that their memory was as good as the young adults'. So recognition memory may be just as much affected by age as recall, or almost as much. Perhaps many previous studies failed to find age differences because this biasing factor was not taken into account.

Another argument, though complicated, is equally compelling. The finding of little or no age difference on cued-recall and recognition tests, compared with free recall, does not inescapably show retrieval is at fault. These results are also compatible with even the opposite interpretation: they could just as easily be explained by deficits localized in the acquisition stage.

For example, having a good technique for organizing material so it can be remembered easily is part of the acquisition, or learning, phase of memory. But, age differences in the adequacy of this strategy are likely to show up mainly in the free-recall situation. When recognition and cued-recall tests are used, there is less need for a good encoding technique. Because external cues are provided, these approaches lessen the need to use one's own internal system of encoding material for easy access.

So older adults' poorer performance on recall tests than on other memory tests may really be due to poorer learning skills. Recall measures are the only ones sensitive to differences in a person's initial encoding strategy (Smith, 1980).

The example above offers just one of the reasons that pinpointing the nature of late-life memory deficits is so problematic. The retrieval stage is practically impossible to isolate from the stage of initial learning (Arenberg, 1980). Actually, while retrieval may also be impaired (Craik, 1977), much evidence also implicates problems in acquisition in older adults' memory deficits (Poon, Fozard, & Treat, 1978; Smith, 1980; Treat, Poon, Fozard, & Popkin, 1978). For instance, as was just hypothesized, the elderly do seem deficient in their learning strategy, the techniques they use in encoding information for easy recall.

One study (Hulicka & Grossman, 1967) illustrates a particular type of poor approach. The elderly are less likely to use mediators when doing so would be helpful. These researchers compared a young and an old group on the standard paired-associate learning task and found the typical result: the elderly did not do nearly as well. The researchers then questioned the two groups about their way of learning the material and found age-related differences. The young people much more frequently reported using *mediators*—for example, forming a visual image including the items of the pair or linking the disparate words by imagining them in a sentence.

This technique aids learning. When the researchers gave special instructions in using mediators, the performance of both the young and the old improved. However, the elderly were helped more, and thus age differences in performance were reduced. So one reason older people do poorly on memory tests is that they are less likely to use good acquisition strategies.

In addition to this poor internal style or approach, external aspects of the learning situation may handicap the older adult. One of these influences we might predict from what we already know: when the learning environment demands speed, older people will perform most poorly.

The impairing impact of having to respond quickly was demonstrated in a test involving paired-associate learning (Canestrari, 1963). Older and young adult subjects were tested under three conditions. The first two involved a timed response; subjects were asked to produce the correct word within either a 1½-second or a 3-second interval. The last did not require speed; subjects could take as long as they wanted to study the pair and also could answer at their own pace. Age differences were most marked under the first two conditions. When subjects had unlimited time, the elderly did take longer to respond. Their memory, though, was much less deficient.

Each of these studies has theoretical importance; they help us get to the root of the deficiency older adults may show. But they also have clear practical implications. To facilitate memory, it might be helpful to teach the elderly better encoding strategies. To enhance recall, we should make sure older adults are allowed as much time to remember (and learn) as they want.

### *The Tenuous Tie between Laboratory and Life*

Ideally we would hope most empirical research on memory and age would have potential real-life applications, as the studies just described do. Investigations designed to answer abstract questions should translate into prescriptions for remedying actual deficits that older adults show. Unfortunately, though, efforts to link laboratory findings with practical action are just beginning to be made (Erikson, 1978; Erikson, Poon, & Walsh-Sweeney, 1980; Fozard & Popkin, 1978). There are several reasons that making the transition from academic research to real-world problems has been so difficult.

**Problems Inherent in Memory Studies.**   First, as our earlier description of the research implicating retrieval demonstrates, there is no consensus about the specific memory difficulties that older adults actually have (Poon, Fozard, Cermak, Arenberg, & Thompson, 1980; see Recommended Readings). Investigators not only argue about whether the deficit resides in encoding, storage, or retrieval but even dispute the utility of this basic scheme for viewing and understanding the older person's problem (Salthouse, 1980). The lack of agreement, not just about what results mean but about the whole way to view memory in the elderly, impedes action. Without a consensus even on how to begin to conceptualize what may be wrong, it is difficult to envision a remedial plan.

Then there is the critical question of validity posed at the end of our vignette. Is performance on standard memory studies an adequate index of behavior outside? Concern here centers on the same two areas as for IQ tests: extraneous influences peculiar to being evaluated may explain much of the poor performance of the old, and the actual content of laboratory memory tests may be too irrelevant to the real world.

One paramount test-taking influence was apparent in our clinical case. Mrs. Johnson had a memory problem only under the stress of taking an examination. Under less anxiety-provoking conditions, her ability to recall information was actually remarkable. In other words, any situation in which memory is being formally evaluated is likely to be a poor showcase for an older person's general ability. In addition to excessive anxiety and the other detrimental ways the elderly approach tests, as discussed in Chapter 4 (see Woodruff & Walsh, 1975), one other impairing influence, being particularly likely to appear in memory studies, needs special mention. The typical way of empirically evaluating memory is to make the information to be remembered as meaningless as possible. So, on paired-associate tasks subjects may be asked to memorize pairs of completely unrelated words. They may be instructed to learn lists of nonsense syllables or unrelated letters or numbers. The rationale for using stimuli of this type is that it permits investigators to evaluate memory in a pure, uncontaminated form. However, this laudable objective may be least likely to occur when this very strategy is used with the old.

In one revealing study (Hulicka, 1967) the standard approach was first attempted with a group of elderly and young adults. Subjects were asked to memorize a list of unrelated paired associates. However, the investigator soon found that this request evoked strong resistance among the older subjects. A full 80% refused to complete the study. Many gave as their reason that they could not participate in doing something that made so little sense. Only when the requirement was changed to make the task more applicable to real life did the older group consent to participate. Then the investigator was able to interest them and motivate them to do their best.

So the traditional way of assessing memory may be counterproductive when applied to the elderly. Rather than illuminating ability in a pure way, it may actually allow a memory-extraneous influence to have its maximum effect. Older people are likely to be less motivated when the test content seems meaningless or irrelevant. They then may be revealing not their memory but mainly the extent to which they are able to become interested in the research when they participate in academic memory studies.

This same meaningless content may limit the adequacy of the standard approach in a second important way. Memorizing nonsense syllables or unrelated words is something a person would never be asked to do outside the laboratory. There is a real question, then, whether the typical procedure is at all ecologically valid, as it is so maximally removed from memory in real life (Hartley, Harker, & Walsh, 1980).

Concerns about ecological validity have a basis in fact. Training on typical laboratory tasks does not translate into improvement on tests more similar to the requirements of the real world. In the investigation demonstrating this is so (cited in Erikson et al., 1980), elderly subjects were first given practice memorizing paired associates. This made it easier for them to memorize other lists of paired associates. However, there was no generalization to other, more common tasks such as remembering a grocery list, a disappointing lack of transfer that suggests the connection between skill in the laboratory and performance outside is more tenuous than we would have hoped.

So in measuring memory, the current prescription is for the need to devise more ecologically valid tests which might include, for example, recalling the content of a conversation or the location of a place (Hartley et al., 1980). These are the kinds of demands a person is more likely to be exposed to in the course of actual living. Tests of this type might better highlight the real problems a person has.

**Problems Inherent in the Differing Goals of Experimenter and Clinician.**    Actually, we should not expect that laboratory findings will often directly apply to a given person's difficulty. The purpose of these studies is quite different. As our earlier discussion shows, researchers who study memory in the laboratory are often trying to isolate one (usually purely cognitive) aspect of poor performance and then generalize about its impact for most individuals. Gerontologists interested in clinical intervention have a different goal. Their focus is not on finding an abstract truth but on looking at a particular, special individual. In addition, they want to understand that person's problem as a totality, to explore all its possible determinants and manifestations.

In fact, one general "truth" about memory in older adults is the very existence of individual variability (Erikson, 1978; Erikson et al., 1980). Different people manifest diverse types of deficits, which, in turn, may have quite variable causes. This is clearly illustrated in our vignette. Mrs. Johnson's impairment was quite personal; it appeared only in a special context. Moreover, its basis was not cognitive at all but resided in a motivational difficulty—too much anxiety. Finally, as in

Mrs. Johnson's view of her memory at the party, what was for her clear evidence of a problem was not a deficit at all. Mrs. Johnson, like many older adults, really had no memory difficulty. Because she was highly attuned to the possibility, though, she saw signs of declining ability in instances of forgetting that a younger person would have laughed off. Her gloomy convictions were dependent on her general morale rather than on external events signaling an actual problem did exist.

The crucial importance of mood or life satisfaction to perceptions of poor memory is far from limited to our clinical vignette. In a quite telling study, researchers (Kahn, Zarit, Hilbert, & Niederehe, 1975) discovered a surprising phenomenon when they correlated memory complaints in a large group of older subjects with objective memory tests and depression. Subjective concerns were not related to a person's real level of impairment. Instead, they were associated only with depression; the more unhappy individuals were, the more likely they were to believe their memory was poor.

So a person's convictions about his or her failing memory should not be automatically accepted at face value. As was true in our vignette, they may be more diagnostic of low morale. Indeed, this same low morale, rather than a lack of inherent ability, may cause actual deficits. As will be discussed in detail in Chapter 8, one symptom of depression in the elderly is memory impairment, problems in remembering that may be so severe they can lead to a mistaken diagnosis of senility.

Obviously, then, if we limited our inquiry to the purely cognitive aspects of memory, as academic researchers often do, we might be missing a person's true problem. Real-world deficits are localized not just in poor acquisition or retrieval but also in poor motivation or, as here, in poor mental health.

### *Interventions*

For this reason many authors (Erikson et al., 1980; Fozard & Popkin, 1978; Poon et al., 1978) suggest that as a prelude to giving concrete help there should be a thorough effort to understand many aspects of the individual's psychological functioning. Impairments in specific aspects of memory, such as acquisition skills, should be assessed. The impact of depression, excessive anxiety, and all other factors that might affect performance should also be considered. The person performing the evaluation should carefully define the particular situations in which memory problems occur. The evaluator should, if possible, use assessment devices that reflect real life. Only when the older adult has been examined in this comprehensive way can the diagnostician best know how to intervene. The following are some treatment strategies that might be used, depending on the results of the assessment.

**Training the Person.**    If it is determined that deficient learning skills are responsible for the person's poor memory, then findings directly gleaned from laboratory research can be used to help. Two approaches in particular have been demonstrated to be effective—simple practice and special training.

One study (Hultsch, 1974) illustrated the value of pure practice in improving subsequent learning. Experience in memorizing lists reduced the time it took to learn subsequent lists. The original purpose of this research was to show that age differences in memory are due partly to older adults' lack of practice, so it was hypothesized that the elderly would benefit the most from experience. This turned out not to be true; practice helped all age groups. However, though negative with regard to age differences, this finding is important with respect to offering actual help. To improve memory, we might simply give older adults who need it regular memorization experience. Simple exercises enhance a person's skills.

Another effective avenue is more active: directly teaching the person new, more helpful learning strategies. This approach, called ***cognitive skill training,*** usually entails instructions in mediational techniques. Cognitive skill training was used in the study described earlier demonstrating that older adults have difficulties in their ability to encode information.

The cognitive skill approach has been used successfully in a variety of studies (Poon, Walsh-Sweeney, & Fozard, 1980; Treat et al., 1978). In one in particular (Treat & Reese, 1976) it actually erased performance differences between the young and the old. Here, elderly and young adult subjects were assigned to one of three imagery conditions. In the first they were provided with specific visual images that would link the paired associates (for instance, for the pair *tree–shoe* they were told to imagine a tree growing out of a shoe). In the second they were instructed in this technique but told to form their own images. In the last, the control group, they were given no specific training.

---

**BOX 5-1.   Memory Training and Memory Complaints**

Since cognitive skill training improves memory, naturally we would expect this objectively better performance to lessen an older person's fears. Seeing that their memory is so much better, elderly individuals who have undergone this training should complain less about their failing ability.

However, our earlier discussion suggests this quite reasonable hypothesis might not hold. If memory complaints result more from depression than from actual performance, objective improvement might have little impact on a person's concerns.

Zarit, Cole, and Guider (1981) examined the truth of these competing ideas. They assigned elderly subjects either to a memory training group or to a current-events discussion group. Subjects exposed to both conditions had the idea that the sessions would be helpful. As expected, though, actual recall improved only for those in the first group.

In contrast, subjective memory complaints were lessened equally after participation in either condition. This result shows once again their lack of relation to objective reality. It also demonstrates something else of crucial importance: simply the belief in having received help may be enough to allay one's fears.

Interestingly, although either type of instruction was helpful, when given as much time as needed to respond, the elderly in the self-generated-imagery condition performed as well as the young. This illustrates that for older adults the most effective method for enhancing memory may be merely to provide general training in how to use mediators.

The training might be used in conjunction with regular homework assignments. It has also been suggested (Treat et al., 1978) that an optimal approach would be to conduct the instruction in groups. This would have the same benefit as using a group to modify Type A behavior: members would be able to reinforce one another for continuing to use the techniques. Group sessions would also engender an atmosphere of hope, in which change was viewed as possible. Perhaps most important, ongoing memory groups would supply reinforcement for competent performance that the person's normal environment might not provide. Actually, this very environmental lack may be another factor contributing to some of the memory deficiencies observed in older adults (Kahn & Miller, 1978).

**Modifying the Environment.**    Two studies of nursing home residents (Langer, Rodin, Beck, Weinman, & Spitzer, 1979) clearly demonstrated the importance of an impoverished external environment. The investigators were able to enhance residents' memory by applying a behavioral perspective. The unstimulating environment of the home had caused excess disabilities. Reinforcement for good memory, then, might reverse some of what looked like a purely physiologically caused deficit.

In the first study residents were individually engaged four times during a six-week period in a 30- to 40-minute discussion designed to stimulate their memory. There were two experimental conditions: in one the interviewer revealed a good deal about herself, and in the other self-disclosure was low. At the end of each session, residents were instructed to think about current occurrences in their life so they could discuss them during the next interview. It was felt that residents exposed to the high-disclosure condition would be more motivated to remember these events, as disclosure by the interviewer would be a reinforcer eliciting better memory.

In fact, this group did improve on subsequent memory tests. Nurses also rated residents in the high-disclosure condition as generally more aware and active. The low-disclosure interviews were not effective at enhancing memory. Subjects did no better than those not interviewed at all.

In the next study a more tangible reinforcer was used—chips that could be redeemed for gifts. Residents were visited nine times during a three-week period. Once again there were two experimental conditions. In the first residents were reinforced contingent on their remembering facts such as the names of nurses on the floor or what they had eaten for breakfast. Residents in the second condition were also given the chips, but their reinforcement was not contingent on good performance.

Needless to say, once again contingent reinforcement produced improvements. Subjects exposed to the first condition showed better recall. Further, their enhanced performance was not limited to the specific material they had been rein-forced for remembering but generalized to other facts about the institutional environment.

Two cautions limit our applying these findings to the memory problems that more typical elderly people may show. First, these residents had pathological im-pairments, symptoms much more severe than the mild deviations being discussed in this chapter. Second, they were living in a quite atypical setting. Nursing homes are an extreme in deficient environments, as few cognitive demands are made on a person at all. However, it does seem reasonable that a highly stimulating situa-tion for remembering such as Mrs. Johnson encountered in school might help prevent excess disabilities in normal community-dwelling elderly people too. In sum, as was true for physical performance and intellect, an external world encour-aging optimal functioning is the ideal.

## Creative Achievements

As we just saw, confusion about the exact nature of the problem is characteris-tic of research on memory and age. However, there is little controversy about the fact that real decline often occurs. The same is true of at least one aspect of intelligence discussed in the previous chapter. No matter how heated the debate over the issue as a whole, there are few disagreements that fluid intelligence in particular is negatively affected by advancing age. This uniformity of agreement has an unfortunate implication for our current discussion. Fluid intelligence in-volves inventiveness of thought and the ability to arrive at an original solution, the very skills that seem the core element of creativity. We might therefore expect that, in a parallel way to fluid intelligence, as a person aged, he or she would become less capable of doing creative work.

However, age is likely to have a more complicated relationship to creativity because, to make an original contribution in any area, fluid intelligence can't be enough. A person must be motivated and enthusiastic. It would help to have the physical stamina to put in long hours and the financial resources to make it possi-ble to devote a good deal of time to creative work. It would be good not to be too emotionally sidetracked—pulled, for example, by commitments to family, co-workers, or other interests.

Requirements intrinsic to the content of one's profession should also play a part. For example, having a backlog of knowledge and experience might affect creativity to varying extents in different fields. To make a contribution, it might take more time or be more essential for a person in some areas than in others to learn what had already been done (Zuckerman & Merton, 1972). In particular professions a long training period and extended practice in honing creative skills would be important. In some, even time living would be a critical plus—those in which, as in our vignette, maturity and wisdom would enhance the quality of a person's work. Factors apart from actual content might also be crucial in a given profession—for instance, how competitive the field was and the opportunity it offered people at different life stages to do original work.

So, it is likely to be more difficult to predict the life period of maximum creative achievement than a simple equating of creativity with fluid intelligence suggests. We have to consider a host of other influences, some intrinsic to the person's biological and psychological capacities at different stages of life and some a function of the field itself. In fact, the perhaps overriding impact of the field on the probable best age for creative discovery suggests that we organize our discussion in just this way. So after a description of the initial work in this area and the controversy it caused, we will go on to consider creativity in the two major areas of scholarship, the arts and sciences, separately.

### The First Findings and the Resulting Controversy

The first major attempt to look systematically at creativity in relation to age was published in 1953. In this controversial book, *Age and Achievement*, Lehman set forth the fruits of an exhaustive investigation into the peak period of creative achievement in a wide variety of fields (see Lehman, 1960). He examined performance in traditional scholarly areas and also in nonacademic ones such as athletics, typing, and chess. He studied the ages at which college presidents, heads of large corporations, and Supreme Court justices had occupied their posts. He examined movie directors, foreign diplomats, and the authors of notable church sermons.

The findings of his that generated the most debate, though, involved original work in the arts and sciences. Paralleling the cross-sectional findings on IQ scores and age, he discovered that young adulthood was the time of maximum creativity. After the thirties a person's chances of producing a significant contribution seemed to decline rapidly. Furthermore, this negative picture was fairly consistent; it held across specialties as diverse as poetry and physics. The following illustrations give an idea of the alarming age decrement he found in certain fields.

Chemists aged 40 to 45 produced only one-half as many significant contributions per person as those a decade younger. By age 60 to 65 their production was a mere 20% of the peak rate. An even more striking loss was evident in the work of orchestral composers. Here by age 55 to 60 the productivity level per person was only 20% of the maximum (see Dennis, 1956).

Of course, as with the initial data on IQ and age, the validity of these gloomy statistics was almost immediately questioned. Lehman had arrived at his figures using a questionable strategy that at first glance seems quite reasonable. He looked through several textbooks and histories in each field and copied down each work listed. He then determined the age of the person who had made the contribution by looking up his or her birthdate and subtracting that from the date of the work. If the various histories he consulted tended to agree in listing the contribution, he included it in his calculations. Finally, he divided his age listings by the total number of creators in that field living at the time (Lehman, 1960).

This methodology has been criticized for several weaknesses (Dennis, 1956, 1958, 1966). First, it does not consider that there may be a bias in the citation style of the textbooks themselves. For instance, it seems possible that a compiler, particularly in a scientific field, might be prone to list a person's youthful pioneering breakthrough rather than the just as creative later work necessary to validate its premise. Moreover, there is a natural tendency, in compiling a history, to include past productions at the expense of current ones because in both the arts and sciences a work is certified as important only after it has stood the test of time. This very practice leads to spurious evidence of an age decrement in examining the work of creators living now. A currently older person's earlier work would be included in the anthology; his or her recent work, even if just as good, would tend to be omitted.

Then, there is a crucial problem specifically for the sciences in judging age/ creativity relationships from citations in texts: in this whole area of inquiry there has been a steady increase in the competition. In successive years more and more works are produced and more and more workers enter the field. The rapid growth rate, as Table 5-1 shows, means that over time an increasingly smaller percentage of the total works produced can be listed in a history—which, in turn, means that each older creator had an easier job getting his or her early contributions in. The creator's youthful work may in fact be better. But it may also have been cited because of mere competitive advantage, the smaller field of competitors itself.

**TABLE 5-1.** Percentage of scientific publications cited in six sourcebooks, by decade of publication.

| Decade | Number of Publications | Percentage Cited |
|---|---|---|
| 1810–1819 | 13,085 | 0.2 |
| 1820–1829 | 20,866 | 0.1 |
| 1830–1839 | 29,608 | 0.1 |
| 1840–1849 | 43,125 | 0.1 |
| 1850–1859 | 43,325 | 0.1 |
| 1860–1869 | 80,421 | 0.05 |
| 1870–1879 | 106,001 | 0.06 |
| 1880–1889 | 178,390 | 0.03 |
| 1890–1899 | 198,038 | 0.02 |

*(Source: Adapted from "The Age Decrement in Outstanding Scientific Contributions: Fact or Artifact," by W. Dennis. In* American Psychologist, *1958, 13, 457–460. Copyright 1958 by the American Psychological Association. Reprinted by permission of the publisher.)*

Perhaps the most serious shortcoming of *Age and Achievement,* though, is that its author failed to control for the very different longevities of his creators. People who die young are obviously deprived of the chance to create when old, but data for these short-lived creators are included in the statistics along with figures for those who did have this opportunity, the long-lived. The effect is a built-in favoritism for the early decades. Only the small long-lived number in the sample have a chance to demonstrate that creative work can occur later in life (Dennis, 1956;

Riley & Foner, 1968). A simple stratagem might be used to give the later years their fair weight—confine our analyses to creators who have lived a full life span.

Dennis (1966), who came up with the compelling criticisms of *Age and Achievement*, did just that. He examined the productivity of 738 persons in various artistic and scientific specialties, all of whom had lived to age 79 or beyond. In addition, rather than employing the possibly skewed information presented in texts, in most cases he used as his sources simply listings of every published work in the field. This means his statistics are of something very different from what Lehman examined. They are of pure creative output, not necessarily of the best work produced.

As Table 5-2 shows, Dennis's approach yielded quite divergent facts from those presented in *Age and Achievement*. For most professions midlife, the forties and fifties, is the most productive time. In fact, the sixties are the most creative decade in the two scholarly areas where we might expect wisdom to count for the most, history and philosophy. In addition, rather than declining sharply, productivity gradually slopes off. In many areas it declines only minimally even at the oldest ages.

The table also reveals an interesting pattern of variability among the three broad areas of inquiry. In general, declines occur earlier in the arts than in the sciences. Output in the sciences falls off earlier than for scholarship. In addition, there are provocative differences across professions within each area. More recent

**TABLE 5-2.**   Production of creative works in selected fields in each decade of life by persons living to 79 and above.

| Field | Number of Persons | Number of Works | Percentage of Work Produced during Decade | | | | | |
|-------|------------------|-----------------|------|------|------|------|------|------|
| | | | *20s* | *30s* | *40s* | *50s* | *60s* | *70s* |
| History | 46 | 615 | 3 | 19 | 19 | 22 | 24 | 20 |
| Philosophy | 42 | 225 | 3 | 17 | 20 | 18 | 22 | 20 |
| Scholarship | 43 | 326 | 6 | 17 | 21 | 21 | 16 | 19 |
| Means | | | 4 | 18 | 20 | 20 | 21 | 20 |
| Biology | 32 | 3456 | 5 | 22 | 24 | 19 | 17 | 13 |
| Botany | 49 | 1889 | 4 | 15 | 22 | 22 | 22 | 15 |
| Chemistry | 24 | 2120 | 11 | 21 | 24 | 19 | 12 | 13 |
| Geology | 40 | 2672 | 3 | 13 | 22 | 28 | 19 | 14 |
| Invention | 44 | 646 | 2 | 10 | 17 | 18 | 32 | 21 |
| Mathematics | 36 | 3104 | 8 | 20 | 20 | 18 | 19 | 15 |
| Means | | | 6 | 17 | 22 | 21 | 20 | 15 |
| Architecture | 44 | 1148 | 7 | 24 | 29 | 25 | 10 | 4 |
| Chamber music | 35 | 109 | 15 | 21 | 17 | 20 | 18 | 9 |
| Drama | 25 | 803 | 10 | 27 | 29 | 21 | 9 | 3 |
| Libretta writing | 38 | 164 | 8 | 21 | 30 | 22 | 15 | 4 |
| Novel writing | 32 | 494 | 5 | 19 | 18 | 28 | 23 | 7 |
| Opera composition | 176 | 476 | 8 | 30 | 31 | 16 | 10 | 5 |
| Poetry | 46 | 402 | 11 | 21 | 25 | 16 | 16 | 10 |
| Means | | | 9 | 23 | 26 | 21 | 14 | 6 |

*(Source: Adapted from "Creative Productivity between the Ages of 20 and 80," by W. Dennis. In* Journal of Gerontology, *1966, 21, 1–18. Copyright 1966 by The Gerontological Society. Reprinted by permission.)*

work on this fascinating topic has focused on the question of how reliable these figures and differences are and has generated some hypotheses to account for the patterns that do exist.

### In the Arts

The little research here has been done almost singlehandedly by one person (Simonton, 1975a, 1975b, 1977a, 1977b). In a series of studies this psychologist explored a variety of factors that might influence productivity in the arts. Two of his investigations focused in part on the critical variable of age.

In his initial study Simonton (1975a) looked specifically at literary creativity—the production of poetry, imaginative prose (fiction), and informative prose (non-fiction). He chose literature because its universality and its distinction of being the oldest enduring creative endeavor afforded the opportunity to look at age/creativity relationships in many historical eras and across a variety of cultures. Also, literature seems an ideal medium for studying the influence of age on creativity because here (as with some other art forms too) competence seems more closely tied just to individual skills. Producing high-quality work in the sciences is more dependent on externals—for example, having access to laboratory facilities, getting grants, or being at the appropriate career stage to concentrate on research.

Simonton examined the production of high-quality work by both long- and short-lived creators, using a special technique to control for the biasing influence of longevity differences. His conviction was that the stratagem of considering only long-lived individuals was too limiting. Only about 15% of great writers have lived past 80. Those who have were likely, he reasoned, to be unrepresentative in ways other than unusual longevity too.

Luckily, his procedure of examining age/creativity relationships in many settings and times was a built-in control for competitive advantage. In literature, unlike the sciences, the number of creators is not steadily increasing. Here there is probably more of a wavelike fluctuation: in a particular time and place the field becomes more crowded and then, after reaching a peak, gradually less so. By considering many milieus then, conditions favoring achievement in youth would be automatically counterbalanced by others promoting the opposite.

Using a large sample of creators whose names and work had been culled from histories and anthologies, Simonton discovered different age/creativity relationships among the three literary media. As originally hypothesized, poets tended to produce their best work when youngest (at a modal age in the late thirties). The peak age for producing imaginative prose was next (the early forties). Informative prose peaked last (at a modal age of 50). When longevity and other variables were controlled for, the marked difference between the two types of prose shrank to an insignificant two years; but a significant tendency remained for poets to be more productive at a younger age than prose writers.

This poetry/prose difference is consistent with our intuition. Writing poetry has the reputation of being an activity of youth, actually a practice more likely to be associated with adolescence rather than even, as here, the thirties. In fact, the reasons for this stereotype may be the real reasons that achievement in this medium does flower earlier. We link both youth and poetry with subjectivity and deeply felt emotions and with playfulness, the attempt to break with established patterns, and flexibility (Simonton, 1975a). Writing a book, whether fiction or nonfiction, demands more discipline. Writing a novel (or even, as in our vignette, a short story) may require maturity, a knowledge of people and situations gained in part through life experience. How the art form itself fits in with individual development, then, may best explain the age differences in these types of literature.

The overwhelming impact of just the medium and the person on creative productivity was only emphasized by another finding of this interesting study. Though looking at very different cultures in widely divergent times, Simonton found an amazing similarity in his results. The peak modal ages for producing prose and poetry were the same in almost every culture and historical epoch, showing that environmental conditions or social norms have surprisingly little impact on at least these two major avenues for creative expression.

One aspect of this research may seem problematic: its findings are quite different from those presented in Table 5-2. According to the table, for example, production of informative prose (histories and other scholarly works) peaks in the sixties, a full decade later than is reported here. Ages of maximum productivity for novels and poetry are similarly older. One possibility is that this differential is caused by differences in what was being measured. Simonton measured high-quality work; Dennis, pure activity. If so, however, it seems that as a person ages, creative output may increase but its quality decline.

The *Age and Achievement* debate centered in part on just this issue. In response to Dennis's statistics on creative output, Lehman, the author of the controversial 1953 book, countered that data on mere activity in no way negated his results. True, output may rise or remain relatively constant as a person ages—but the production of good work still declines. Dennis disagreed. He asserted it was only reasonable to assume that more work equals more high-quality work too (1966). Logically, the number of major works should be a constant proportion of the total produced. It was partly to test the validity of these two contrasting contentions that the next study was devised.

In this investigation Simonton (1977a) examined the productivity of ten of the most eminent composers of classical music. Reasoning that ability increases with age but energy wanes, he predicted that as these creators advanced in years, the proportion of major works, rather than decreasing or remaining stable, should rise. Because age means less energy and motivation, fewer works should be produced; but because accumulated experience should mean enhanced competence, more of the works produced should be of high caliber.

Examining the ratio of major works to total works during each five-year period in the lives of these ten geniuses, Simonton found that the hypothesis of stability, or a constant proportion, best fit the data. In addition, for this most select sample possible, productivity was highest in the early thirties. After a steep rise to that age, it sloped off, but gradually.

This optimistic result mirrors that in our vignette, on a much grander scale. For musical geniuses, age far from equals obsolescence. True, there are some losses after the thirties; however, continued productivity and the production of highly creative work are the clear prevailing pattern throughout life.

### In the Sciences

If continued creativity occurs among the most brilliant innovators in music, then this has fascinating implications for a widespread belief among scientists. It is a widely held prejudice among scientists, particularly in the physical sciences and mathematics, that the great breakthroughs are made by people at a remarkably young age. Even the thirties are seen as the death knell of creativity; really important discoveries are expected to be made by the very young. To buttress their contention, the many people within and outside the scientific community who hold this idea cite the examples of Newton and Einstein. Both these geniuses formulated their revolutionary theories while only in their midtwenties.

This belief in early obsolescence may have particularly malignant effects when applied to scientific creativity. The support of the outside community is more crucial to achievement here than in the arts. If this idea is incorrectly institutionalized as fact, it may be more difficult for older scientists to get even good work accepted and, more important, to obtain the facilities and financial support necessary to make actual discoveries. We must disentangle the influence of variables other than pure creative capacity on achievement in the sciences; as with intelligence, ability-extraneous influences may load the dice against older scientists, making it falsely appear that they are less capable of doing high-quality work than the young.

One article (Reif & Strauss, 1965) makes a compelling case for the importance of some of these pressures, externals apart from competence that militate against creativity except early in a person's career. The authors' hypothetical scenario centers on the detrimental effect of rapid scientific discovery on older workers. Particularly in the physical sciences, the exponential accumulation of knowledge makes what students learn during their training relatively obsolete soon after they leave school. True, scientists may be up to date in the particular area that is the focus of their own research. However, if, as may be likely, their specialty goes out of fashion or their findings are eclipsed by others', they may find themselves at a dead end.

At this point, Reif and Strauss posit, the scientist has two alternatives: to change specialties or to go into nonresearch work. The first is much more difficult. Taking this road means one must reeducate oneself and compete with younger scientists who have enthusiasm and recent training in the new area. Besides, by this time the scientist probably has a family to support, and changing fields would mean taking a salary cut. The only reasonable alternative is to abandon research work and take a job in administration, public service, or private industry where the pressure to be creative is not as intense. In fact, even the most eminent scientists are prone to make this shift later in their careers. It may simply become too difficult to refuse the lucrative and prestigious positions outside research that are offered to these high achievers as a very consequence of their early creative competence itself.

A recent study implies that this hypothetical impetus away from research may actually exist. Shin and Putnam (1982) demonstrated what we might intuitively think to be true: the most prestigious nonresearch leadership positions in the academic community are usually occupied by people relatively late in their careers. Shin and Putnam looked at the mean age at selection of university presidents and the heads of national professional organizations such as the American Psychological Association. Examining the years 1901–1975 and using a sample of 12 of the most important universities and associations, they found a kind of reverse ageism. With a mean age at selection of about 51 for university presidents and 57 for the heads of associations, a kind of gerontocracy did exist. Furthermore, this situation is even more prevalent now. When data for the three successive 25-year periods were looked at separately, there was a clear trend toward older appointees over time, a tendency that could not be completely accounted for by age changes within the scientific community itself.

A second aspect of this research is relevant to the idea that it is in the hard sciences and particularly those that are most mathematical that creativity flowers early. The investigators also examined the mean age at selection of a third group, Nobel Prize winners. Recipients in physics, chemistry, and physiology or medicine, on the average, were in their early fifties—a full ten years younger than those who received this highest honor in literature. Considering that it takes some time after a discovery is made to win the award, we would suspect that these scientists had done their groundbreaking work at a relatively young age.

There was also a differential depending on the rigor of the particular science. Winners in physics tended to be a few years younger than those in chemistry. Recipients in chemistry were slightly younger than those in physiology or medicine. The variations here are quite small. However, they do fit in with the prevailing prejudice—and they had already been predicted by the following rationale.

Zuckerman and Merton (1972) had hypothesized some years earlier that the codifiability of a discipline should have a significant impact on the modal age at which discoveries are likely to be made. By **codifiability** they meant something almost identical to scientific rigor: the extent of consensus about the truth among workers in the field, the degree to which knowledge in the profession is encompassed into succinct theories rather than a mass of descriptive facts.

In more highly codified fields, they reasoned, several factors conspire to favor the young. The more compact body of knowledge makes it easier to master the content of the area at an early age. This very parsimony, as well as the high degree of consensus, also makes obsolescence a greater danger. Because more people are likely to be working on the same problem, an established individual's research is more likely to be challenged. When this challenge is successful, unlike the situation in a looser discipline, the work is immediately outmoded and definitively rendered wrong.

So the findings about Nobel Prize winners may be accurate because they make such good theoretical sense. But this means the gloomy predictions about older scientists and the *Age and Achievement* findings too may be correct. We cannot assume that the evidence discussed earlier on continued high output negates this possibility. It may be that in the sciences, unlike the arts, pure productivity is really unrelated to the production of high-quality work. Luckily, however, in the sciences too the presumption of an early loss in creativity has finally been put to rest. Furthermore, it has been disproved for the very group to whom it could have done the most harm, typical working scientists, not the tiny handful of geniuses at the top of each field.

The definitive investigation revealing that this idea is truly a myth (Cole, 1979) had two parts. First, Cole used a cross-sectional approach. He selected a random sample of scientists of varying ages and examined their productivity (both total output and production of high-quality work) over a five-year period. He chose disciplines within both the physical and social sciences for his analysis, to test the truth of the codification hypothesis as well.

Using as his index of quality the number of times a paper had been cited by others (information published in a reference work called the *Science Citation Index*) and automatically controlling for competitive advantage by focusing on a single time period, Cole discovered that age had only a slight curvilinear relation to creativity. Productivity usually rose to a peak in the early forties, leveled or declined slightly to about age 50, and then dropped off quite slowly after that. Furthermore, as was true in the study of eminent musicians, the curves for total output and for high-quality work, though differing in steepness, were quite similar. Contrary to the codification hypothesis, so were the general shapes of the curves for disciplines varying greatly in scientific rigor.

In his next phase Cole used a longitudinal strategy and chose one particular field, mathematics. He selected this specialty because here, even more than in any other science, youth is thought to be a prime requirement for creativity.

He selected a random group of mathematicians who had obtained their Ph.D.s between 1947 and 1950 and followed their careers for the next 25 years, looking once again at both total output and the production of high-quality work, gleaned from the *Science Citation Index*. Breaking down this span into five-year periods, he found a surprising and encouraging result. There was basically no change in the total level of scientific output over this period. Using the best measure to control for competitive advantage, the *Science Citation Index* of 1975 (the end of the 25-year period), there was also basically no change in production of high-quality work.

This careful research, then, offers powerful evidence of continued scientific creativity in later life. In fact, the findings concerning the mathematicians are particularly compelling because they show no decline in the very field where youth is believed to count the most. Perhaps if we looked longitudinally at the work of scientists in less rigorous disciplines, we would arrive at an even more encouraging result—more activity and better-caliber work in the later years.

So this is the answer to our major question about age and scientific creativity. However, we have neglected another of probably greater personal interest. Does high or low achievement tend to be a lifelong pattern? If a person is highly creative when young, how likely is this to continue through later life? Looking at age groups in the aggregate does not give us this information, but the very methodology used in the study of mathematicians can.

---

**BOX 5-2. Inherent Talent versus Positive Reinforcement and Scientific Creativity**

The fact of stable individual differences in productivity does not explain how these differences come about. One possibility is that strong publishers are inherently the most talented and able. Another idea, much less elitist, looks to the environment: those scientists whose initial efforts are reinforced will be motivated to continue to work. They will want to increase their output and also will be given the best resources to make further discoveries. Others whose initial effort does not get the hoped-for response will tend to publish less. Discouraged by their failure, they also will not have access to the facilities encouraging high-quality research.

One sign that reinforcement or "accumulative advantage" is indeed important might occur if we discovered productivity differences becoming increasingly unequal as a given cohort of scientists in a discipline aged. Though not negating the importance of inherent ability, this result would illustrate the truth of the adage "Success breeds success" as applied to the sciences.

In fact, among a sample of mathematicians, physicists, and chemists, this very pattern of increasing divergence was found. As the groups aged, after initial uniformity, there was more and more inequality. Strong publishers became stronger; weaker ones produced less. In some cases, the increasingly less productive scientists eventually stopped publishing at all (Allison & Stewart, 1974).

---

Because Cole was doing a longitudinal study, he could follow the publication patterns of individual mathematicians over the 25-year span, looking for evidence of just this consistency or change. He first classified the mathematicians as strong publishers, weak publishers, or nonpublishers on the basis of their publication records during one five-year period. Then he noted whether they maintained the same relative ranking during other periods.

This simple procedure showed that stability was the rule. Rarely did a scientist shift more than one category; almost half the sample never changed ranks at all. But does the same continuity occur beyond midlife, and is stability also characteristic of other aspects of behavior as a person ages? These are two of the main questions we will be considering in the next chapter.

## Summary

Memory decline is generally believed to be a universal concomitant of old age. Its existence has been documented in laboratory studies. These investigations, which almost always show older adults perform more poorly than the young, are usually designed to pinpoint the actual root of the deficit older adults show.

According to the current information-processing model, memory involves three stages, or stores. The first, called the sensory store, holds only a rapidly decaying, modality-specific copy of the incoming information. The amount of information that can be maintained in awareness at one time comprises the next store, called primary memory. When rehearsed, this information enters the third and most important memory system, secondary memory.

The elderly have impairments in secondary memory. Investigations have been designed to localize this deficit in one of three processes or in a combination of them: acquisition (getting information into the system), storage, or retrieval (getting information out of secondary memory). The fact that age differences are minimized on tests in which cues are given seems to suggest retrieval is at fault. Providing cues eliminates the need to retrieve information. However, an explanation involving poor acquisition can also account for this finding, as it seems impossible to empirically separate adequacy of learning, or acquisition, from retrieval. Actually there is evidence that suggests older people have deficits in their acquisition strategy too. Not only do they use poor techniques for memorizing information, but their performance is particularly deficient under pressure to learn and respond quickly.

These results suggest clear prescriptions for help: teach the elderly good encoding strategies and give them as much time to learn and remember material as possible. However, only rarely have laboratory memory studies translated into concrete ideas for intervention such as these. Making the transition from lab to life is difficult because researchers disagree about the nature of the deficit older people have. In addition, questions are increasingly being raised about the validity of academic memory studies.

Another reason memory-stage studies may not be helpful for an individual is that noncognitive influences may be causing the problem. Prime among these is poor morale. For instance, depression may produce both memory complaints and real deficits in performance. So, a comprehensive examination of many aspects of the person's psychological functioning needs to be made in order to know how best to intervene.

If the problem is specifically in a cognitive difficulty such as poor acquisition skills, then information gleaned from academic memory studies may be directly applied. Research has shown that pure practice may be helpful, so the older person might be given memory exercises to do regularly. Cognitive skill training—direct instruction in techniques to facilitate memorization—has also been shown to be effective. This type of training may be best done in groups so that members can reinforce one another for optimal performance.

A behavioral perspective suggests memory deficits may exist to some degree because of this very lack: the typical environment of the older person does not support optimal functioning. The environmental contribution to poor memory was demonstrated in studies in nursing homes, where both interpersonal and more tangible reinforcement contingent on good recall produced improvements in residents' memory. Even though these elderly subjects had pathological deficits and were living in an extremely impoverished setting, the same principle should apply to community-dwelling elderly with more minimal difficulties. It would help to have the environment not permit the development of excess disabilities.

On the surface, the fact that fluid intelligence declines after adulthood suggests that so may a person's chance of producing creative work. Originality and inventiveness seem at the core of both fluid intelligence and creativity. However, many other factors may be just as crucial in determining the age at which creativity is most likely to flower—some influences intrinsic to the individual, others to the special requirements of his or her chosen field.

The first effort to explore age/creativity relationships yielded depressing results. In an exhaustive examination of many areas of endeavor, one author demonstrated that the period of maximum creativity usually occurred quite early in a person's career. After the thirties, the probability of making a significant contribution rapidly declined. However, these findings are based on questionable methods. In another study controlling for some of these methodological problems, the age of peak creativity was shown to be much later, in the forties or fifties and in some cases even beyond. Furthermore, rather than rapidly declining, productivity usually sloped off only gradually, even at the oldest ages. These findings, however, pertained to amount of creative output, not, like the first, to high-quality work.

Two more recent studies examined age/creativity relationships in the arts. In the first, focusing on literature, the investigator found that the peak period for creative expression was earlier for poetry than for prose. High-quality poetry was most likely to be produced in the late thirties. For prose, the forties were the time of peak creativity. In a study of eminent composers, the thirties were the most creative time. However, for this sample of musical geniuses, there was only slight diminution of creative output with age.

A widely held prejudice, particularly in the physical sciences, is that older people are less capable of doing creative work. This idea is particularly dangerous, as it may deny older workers the resources to make scientific discoveries. Actually, the fact that knowledge in the sciences accumulates so rapidly may confer an advantage on younger workers. The older scientists' research is in danger of becoming obsolete. When this happens, or even when it does not, it is easier for older scientists to accept positions outside research.

Two definitive studies have shown that scientific creativity wanes little or not at all through midlife. The first, an investigation of scientists in six diverse disciplines, found only small declines in both productivity and the production of high-quality work with age. The second, a retrospective 25-year-long investigation of mathematicians, revealed no decline at all; this study also showed that individual scientists characteristically had stable productivity patterns.

## Key Terms

| | |
|---|---|
| *Paired-associate technique* | *Secondary memory* |
| *Free recall* | *Encoding, storage, and retrieval phases (or* |
| *Cued recall* | *stages)* |
| *Recognition* | *Mediators* |
| *Sensory store* | *Cognitive skill training* |
| *Primary memory* | *Codifiability of a field* |

# Recommended Readings

Cole, S. Age and scientific performance. **American Journal of Sociology**, 1979, *84,* 958–977.

*The two definitive studies described in this chapter, dispelling the idea that scientific creativity wanes with age. Moderately difficult.*

Craik, F. I. M. Age differences in human memory. In J. E. Birren & K. W. Schaie (Eds.), **Handbook of the psychology of aging**. New York: Van Nostrand Reinhold, 1977.

*Comprehensive review of laboratory research on memory and age. Difficult.*

Poon, L. W., Fozard, J. L., Cermak, L. S., Arenberg, D., & Thompson, L. (Eds.). **New directions in memory and aging**. Hillsdale, N.J.: Erlbaum, 1980.

*A diverse collection of highly technical articles. One section shows the different perspectives that experts bring to viewing and understanding age deficits in memory. Another section illustrates how memory research can be translated into giving practical help and how such practical programs might proceed. Difficult.*

# PART FOUR

# PERSONALITY

# CHAPTER SIX

# Internal Aspects of the Person: Change, Consistency, and Some Specifics

Within the past few years Mr. Smith, a 55-year-old factory supervisor, has noticed a definite change in his values and sense of priorities. Now he is just where he always wanted to be in his career, and yet he no longer has the same drive or need to achieve at work as he used to. For example, he has a good deal more paperwork to complete since his recent promotion but finds he is reluctant to take work home to finish on evenings and weekends. In contrast to his feelings just a few years ago, he is resentful of working more than a 40-hour week because that will interfere with time spent with his family.

This inner change seems particularly surprising, as it has upset some firmly held beliefs he has always had about himself. Mr. Smith always enjoyed working hard and felt that competitiveness and the need to achieve would be a driving force throughout his life. In part he connects this to the trauma of having grown up during the Depression. Besides, he still shamefully remembers his experience, as a young married man returning from the war, of not being able to adequately feed himself and his wife. He recalls the overwhelming relief he felt when his present company offered him a job, one that, though menial, offered security and a chance to advance. At that time he gladly gave up his dream of being a professional artist. His motivation never to be vulnerable like that again drove him to put in the long hours necessary to reach his present position from that of a messenger boy.

The interesting thing to Mr. Smith, however, is that even though he has always abhorred the prospect of being vulnerable in any respect, he is now willingly developing some traits that seem to fall into that category. He notices he does not really want to be in control in the same way he had before. In particular, this change is evident in his relationship with his wife. He was always the unquestioned boss in the house but now finds his authority eroding somewhat. At times he actually wants to defer to her. This transformation troubles him because he is no longer the utterly "masculine" person he always prided himself on being. But he cannot help seeing it simultaneously as a sign of maturity. At the very least, his new ability to compromise has led to a much more interesting marital relationship.

In fact, on balance he feels this new shift is a change for the better. He has lost his sense of power, certainty, and purpose, his zest in active combat, but he has also gained what he feels is a more balanced perspective on life. A perfect example is the election, in 1980. A few years earlier he would have been irate about the disturbing elitist trend it signaled—the country's willingness to retreat from the hard-won social gains his parents' generation fought to establish by electing Roosevelt. Now he is able to accept the current political climate with at least a measure of calm. His son feels this means he is becoming narcissistic, withdrawing from his former empathy and concern with the problems of others. Mr. Smith, however, would like to think it really means something very different. He knows from experience what he could not understand when he was younger. This conservative political trend too is a phase that will pass.

What is fascinating, though, is to puzzle over the reasons for this marked personality transformation. His bias is to assume it is a point of view gained simply from having lived 55 years, but he is willing to admit it also could be something else. The shift does seem to have coincided with that last promotion and that last child leaving for college. And he cannot discount the impact of his father's death last year in causing him to reevaluate his combative, work-oriented approach to life. Or it could simply be "hormones" or a subtle loss of physical stamina he has felt recently. Another possibility is that he is really preparing psychologically for retirement, even though he does not expect that event to occur for another ten years.

Not only is it impossible to assign a cause to his new orientation, but Mr. Smith also finds it impossible to determine how much he really has changed. He feels like a radically different person from who he was even ten years ago, but in his new, more measured spirit he can also entertain the idea that he has changed less than he thinks. This possibility, in fact, hit him particularly strongly when he recently met an old friend he had not seen for 15 years. During those years the friend had made a good deal of money, moved to London, and acquired a new wife. However, in spite of these radically different life circumstances, he seemed to have changed remarkably little. There were the same mannerisms, the same interests, even the same problems. At the neighborhood bar where they stopped to reacquaint themselves, the friend (though he did not know it) confided identical complaints about his second wife that Mr. Smith remembered having heard about the first. Mr. Smith certainly had learned more about life in this interval than his friend. He could not help wondering about this, though, when the friend had the nerve to say as they parted "I'm amazed at how little you've mellowed since I last saw you. You seem to have the same intense commitment to your work, dominant relationship with your wife, and strongly held political ideas you did before."

Nowhere is the need for the pluralistic life-span developmental approach in the psychology of aging more evident than in the area of personality. In research examining how people's values, interests, needs, and activities change in the latter part of life, we find support for most of the theories described in Chapter 1. Most important, as implied in our vignette, we find diversity in development, change coexisting with stability, decremental signs and their opposite. This research evidence, in particular that from a landmark study of personality and the theory and controversy it spawned, is described in the first part of this chapter.

Our general focus on change and consistency, however, misses some crucial specifics, ingrained ideas most of us have about the way an older adult's whole orientation is likely to differ from a younger person's. Two of these most commonly held beliefs are spelled out in the ageism quotation at the beginning of this book: that sex is not important in old age, in contrast to youth; and that older people think a good deal, actually excessively, about the past. So, rather than catalogue how more limited aspects of personality may change in older adults, in the second half of the chapter I have chosen to focus just on these two general facets of behavior. Because they are such crucial components of the stereotype of old age, it seems particularly important to examine research on late-life sexuality and thoughts about the past in a quite complete, in-depth way.

## Change and Stability in Personality and Lifestyle

### *The Kansas City Studies of Adult Life: Focus on Change*

The first comprehensive, and probably the most influential, investigation specifically of personality and social behavior in middle and later life was undertaken in the mid-1950s by a team of social scientists at the University of Chicago. These investigators (Cumming & Henry, 1961; Neugarten & Associates, 1964) were interested in some questions that were theorized about at the time but whose answers were virtually unknown: How do attitudes, activities, and general personality processes change as a person makes the transition from middle to old age? To get their data, they chose a typical urban American environment, Kansas City, and used a fairly specific group of Americans, noninstitutionalized White males and females aged 40 to 90 from all social-status levels who were in good health.

Eventually over 700 people participated in the Kansas City Studies of Adult Life. The first study, from which almost all the information on personality was culled, was cross-sectional. The second phase was a short (six-year) longitudinal investigation involving several rounds of testings.

To measure personality, the researchers used objective tests, interviews, and, because their orientation was psychoanalytic, a projective measure designed to tap unconscious processes, the Thematic Apperception Test (TAT). From the first two types of data they found evidence suggesting that a person's basic style of personality remains stable from middle to old age. However, when they used the TAT, their test measuring aspects of personality that lie further below the surface, they found fascinating evidence of change. They therefore concluded that while the outer, more conscious, or what they called "socioadaptational" aspects of personality remain stable as a person ages, some inner, unconscious, or what are called "intrapsychic" processes might not. The researchers found these intrapsychic shifts by using the TAT in a nontraditional way.

**Intrapsychic Changes.**   The TAT is typically used to diagnose psychological problems in clinical (mental health) settings (see Chapter 8). The test consists of a series of pictures, which a clinical psychologist shows to the patient one by one. The patient, instructed by the examiner to tell a story about each scene, is believed to reveal his or her unconscious concerns and world view by the type of story told.

In evaluating a patient's TAT responses, clinical psychologists usually want to get as complete a picture as possible of psychological functioning and so look for general patterns that emerge in the material. In contrast, the Chicago researchers were looking for just those ways personality might change in normal adults as they aged, so they looked only at certain delimited aspects of the Kansas City respondents' stories.

They discovered that age differences in the stories suggested that two major changes were occurring in psychological functioning. The first was a shift toward what they called **interiority** (Neugarten, 1964). It seemed that as people aged, they became increasingly less interested in the outside world and more preoccupied with themselves. This change toward interiority was revealed by differences in the "ego energy" and "mastery style" of older subjects' stories.

By **ego energy** the investigators (Rosen & Neugarten, 1964) meant the extent to which a story reflected active, energetic involvement in life rather than passivity and withdrawal. They measured this dimension by noting whether protagonists not actually on the TAT card were introduced, whether conflict was described, and what level of action and intensity of feeling the stories contained. In three successively older age groups (40–49, 50–59, and 64–71) there was a steady decline in ego-energy ratings. Older respondents told stories that involved less conflict, contained less feeling and activity, and were more confined to characters actually on the card. This meant, according to the theory underlying the test, that an unconscious pulling back from active involvement in life was occurring at least by late middle age.

The dimension called **mastery style** was somewhat different (Gutmann, 1964). Here another change suggestive of interiority seemed to be occurring. Subjects' stories were categorized under three mastery styles that formed a continuum from most to least involved in competently mastering the environment and so most to least psychologically healthy. Stories having an active mastery theme portrayed protagonists who achieved success (or at least viewed success as possible) on the basis of competence and one's own initiative. In those having a passive mastery orientation, the hero, even if he or she was successful, triumphed because of luck or the help of others, not his or her own efforts. In other words, these two types of stories represented very different world views. In the first, the locus of control and power was in the person; in the second, the individual was frail and at the mercy of the vagaries of the environment.

Responses having the third orientation, magical mastery, were judged the least adaptive and healthy. These stories ignored or misinterpreted the actual scene on the card, indicating that the storyteller had retreated from the outside world to such an extent as to forgo reality in favor of fantasy.

The following description of types of stories told in response to one TAT card (adapted from Gutmann, 1969, pp. 12–13) illustrates the three mastery themes. The card depicts a vigorous, muscular figure, possibly nude, who could be going up or down a rope.

*Active Mastery Story Types**

1. The hero demonstrates his strength usually in successful competition. However, the rope may break at the moment of triumph, and the respondent may deride the hero as a showoff.

---

*Adapted from *The Country of Old Men: Cultural Studies in the Psychology of Later Life*, by D. Gutmann. Copyright 1969 by The Institute of Gerontology, University of Michigan-Wayne State University. Reprinted by permission.

2. The hero strives vigorously, sometimes zestfully, toward a self-determined productive goal. He does not compete against others or flaunt his strength.

*Passive Mastery Story Types*
1. The hero is immobilized by environmental forces that do not collaborate with his action or that block it—the rope is slack, the cliff is slippery.
2. The hero is threatened by destructive external forces or forces turned against himself (suicidal), or he is out of control and a threat to others (homicidal).
3. The hero climbs, though without much involvement, for conventional purposes.
4. The hero lacks force to match his purpose; he is tired or ill.
5. The hero has pleasure or security-seeking purposes: he plays on the rope or climbs to see something, to get food, and so on.

*Magical Mastery Story Types*
1. The hero is not erect, the rope is not a rope.

Mastery styles showed the same shift with age as ego energy. In the three successively older groups, more and more stories had passive or magical mastery themes.

Taken together, these findings suggested to the research team that, as part of a natural developmental process in late middle age, individuals begin to withdraw psychologically from involvement with the external world. Even though they may, as in our vignette, be at the pinnacle of a career, they become less interested in activity and achievement. From a traditional psychoanalytic perspective, this shift to interiority, because it signals passivity and a lessened appreciation of reality, is pathological. However, the investigators felt it may not have this meaning when we look at it as a preparation for life's last stage (Gutmann, 1969). The researchers viewed this shift as adaptive, a necessary emotional precursor enabling a person to accept the role losses and limitations in activity to occur several years later, in the sixties and seventies.

The second intrapsychic change the investigators found was elicited by using a specially drawn TAT card picturing a young man, a young woman, an old man, and an old woman (Neugarten & Gutmann, 1964). There were fascinating age differences when subjects were asked to describe the older figures. Whereas younger Kansas City subjects (age 40–54) portrayed the characters' personalities in a stereotypical way, seeing the male as aggressive and dominant and the female as gentle and submissive, for the older group (age 55–70) this description was reversed. Older subjects saw the woman as the powerful, controlling figure; the man was viewed as passive, submissive, and sweet. The researchers concluded that, probably because of the same intrinsic developmental process, an inversion of sex roles occurs in late life. "Women as they age seem to become more tolerant of their own aggressive egocentric impulses; whereas men as they age of their own nurturant and affiliative impulses" (Neugarten & Gutmann, 1964, p. 89).

**Conclusions and Cautions.**    These two changes, toward interiority and toward an inversion in sex roles, echo in an almost uncanny way Jung's clinical hunches (see Chapter 1). Jung hypothesized that exactly these two personality shifts should occur in midlife, although he viewed interiority in an unambiguously positive way, as a progressive development toward greater maturity. These changes were the ones that puzzled Mr. Smith—his decreasing interest in achievement, his increasing sense of vulnerability, his perception of a difference in his marital relationship.

The Kansas City findings, however, though fascinating, are based on 25-year-old cross-sectional data. Even the ideas of the cohort doing the research seem dated. In the 1980s there is simply not the same emphasis on defined sex roles there was in the late 1950s. Also, today psychologists are less likely to assume that the theory underlying the TAT is correct—that a person reveals a basic personality or unconscious world view by the types of stories he or she tells. In addition, the researchers' inference of interiority based on their categorization scheme seems suspect for other reasons. For example, the ego-energy dimension is highly vulnerable to criticisms of not being valid. It may not reflect real-life withdrawal; it just as easily could be tapping something else. For instance, older subjects may have received lower ratings on this scale because, being less comfortable taking tests (see Chapters 4 and 5), they produced more concrete and so less energetic stories. The features of TAT stories used as indexes of ego energy might easily be, in truth, indexes of verbal fluency or literary ability, both of which may also differ by age because of simple cohort differences in years of schooling. For these reasons we must view the Kansas City research with caution and look carefully for evidence that corroborates its results (see Box 6-1).

A final important issue this research raises is that of causality. At least originally the Kansas City researchers suggested these changes were universal and internally programmed. They were independent of external contingencies that might operate in a particular society to engender them (Neugarten, 1977). However, as most cultures do encourage older adults to withdraw from active involvements and may also implicitly foster the sex-role reversal the researchers found, this conclusion is not necessarily warranted. The question of what may cause these changes, if in fact they do currently occur, is unanswered. It is the fascinating one Mr. Smith was grappling with in our vignette.

**Lifestyle Changes.**    In the other area they were looking at, age changes in activities, the researchers also found shifts. These differences in actual external involvements paralleled the internal progression to interiority but happened about ten years later.

From about the midsixties on, the average number of roles that older age groups had, such as "mother" or "worker," decreased steadily. Successively older groups spent progressively more time alone each day. They had fewer and fewer contacts per month. In addition, their whole attitude toward life suggested they had pulled back from an interest in external involvements. This lifestyle change, in conjunction with its equivalent intrapsychic harbinger, led two of the research-

**BOX 6-1.    Support for the Kansas City Findings**

More recent studies using different populations and different measures have tended to support the validity of the Kansas City results. For example, as part of a large cross-sectional study done in the late 1960s examining a group of lower-middle-class Americans at different life transition points, Lowenthal, Thurnher, Chiriboga, and Associates (1975) discovered that the oldest men tested, those in their early sixties and at the brink of retirement, had a very different set of values than the younger men. Like the late-middle-aged males in the Kansas City sample, they were more interested in interpersonal than in work-oriented concerns. They too were more interested in easy contentment than in active struggle.

Another piece of research, this time examining life-span changes in daydreams among men and women, found a parallel shift. There was a decline in the frequency of achievement-oriented daydreams (and daydreaming in general) in older men. Also corroborating the Kansas City findings, achievement-oriented themes in women's daydreams became more prominent after age 40 (Gambria, 1979–80).

Cross-cultural studies using the Kansas City methodology for measuring mastery style have demonstrated the same change toward passive and magical mastery among older men in several primitive societies (Gutmann, 1969). Diverse cultures share the idea that older women are assertive and older men passive (Gutmann, 1977). All these instances suggest the Kansas City results are not peculiar to this sample or artifacts of invalid indexes. These changes may, as the researchers suggest, be universal, operating in very different societies at very different times.

Still, we should remain cautious. A good test of at least the sex-role finding of the Kansas City research awaits a longitudinal study of today's young adults. What impact do current shifts in women's and men's traditional roles have on the characteristics and concerns of the sexes, both in early adulthood and as they age?

ers (Cumming & Henry, 1961) to formulate a hypothesis that has perhaps been the most hotly debated and strongly criticized idea about aging in the field—
*disengagement theory.*

### *Disengagement: The Hypothesis and the Debate*

**Assumptions of the Theory.**    According to this now-famous theory, in late life there is

> an inevitable mutual withdrawal or disengagement resulting in decreased interaction between the aging person and others in the social system he belongs to. . . . When the aging process is complete the equilibrium which existed in middle life between the individual and his society has given way to a new equilibrium character-

ized by a greater distance and altered type of relationship [Cumming & Henry, 1961, pp. 14–15].

Looking carefully at this statement, we can see that disengagement is viewed as a universal process intrinsic to a person's being chronologically at the last stage of life. Furthermore, although the quotation does not state its basic worth, the strong implication is that because it is normal, it is best or ideal for older people to disengage.

The validity of all these assumptions has been questioned. There is evidence contradicting the idea that disengagement predictably occurs in late life. There is a study refuting the idea that it is basic simply to chronological age. Finally, and most important, there has been a tremendous controversy about the last assumption of the theory in particular—that disengaging from the world is the ideal way for an older person to live.

**Critique and an Alternative Theory.** Findings from the Duke study (among others) show that disengagement does not always occur. Over a ten-year span the Duke researchers (Palmore, 1968) found no reduction in volunteers' external activities, particularly among males. Even though many men retired during the study and so lost a major role, they compensated for this change by increasing their involvements in other areas. This finding of no decrease even over this long period is clearly discrepant from what the theory would predict.

The Duke elderly, as we know, were a relatively physically elite group. In fact, in cross-sectional studies testing more disabled older people, evidence of disengagement is often the rule. This implies that, far from being part of some inner timetable tied to chronological age, the process may really be engendered by stresses that are more likely to befall a person as he or she gets older.

In fact, this was shown to be so when two researchers (Tallmer & Kutner, 1969) correlated indexes of disengagement with a variety of age-associated difficulties, such as being widowed or being in poor health. Among the large group of people they tested, they discovered that it was these changes that were associated with disengagement, not age itself. True, disengagement did occur with increasing frequency at older ages, but this did not mean it was simply a function of a person's having lived a certain number of years.

If a person withdraws from society partly in response to often-negative life events, though, then being disengaged may be far from an ideal state of affairs; so the third assumption of the theory too seems wrong. Actually, this final postulate, that disengagement is best, is counterintuitive. Older people themselves are more likely to view its opposite, "keeping active," as the key to successful aging. For this reason, and because particularly this tenet of the theory seemed to justify the ageist practice of forcing people to withdraw from society in late life (Cath, 1979), another idea about optimal aging was almost immediately proposed. It is called *activity theory.*

Activity theory is the exact opposite of the disengagement point of view. This hypothesis states that being involved in a variety of roles and activities is the ideal way for an older person to approach life. The theory also makes a clear prediction about activity and morale: older people who are active should be more satisfied than those who are disengaged (Lemon, Bengston, & Peterson, 1972).

**The Activity/Disengagement Controversy.**    A good deal of effort in the years immediately after these hypotheses appeared was devoted to testing which statement about ideal aging was accurate. Early on it was found that a good test of the competing conceptions was not so easily made. For one thing, the activity/disengagement continuum was not unitary. Being highly involved with family was unrelated to the extent to which a person was involved in other areas of life (Carp, 1968). Moreover, the indexes used to tap engagement were themselves far from perfect. Simple quantitative measures like number of contacts an individual had with others per week were being used to assess a really more emotional phenomenon—how intensely involved in the outside world a person felt. Even more basic, it soon became obvious that the whole argument itself was much too simplistic. Although most studies did reveal a small positive relationship between activity and morale, as we might imagine from the simple fact of its being related to morale-elevating influences like being in good health (Larson, 1978), others generally did not (Lemon et al., 1972). Clearly disengagement was best for some people and activity was best for others.

Personality, as we might imagine, is central to understanding who will be most satisfied being active or disengaged (George, 1978). This was first demonstrated in a further study done by the Chicago group using the Kansas City subjects. Neugarten, Havighurst, and Tobin (1968) looked at levels of activity and life satisfaction in relation to a person's basic personality style. Among the most well-adjusted, or what they called "integrated," respondents, they found a mix of active and disengaged elderly people, all highly satisfied with life. In the least psychologically healthy, or what they called "unintegrated," personality types in their sample, disengagement coupled with low morale was the rule. So a person's life satisfaction seemed a function not of activity level itself but of who he or she was. Disengagement could be a highly satisfying lifestyle in a well-adjusted person; it could also be an unhappy way of life in a disturbed individual.

Looking at activity or disengagement in this context also showed the researchers something else of importance. Certain people seemed to be disproportionately active or disengaged. The Kansas City subjects classified as "armored defended" individuals, who were highly achievement-oriented but also kept their feelings under tight control, were likely to maintain a high level of activity. Those typed as "passive-dependent" were more likely to be the opposite. So it became clear that disengagement, far from being either universal or just dependent on life events, was also a freely chosen option. It was something embraced or discarded in part because it fit a person's preferred way of conducting his or her life.

The Chicago research implies what seems only logical. It is unrealistic to view personality and lifestyle in old age in a vacuum, as if people reached late life shorn of their former habits, traits, and needs. The way individuals act after their 65th birthday is likely to be compatible with the way they shaped their lives before.

This brings us to a topic so far largely neglected in our discussion—the extent to which a person remains the same as he or she ages.

### *Focus on Stability*

This chapter's vignette illustrates a common perception when talking with old friends we have not seen in a long time. We are often struck by the fact that in many ways they seem to have changed little. This idea, that in large part personality during adulthood does not change, is also central to psychoanalytic theory. As discussed in Chapter 1, traditional psychoanalysts have little interest or belief in late-life development. They feel personality is fixed and remains basically the same from childhood. To test the truth of this last assumption would be too heroic a task. However, the Duke Longitudinal Study does provide us with information relevant to the more limited question implied at the end of our vignette: How much do adults really change as they age?

Duke researchers (Maddox & Douglass, 1974) did not examine this question in a complete way but only measured stability in certain aspects of their respondents' behavior over a ten-year period in relation to others in the sample. However, in the areas they did look at, consistency did appear to be the rule. For example, elderly subjects rated as depressed tended to remain depressed in subsequent testings (see Chapter 8). They maintained their relative rankings on measures of life satisfaction as well as other attitudes. As mentioned earlier, their activity levels also tended to remain the same. All in all, the Duke research offered a good deal of evidence of continuity in adult life, at least over a short period. This finding has been corroborated in the few studies that have longitudinally measured aspects of adult personality over even longer periods (Costa, McCrae, & Norris, 1981; Leon, Gillum, Gillum, & Gouze, 1979).

That a person's way of approaching life may survive even what seems to be a profound situational change is shown by an interesting study of the publication patterns of retired professors. Havighurst, McDonald, Maeulen, and Mazel (1979) compared the number of publications a large group of social scientists had produced since retirement with their publication level in the years just before. They found a striking degree of consistency between these two figures. People who were highly prolific before retirement continued to be highly productive after. Those who had had fewer publications earlier also maintained this pattern. In fact, the act of formally retiring itself had little impact on the publication activities of the most productive of the social scientists. They continued to be just as interested in research and writing as they had been before.

As was true of the mathematicians described in Chapter 5, there were signs of quite long-term stability in the subjects' way of life. The highly prolific professors, it was discovered, had become interested in and established in their careers earlier than those whose postretirement publication level was low. This implies that their high productivity also had been a lifelong pattern, one that developed early and then was maintained through adulthood and into retirement.

For college professors, however, there are two forces operating to encourage maintaining the same style of life after retirement. Professors are usually working because their job is intrinsically pleasurable, and there are no barriers to continuing the same activity if they want to even after being formally retired. As few occupations have these dual continuity-enhancing attributes, we might expect that for other workers retirement may cause a more abrupt change in the way they live.

This point raises the idea that diversity should be the real key to understanding the degree to which people change or remain the same in adulthood. Individuals may change to either a little or a great degree as they age, depending on who they are, the events they have been exposed to, and the particular aspects of personality or lifestyle examined. Also it seems likely that, as in our vignette, some may evolve or develop in a positive way and some may change for the worse.

For this reason it seems appropriate to end our discussion with an example that captures this diversity: the sole in-depth longitudinal investigation of personality and lifestyle that spans a 40-year period during adulthood (Maas & Kuypers, 1975).

### Follow-Up of the Berkeley Guidance and Growth Study Parents: Change and Stability

As part of two large-scale studies of infant development and parent/child interactions, a good deal of information had been gathered about the lives of a large group of upper-middle-class parents of children born in Berkeley, California, in 1928. Researchers in the 1960s therefore had an unusual opportunity to examine these people in their seventies and see how their current personalities and ways of life might relate to their personalities and lifestyles as young adults. Restrictions in this sample, the need to make inferences from very different measures, and other problems make any conclusions from this research highly tenuous and speculative. However, the findings reveal some fascinating insights into factors producing consistency and change as adults age.

On the basis of their 1960s interviews and tests, the researchers grouped the subjects, looking at males and females separately, into several lifestyle types and several personality types (see Table 6-1 for examples). Using this typology, they then looked for early adult antecedents of these late-life patterns of living and personality styles.

Maas and Kuypers did find a good deal of continuity in lifestyle over this long span, but only for fathers. For example, "hobbyist" fathers as young adults had always been highly active in projects outside the home and never family-centered. The "unwell-disengaged" had been sickly even in their early thirties. In contrast, the lifestyles of the mothers more often changed radically. Among these shifts were two particularly interesting ones.

Mothers now typed as having "work-centered" lifestyles, characterized by high energy and high commitment to a job, were discovered as young adults to often

**TABLE 6-1.**    Examples of two personality and three lifestyle groups for mothers and fathers.

| | Group Label | Characteristic Items |
|---|---|---|
| **Personality (Five groups in total for mothers; four for fathers)** | | |
| *Mothers* | Person-oriented | Behaves in giving way; sympathetic or considerate; has warmth; is compassionate; arouses liking and acceptance. |
| | Fearful-ordering | Basically submissive; favors conservative values; uncomfortable with uncertainty, complexity; basically anxious. |
| *Fathers* | Person-oriented | Behaves in giving way; cheerful; dependable and responsible; straightforward, forthright, candid; productive, gets things done; submissive. |
| | Active-competent | Interesting, arresting person; critical; skeptical, not easily impressed; rebellious and nonconforming; verbally fluent; masculine in style and manner. |
| **Lifestyle (Six groups in total for mothers; four for fathers)** | | |
| *Mothers* | Husband-centered | Life focused on husband and marriage. |
| | Uncentered | Few interests; nonengagement with others in giving or receiving relationship; most not married. |
| | Work-centered | Highly involved with and satisfied with work. |
| *Fathers* | Family-centered | Life revolves around marriage, parenting, and grandparenting. |
| | Hobbyist | Leisure-time interests and activities most important. |
| | Unwell-disengaged | Ill, withdrawn; unsatisfied with life and marriage. |

*(Source: Adapted from* From Thirty to Seventy, *by H. S. Maas and J. Kuypers. Copyright 1975 by Jossey-Bass, Inc., Publishers. Reprinted by permission.)*

have been depressed and apathetic. It seemed as if their early adult life circumstances, as full-time housewives, never quite fit their real talents or interests. When freed of this role in late life, then they could truly blossom. In contrast, another group called the "uncentered," who were unfocused and unhappy as older adults, had been highly satisfied in their job of young housewife. Unfortunately, they were unable to replace their formerly family-centered way of life when circumstances demanded that they change. Being unsuited to and unable to adapt to their new life situation (usually widowhood), they were floundering in old age.

The researchers explained these differing patterns of continuity and change for males and females as due to differences in the extent to which external circumstances shifted for each sex. For example, other than retirement, no marked external events had occurred that might have operated to change the life patterns of these all still-married men. In contrast, there were often radical changes in what the researchers called "contexts" for women, external contingencies that forced alterations in the way they lived. For example, in later life some of the women had to enter the job market for the first time to make ends meet. They could no longer live lives focused on their families, as their children had left home and often their spouses had died. So these greater context differences seemed to account for the greater change specifically in the way the women lived.

In contrast to the sex differences in lifestyle, personality consistency was more evident among women than men. This difference seemed really an artifact, a function of the fact that stability was most evident in older adults who had pathological late-life personalities, and unfortunately more among the group of women were typed in this way. In an extremely provocative finding, better-functioning men and women showed little similarity to who they had been as young adults. However, there were clear early adult antecedents for those whose older adult personalities were the poorest functioning. In this group, poor adaptation and coping was a consistent pattern. This had also been clearly in evidence from early adulthood.

To summarize, this limited and fragmentary study illuminates what we intuitively might think should be true: there are likely to be diverse patterns of stability and change in personality and lifestyle throughout adulthood. In addition, it suggests some possibilities for predicting when change or stability may be most likely. Radically different external circumstances, not unexpectedly, seem to force lifestyle changes. In the absence of these change-inducing forces, a person's basic interests and activities are more likely to remain the same. In addition, psychopathology in particular in late life seems to have clear early adult antecedents. This finding, if accurate, has the clear practical implication for our working to change psychological problems we may have as soon as we can.

## Specific Aspects of Personality and Lifestyle

### Sexuality

Sexuality encompasses many diverse behaviors, ways of acting that are, for some of us, life's greatest pleasures. These include not just having sexual relations but the enjoyment we get from dressing to look sexually attractive, from flirting, from fantasy. For many of us the idea that we are sexually appealing is central to our way of thinking about ourselves. Much of the way we relate to the other sex has an underlying sexual theme.

All these ways of behaving, though, are expected to change at a certain age. There is an ill-defined but definitely evident time beyond which there is at least subtle pressure to forgo all expressions of sexuality lest a person feel, at the minimum, faintly uncomfortable and, at the extreme, grotesque. Simply put, older people, particularly older women, are still often expected to be asexual. Even in our anti-Victorian age we still have some very firmly held ideas that sexuality in late life is abnormal and even a cause for disgust.

This assumption of asexuality is highly evident when we look at a good barometer of our attitudes and anxieties, the jokes we tell. Palmore (1971a) copied jokes about aging from various anthologies and sorted them according to their content. Jokes about late life not infrequently had a sexual theme. Many dealt with the waning sexual abilities of the older person or with surprising evidence that they were intact. An example of the latter is the following (Cumming & Henry, 1961, p. 18):

> An old man who had just married a twenty-year-old went to his doctor for advice because he wanted to keep his bride happy. . . . The doctor advised him to get a young female companion for his wife as a roomer in their home. Three months later the doctor saw the old fellow again. "How's your wife?" the doctor inquired. "Fine, she's pregnant." "And your roomer?" "Well, she's pregnant, too!"

It is apparent that even this most positive example of elderly sexuality is really negative. The joke would not be funny if told about a younger person. Its humor resides in its being so unexpected; older people are simply not believed to be this sexually active or capable.

The problem with the idea of incapacity and related assumptions about sexuality in old age is that, as with any stereotype, they limit people to behaving in a certain way. Moreover, these fixed beliefs serve as self-fulfilling prophecies, at least to some extent engendering the very behavior they predict. Having sexual desires, wanting to act on those feelings, and being able to respond adequately in a sexual situation are intimately dependent on how a person feels about himself or herself. If older adults are told, even by innuendo, that they are sexually unattractive or incapable, than this can only have the most negative effect on their interest, activity, and actual behavior.

So, understanding that it is impossible to tease out the impact of this external, societal view on the person from true decrements that result from age, let us now look first at the last aspect of sexuality just mentioned—actual sexual behavior.

**Age Changes in the Sexual Response.**    As is well known, Masters and Johnson (1966) were the first to investigate the actual physiology of the sexual response. Among the approximately 700 subjects who consented to engage in sexual behavior in the laboratory and so furnish data for their landmark study of normal sexuality were a small group, 39 couples, in which at least one partner was over 50. Masters and Johnson called these couples their geriatric sample. However, only 20 of these men and 11 of the women really deserved this name, being over age 60.

In view of the particularly strong cultural prohibitions for this cohort against volunteering for such studies, we might expect that, even more than Masters and Johnson's other subjects, their "geriatric sample" was a highly select group. These volunteers were probably much more sexually sophisticated than their similar-aged peers. Their responses, then, probably show us more what is possible in sexual performance as one ages than what is typical, and how this compares with what is physiologically more likely in youth.

Looking at the women first, there were several changes in what might be seen as the intensity of sexual responsiveness. In the older women, for example, breast size did not increase with sexual arousal, as it does in the young. The sex flush (a pinkish rash that normally occurs as part of sexual excitement) was not as prevalent. Contraction of the rectal sphincter during orgasm, generally an indication of an intense orgasmic experience, rarely occurred.

In all older women there are general changes in the vagina that occur after menopause and may affect the sexual response. As a result of decreased hormone levels at menopause, the walls of the late-middle-aged woman's vagina become thinner, pinkish rather than reddish, and generally more fragile. The vagina also becomes shorter and narrower and loses some of its expansive ability (Corby & Solnick, 1980; Weg, 1978). In addition, Masters and Johnson's observations revealed that the rate and amount of vaginal lubrication during sexual arousal were

---

**BOX 6-2.  Age Differences in Attitudes toward the Sexual Consequences of Menopause**

Except for causing the changes mentioned in the text that may make intercourse more painful, there is little evidence that menopause, with its marked drop in estrogen and progesterone levels, negatively affects sexuality. However, many people do assume that, for either physical or psychological reasons, it does have detrimental consequences, particularly for sexual desire. Research shows that the likelihood of a woman's having this idea depends on her age.

Neugarten, Wood, Kraines, and Loomis (1968) devised a questionnaire tapping perceptions of menopause and administered it to women of different ages. Respondents were asked whether they agreed or disagreed with statements about how menopause affects a woman in many areas of her life. Among the statements were two about its sexual impact: "If the truth were really known, most women would like to have themselves a fling at this time in their lives" and "After menopause a woman is more interested in sex than she was before."

As we might have guessed, the younger, still-menstruating women were in many respects more negative about how women felt during and after this change than those who had undergone or were currently reaching menopause. These more negative perceptions extended to the sexual area. Only 8% of the youngest women (aged 21–30) agreed with the first statement about menopausal women's sexuality and 14% with the second. Among women of typical menopausal age or actually in the process of undergoing menopause (aged 45–55), the comparable figures were 32% and 35%.

The percentages just mentioned show that women likely to be undergoing menopause have very mixed sexual reactions to the experience. Compared with the percentages for 21–30-year-olds, they also reveal that the sexual effects of menopause are viewed by younger women in an excessively gloomy light. As one older participant in the study creatively put it, experience in this area allows a person "to separate the old wives' tales from that which is true of old wives" (Neugarten et al., 1968, p. 200).

less in their older subjects. These changes make intercourse more painful for some older women and so may lessen sexual enjoyment and even cause some women to avoid sex.

However, the researchers found only minor age changes in responses most clearly indicative of female sexual performance and pleasure. For example, the clitoral response to sexual stimulation was virtually unchanged. This is important because the clitoris is generally thought to be the actual center of sexual arousal. Also, the older women were just as capable of orgasms as the younger group. On the average, though, they did have fewer orgasmic contractions and less prolonged orgasms than the young.

Interestingly, this last difference was not true of the three most sexually active older women in the sample. Their orgasmic response was indistinguishable from the 20- to 30-year-olds', and these women responded to stimulation with as copious and rapid vaginal lubrication as the young adults. This may mean only that this small group was particularly highly physiologically elite. However, it also implies that in the sexual arena, as elsewhere, some of what look like pure aging effects may be in part the effects of practice. The limited instances in which older women did appear to be less responsive may have been due to some extent to their engaging in sex less frequently. Regular sexual activity, then, like other forms of exercise (see Chapter 3), may be an antidote to physiological losses that occur with age.

To summarize, Masters and Johnson's findings on the sexual response in the aging female were quite positive. They showed only relatively minor changes in responsiveness compared with the young. The investigators concluded with a brief but important statement: "There is no time limit drawn by advancing years to female sexuality" (Masters & Johnson, 1966, p. 247).

Their findings were not as encouraging for men. The males they studied did show pronounced physiological changes. Some were similar to the auxiliary ones experienced by the women, a loss in the sex flush and fewer rectal-sphincter contractions at orgasm. Unlike the women, however, the men also showed changes entailing clear differences in coital behavior itself.

There were a variety of changes in the erectile response. The older men took longer to have erections. Once attained, their erections could be maintained for a longer time without ejaculating. These differences actually are signs of an overall decline in the resilience of the erectile system, a fact demonstrated by a later piece of research.

In this more recent study (cited in Solnick, 1978), using a device attached to the penis, investigators directly measured the erectile responses of samples of young men (aged 19–30) and older men (aged 48–65) as the groups watched an erotic movie. Erections occurred, on the average, six times as fast in the younger men, and the whole character of their responsiveness differed. They could rapidly achieve and then partially lose an erection only to respond rapidly again when stimulated by another scene. In contrast, the older men tended to achieve an erection gradually and steadily and were slower to rebound after a partial loss. Moreover, their erections never reached the maximum levels measured in the younger subjects.

Masters and Johnson's research also showed that the ejaculatory process was different in the older male. The older men had much less intense ejaculations. If a man had maintained an erection over a long period, ejaculation sometimes resulted in a seepage of seminal fluid rather than an expulsion.

Penile detumescence after orgasm was very rapid in Masters and Johnson's older subjects. Rather than occurring in two distinct stages, as in the young, it appeared to happen all at once. Finally, many males in their middle and late fifties and their sixties found they could not redevelop an erection for some 12 to 24 hours after a previous ejaculation. This too was in marked contrast to the younger men.

Taken together, though, these changes far from suggest that the sexual response is absent in older men. In fact, because erections can be maintained longer before ejaculation need occur, it has been suggested that the older man may even, from the woman's point of view, be a superior sexual partner (see Corby & Solnick, 1980). This evidence, coupled with the more encouraging data for older women, should give us a framework for looking at studies examining the two other aspects of sexuality mentioned earlier—the degree of sexual interest and activity reported by older adults.

**Sexual Interest and Activity.**   Getting accurate information about the extent of sexual interest and activity in any age group can be problematic. First, a researcher must get people to agree to answer questions about this normally most private topic. Those who do, as in Masters and Johnson's research, may be a more capable subgroup of the cohort at large. In addition, during these interviews, the temptation to be less than honest may be particularly strong. Questions about sexual feelings and behavior may be not just embarrassing but often central to one's self-esteem.

These problems are only magnified when an investigator's subjects are elderly (Botwinick, 1978). Here, at least for the current cohort of older adults, the prohibitions against discussing sex are most ingrained and intense. Here there may be the most additional pressure to fabricate, either to counter or to comply with the firmly held stereotypes about how older people should behave. With these cautions in mind, let us once again turn to information from the Duke Longitudinal Study. In this area too the landmark Duke investigation furnishes us with some of the best data we have about behavior in later life.

As part of a psychiatric interview Duke volunteers were asked to estimate the frequency with which they had intercourse or, if they had stopped having sexual relations, to say when and explain why. They were also asked to rate the intensity of their present interest in sex and compare it with the strength of their sexual feelings as a young adult. These very simple inquiries yielded a good deal of information both about late-life sexuality and about factors influencing sexual interest and behavior (see Newman & Nichols, 1960; Pfeiffer, Verwoerdt, & Wang, 1968; Verwoerdt, Pfeiffer, & Wang, 1969).

For the men both cross-sectional data and repeated interviews over a ten-year period revealed the following: About three-fourths of Duke respondents in their sixties reported they still engaged in sexual intercourse, and a somewhat higher proportion said they still had sexual feelings to a mild or moderate degree. In fact, respondents seemed to maintain the same levels of interest and activity throughout this decade. In the seventies, however, there were sharp declines in the percentages reporting continued sexual feelings and continued sexual relations. Finally, among subjects in their eighties and nineties, most (about four-fifths) no longer engaged in intercourse. However, even among this oldest group half reported they still continued to have sexual feelings to some extent.

The longitudinal design offered the Duke researchers the opportunity to see how individual patterns of sexual behavior might vary from this prevailing picture of marked decline in the seventies. Looking at individual subjects over a three-year period, they found that about 20% or more of the men reported the opposite trend. For this not insubstantial group, with the passage of time there was increased interest in sex and more frequent activity. In other words, the evidence here clearly disputes the blanket idea that declining sexuality is an inevitable concomitant of advancing age.

For the women, the most striking finding was their much lower level of sexual interest and activity compared with the men's. This is clearly shown, for example, by the percentage of each sex reporting continued sexual interest at the first Duke testing. While 77% of the Duke males aged 60–65 said they still had sexual feelings, only 50% of the women this age reported they did. For reasons made more comprehensible in the next section, this disparity is even more evident between men and women in their late sixties; here the figures were 74% and a meager 23%.

These numbers may be partly a function of differences in response style. For cultural reasons we might think males would tend to overemphasize and females to underreport the extent of their sexual feelings. However, because of what we know about the physiological potential of older men and women, these data also suggest that psychological and social influences may have a particularly inhibiting effect specifically on female sexuality. Before turning to this issue, though, let us look at another Duke study that provides a broader perspective on this late-life information—one examining patterns of sexual interest and activity in a younger group of women and men.

As part of a second comprehensive Duke investigation, looking at aspects of aging in volunteers aged 45–69 (see Chapter 1), Pfeiffer, Verwoerdt, and Davis (1972) asked these mainly younger subjects the same questions about their sexual feelings and activity as in the first study. In this group, interestingly, they found the identical male/female disparity they had before. Men reported higher sexual interest and more frequent activity than women of the same age; for both sexes declining sexuality was the pattern reported in successively older age groups.

However, in this largely middle-aged sample, sexual interest and activity generally were quite high. For instance, at least until about age 60 the majority of the men reported having intercourse once or more a week. An even higher majority rated their interest in sex as strong or moderate. For the women the figures were lower but still high enough to show clearly that sex often played an important part in respondents' lives.

This study revealed another interesting finding specifically with regard to a person's perceptions about his or her sexuality. At about age 50 half the men and somewhat more than half the women reported they had noticed a decline in the frequency of their sexual relations and in the intensity of their interest in sex. In another part of the investigation, the researchers (Pfeiffer & Davis, 1972) looked specifically at factors related to continued high levels of sexual activity and interest in the women and men. These data, as well as corroborating evidence from the earlier study confined to the elderly, give us a good deal of insight into the reasons behind the late-life patterns of sexual interest and activity just described.

**Factors Affecting Sexuality in Later Life.**   In the second Duke study, subjects were asked to rate their sexual interest and activity in the past. They were questioned about the extent to which they had enjoyed sex as young adults, the frequency with which they had had sexual intercourse, and the level of their previous interest in sex. For both men and women all these assessments were highly related to continuing to report high levels of sexuality in the present. Simply put, continuity seemed to be operating here too. People who reported being highly sexually oriented when young continued to report being highly sexually interested and involved as older adults. This finding, although it would need to be confirmed by a longitudinal study, suggests that a simple prescription for remaining interested in sex in later life may be to be very interested and sexually active as a young adult.

Unfortunately, at least for the women, there was another important condition influencing later-life sexuality that was even less under the person's control. This was the availability of a partner.

---

**BOX 6-3.   Effects of Hysterectomy on Sexuality**

Hysterectomy, the most commonly performed operation in the United States, involves at minimum the surgical removal of a woman's uterus and cervix. Usually the ovaries and fallopian tubes are also removed. This more extensive procedure, which induces menopause in a still-menstruating woman, is called a total hysterectomy.

This operation, more than any other, has been the target of controversy. Its supposed overuse has evoked the ire of women's groups and other critics of the medical establishment. It is statistics like the following that seem particularly irksome. During the ten-year period from 1968 to 1977, the number of hysterectomies performed increased by 47%. If the current increases persist, 40% of American women will have the operation by age 50 and 50% by age 65 (Block, Davidson, & Grambs, 1981). Concern for preventing unnecessary hysterectomies arises partly from the physical danger involved; the operation, though relatively safe, does carry the danger of complications and a small mortality risk. It also involves fears about how the operation will affect the quality of a woman's life. A prime concern is that hysterectomy, for either physical or, more likely, psychological reasons, will lead to sexual problems.

That negative psychological responses may occur is strongly suggested by psychoanalytic formulations about the symbolic importance of the uterus to a woman. According to several psychoanalysts, the uterus (and understanding one has a uterus) may play a central role in a woman's feeling feminine; so operations like hysterectomy or, for similar reasons, mastectomy are a cause for particular concern (Broderick, 1978).

To test whether sexual deterioration does occur after hysterectomy and, if it does, to determine why, a retrospective study was made of women who had undergone this operation at least six months previously (Dennerstein, Wood, & Burrows, 1977). A female investigator interviewed 89 married women who had had total hysterectomies for reasons other than cancer about changes in their sexual desire and sexual relations that could be attributed to the operation.

In common with the findings with regard to menopause mentioned earlier, these women reported varying sexual responses to their surgery. A full 34% said sexual relations after the operation had improved; 29% said their sexual responsiveness was unchanged; 37% said the operation had had a negative effect on their sexuality. So the sexual effects of hysterectomy are much less uniformly dire than we would predict; however, we still want to know why a significant percentage of women do suffer impairments in their sexual responsiveness after the operation.

Among this group, psychological expectations appeared to play a major part. For example, as might be expected from our earlier discussion of the sexual effects of menopause, replacement estrogen administration after the surgery had no effect on sexuality. In contrast, how a woman had felt about the procedure clearly did. Women who said they had felt before the operation that it would alter their sexuality were those who were most likely to experience actual declines. This means that a self-fulfilling prophecy is operating. We need a longitudinal study to test this proposition in a methodologically adequate way. However, it does seem that if a woman expects a negative outcome from the procedure, then she is likely to get that result.

---

The second Duke study showed that the only factor predicting continued sexual relations for the women in the sample, other than age and past sexual enjoyment, was marital status. Women who were married were much more likely to be having intercourse than women without a spouse. The extent of this disparity and the magnitude of its difference from the situation of men is best revealed by some sobering statistics from the earlier Duke investigation, confined to the elderly (Verwoerdt et al., 1969). A considerable percentage of the Duke female respondents were currently without a husband, and only about 4% of this large single group reported that they were still having sexual relations. In contrast, more than 40% of the Duke females who were still married said they continued to be sexually active. For the Duke males, however, being single had no such inhibiting effect. A full 82% of the relatively tiny number of Duke males without a wife said they were still having intercourse. In fact, this figure was somewhat higher than even for the married men in the sample.

So one major reason for the lower incidence of sexual activity specifically in older females seems to be the social fact of lack of opportunity. Not only are many middle-aged and elderly women widowed, but they are often barred from having sexual intercourse outside marriage by the scarcity of available men and, at least for this cohort, an upbringing that is likely to have stressed nonmarital sex as wrong. Just as important, they are limited by the all-important perception our society shares that aging women, much more and much earlier than aging men, are not sexually desirable and so should not be picked as sex partners.

Specifically, many of us share the idea that women are no longer sexually attractive when they begin to show clear physical signs of age, usually in their forties. For men, however, sexual desirability is much more a function of the individual's power and status, so it may actually increase in middle age. It is not until some 20 years later, when retirement means that a man has lost this key to his attractiveness, that our society begins to see him too as a relatively poor sexual choice (Block, Davidson, & Grambs, 1981).

Aging women without a partner because of their much larger numbers, coupled with their undesirability to men, do compensate for this lack somewhat by increasing the frequency of masturbation (Christenson & Gagnon, 1965). However, we might expect that another adaptation many make would be to decide they are no longer interested in sex. This, then, may partly explain why in the area of sexual interest middle-aged and elderly men and women differ so greatly. The Duke findings here may partly reflect simply the differential reinforcement of later-life sexual feelings for males and females.

The primary importance of a partner for sexual activity in women is not confined to those who are single; it is also seen in the currently married. The interesting fact is that even in elderly married couples the man is the one most likely to determine whether sexual relations continue to occur. When Duke researchers in the first study (Pfeiffer et al., 1968) questioned the eight married couples who had stopped having intercourse about their reasons for doing so, there was a good deal of shared agreement that the man was the cause. Six couples agreed the husband was responsible; one concurred in attributing the cause to the wife; and one couple disagreed, each spouse taking the responsibility.

Even for couples who continue to have sexual relations, the husband is the determining factor. This point was brought home by an ingenious study that looked at female sexual activity in the context of making a point about the late-life consequences of the typical practice for women to marry older men (Christenson & Gagnon, 1965).

Married women aged 50 and over were asked to estimate how often they had sexual intercourse. These reports were then looked at in the light of whether the husband was older, younger, or the same age. There was in fact a significant difference depending on this variable. In every age group, women with younger husbands reported the most frequent relations; those with older husbands reported the least. We might easily argue that more sexually liberated females, those who would be more inclined to continue sexual activity into late life, are more likely to flout convention by choosing younger spouses. However, at least for this cohort of older people, the husband is most likely to be the person who initiates sex; and, of course, we now know that the younger he is, the more likely he is to want to engage in sexual activity. So our study suggests that, aside from consid-erations of longevity, if a woman wants a highly active sex life, it may be best (at least in the abstract) for her to choose a younger mate.

The likelihood that in the cohort now elderly the husband sets the sexual pat-tern may account for the differing sexuality found in both Duke studies between men and women of the same age. Women are more likely to marry, and so to have their sexual activity dictated by, men in an older group (Newman & Nichols, 1960). In fact, because male sexual activity in the first Duke study fell off steeply in the seventies, we would expect the most male/female disparity in sexual inter-est and activity exactly where it was found—between women and men in their late sixties. This is because women in their late sixties are most likely to have husbands in their seventies.

Why, however, was there this marked drop in sexual interest and activity in the Duke men specifically in their seventies? The answer seems to lie in a critical factor the researchers (Pfeiffer & Davis, 1972) found that influenced sexuality spe-cifically for men—their health.

In the second Duke study, for males, both self-reports of good health and more objective indexes were correlated with continued sexual interest and activity. As the probability of a person's being in poor health increases markedly in the seven-ties (the person becomes old-old), this seems to explain the steep drop in sexual desire and activity reported at that age. However, not many age-related health problems directly cause losses in sexual capacity. Diabetes, which can affect erec-tile performance, and in some cases genital or colon surgery are among the few (Corby & Solnick, 1980; Weg, 1978). More often poor health is limiting in a more circuitous way: drugs taken for a chronic condition may affect a person in this crucial area of life. Unfortunately, medications given for problems common in older people, such as depression or high blood pressure, can have the side effect of decreasing sexual interest or impairing actual sexual behavior (Comfort, 1980).

In addition, feeling sick can have a significant indirect impact on older people. It may make them too tired, too listless, or too depressed to be interested in sex. Then there is a sometimes central element of fear—the idea that with certain physical conditions sexual intercourse is too strenuous and can lead to sudden death (Weg, 1978). The perhaps overriding impact of these more psychological reasons that ill health may inhibit sexuality was revealed by another Duke finding. Subjective ratings of illness related more highly than objective measures to reports of declining sexual interest and enjoyment in the men. In other words, it was a man's belief he was ill that was most crucial to his losing sexual desire and a sense of pleasure in sex.

Anxiety over sexual activity occurs perhaps most reliably when a person has a certain very common chronic condition—heart disease. Bloch, Maeder, and Haissly (1975), studying a large group of subjects (male and female) 11 months after a heart attack, found a marked drop in the reported frequency of intercourse from about 5 times per month before hospitalization to 2.7 times per month at the time subjects were questioned. This decrease was not related to the results of exercise tests, however. Instead, it appeared determined by three influences in particular: the person's being depressed, fearing a relapse, and fearing sudden death during intercourse.

The common belief that intercourse can cause a heart attack often prevents not just heart patients themselves but also their partners from fully enjoying sex (Corby & Solnick, 1980). However, documented cases of death occurring during sexual relations from this cause are rare (Butler & Lewis, 1973). In fact, intercourse is less stressful on the heart than the stress test done to assess heart functioning in the doctor's office. A general rule is that some level of sexual activity can be resumed about three months after a heart attack and that a person with heart disease who can comfortably climb a few flights of stairs or take a brisk walk around the block is safe in resuming sexual relations (Corby & Solnick, 1980).

The second Duke study found that several factors in addition to health were related to high sexual activity and interest in the men. They included high socio-economic status and, as just implied, high morale. We can add to this Masters and Johnson's (1966) list of other influences that they felt diminished sexual interest in aging men: monotony arising from having a single sexual partner for many years; overfocusing on economic pursuits; mental and physical fatigue; and overindulgence in food and drink.

Lastly, Masters and Johnson stress another factor of particular importance in inhibiting older men—fear of not being able to perform. As unfortunately this anxiety often leads to the feared result, this is all the more reason for our trying to avoid the assumption of incapacity in older males so evident in the joke at the beginning of our discussion.

**Interventions.**   Promoting increased sexual expression should not be a goal for all older people. To decide that every older adult must be sexually interested or active is as much a way of stereotyping a person as to decide its opposite. However, because of the pressures on the elderly not to be interested in sex, this aim may often, even more than for young people, be a good one. Interventions to enhance sexuality in old age have focused on the three areas that seem important: changing the responses of the person, changing the responses of society, and changing the external situation of older adults.

1. *Changing the person.* After demonstrating age changes in erectile functioning, the author of the study that noted this loss attempted to both reverse it and increase sexual interest as a whole in a sample of older men (Solnick, 1978). His technique was to use fantasy practice combined with biofeedback.

He first divided his subjects, men aged 45–55, into two groups. Both were exposed to five training sessions during which they were asked to fantasize to erotic stimuli, but only those in the biofeedback group were given information about their erectile response.

At the end of the study both sets of subjects showed significant gains in the rapidity with which they achieved erections. They also reported increases in the average amount of time they spent having erotic daydreams and in fre-

quency of intercourse. Finally, the gains, even though not statistically significant compared with the other group, were most pronounced for the men in the
biofeedback condition. This indicates that not just sexual activity and fantasy
but even what looks like an irreversible age-related loss, impaired erectile
responsiveness itself, is amenable to reversal by even a relatively brief psychological intervention.

2. *Changing society.* While it is important to educate everyone to have more
tolerant attitudes toward sexuality in older people, a good place to start this
effort is with nurses. As a group, nurses are highly involved with older people.
They also have a good deal of control over expressions of sexuality in institutionalized older adults. The importance not just of training this group but of
making that learning experience more than intellectual is clearly evident in
observations such as the following. As part of a nursing home survey, Wasow
and Loeb (1978) found that the personnel in one institution expressed very
positive feelings about the right of older people to sexual expression. Their
actions, though, spoke differently. When an elderly couple at the institution
escaped and got a room at a motel, the staff, agitated, immediately wanted to
call the police to get them back.

To change this type of ingrained emotional response, a nursing educator
(Monea, 1978) uses an experiential teaching technique. She first tells students
to close their eyes and fantasize themselves as a disabled older person. They
are asked to imagine how the illness affects their sexuality and how caretakers
respond. Then, still with eyes closed, each person is given clay and instructed
to sculpt it into an image reflecting his or her feelings. Next, participants open
their eyes, write down a description of the sculpture, and choose partners for a
ten-minute discussion of the experience. Finally, the students meet as a group
to expand on the feelings the exercise has elicited. No formal evaluation has
been done of its effectiveness. However, it is hoped that, through feeling what
it is like to be an older person in the situation, students will be able to overcome their deep-rooted aversion to expressions of sexuality in older people.

3. *Changing the situation.* The main situational problem inhibiting late-life
sexual expression is the difficulty older women have—the simple lack of available men. Suggestions to remedy this have been made, such as serial relationships or homosexuality (see Corby & Solnick, 1980 for review), but they are
unrealistic. They are unlikely to be easily implemented or enacted in anything
like a widespread way even when the present sexually liberated cohort of
young adults reaches late life. There is, however, a very simple barrier to sexual expression among one group of elderly that can be more easily changed—
the practice of segregating men and women on different floors of nursing
homes.

In some institutions there is little chance for sexual contact because male
and female residents live on separate floors. In one nursing home the effects of
changing this practice were assessed (Silverstone & Wynter, 1975). It was felt
that if men and women lived in closer proximity, there would be a change for

the better in the whole atmosphere of the unit. In addition, rather than prohibiting sexual expression, this procedure would at least allow its possibility. Because the residents themselves showed some initial resistance to this change, it was introduced gradually as additional beds became available. Once implemented, however, there was a real difference in the ward behavior of the residents of the heterosexual floor compared with an adjacent all-female one. Male residents on the sex-integrated floor were better groomed and more cooperative and generally functioned at a higher level.

### Reminiscence

When we hear an older adult reminiscing about his or her youth or lamenting the passing of the "good old days," we are likely to be far from surprised. The elderly are expected to behave in this way. A well-established idea is that in old age a person has a completely different temporal orientation. Feelings, thoughts, and interests are much more focused on memories; a person's main concern is the past rather than what is now or what will be.

This idea seems to fit with everyday observations. Older adults really do seem to talk more about the past than the young. However, this behavior also seems reasonable in the context of our underlying negative attitudes about old age itself. It is easy to imagine the elderly dwelling on what may seem to us a happier time. Reminiscing, then, seems predictable in older adults as a simple response to their stage in life—a way to find solace in the face of a nonexistent future and what may seem, from our perspective, an unpalatable present.

In contrast, far from being an escape, thinking about the past takes on a new and positive purpose when looked at in an Eriksonian framework. As you may remember from the discussion of his theory in Chapter 1, Erikson too suggests reminiscing is an important activity in old age. However, he believes that thoughts about the past serve a very different aim: to allow the person to reach the ideal of ego integrity by coming to terms with what he or she has and has not achieved in life.

The critical value and universal nature of this type of reminiscence in particular, however, were only later fully spelled out, by psychiatrist Robert Butler, the former director of the National Institute on Aging, whose ageism statement begins our book. Drawing on Erikson's ideas, Butler hypothesizes that in old age what he calls a *life review* is set into motion, prompted by the older adult's becoming aware of his or her closeness to death.

> Only in old age can one experience a personal sense of the entire life cycle. This comes to its fullness with the awareness of death in the forefront. . . .[This is] the process of the life review prompted by the realization of approaching dissolution and death. The life review is characterized by a progressive return to consciousness of past experience, in particular the resurgence of unresolved conflicts which can now be surveyed and integrated. . . .If unresolved conflicts and fears are successfully reintegrated they can give new significance and meaning to an individual's life in preparing for death and mitigating fears [1974, p. 534].

As this statement shows, life review is different from simply thinking about the past. Rather than just recalling events, the person is using memories in an Eriksonian sense—becoming able to accept death by getting closure on his or her life, particularly its difficult aspects.

Butler's proposition, that this evaluative review of one's life is important to psychological health in old age, has been empirically tested. Before looking at studies that explore its value, however, we need to verify his (and most likely our) first assumption about thinking about the past. Is it in fact more frequent in older adults?

**Prevalence of Thoughts about the Past.**    In one investigation (Cameron, 1972) three large samples of subjects of varying ages were approached and asked what they had been thinking about within the last five minutes. The elderly subjects reported no more thoughts of the past than the other age groups. There was only a slight difference in the responses of the elderly. The percentage of older adults reporting thoughts of the future was somewhat less. For older respondents these thoughts were replaced by proportionately more thoughts of the present. For all age groups, thoughts about the present were most common. Thoughts about the past ranked a poor third.

This negative result was supported by two investigations in which subjects of various ages were asked to fill out a comprehensive questionnaire about their daydreams (Gambria, 1977, 1979–80). This procedure revealed a good deal of other interesting information not only about life-span changes in the content of fantasies but also about their time setting. In only one of these studies (Gambria, 1979–80) was there a slight tendency for older female respondents to report more absorbing daydreams about the past and an increase in the proportion of fantasies of this type. However, even this difference was quite small, and daydreams of the future and present were also found with equal frequency in the elderly group. Moreover, contrary to the supposition that older people are absorbed in the past, in the oldest subjects daydreams were actually least compelling and frequent. In fact, there was a steady decline in the amount of daydreaming and absorption in daydreams reported in successively older age groups, beginning in the twenties.

The negative results of these studies seem particularly surprising. Why, then, does the past seem so apparent a theme in discussions we have with older people? The answer may lie partly in what we ourselves do. Particularly in superficial social encounters, we may be more prone to ask older adults questions about what they used to do rather than about what they do now. Even when discussing impersonal topics like the state of the world, the temptation with an older person is to inquire specifically about how things today compare with how things used to be. This kind of direct invitation to discuss the past, absent in our conversations with younger people, may also be eagerly seized on by the other side. The older person's past may be one of the few topics that can be easily discussed with someone of possibly different interests at a disparate stage of life. What is happening now may simply offer less opportunity for finding a common conversational ground.

Lastly, there is the all-important factor of selective perception. When the elderly comment about the past, we may be highly attuned to it because it fits in with our preconceived idea of how they are supposed to behave. Similar talk in younger adults, because it is not seen as characteristic, may not be noticed in the same way.

**Adaptive Value of Past-Oriented Thinking.**    Even if it is not endemic to late life, it still may be good psychologically for the elderly to think about the past. In other words, even if its universality is in question, we need to examine the truth of Butler's second idea about reminiscence: is engaging in a life review important to mental health in old age?

To be fair to Butler, as with the research just described, most investigators examining this question have not specifically measured life-review activity. Instead, they have correlated measures of psychological health with indexes of a person's propensity simply to talk or think about his or her past. However, even when these simple measures of reminiscing are used, some positive relationships have been found between past-oriented thoughts and good adjustment. Older people who think or talk more about the past are likely to be less depressed (McMahon & Rhudick, 1967), to show evidence of more ego integrity (Boylin, Gordon, & Nehrke, 1976), and to have better personal-social adjustment (Havighurst & Glasser, 1972). Unfortunately, these associations are modest, and these studies are correlational. At the minimum, then, they do not show us whether in fact thinking about the past causes good adjustment. It may be incidental to or even, just as logically, a consequence of a person's being satisfied or well adjusted in late life.

With these cautions in mind, let us turn to the only correlational study in the literature that took care to measure life-review activity in itself. Coleman (1974) taped extensive interviews with elderly people (most in their eighties) who lived in the English equivalent of congregate housing. He then coded his respondents' talk about the past into three discrete types: simple reminiscence (the number of references to the past the person made), life reviewing, and what he called informative or teaching reminiscence (using the past to make a point or instruct the listener).

Using this scheme, he found that people who engaged in a large amount of life-review behavior were not necessarily in better mental health overall. However, this type of reminiscence did seem to be associated with good adjustment under certain circumstances—namely, if a person reported being dissatisfied with his or her past life. Respondents who said they had been unhappy in the past and who engaged in life review were well adjusted at the time of the interview, while those who reported a low level of previous life satisfaction and were rated low in life-review activity were currently functioning poorly psychologically. So it may be that life review has particular value mainly for the purpose of helping someone come to terms with an unhappy past.

In fact, there is no reason simple thoughts about the past too should not have positive psychological value. For instance, they might offer comfort and psychological support to an older adult unhappy with his or her present situation. In an interesting study this consoling use of the past, at least for some elderly people, seemed evident. Older people classified as reminiscers (those who talked and thought a good deal about the past) seemed to use this ability to restore their self-concept following a threat to their self-esteem. After being criticized, they showed more consistency between their past and present self-concepts than a group classified as nonreminiscers (Lewis, 1971).

Of course, this use of the past to restore self-confidence is far from confined to older adults. After a failure many of us may try to review the past for memories of previous successes to raise our self-esteem. However, this approach may be particularly valuable for older adults because they have such an extensive set of memories to draw on. Also, by recalling the past, the elderly can enhance their sense of self-worth in another way: by identifying not just with what they as individuals have achieved but with what their generation as a whole has accomplished. Using the past in this last way, to identify with one's cohort, and using it for life review have each been encouraged, using different techniques.

**Interventions.**    To stimulate life review, Butler (Lewis & Butler, 1974) has older adults compose an autobiography, if possible revisit places where they lived as a child, and discuss mementos of their life they have collected. These and related techniques help the person come to terms with his or her personal past. In contrast, a group approach seems particularly appropriate for stimulating generational solidarity. In one group the leader encourages older adults to reminisce together about their personal experience of historical events, such as the Depression or World War I. Although this collective exploration does not preclude life review, ideally what is gained here is a sense of community, a pride in one's age group that can counteract expressions of ageism on the outside (Ebersole, 1978).

## Summary

The Kansas City Studies of Adult Life, begun in the mid-1950s by a group of researchers at the University of Chicago, were the first comprehensive investigations of personality and lifestyle in middle and old age. Using a variety of indexes of personality and evaluating a large sample of community residents aged 40 to 90, the researchers found stability in the outer, or what they called "socio-adaptational," aspects of personality with age. However, when they used a test measuring unconscious personality processes, the TAT, they found evidence of changes.

Two major transformations seemed to begin by late middle age (the midfifties). A progressive change in the "ego energy" and "mastery style" of older subjects' TAT stories suggested that a psychological pulling back from the external world might be taking place, a shift the researchers called increasing "interiority." A reversal in the TAT descriptions of an old man and an old woman pictured on a specially designed card suggested there might be an inversion in traditional sex roles in later life. These findings support Jung's clinical formulations. Though 25 years old and arrived at by easily criticized methods, they have been corroborated by other studies. We do not know, though, whether these changes are caused by external events that may be age-related in our society or are intrinsic to a person's having lived a certain number of years. We also are unsure particularly whether the sex-role transformation will manifest itself in the present cohort of younger adults.

The Chicago investigators also found that, beginning in the midsixties and increasing thereafter, there was a marked reduction in external involvements. This overt evidence of withdrawal, coupled with the intrapsychic shift to interiority evident ten years earlier, led two of the researchers to formulate a famous proposal about aging called disengagement theory. According to this theory, there is a universal process intrinsic to later life whereby a person withdraws or retreats from active involvement in society. The theory implies that because disengagement is natural, it is also ideal in old age.

The assumptions that disengagement is universal and is set in motion purely by a person's being a certain age have both been shown to be false. The third tenet of the theory, that disengagement is ideal, has provoked a storm of criticism and has led the opposite idea about ideal aging to be put forth, called activity theory: that people who are most involved in society are aging ideally and so should have the highest morale in late life.

A good deal of research designed to test the truth of these competing conceptions has revealed, not unexpectedly, that neither way of approaching old age is necessarily better. Some people have high morale being disengaged; others are happy being active. Morale in late life depends more on personality than on how active or withdrawn an older adult is. Moreover, personality predicts who will choose to disengage or to remain involved in the outside world.

Actually, a variety of studies have shown that in many respects personality and lifestyle remain stable as a person ages (at least during middle and old age). One study, for example, found that retired professors maintained the same pattern of either high or low publication they had in previous years.

A longitudinal study spanning 40 years shows evidence of both change and consistency in personality and lifestyle during adulthood. In this investigation subjects initially examined in their thirties were retested in their seventies. The (highly tentative) conclusions of this research are that radically shifting environmental contingencies, such as widowhood or financial reversals, engender discontinuous lifestyles. When external changes have not occurred, a person's interests and activities are more likely to remain stable. Personality shows continuity over this long period only for individuals who are emotionally disturbed.

In large part our society expects older adults, in particular women, not to be sexually active or interested in sex. This widespread assumption is clearly revealed by the frequency with which jokes about late-life behavior have a derisive sexual theme. The stereotype, though, unfairly confines older people and also is to some extent a self-fulfilling prophecy, inhibiting sexual potential in later life to an unknown degree.

Masters and Johnson investigated age effects on the sexual response in older couples. They found relatively few physiological changes for females but did discover some more pronounced ones for males. Men showed deteriorative changes in their erectile response and ejaculatory capacity. Despite these signs of reduced responsiveness, their capacity for sexual behavior was in no way absent. The conclusion is that some limitations in sexual responsiveness do occur with age, more for males than females, but that these far from warrant ascribing sexual incapacity to older adults.

The Duke Longitudinal Study provides us with information about two other aspects of late-life sexuality—the extent to which older people report continued sexual desire and the extent and frequency of their sexual relations. For males, a sharp decline in sexuality was found in the seventies. However, even in the eighties a significant percentage of the Duke male respondents still reported sexual desire and at least occasional intercourse. And even though declining sexuality was the rule, about 20% of the male sample actually showed increased sexual interest and activity over a short period. For women, levels of sexual interest and activity were much lower than for men at all comparable ages. A second Duke study questioning middle-aged adults revealed identical trends, as well as looking specifically at factors relating to high levels of sexual interest and activity in men and women.

For both sexes, reports of sexual interest, enjoyment, and activity when young were positively related to current level of sexual interest and behavior; in other words, high or low sexuality appeared to be a lifelong pattern. For women, an extremely important influence on both interest and activity was the availability of a partner. Women respondents without a spouse rarely reported sexual activity and infrequently reported sexual interest. Furthermore, when an older woman is married, her partner tends to determine her level of sexual activity. The man is usually responsible for stopping sexual relations and for their frequency when they continue to occur.

The Duke study revealed that for males a primary factor in continued sexual interest and activity was health. Very few physical problems are directly responsible for total loss of sexual interest or capacity. However, some drugs commonly given to treat age-related conditions may have an inhibiting effect on sexuality. The impact of subjective perceptions is also critical: a person who feels he or she is ill is less likely to be sexually active or interested. Psychological precipitants of decreased sexuality are not uncommon in both heart-attack victims and women who have undergone a hysterectomy. In people who have suffered a heart attack, one prevalent fear causing a person to give up sex is that intercourse will precipitate another. This idea is largely a myth. Another fear, anxiety about being unable to perform, is a major cause of impotence and loss of sexual interest in aging men.

Interventions to enhance sexuality have included efforts focused on increasing responsiveness in the individual, educating others, and changing an external situation to permit sexual expression. Using biofeedback and fantasy practice, one investigator was able to increase both erectile responsiveness and sexual interest and activity of aging men. Using an experiential approach, a nursing educator trains students to be more accepting of sexuality in old age. Finally, integrating the sexes on one floor of a nursing home resulted in improvements in behavior and mood among residents.

The belief that older adults think a good deal about the past is prevalent in the general population. This idea is implicit, too, in Erikson's theory: reminiscing about what has been achieved in one's life is necessary for a person to achieve ego integrity. Butler, drawing on Erikson, has explicitly focused on the importance of this self-evaluative activity in late life. He hypothesizes that a life review is critical to mental health in old age and that reviewing one's past is an automatic process set into motion by the older person's inevitable awareness of impending death.

Interestingly, there is little or no empirical support for the idea that older people are more absorbed in the past than other age groups. There is limited evidence, however, that thinking (or talking) about the past is correlated with good adjustment. In the one study specifically looking at the value of the type of reminiscence called life review, this activity seemed beneficial, but only when a person needed to come to terms with a past he or she viewed as negative. Finally, reminiscence in some people may be effective as a technique for restoring self-esteem in the face of a current failure. In older people self-esteem may be enhanced both by reviewing the past for personal successes and by using it to identify in a more general way with the accomplishments of one's age group as a whole.

To encourage life review, Butler asks older people to write an autobiography, revisit places where they have lived, and discuss mementos of important events in their life they may have kept. Groups have also been formed whose major focus is to enhance generational solidarity. Here members reminisce about their personal experience of shared historical events.

## Key Terms

*Interiority*  
*Ego energy*  
*Mastery style*  

*Disengagement theory*  
*Activity theory*  
*Life review*  

## Recommended Readings

Maas, H. S., & Kuypers, J. A. ***From thirty to seventy: A forty-year study of adult life styles and personality***. San Francisco: Jossey-Bass, 1975.
*The Berkeley parents follow-up study. Interesting reading both for case descriptions and for methodology. Moderately difficult.*

Neugarten, B. L., & associates (Eds.). ***Personality in middle and late life***. New York: Atherton, 1964.
*All the Kansas City investigations of personality. Includes detailed description of concept of interiority. Moderately difficult.*

Solnick, R. L. (Ed.). ***Sexuality and aging***. Los Angeles: University of Southern California Press, 1978.
*Collection of articles. Includes large section on interventions (including first two discussed in text). Not difficult.*

CHAPTER SEVEN

# *External Aspects of the Person: Life Transitions*

Mr. Smith was 64 when he died. The year before, his long-standing emphysema had gotten so bad that he had been forced to give up his job as a factory supervisor. Although Mr. Smith had continued to love working in the mill, it eventually became just too tiring to do a full day's work. Besides, he had more than enough money from Social Security, his pension, and savings to retire and had, for at least the last ten years, looked forward to leaving work as a chance to indulge in his lifelong interest, landscape painting. Mr. Smith's youthful fantasies of being a professional artist had once had to yield to reality—the need to support himself and his new wife. Before retirement he dreamed of the new chance to translate them into action in this, the last phase of his life.

Mr. and Mrs. Smith had been high school sweethearts. They had married when both were 18 and had lived in the same neighborhood in Brooklyn for their entire married life. In fact, they had just invited their many friends to a huge wedding anniversary party eight months before Mr. Smith's death.

The last year of their marriage was bittersweet for the couple. Mr. Smith's retirement, far from creating problems between the two as they had feared, actually brought them even closer. They had always been an intimate couple but during this year seemed to become almost totally entwined. They reveled in the chance to spend so much time being with each other.

During this last year, however, Mr. Smith's health deteriorated rapidly. Far from enjoying his new freedom from working, then, he also found being retired a disappointment. Most days he was too ill even to paint. Because during the last few months he was completely bedridden, Mrs. Smith too was robbed of the chance to fully enjoy her time with him. She was forced to serve as a full-time nurse and suffer the pain of watching her husband approach death.

Even though she refused to hire professional help, Mrs. Smith might have asked her daughter for support with the caretaking at this time of obvious need. However, her daughter worked full-time as a lawyer and had her own family to raise. To Mrs. Smith, asking her son or only sister was also out of the question. She believed the stereotype that sons should not do this "traditionally female" job, and she and her sister had never been that close. She clearly could not ask her many friends, either. Inflicting demands on family was hard enough; it was impossible to burden people who were not blood relatives with such intimate requests.

Mrs. Smith felt the same way about her relatives and friends after her husband died: she could not really burden them with her problems. Often she felt reluctant to mention her husband's death with friends for fear she would start to cry. She also noticed that they too avoided the topic. Her son helped with the funeral arrangements and somewhat with finances. Her daughter was a source of emotional support. However, she quickly realized she had to come to terms with the loss of her husband on her own and learn for the first time how to face life as a single person.

This was frightening to Mrs. Smith because she had gone straight from being a schoolgirl living with her parents to being a wife. In addition to depending on her husband's actual physical presence in the house, she had counted on him for so many little things—chores as different as doing the taxes and taking out the garbage. Most important, though, she missed him terribly as her closest companion and best friend. Sometimes she longed for him so much that she actually felt he was beside her in the room.

During the first few months her grief was intense. Even though she knew her husband was dead, Mrs. Smith kept feeling he was still alive somewhere. She had other strange obsessions and ideas and at times thought she might be going mad. Gradually these feelings decreased in intensity and she was able to begin adapting to her new life. She discovered that she had little in common now with some of her married friends and so had to make new ones in her same situation. She found these new widowed friends by getting a part-time job, which enabled her to meet people. She also learned to take care of most things herself and felt pride and some surprise at her strength and ability to cope. This is not to say she stopped missing her husband or felt she really ever got over his death. Her family and new and old friends were important, but they did not begin to make up for his presence, a presence she felt most acutely when enjoying her new hobby—landscape painting.

Three of the most radical changes that can occur in a person's life happen most frequently to older people: retiring, losing a spouse, and having to enter a nursing home. In addition, for the elderly these first two changes are widespread, predictable events. Institutionalization is less common but is more prevalent than we might expect; it is likely to affect the lives of more people in the future as the numbers of old-old increase.

Any view of today's elderly would be impoverished, then, without focusing on these events in some depth. Understanding these transitions will enrich our knowledge about the day-to-day lives of older people. It will help us understand the falsity of conceptions of aging that stress the older person's rigidity and incapacity in the face of change. It will help us evaluate further the validity of psychoanalytic theory with its clear implication that retirement, widowhood, and institutionalization are stresses that should precipitate psychological problems in many older adults. Finally, it will give us additional information about the truth of the empirical evidence on change and consistency presented in Chapter 6 and the blanket ideas about ideal aging described there—that either disengagement or keeping active is best in late life.

## Retirement

Retirement is currently an expected transition for almost all older workers. This was not always so. Before Social Security was instituted, people were expected to continue working into old age though fewer lived to 65, the now "classic" marker of late life and retirement.

Industrialization and a prosperous economy that became able to support non-working members have made retirement possible (Sheppard, 1976). During this century older workers have been pushed to retire because of the rapid increase in the number of large industrial firms. In addition to having fixed rules governing hiring and firing, these companies often had to develop a structured mechanism for allowing younger people to advance and gracefully getting rid of those who could no longer perform. Their solution was compulsory retirement at a given age. At the same time, older workers have been pulled to retire because of the feasibility of living without working. The establishment and growth of the Social Security system, the increasing availability of pensions, and the development of laws and programs geared to helping older people financially have all made it increasingly possible and attractive to retire (Foner & Schwab, 1981).

The fact that retirement is expected, however, does not mean it is universally thought to be a pleasant transition. The idea still lingers that being retired is bad for most people psychologically and even physically. Because, at least for American men, work is thought to be a central self-defining activity, retirement is expected to be emotionally traumatic, fraught with overtones of being dumped and deprived of membership in adult society (Thompson, 1973; Withers, 1979). This trauma, in turn, coupled with inactivity, is thought to lead to illness and hasten death. These negative conceptions about retirement are not just popular stereotypes but permeate the aging literature. Activity theory, for example, strongly implies that retirement should be bad for the older person.

In contrast to these ideas is the increasingly prevalent conviction that retirement is really a positive life transition, a healthful and health-enhancing rest from the stress of having to work (as noted in Ekerdt, Bosse, & LoCastro, 1983). This view of retirement as a desired and desirable state is becoming increasingly publicized as the debate has raged over the prospect of cutting Social Security benefits. Suddenly we are becoming aware that surveys show the majority of old and young workers look forward with pleasure to retirement (Fillenbaum, 1971b; Foner & Schwab, 1981; Kimmel, Price, & Walker, 1978; Prentis, 1980). Now it is argued that having to work may be bad for the older person!

In a later section, we will explore the veracity of these contrasting ideas. Before looking at the effects of retirement, however, we need to understand some influences on the decision to stop work itself.

### *The Decision to Retire*

Participation of people over 65 in the labor force has been declining steadily over the past several decades (Sheppard, 1976). In addition, there has been an increasing trend toward early retirement. As Figure 7-1 illustrates, the surprising statistic is that most people now retire before age 65. In fact, the average retirement age is now closer to 60 (Allan & Brotman, 1981; Foner & Schwab, 1981).

The reasons people choose to retire or continue working vary greatly. An important component of the decision is financial —whether or not the person has the income to live. Some people may be pulled out of the job market by subtle pressures on them to retire or by the mandatory retirement policies that still exist.

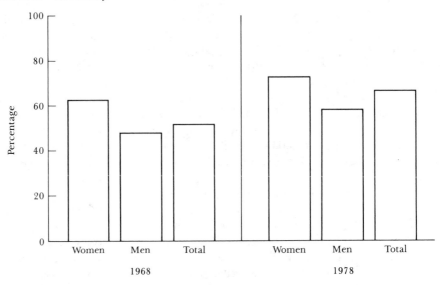

**FIGURE 7-1.** Percentage of total Social Security claimants awarded re-
duced payments because of retirement before age 65 by sex, 1968 and 1978.
*(Source: From* Chartbook on Aging in America *by C. Allan and H. Brotman.
Copyright 1981 by The White House Conference on Aging.)*

Some may leave work owing to a more internal pressure—poor health. Another
important aspect of the decision is psychological—how much one likes or dislikes
a job, feelings about the prospect of retirement, commitment to the value of work.
As our vignette suggests, several of these influences may operate simultaneously
when a person decides to retire or remain on the job. We will examine each
separately.

**Financial Influences.**    The availability of Social Security provides the primary financial impetus allowing people to decide to retire. Social Security benefits
constitute the average retiree's major and sometimes sole source of income (Foner
& Schwab, 1981; see Figure 7-2). A person pays into the Social Security system
during his or her working years and then gets benefits on leaving the work force
at age 65. The number of categories of Social Security beneficiaries has steadily
increased since the system was established in 1935. Recipients now include many
who were not eligible during the program's early years; among these newer beneficiaries are people as young as 62.

At age 62 a person can now collect most (80%) of the benefits he or she is due at
age 65. This fact alone partly explains why so many people now retire early. An
additional probable influence on retirement at age 65 is that Social Security recipients between 65 and 70 who work are penalized if they earn over a certain
amount. They have to forfeit some or all of their benefits, depending on the

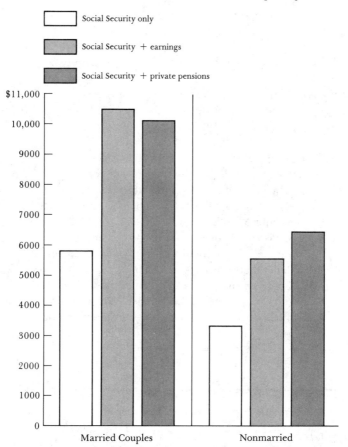

**FIGURE 7-2.**   Median income and income source of older households by marital status, 1978. *(Source: From* Chartbook on Aging in America *by C. Allan and H. Brotman. Copyright 1981 by The White House Conference on Aging.)*

amount of income they earn. A final incentive may be the size of the Social Security check itself. Although the typical allotment provided by the program is not large, it is adequate and has risen substantially over the years.

However, the Social Security system also includes incentives to discourage retirement. As of 1982 a person over 70 who works can earn an unlimited amount and still collect all of his or her benefits. A worker who delays receiving benefits until after age 65 receives a bonus for each year he or she delays (Gelfand & Olsen, 1979). Although it is clear from Figure 7-1 that these inducements have not worked to stem the tide of retirements before 65, retrenchments in the system may do so in the near future.

Another financial incentive to retire, for many people, is money from pensions to boost one's income (see Figure 7-2). For example, in 1976, 31% of retired people were receiving this additional source of support. Savings, tax breaks, and government programs (like Medicare) favoring the elderly also help make retirement feasible by extending the older person's income.

That adequate finances are an important component of the decision to retire is obliquely suggested by the finding that single men (who presumably have fewer expenses) are more likely to retire early than married men (Ireland & Bond, 1976). It is directly shown by the many surveys revealing that retirees often list "enough income" as one primary determinant of their decision to leave work (Foner & Schwab, 1981; Pollman, 1971).

**Job Influences.**    While the prospect of adequate finances entices people to leave their jobs, the older person may also be forced to retire by mandatory rules or less obvious forms of age discrimination at work. As just mentioned, mandatory rules helped to institutionalize retirement as an expected life event. These policies, which often required retirement at age 65, were widespread in American industry until the recent past. They had always been controversial for the reasons specified in Box 7-1, and a growing outcry against their unfairness to older workers finally forced the federal government to step in.

In 1978 Congress amended a 1967 act outlawing age discrimination for workers under 65 to include many workers under 70. Except in jobs where age can critically affect ability to work, this new law states, retirement cannot be forced before age 70 in most industries. In addition, the amendment abolishes any mandatory retirement age at all for most federal employees.

---

**BOX 7-1.    Compulsory versus Flexible Retirement**

Mandatory retirement policies are both defensible and easy to criticize. The following arguments for and against these rules were taken from an article (Palmore, 1977) that concludes that the case for *flexible retirement,* or allowing people to leave the work force at their own pace, is most compelling. What do you think?

1. *The case for compulsory retirement:* It is simple and easy to administer. It prevents capricious discrimination against individual workers. Its predictability allows people to plan for retirement far ahead. It allows younger workers to advance and saves face for older workers who can no longer perform their jobs adequately.

2. *The case for flexible retirement:* It is nondiscriminatory, nonageist, and equitable, as age is in no way synonymous with inability. It better utilizes the skills, potentials, and experience of older people and so would increase our national output. It increases the income of the aged and reduces the burden on the Social Security system. It eliminates resentment, anger, and unhappiness among workers forced to retire against their will and thus increases the life satisfaction and even longevity of reluctant retirees.

Common sense and popular opinion suggest, though, that workers as they age may still often be pressured to leave the job. For example, the majority of employers responsible for hiring and firing sampled in a national Harris poll said they believed older people were discriminated against in the workplace (reported in Tibbitts, 1979). Subtle pressures on older people to retire are difficult to measure directly. However, they can be inferred by looking at the hiring (not the firing) practices of people who must choose between young and older job applicants.

One reviewer (Sheppard, 1976) reports a variety of studies showing that older workers are less likely than the young to be rehired after industry layoffs. This is true even in high-status professions and when the effects of education are controlled for. He suggests that not only does this mean that on-the-job discrimination also occurs, but it explains some proportion of so-called voluntary early retirement. It is likely that many laid-off job seekers approaching the early retirement age simply opt to take this avenue when they cannot find new work.

**Health Influences.** Illness as an influence on why people retire should also be important if for no other reason than that it was a rationale for instituting the Social Security system in the first place. The need for Social Security was sold to the public because it was recognized that older people often could not work because of poor health and yet needed to live.

Chapter 2, however, suggests that only a certain type of ill health should affect a person's ability to work. People with conditions causing functional disabilities, not simply chronic diseases, are likely to need to leave work for health reasons. Our vignette underscores this point: Mr. Smith was forced to leave his job only when his long-standing chronic condition actually impaired his ability to perform.

Because, like Mr. Smith, a significant number of older people have functional impairments (see Chapter 2), we would expect many to retire because of poor health. In fact, in surveys health is high on the list of reasons retirees mention for leaving work (Foner & Schwab, 1981). This is particularly true of men who choose early retirement, as a ten-year longitudinal study of retirement in the United States, conducted by the Social Security Administration, revealed clearly. In this investigation, called the Retirement History Study, early retirees (age 58–63) were asked why they had chosen to leave the work force. Fully 65% of the males but only 38% of the females cited poor health as the crucial factor in their decision to retire (Ireland & Bond, 1976).

The magnitude of this male/female disparity might cause us to view the answers of some of these men with suspicion. It seems that this cohort of male early retirees in particular might feel pressured to justify their decision. Poor health, we might think, is a more acceptable reason for having prematurely abandoned the expected role of worker than others that might really be more accurate—for example, being fired or more subtly pressured to leave the job.

It is likely, however, that many men who retire early really are in poor health. We know simply because of their lower life expectancy that aging men are less healthy than aging women. We also know (see Chapter 2) that this cohort of older people in America are generally accurate or even optimistic reporters of their physical condition. Finally, there is some objective evidence from the Retirement History Study to validate these early retirees' claims. Early-retiring respondents in the study were more likely to have been hospitalized in the year preceding their leaving work than those who retired at an older age (Foner & Schwab, 1981).

And yet there are also signs that some early retirees may magnify the extent of their disabilities as a rationale for leaving work. The Retirement History Study data, too, bear out this opposite view. Although it is true that early retirees overall were hospitalized more often than those who remained at work, many respondents in the study who stayed on the job had physical impairments identical to those of many of the same early retirees, or even more severe ones (Foner & Schwab, 1981). So poor health may sometimes become crucial when a person encounters discrimination at work, for example, or finds working unattractive. This latter possibility brings us to the importance of attitude toward one's job as an influence on the decision to retire.

**Attitudinal Influences.**    It is likely that disliking one's job would predispose a person to retire early. Conversely, being happy with one's work should go along with making the opposite decision: to retire late. Another idea is just as reasonable: workers who are favorable to the thought of being retired will tend to leave the labor force sooner than those who feel negatively about the prospect of making this life change. Finally, it only makes sense that one's attitudes toward work and toward being retired should themselves be related. People who are highly committed to their work should also be most adverse to the idea of living without working. Those who dislike their jobs should be most favorable to the thought of being retired.

There is evidence that people who are committed to their jobs and dislike the idea of retirement leave work later. People with higher education and less financial need, factors possibly implying a greater job commitment, tend to retire late (Fillenbaum, 1971a).

A major longitudinal study of retirement, to be described in some detail next (Streib & Schneider, 1971), also found that an aversion to the idea of being retired went along with a person's leaving the work force late. Respondents who said they were initially reluctant to retire did in fact delay stopping work. Those who said they were willing to retire were most likely to leave their jobs early.

Surprisingly, however, a person's attitudes toward work and retirement are not related in themselves. Workers who say they like their jobs feel just as favorable toward the idea of being retired as those who do not (Fillenbaum, 1971b; Glamser, 1976). This unexpected finding makes more sense in the context of the recent revolution in the way retirement is viewed in our society. Retirement has now become an expected life change, a transition viewed as appropriate, even intrinsic to old age. This shared perception of near inevitability may in itself explain why, for Americans, feelings about one's retirement have become divorced from feelings about one's work.

We might argue, however, that this cohort of men in particular, when actually faced with the immediate prospect of retiring, should react more negatively to the loss of what is the traditionally central male role than they do. The idea that leaving work becomes palatable to older men makes sense, though, in conjunction with the material on personality changes presented in the last chapter. An intra-psychic shift toward more home-oriented, traditionally feminine values does ex-plain why facing retirement seems relatively nontraumatic for older males. In addition to this probable psychological reorientation in late midlife, a fascinating piece of evidence suggests that the work role specifically may become less central psychologically to men as they approach their retirement years.

One study (Cohn, 1979) had this implication, although, being cross-sectional, it could only suggest that shifts in the centrality of work occur when retirement becomes relatively imminent. The researcher asked men of different ages about the degree of intrinsic satisfaction they got from work. He then related their an-swers to a measure of overall satisfaction with life. Just as many older as younger men reported intrinsic satisfaction with their work, but only in the younger men was a high level of work satisfaction positively related to overall happiness. For the older men, in sharp contrast, joy in work was uncorrelated with overall joy in life. In other words, although satisfaction with one's job does not decline with age, the emotional importance of one's work may diminish in just this way. As men ap-proach retirement, whether they enjoy work becomes psychologically less rele-vant. Work well-being is less central to general well-being.

### Consequences of Retirement

What are the financial consequences of not working? Is being retired good or bad for one's health? How do older people adapt psychologically to this major life change?

Some answers to these questions were already available more than 20 years ago, as a major study of retirement had already been completed in the late 1950s. In this ambitious, nationwide, seven-year longitudinal investigation, called the Cor-nell Study of Occupational Retirement (Streib & Schneider, 1971), male and fe-male retirees were followed from the year before they left work through their first few retirement years. Respondents in a variety of professions and work settings were included. Many of the study's major findings are true to this day.

**Financial Effects.**   The Cornell researchers found that although there was considerable variability, in the first year of retirement, respondents' income dropped, on the average, about 50%. This figure is similar to the results of more recent assessments of how retirement affects people financially (Foner & Schwab, 1981). Many retirees do not seem as unhappy as we might think by this new state of affairs. At least this was true of the Cornell sample. The majority said that their income, even though lower, was clearly adequate to meet their needs.

A lack of verbalized upset in the face of marked negative financial changes, as we will see, has been found to be true too of widows, many of whom must adjust to a much lower income after their husbands' death; but it seems at first glance to be surprising. Adapting to economic reversals is generally thought to be quite stressful. Retirement and widowhood, however, are *expected* to lead to reductions in one's standard of living. This very predictability itself may make adjustments easier, as may the fact that here modeling can so effortlessly occur. Many of the older person's peers are retired or widowed and likely have been observed adapting in a similar way.

**Health Effects.**    In contrast to its often profound effect on finances, retirement seems to have no negative consequences for health. This lack of relationship was found both in the Cornell study and in other research (Atchley, 1979). Health declines at the same rate after retirement as it does before. In fact, the Cornell researchers discovered that, for respondents in unskilled occupations, health actually seemed to improve after leaving their jobs.

The same is true of statistics on deaths, but only for people who retire at the appropriate time (Haynes, McMichael, & Tyroler, 1978). Mortality does not rise at a higher-than-expected rate immediately after people reach the classic retirement age. Early retirees, though, do show higher-than-average death rates in the first year after they stop work. This finding too makes sense if we remember that a main reason people choose to retire early is poor health. In fact, the finding is another sign of the general validity of this rationale most often given by early-retiring men for leaving work.

**Effects on Morale.**    As with health, the Cornell researchers and others (George & Maddox, 1977; Thompson, 1973) have failed to find a change in morale after retirement. The only negative effect of leaving work on a retiree's life satisfaction revealed in the Cornell investigation was fairly trivial—a slight increase in feelings of uselessness the year after retirement.

Actually, retirees may even be happier than they expected. Some Cornell respondents said they were surprised at how easily they appeared to be adjusting. They had felt making such a radical life change would be more difficult than it actually was.

**Factors Influencing Retirement Adjustment.**    This generally rosy picture of how retirees adapt, though, needs some qualification. As our discussion of subjectively rated health in Chapter 2 reveals, some of this cohort of elderly may have a bias against complaining, which could influence their responses to questions about the quality of life after retiring.

In addition, the findings just cited deal with averages. Some elderly people are clearly not happy with their lives as retirees. This is most true of those with health or money worries (Foner & Schwab, 1981; Glamser, 1981). As indicated by the discussion of personality continuity in the previous chapter, this dissatisfied group also may (although this is only speculation) include people who are unsuited in less tangible ways to life in their new role.

**BOX 7-2.  Wives of Retirees**

Of course a paramount question is the effect of leaving work on the person who has traditionally been the worker, the husband. A related concern, however, is just as important. How does a wife adapt to her husband's retirement? As in our vignette, couples may be concerned about the effects of retirement on even the best marriage. Wives in particular may worry about their ability to cope with a life partner suddenly transformed into a full-time companion.

Two researchers (Keating & Cole, 1980) examined just this issue, looking at, among other things, how women adapted to their husbands' being retired. The subjects in this research were male teachers (and their wives), aged 63–68 who had left the labor force within the past three years.

Retirement did affect these middle-class marriages from the wife's point of view. However, its impact was as likely to be positive as negative. Most women complained about a loss of privacy and increased demands on their time. Many, though, said these negative effects were offset by increased marital closeness and enhanced feelings of being needed. Some women mainly resented their husbands' being around, but most thoroughly enjoyed this greater contact and appreciated the increased chance to nurture their spouses that retirement brought.

Research cited in the last chapter illustrates that people tend, in some measure, to carry over their dominant lifestyles as adults into old age. If we accept the evidence that continuity may characterize many aspects of adult behavior, then we might predict that people most easily able to make the transfer of previous interests to retirement would be likely to be happiest in their new life situation. For example, the professors described in the previous chapter were able to make this change smoothly and directly. Their solution was to continue to work and publish in much the same way after being formally retired as before. Other groups may be able to make this translation just as easily, though in a more indirect manner. For example, workers whose jobs and preretirement activities had involved dealing with people might easily be able to fit into the more interpersonally focused activities of this new life stage (Atchley, 1971). Even having an adult hobby compatible with retirement might foster positive adjustment. Mr. Smith's painting is a perfect example. Conversely, it seems only reasonable that when the options in retirement are totally foreign to a person's previous interests, he or she may well have the most trouble fitting happily into the role of retiree.

Interestingly, people do seem to know beforehand whether being retired will be good for them. The Cornell investigators found that a person's prior positive or negative attitude toward the prospect of being retired was the best predictor of eventual adaptation to this new way of life. Cornell respondents who said they were willing to retire were happier later than those who initially expressed an aversion to leaving work. Another group of researchers (Kimmel et al., 1978) found that previous attitude was much more important to postretirement adjustment than whether retirement had been voluntary.

### *Interventions*

Our discussion of personality continuity implies that at least some workers might be helped by preparing in advance for retirement. At the very least, if preparation occurred early enough, it might enable some people to change before-hand and develop interests compatible with what is possible in this life stage. Alternatively, options in retirement themselves could be broadened—for example, by including possibilities for retirees to do more varied things and things more akin to work. There have been efforts to address these dual needs.

Preretirement programs focus on preparing older workers for retirement in advance, facilitating what sociologists call **anticipatory socialization** to the retirement role (Foner & Schwab, 1981). Anticipatory socialization is the process of learning a role before one enters it. This type of active learning, it is thought, helps people adjust to all major life transitions, not just retirement, by mitigating the discontinuity involved in making these often marked shifts.

Preretirement programs may be relatively limited, involving just, for example, explaining Social Security to prospective retirees; or they may be extensive, involving many sessions devoted to exploring various aspects of life as a retired person. One study (Glamser & DeJong, 1975) compared the effects of no program, a brief one, and a more in-depth effort in getting workers to think about and prepare for retirement. Male industrial workers in their last years of employment were assigned to one of three groups: eight sessions of intense peer discussions exploring all facets of retirement, one 30-minute session devoted to explaining retirement benefits, or no intervention. Workers in the eight-session group were stimulated to make specific plans for their retirement as a consequence of this intensive experience. The minimal individual session, in contrast, elicited no such changes. It was as ineffective as no intervention at all in encouraging preretirement planning.

It is highly unlikely, though, that redirecting a person's basic interests is attainable even through the most intensive preretirement program. Perhaps partly because these groups must therefore have limited goals, perhaps partly because so many people are happy being retired anyway, preretirement sessions have failed to demonstrate that they actually do enhance satisfaction after leaving work (Foner & Schwab, 1981; Glamser, 1981). However, the programs, at the minimum, can serve a very useful function. By informing workers and getting them to prepare for such a momentous transition, they should ease anxiety. In fact, one outcome of the study just mentioned was that workers exposed to the eight-session preretirement group said they felt much less apprehensive about the prospect of leaving work than before.

There are many current efforts to fulfill our second suggestion—to broaden possible roles for retirees. For example, many colleges are now competing for retired students, and there are impressive educational programs specifically for retired adults (Bynum, Cooper, & Acuff, 1978). Opportunities for retired people to do volunteer work are also expanding, as are the possibilities of getting some pay for these jobs. The following are three of the best-known volunteer programs for older people, all sponsored by the federal government (Holmes & Holmes, 1979).

The Retired Senior Volunteer Program gives older people the chance to volunteer in places such as hospitals, prisons, and schools. Participants are reimbursed for their transportation, meals, and other expenses related to their service. The Foster Grandparent Program is designed specifically for the low-income elderly. Participants are paid a small stipend to work with physically and emotionally handicapped children in various institutional and private settings. Finally, a volunteer program for retired businesspersons, the Service Corps of Retired Executives, enables executives to use their business skills directly in helping others. Volunteers serve as advisers to small businesses and community organizations.

## Widowhood

Like retirement, losing a spouse is a common occurrence for older people. In contrast to retirement, however, there are no surveys proclaiming the value of this unwelcome transition or programs designed to prepare people psychologically for this traumatic event. Also in contrast to retirement, the passage to being widowed is not helpfully institutionalized to occur at a particular age. Dealing with the death of a spouse, though, is predictable in one way: as in our vignette, it is most likely to befall women, because of their higher life expectancy and their tendency to marry older men.

The importance of widowhood in a woman's life is clearly revealed by some simple statistics. In 1975 there were over 10 million widows in the United States— fully 1 out of 7 or 8 women over age 18. The same census revealed that of the more than 67.8 million men over 18, only 1.8 million were widowers (Lopata, 1979). Because of this disproportion, most of the research on death of a spouse looks specifically at how females adapt. Our discussion too will focus mainly on widows, although we will also review some studies involving widowers.

The chances of being a widow increase with age. Among women just about to enter the ranks of the young-old (60–64), a recent census revealed that 25% were widows; among the very aged (women over 85), the corresponding figure was 75% (Lopata, 1979).

Being a widow means, first of all, mourning the painful loss of a life companion. After recovering from the acute shock of this loss, it also can mean making a change in most aspects of one's life. Relationships with friends often must be modified or broken, as many friendships during marriage are predicated on being part of a couple. Other ties can be attenuated or lost—relations with one's husband's relatives, for example. If children are absent or grown, the widow usually has to adapt to living alone, often with reduced income. She needs to make herself over from a person who has for much of her life been dependent on someone else for concrete and emotional support to a person who has mainly herself to depend on (Lopata, 1973). Being widowed also means reorganizing central aspects of the way the woman thinks about herself, remaking an identity whose root, at least for many of today's widows, had encompassed the idea of herself as a married person. A psychiatrist (Parkes, 1972), whose research on widows during the first year of bereavement we will examine in the next section, beautifully describes how

---

**BOX 7-3.    Chances of Remarriage for the Elderly and the Widowed**

Clearly the large numbers of widowed women bode ill for the older widow who wants to remarry. They should cause joy to the widower who wants to find a mate. Just how common is remarriage in a given year in older Americans? Specifically, what are the chances of widows and widowers of different ages being able to find a spouse?

To answer the first question, Treas and Vanhilst (1976) looked at statistics from 47 states for the year 1970. They found the following patterns. Marriage after 65 was unlikely for people of both sexes, especially, as we might expect, for women. Whereas fewer than 3 of every 1000 single women aged 65 and over married in that year, the corresponding figure for men was 17. In addition, also as we would imagine, many more men married younger women than older women married younger men. A full 20% of the elderly grooms had brides 55 or younger; the corresponding figure for women was less than 3%.

Cleveland and Gianturco (1976) examined the second question, remarriage chances specifically for the widowed of different ages, by looking at all marriage certificates in North Carolina from April 1970 through March 1971 and comparing data on widows and widowers who married with their total number of a corresponding age in the state that year. Not unexpectedly, remarriage probabilities for both sexes proved to be high for people widowed young (under 35) and steadily decreased for successively older age groups. Also not unexpectedly, the remarriage chances decreased faster for widows than for widowers. In fact, the researchers calculated that while widowers between 65 and 74 had about one chance in four of remarrying, the remarriage probability for elderly White widows was a meager 0.004.

---

some basic perceptions can be altered after the death of a spouse: "Even when words remain the same their meaning changes—the family is no longer the same object it was. Neither is home or a marriage" (p. 93).

In our vignette we can see how Mrs. Smith had to cope with these internal and external changes. Now we will see how typical her behavior and adaptations are of most widows.

Unfortunately, though, comparisons are sparse. In marked contrast to the many studies dealing with retirement, very few explore how people deal with the loss of a spouse. Inquiring into such a sensitive area may be difficult for researchers. Many may balk at the prospect of scientifically probing into another's pain. However, those brave enough to research this difficult topic have found many of their respondents surprisingly willing subjects (Lopata, 1973). It is often a welcome comfort for widows and widowers to talk openly about this difficult experience.

Most studies of being widowed usually focus on one of the following two areas: they either attempt to understand the period of mourning itself, looking at the symptoms of acute grief and what impedes or facilitates the bereaved person's ability to eventually come to terms with the loss, or they examine the widowed state itself, looking at the personalities, relationships, or activities of widowed people who have passed the period of acute mourning. Investigations of the period of bereavement tend to be undertaken by psychoanalytically oriented mental health clinicians interested at least partly in helping people cope by understanding normal and abnormal mourning. The landmark studies of the widowed state were done by Lopata, a sociologist interested in examining various aspects of the role of widow in contemporary urban America.

### *Bereavement*

**Normal Mourning.**   Writing during World War II, a practicing psychiatrist (Lindemann, 1944) was the first person to systematically investigate reactions after the death of a loved one. In focusing on bereavement as an area worthy of study, his goal was to see whether there was such a phenomenon as normal mourning and so identify those whose reactions were abnormal and could make them at risk for eventually adapting poorly to their loss. From his clinical observations of a large number of grieving people, he identified certain symptoms as characteristic of bereavement. These included the common physiological signs of any upset—for example, crying or problems in eating and sleeping—as well as some psychological responses that were not so typical. Mourners, Lindemann observed, were often troubled by guilt that they had not done enough for the now-lost loved one while he or she was alive. They often felt angry at or distant from others, even those they normally cared about. Perhaps most interesting, they typically were preoccupied with the image of the deceased person, at times so intensely that they almost hallucinated the person's presence or felt the deceased was alive in some way. This last reaction in particular, we might remember, frightened Mrs. Smith, who saw it as a sign of impending mental breakdown.

These early observations were corroborated and extended by the findings of another study by a psychiatrist of acute mourning, this time involving just widows (Parkes, 1972; see Recommended Readings). Parkes reported in depth on the responses of a small group of London widows during their first year of mourning. He too found that excessive anger, inappropriate guilt, and a sense of the lost spouse's actual physical presence were all predictable symptoms of bereavement. In addition, he discovered that the women he examined were frequently obsessed with the events of the death itself and experienced the need to repeatedly go over the circumstances immediately preceding their loss. The bereaved widow also often felt the compulsion to search for her dead husband even though she knew she was being irrational. On occasion a widow showed an almost total sense of identification, feeling her dead spouse was actually part of herself. An example of this latter reaction is revealed by a poignant statement made by one of the London respondents: "My husband is in me right through and through. I can feel him in me doing everything. . . . I suppose he is guiding me the whole of the time" (Parkes, 1972, p. 89). We might conjecture that even an identification this intense could be adaptive for this widow and others in need. It may be a way both to deny the full impact of the loss and simultaneously to give the person the strength to take on needed jobs once performed by a spouse. Mrs. Smith's hobby, too, is a clear example of how identification can serve a related function—to broaden a person's interests.

Parkes was interested not just in the manifestations of grief but also in its course and eventual outcome. His observations showed that bereavement reactions generally were predictable in this respect too. With some variation, he found that acute grief consisted of an initial period of numbness followed by waves of intense yearning and pining alternating with periods of depression and apathy. As time elapsed, the pining tended to decrease in intensity and frequency, although it could always be reevoked at reminders of the dead husband. Eventually most widows were able to begin to remake a new life.

**Abnormal and Overly Intense Mourning.**    In both studies some members of the sample adapted poorly to their loss. Lindemann's observations led him to the idea that one influence in particular seemed important in how easily a person could recover. People who initially broke down and let themselves experience the full impact of the death seemed to adjust best to the trauma. Those who at first denied or minimized its importance seemed to suffer particularly severe and unremitting negative psychological reactions later. He coined the term *grief work* to describe this phenomenon of intense mourning and suggested that undertaking grief work was crucial to the bereaved person's eventual ability to come to terms with the death (Lindemann, 1944).

Parkes's study too suggested that aborted grief work was associated with poor emotional adjustment. The bereavement responses of the London widows seemed to fit into three patterns. In the first, the widow became severely disturbed within a week of her spouse's death, was highly upset for about two months, and then appeared to recover, showing only mild signs of disturbance after three months. Widows showing the second pattern got most upset during the second week of bereavement and then rapidly improved. Those experiencing the third type of mourning response were rated as most disturbed and least able to function well at the end of the first year of bereavement. This group tended to have delayed grief responses, appearing relatively calm and untouched by their loss during the first few weeks.

On the basis of these and other observations of the bereaved (see Greenblatt, 1978), counselors now encourage people who have experienced the death of a loved one to mourn actively and openly. For example, intervention programs for widows are often designed specifically to help grief work take place. They involve sessions devoted to the widow's talking about her loss and giving full vent to all her feelings. This approach counteracts the tendency so prevalent in our vignette. Friends and relatives of the bereaved often avoid this painful topic to spare their own, and what they think are the widow's, feelings.

Clearly, then, an emphasis on grief work is often a good thing. It prevents the bereaved person from having to stifle his or her feelings. However, it too may have its pitfalls. Assuming that one mourning style suits everyone does not do justice to the importance of individual differences, the diversity of human beings.

Most crucial, there is little empirical evidence that open, intense mourning is best. The London sample was too small to make this generalization. Lindemann's conclusions about the importance of grief work were based on clinical observations, not systematic tests. Finally, as we know by now, even a firmly documented correlation of grief work with good eventual adaptation would far from prove a causal link. A multiplicity of influences, as Table 7-1 suggests, seem likely to affect how easily a person recovers from this painful life event.

Two possibilities listed in the table have received a disproportionate amount of attention: the mode of a spouse's death (that is, expected or unexpected) and the age of the widow or widower at the time of the loss. Several studies have shown that sudden, unexpected deaths are most traumatic for the widowed or any person who has lost a loved one. Research has also suggested that older people tend to adapt better than the young or middle-aged to losing a marital partner (Ball, 1976–77; Clayton, 1979; Parkes, 1972).

**TABLE 7-1.** Hypothetical determinants of the outcome of bereavement.

---

**Antecedent**
Childhood experiences (especially losses of significant persons)
Later experiences (especially losses of significant persons)
Previous mental illness (especially depressive illness)
Life crises prior to the bereavement
Relationship with the deceased
  Kinship
  Strength of attachment
  Security of attachment
  Degree of reliance
  Intensity of reliance
  Intensity of ambivalence (love/hate)

**Mode of death**
  Timeliness
  Previous warnings
  Preparation for bereavement
  Need to hide feelings

**Concurrent**
  Sex
  Age
  Personality
    Grief proneness, inhibition of feelings
  Socioeconomic status
  Nationality
  Religion
  Cultural factors
  Familial factors

**Subsequent**
  Social support or isolation
  Secondary stresses
  Emergent life opportunities

---

*(Source: From* Bereavement: Studies of Grief in Adult Life, *by C. M. Parkes. Copyright 1972 by International Universities Press. Reprinted by permission.)*

Both these findings make sense if we once again invoke the related concepts of anticipatory socialization and modeling. When a death is expected, one has time to prepare oneself for one's new role, life without a partner. This anticipatory socialization for life alone is felt even to include some of the necessary grief work that usually occurs after the death (Clayton, Halikas, Maurice, & Robins, 1973).

The same is true of the elderly, as death in an older person is also in a sense always expected and so at least potentially prepared for in advance. For instance, older and late-middle-aged women in particular have ample opportunities to be socialized to the role of widow by modeling, watching the experiences of their friends. Empathizing with friends who are mourning a spouse's death is a kind of implicit rehearsal and preparation for one's own widowhood. At the very least it points up the likelihood of the same event happening to oneself. In contrast, the young widow or widower lacks the chance to have this vicarious experience, and so being widowed, when it happens, is likely to be shocking and totally foreign.

This line of reasoning suggests, however, that if anticipatory socialization for a spouse's death occurs to some extent for most elderly individuals anyway, then the mode by which that death occurs may be irrelevant to the older person's ability to cope. In other words, for the elderly, we might predict, since death is always expected, sudden deaths should be no more traumatic than prolonged ones. In fact, if we consider the debilitating effects of caring for an ill marital partner, so evident in our clinical vignette, we might even suggest that elderly widows and widowers would be less able to adapt when their spouses' death occurred after an extended illness.

There is some evidence that this is so. In one investigation in which the intensity of grief experienced six months after being widowed was rated, it was mainly for the younger widows and widowers that more severe symptoms were associated with sudden rather than extended deaths (Ball, 1976–77). In another study, in which most of the widowed were over 60, those experiencing the prolonged fatal illness of a spouse actually had more physical and psychological reactions one month after the loss than those whose spouses had died more abruptly (Clayton et al., 1973). In this latter study, though, the two groups of widowed subjects had adapted equally well at one year. This means that the negative impact for the older person of dealing with an extended illness may be confined to the initial period of bereavement.

**Consequences of Bereavement.**   Our discussion so far has neglected an important question: What actually are the detrimental consequences for most people of experiencing the profoundly stressful event of a spouse's death? Likely longer-term negative effects of this trauma might include an increased incidence of psychological problems in general in widows and widowers. Another possibility, suggested by the rating of death of a spouse as the most stressful event on the Social Readjustment Rating Scale (see Chapter 2), is that the first months of mourning could carry an increased risk of disease and even death in the surviving spouse.

Interestingly, the elderly seem to adapt remarkably well, both psychologically and to some extent physically, to bereavement. Clayton (1979), comparing the psychological adjustment of older widows and widowers with that of the still married, found that the bereaved were not appreciably more disturbed in the year after their loss. Compared with older married couples, the elderly widowed do have higher rates of depression (Blazer & Williams, 1980). However, their long-term psychological adaptation seems remarkably good (Heyman & Gianturco, 1973).

This is also true when we look at nonfatal physical symptoms in older people who have recently lost a spouse. Parkes (1972), for example, reported studies showing that younger widows are hospitalized more frequently and visit their doctors with more medical complaints during the first year of bereavement. He could find, however, no comparable evidence that *older* widows had increased rates of disease.

Losing a spouse, though, does seem to affect one group of elderly people in a highly negative way. Like the younger bereaved of both sexes, older men have elevated mortality rates during the period just after a spouse's death. This high-risk period occurs in the first six months of bereavement, as life-stress theory would predict (Jacobs & Ostfeld, 1977). A recent longitudinal investigation suggests that it lasts unless the older widower remarries. In widowers who remarry, the mortality rate once again drops to normal; in those who do not, it stays elevated (Helsing, Szklo, & Comstock, 1981). Although once again we must caution care in inferring causality from this type of research, one possibility is that being married, at least for men, may be good for one's health. Unfortunately, no parallel evidence exists for the salutary effect of marriage on women. There is no hint that women's death rate changes in either direction after losing a spouse.

### Life as a Widow

Intense mourning is only the first phase of the transition to widowhood. It says nothing about what happens to the person after the acute impact of a spouse's death when life must proceed in a new way. To understand what this life is like, we have the benefit of two large-scale, cross-sectional studies of widows. In these landmark investigations, directed by Lopata (1973, 1979; see Recommended Readings), a research team conducted extensive interviews with large numbers of widows in the Chicago area, women of varying religions, ethnic backgrounds, and social classes.

The subjects in the first study were 301 widows over age 50, interviewed in their homes (Lopata, 1973). The sample was selected so that half the group was under and half over 65. These women had been widowed for varying lengths of time. The vast majority were well past the initial period of bereavement; on the average, they had lived without their husbands for 11 years.

The focus of this study was mainly to understand the widows' current life situation, but the research team also questioned them about aspects of their lives with their husbands and the events leading up to and immediately following the husbands' death. Questions were designed to elicit information about the widow's attitude toward and performance in a variety of roles—wife, mother, relative, friend, and participant in organized activities in the community. The widow's overall degree of social isolation was also measured, as was her attitude toward the way others responded to her specifically and widows in general. The following are among the items tapping these latter feelings from a measure called the Relations Restrictive Attitude Scale*:

1. Widows are constantly sexually propositioned even by the husbands of their friends.
2. People take advantage of you when they know you are a widow.
3. Many widows who remarry are very unhappy in that marriage.
4. Sharing one's home with anyone causes nothing but trouble for a widow.
5. My married friends have not been much help to me.
6. When they become widows, women lose status, respect and consideration.
7. A widow has to make her own life and not depend on anyone.
8. Relatives are your only true friends.

The study revealed that the women were living what were actually very independent lives. The vast majority either lived alone or were heads of households. Widows living by themselves complained of loneliness but usually said they preferred the arrangement, particularly when the alternative was living with adult offspring. The personal freedom of living alone was valued, and many widows stated they feared that moving in with children might create too much friction. This spirit of independence also extended to financial matters. Although more than half the widows had experienced a sharp drop in income after their husbands' death, few reported that their finances were really restricted. Even fewer wanted to or actually did receive monetary aid of any kind from relatives.

For many of these widows the role of wife had been, as in our clinical example, central to their adult lives. Fully 20% felt, as Mrs. Smith did, that they had never really gotten over their husbands' death. However, most said they did not want to remarry, citing, among other reasons, their age, fear that they would have to take care of an ailing husband (one-sixth had nursed their husbands at home for at least a year before the death), and their feelings that they could never find a man as good as their late spouses. This last rationale for not remarrying is particularly interesting, as it signaled a general tendency for many widows to romanticize their life with their husbands. Some respondents idealized their spouses' memory almost to the point of sanctification.

Current relationships, particularly with children, seemed more ambivalent and conflict-ridden. Although offspring were very important to most widows, relations with them were rarely uniformly close. Usually one child in particular, most often a daughter, was closest to the woman. Ties with other kin seemed much more peripheral (see also Lopata, 1978a). For example, most women reported that they had a sibling but (like Mrs. Smith) talked to this person infrequently or not at all.

Friends were important mainly to the best-educated widows. Many women reported problems in modifying friendships based on being part of a couple. When

*Adapted from *Widowhood in an American City*, by H. Z. Lopata. Copyright © 1973 by Schenkman Publishing Co. Reprinted by permission.

relationships could not survive the strain of this life change, the widow had to make new friends. Apparently one reason friendships were important particularly to the best-educated widows was that educated women were more adept at making these new adaptations. They were most likely to have the social skills to transform the character of old friendships or build new ones.

---

**BOX 7-4.   Do Divorcees Adjust Less Well to Being Single than Widows?**

Divorce and widowhood have many of the same consequences: the need to mourn a loss, the need to change many aspects of one's life, the need to adapt psychologically to one's changed status. Because widowhood often means the end of a happy situation, we might assume widows should be more bitter about their life situation than divorcees. However, because divorce is often fraught with anger and signals having failed personally, we might more reasonably feel that divorcees would adjust less well. It is they who should feel more negatively about themselves and how others treat them in their new role as a single person.

Lopata and her coworkers had an ideal opportunity to test this question by comparing the responses of her widows on some items of the Relations Restrictive Attitude Scale to those of divorcees (Kitson, Lopata, Holmes, & Meyering, 1980). They merely substituted the word *divorcee* for *widow* in the scale questions. Not unexpectedly, they found that divorcees had a much more negative attitude toward their new life than widows. Divorced women were more likely to feel, for example, that they had lost status (see number 6) or were taken advantage of (see number 2). They were more prone to feel suspicious of others (see number 8). In general, they were more unhappy, which is really no surprise. Divorce, unlike widowhood, is an event tailor-made for feeling bad about oneself and angry toward the world.

---

In fact, education and social class were important variables predicting a widow's overall adaptation to her new life. Lopata found that the least-educated, lower-class widows were most likely to be dissatisfied and socially isolated. She suggested that the traditional upbringing and way of living these women had experienced was partly to blame, as it stressed conformity to rules, dependence, and lack of the need for initiative in making changes. Traditionally reared women, she argued, could adjust well to widowhood only when their new environment remained relatively stable. When being widowed involved having to make many new adaptations, these women had not been equipped by their training to cope. One price they paid was disengagement from others. This social isolation, in turn, was associated with low morale. Lower-class, isolated widows tended to have poor scores on the Relations Restrictive Attitude Scale, a result that is additional evidence against the equation of disengagement with ideal aging.

In addition to serving as another disconfirmation of disengagement theory, this information supports the Berkeley findings of lifestyle continuity throughout later adulthood in the absence of an environment that forces change (see Chapter 6). The Chicago widows clearly transferred their previous approach to life to their new situation. When their external situation meant continuity could not occur, in some cases their coping failed, and they developed problems. (Because Mrs. Smith could cope so well with being widowed, she may have had an upbringing and marriage that, even though protective, also allowed her a chance to develop initiative. Otherwise she might not have had such an easy time making the transformation to independence when her circumstances demanded a new way of living.)

The second study of widows (Lopata, 1979) enlarged on the findings of the first and gave additional insights into some of the gaps in these women's lives. The research team interviewed a large group of widows selected from the ranks of current and former Social Security recipients. The aim this time was specifically to focus on what was called the widow's "support systems": who helped the woman, whom she helped, and how much support she got from and gave to others in important areas of her life.

This investigation also showed that most widows were highly independent. Respondents seldom reported receiving financial aid from friends and relatives or help from anyone with concrete activities such as shopping or housework (see also Lopata, 1978a, 1978b). Children were cited as the most important class of people providing tangible help when it was given and the most important source of emotional support. Interestingly, though, when asked to list the people they were closest to and most dependent on emotionally, widows often named themselves or their dead husbands. Although our vignette shows that a widow can be attached to a dead husband and still live a full, involved life, the limited quality of these responses suggested that many of these women were quite lonely; that is, it indicated their independence may have had a negative tinge, signaling isolation from others.

An identical impression emerged when looking at the widow's social life. In a scale gauging what the research team called the social support system, the woman was asked how often she participated in a variety of common social activities. Over half the widows reported that they never went to public places such as movie theaters; 4 in 10 never entertained; 4 in 10 always ate lunch alone. Financial considerations probably played a large part in restricting these widows. However, their responses do reveal that, for whatever reason, a significant number lived somewhat impoverished lives.

### Interventions

It must be emphasized that these studies are confined to a single cohort. In the future widows may be less fiercely independent, more prone to chance new involvements, and even more willing to risk visiting restaurants or movie theaters alone. Still, the results suggest that widows in this cohort are too isolated. To Lopata, her findings meant they could use societal help. Formal community groups providing information, opportunities to socialize, and even concrete services, she felt, might have made these women's lives easier. Such groups could have given isolated widows lacking social skills ready-made opportunities to form new relationships. They might have obviated the necessity for a widow in need of help with particular tasks to make the difficult choice between doing without any aid and feeling she had to burden family and friends. They might even have provided significant emotional support, particularly during the difficult initial period of bereavement. However, institutionalized help was almost totally absent from widows' lists of supporting influences both in the present and right after their loss. Religious organizations, government agencies, and other community groups whose job it might have been to provide services to widows were rarely mentioned in Chicago subjects' catalogues of support systems (Lopata, 1978a).

This lack is unfortunate, as structured help, particularly from groups set up specifically to help widows and widowers cope, has been shown to be beneficial. A study by Raphael (1977) demonstrates the utility of even a limited form of intervention. Widows under age 60 at risk for poor adaptation to bereavement were randomly allocated to treatment and no-treatment conditions in the early weeks following their husbands' death. At-risk widows were defined as those who seemed to have had ambivalent relationships with their spouses, whose social network was unsupportive, who had experienced several recent life crises, and whose husbands had died traumatically. The treatment consisted of regular, two-hour sessions during the first three months of bereavement, devoted to having the widow openly share feelings about her loss. At the end of a 13-month period, the widows who had participated in the treatment rated themselves as less depressed, reported fewer physical symptoms, had visited their family physicians less often, and generally were better in a variety of ways than widows who had not participated in the treatment.

In view of these results, we might expect that programs offering an even larger range of services could be even more helpful. These multifaceted programs, though, are not widely available. They have the added deficiency of depending on voluntary participation and so possibly missing some of the people most in need. A rare example of one such extensive service was begun in Boston in 1969 (McCourt, Barnett, Brennan, & Becker, 1976).

This program offers regular social gatherings and biweekly seminars dealing with issues pertinent to widowhood. It also operates a telephone hotline staffed by widow-volunteers who counsel callers on a variety of topics. Volunteer widows make weekly home visits, particularly during the first two months of bereavement, to those in need. These trained volunteers listen to the widow or widower, lending support during the difficult initial period following the loss and also afterward if the person appears to be adapting poorly.

There is a good reason that this Boston program and others emphasize the role of peer counselors, not professionals. The less recently widowed can serve as models to the newly bereaved and are often those best able to understand and empathize with their particular emotions and needs. In fact, even if not directly labeled, the use of widow-counselors is an instance of the application in practice of model-

ing. It is a systematic attempt to use this major type of learning to effect psychological change.

## Institutionalization

*Long-term-care* institutions include nursing homes, homes for the aged, and
places by other names that are set up to provide shelter and services for frail older
people in need of some medical care over an extended period. At first glance we
might consider our third transition, the change to living in one of these places, one
that touches the lives of relatively few elderly individuals. As mentioned in Chapter 1, it is estimated that only 5% of people over 65 live in long-term-care facilities.

Unfortunately, this 5% figure is cross-sectional and so in some ways highly mis-
leading. It does not give the probability of a given person's chances, once having
reached 65, of eventually being institutionalized at some point in his or her life.
Kastenbaum and Candy (1973) first revealed this fallacy by using an ingenious
approach. They examined the place of death noted on the death certificates of all
persons over 65 who died in Detroit during a certain year. Fully 24% were listed as
occurring in a long-term-care facility, indicating that the 5% figure, if used to measure the probability of being institutionalized after age 65, is surely a severe under-
statement.

In fact, 24%, too, may be a low estimate. The researchers counted only people
whose deaths occurred in institutions. Their figure leaves out those older people
who at some point lived in these homes and then died somewhere else. A follow-
up study of a group of elderly people who had died within ten years after they
were originally tested as part of another investigation lends weight to this view.
Here the investigators (Vincente, Wiley, & Carrington, 1979), in tracing the lives of
this sample, found that 39% had been institutionalized at some point.

Institutionalization, then, however brief, is likely to be a change experienced by
a significant minority of people once they have lived to age 65. Over 1 million
elderly are currently receiving long-term care. The number of extended-care beds
has increased dramatically over the past 20 years. There are now more beds of
this type in the United States than medical surgical beds. Institutionalization is also
expensive, financed largely by public funds. The system's cost per year now runs
into the billions of dollars (Brody, 1977).

Concomitant with this expansion has been the growing storm of criticism about
abuses in long-term care. Nursing homes and related institutions are generally
viewed as dumping grounds where people are railroaded by an indifferent society.
They are thought to provide scandalously poor care to older people, many of
whom are envisioned as potentially able to function in the community if they
were given the appropriate services. Institutions are seen as neglecting their occupants' valid medical needs or, at the opposite extreme, engendering excess disabilities by overtreating relatively unimpaired residents. Nursing home life itself is
thought to create psychological problems and often hasten death. Are these indict-
ments totally accurate? To attempt an answer, we need to look closely at the
institutions themselves as a prelude to our main goal, understanding the residents
they serve.

### The Institutions

**Types.**   It is difficult to determine what a particular nursing home or home for the aged does from its title. A facility's name gives little clue to the services it provides or the types of residents it accepts. One place called a nursing home may be much like a hospital, offering intensive medical services to seriously ill elderly residents. Another may be more akin to a college dormitory, offering room, board, and just a few nursing services to relatively physically well older people. Homes vary tremendously in size, staff/patient ratio, and philosophy. Their residents also may differ greatly. Some institutions restrict those they accept to one ethnic group or religion or occupation. Many limit the level of physical or mental impairment they will tolerate in their occupants (Manard, Kart, & Van Gils, 1975).

To get reimbursed by Medicaid or Medicare, institutions or beds within an institution must be graded according to the amount of nursing and medical care they offer. The reimbursement rate varies, and the type of reimbursement differs (Medicare or Medicaid), depending on the type of services a place is certified as providing. Facilities or, as is more likely, units within a facility are certified as giving skilled nursing care when they offer a relatively high complement of medical and nursing services. They are rated as intermediate-care or health-related units when they provide fewer of these services. Because intermediate-care settings or beds provide fewer nursing services, they are reimbursed at lower rates, and Medicare will not pay for a resident's stay in one of these settings. Presumably residents needing a given level of care are put in the appropriate place. We will see, though, that there is often an unfortunate mismatch between what a resident needs and the type of care he or she is assigned.

Long-term-care institutions also differ in their type of ownership. They may be voluntary (not run for a profit) or proprietary (run for a profit). Recently, there has been a tremendous increase in the number of chain-owned proprietary homes, so that they now constitute the majority of extended-care facilities. This phenomenon is not without its critics. Proprietary homes have often been the focus of scandals charging patient abuse. Some observers have consequently speculated that the profit motive in running homes, with its necessary emphasis on cost cutting at the expense of quality of services, may contribute to perpetuating substandard institutional care (U.S. Congress, 1974–76).

**Quality.**   The debate over the ability of for-profit homes to be unequivocally committed to providing the best care highlights another critical dimension differentiating long-term-care facilities—their quality. Some institutions provide good service, with staff generally committed to giving humane care. Others are at the opposite end of the continuum—insensitive to residents, inadequately serving their needs (Tobin, 1974).

Researchers interested in understanding which types of places are likely to provide the best care have generally defined and measured high quality in one of two ways. They may rank homes as high-quality on the basis of the amount of objective resources they have. These objective resources include tangible signs of quality such as high staff/resident ratio, breadth of services the home offers, or attractiveness of the home's physical setting. Alternatively, researchers may focus more on intangibles—for example, calling a home high-quality whose residents and staff are satisfied with themselves and where they live or work (Kosberg, 1974).

We might think these two types of indexes should be related. Residents of homes providing the best resources should be most likely to be content with their lives and life situation. Staff members working in a home where they have the tools and time to provide good care should also have relatively high morale.

In a review of the literature on tangible and intangible indicators of quality, Kosberg (1973) noted there did seem to be a relation between these two indexes. Homes rich in observable resources also had staff members who at least verbalized the necessity for providing therapeutic care. In resource-poor homes, even this minimal verbal staff commitment to residents was rarely observed.

The major study Kosberg described, a survey of 214 nursing homes in the Chicago area, also revealed an unsurprising finding about high quality. Homes rated as resource-rich tended to cater to the economically privileged. They were most often located in wealthy suburbs and had a high percentage of private, paying residents (Tobin, 1974; Kosberg, 1973). Interestingly, there was also a relation between the home's ownership and whether it was resource-rich. In common with a previously mentioned belief that for-profit homes are worse, the survey found that resource-rich homes were more likely to be operating under voluntary auspices (see also Gottesman, 1974).

Other surveys, however, have not found an association between a home's type of ownership and the quality of services it provides (Kosberg, 1974), although many have revealed the potent influence of economics in dictating the quality of care (Kart & Manard, 1976; Kosberg, 1973, 1974). Affluent older people get better care for obvious economic reasons. There is also a less obvious reason that they may be better served. Staff practices at homes catering to well-off residents are more likely to come under public scrutiny because these relatively privileged older people tend to have more friends and relatives who visit regularly and are likely to complain if they see maltreatment. Visitors from the outside may thus help to keep the institutional staff accountable. A study in Detroit, using as its index of high-quality care the number of staff contacts residents had, found that residents who had visitors at least once a month received the most staff attention (Gottesman & Bourestam, 1974).

The possibility that outside observers help to make institutional staff more responsible has led to the following proposal and program to combat the difficult problem of nursing home resident neglect or abuse. Barney (1974) has suggested that homes open their doors more to the community, by offering either regular seminars or the opportunity for interested people to do volunteer work with residents. This informal strategy, designed in part to monitor what goes on in these places, it is argued, would be more effective than the main mechanism that exists now—structured government inspections focused mainly on assessing the adequacy of a facility's physical plant.

**The Typical Institution.**   Our discussion until this point has neglected a most basic referent for evaluating institutional quality: we have no idea of what the typical nursing home is like or what the average resident does during his or her stay. To answer these questions, Gottesman and Bourestam (1974) went beyond looking at standard signs of quality, such as staff/patient ratio, to directly measure what it actually is that nursing homes do for their occupants. They observed a random sample of elderly residents at resource-rich and resource-poor homes in Detroit at regular intervals over a two-day period. They noted the particular behavior that was occurring and the physical and mental condition of the person being observed. Their upsetting finding was that more than half the time residents were observed doing absolutely nothing at all (that is, staring into space). Only during 7.5% of the observations were they seen interacting with any staff member. Nursing services went on even less frequently. Only 2% of the contacts observed involved this type of care being given.

At first glance these results reinforce the commonly held view that the institutional environment is malignant. It looks as if elderly residents in nursing homes are being forced to vegetate and live bereft of needed nursing services. However, before we blame the average nursing home for causing resident apathy and berate it for providing substandard care, we should look in some depth at the characteristics of the people these homes serve. It may be that many institutional residents do not need very much nursing care or that other facts about the occupants of these institutions will temper our judgment that their apathy is primarily *caused* by staff neglect.

### The Residents

**Types.**   Nursing home residents vary greatly in background, life experience, temperament, and almost every other characteristic that can differentiate people (Brody, 1973). The characteristics of the "typical" resident will also vary depending on whether we choose to study people admitted to or discharged from facilities or to use as our reference group those currently residing in long-term care. When we choose, as is most common, to profile residents actually living in homes, our portrait is perhaps excessively negative. Those who stay a long time, the most disabled, are overrepresented.

So these caveats need to be kept in mind in making generalizations about the nursing home population. Still, the following general statements about this diverse group may legitimately be made (see Brody, 1977; Gelfand & Olsen, 1979; Gottesman & Brody, 1975; Manard et al., 1975).

As Figure 7-3 shows, institutional residents are likely to be old-old (75+) but are by no means exclusively so. Mainly because of sex differences in longevity, they are also likely to be female. They are disproportionately White. Minorities have a lower life expectancy, and unfortunately institutional care is often not as freely available to non-Whites. As we know because their care is often paid for by Medicaid, residents tend to be poor. Most important, they often have functional disabilities that make them unable to live in the community. The option of institu-

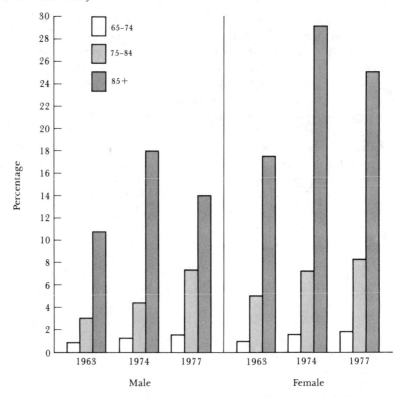

**FIGURE 7-3.** Percentage of the population 65 and over in nursing homes by sex and age group, 1963, 1974, and 1977. *(Source: From* Chartbook on Aging in America *by C. Allan and H. Brotman. Copyright 1981 by The White House Conference on Aging.)*

tionalization is usually considered when a person cannot care for himself or herself adequately and cannot be adequately cared for by others.

Placement in a home, however, may often result as much from a person's having few social supports as from being physically disabled. Social isolation as a reason for early institutionalization is suggested by the fact that a disproportionate number of unmarried elderly persons (widowed, divorced, and never married) live in institutions (Gottesman & Brody, 1975) and these single residents are often significantly healthier than their married counterparts (Barney, 1977). As we saw in our vignette and in our section on widowhood, a spouse often assumes the burden of taking care of a marital partner who cannot function well independently. This option is not available to the single person. So, single older people are sometimes forced to enter institutions when they need only a modest level of caretaking support.

**BOX 7-5.    Do Adult Children Neglect Their Aged Parents?**

Many of us have been exposed to a prevalent popular idea today. In contrast to the past, when older people were cared for by their children, offspring are now thought to often neglect this duty and be unresponsive to their aging parents' needs. This estrangement and lack of commitment explains why many people are institutionalized, so the thinking goes. Nursing homes are filled with people who have been dumped there by uncaring families.

This idea is a myth. It does not fit in with the facts in this text. Elderly people without families are most likely to be institutionalized. Nursing home placement often occurs when a caretaker becomes unavailable or incapacitated. The idea also does not accord with other observations. The decision to put a parent in a nursing home is rarely a choice that families make lightly or without pain. Children often sacrifice tremendously to keep a disabled parent at home before being forced to consider institutionalization (Shanas, 1979b; York & Calsyn, 1977).

National surveys too reveal that children are highly committed to their aging parents. They show that the amount of parent/child involvement is often extensive. Furthermore, the bond between middle-aged child and elderly parent has not weakened much in the last 20 years.

Shanas, whose cross-national findings on health perceptions were discussed in Chapter 2, conducted studies demonstrating this was so (1979a, 1979b). In surveys done in 1957, 1962, and 1975, she examined the visiting patterns of elderly people and their families. Over three-fourths of the aging parents she surveyed in 1975 lived within 30 minutes' distance of an adult child. More than half had seen a child either the day they were interviewed or the day before. More than three-quarters had been visited by a child in the previous week. Needless to say, these recent statistics were not significantly lower than those revealed by the first two surveys.

One reason the idea of uninvolvement may be so prevalent today is that in fact one dramatic, clearly observable change has taken place lately in older-parent/adult-child relations: elderly parents are much less likely to live with offspring than they were even 20 years ago. In Shanas's first investigation, 36% of the aged parents were living in the same house with an adult child; in her last the figure had dropped precipitously to only 18%.

Before we blame children for this state of affairs, though, we need to remember our discussion of widows' lives. Many of the Chicago widows were reluctant to live with their children. They really preferred living alone. Shanas too found that the older parents surveyed said they wanted what she called this "intimacy at a distance," feeling it was better than having conflicts that might arise from living with a child. Separate households, then, appear to result as much from the parent's preference as from neglect by an uncaring offspring.

The encouraging evidence of family support, however, does not mean there may not be cause for concern in the future. Adult children may be just as committed to their parents in succeeding years but, because of societal changes, simply not as able to take care of them as they are today. Our vignette gives an example of the negative consequences of one of these actually positive changes—the broadening of women's roles. Daughters who have a profession may no longer be able to perform their traditional task of being available to help out aging parents. This shift, coupled with an economy necessitating two paychecks and a declining birth rate, should make future cohorts of elderly less able to depend on their families when disabled and so increasingly forced to turn to impersonal, formal sources of help (Treas, 1977).

A study of the reasons prompting admission to an urban long-term-care facility (Brody, 1977) directly highlights the crucial function that not just a spouse but any relative plays in preventing premature institutionalization. Admission to the home was usually sought as a last resort after many physical and life stresses and at the time of a hospitalization for a particular illness, but often the final step had been taken after the person's caretaker had suddenly become unavailable. Admission tended to occur after the death or illness of a spouse, adult child, or child-in-law.

**Personality and Psychopathology.**    On a variety of measures of mental health, institutionalized elderly persons are rated as more disturbed than those living in the community. Various studies have shown they are more passive, are more apathetic, and have lower self-esteem and morale. At least until recently this unfavorable psychological profile was assumed to be due to the detrimental influence of the institution itself (Tobin, 1980). We just saw how easy it is to make this assumption by viewing what occupants of institutions do during the day and by seeing what appears to be the minimal effort made by staff to interact with residents and attend to their needs. Moreover, even the best-run institution of necessity limits a person's option to exercise choices, imposing control shown to be inimical to good mental health (see Seligman, 1975). Residents are told when to eat, where to sleep, and when they may have visitors. On entering, they often are asked to sign a form that robs them of the option of refusing medical treatment (Brody, 1977). This is in addition to the fact that institutionalization means the trauma of forced disengagement—being separated from one's familiar environment, most of one's possessions, and sometimes one's loved ones.

A more accurate assumption, however, is that people who have reached the point of deciding to seek long-term care are already quite different psychologically from older people who have not. The institution itself may engender psychological problems—but problems may also already exist in people before they enter a home.

As part of a longitudinal study of the process of adapting to institutional living, investigators confirmed this proposition (see Tobin, 1980). They compared the psychological functioning of three groups of older people: nursing home residents, community residents who had applied for nursing home admission but were on a waiting list to enter, and community residents who had not applied. The waiting-list sample showed the same psychological symptoms as the older people already in institutions. Compared with the community sample (matched for marital status and degree of physical disability) who had not sought placement, the waiting-list and already-institutionalized groups were identical. They had a lower self-image and were less emotionally responsive and less cognitively intact.

Although people deciding to enter nursing homes may have poorer mental health for many reasons, the investigators suggested that, to some extent, the act of making the decision itself caused these psychological decrements. They reasoned that most older people view institutions as places where one goes to die. For many elderly people, then, choosing institutionalization is fraught with the symbolic meaning of choosing the last station before death.

Although to some extent this belief has reality, it is by no means unequivocally true. Elderly patients are discharged to the community from nursing homes. Many who are discharged do live. But the fact that many older adults do equate nursing homes with death was suggested by responses to a scale tapping latent anxiety about institutionalization (Tobin, 1980). Of 14 elderly community residents to whom the measure was given, 12 revealed negative feelings about the prospect of being institutionalized. These intense, highly unpleasant underlying feelings often coexisted in the context of the older person's manifestly making positive statements about the value of institutions in general for needy elderly.

In addition to the decision to enter the home, the stress of the move itself may affect the person adversely. As discussed in Chapter 2, relocation is sometimes associated with higher death rates, physical and behavioral deterioration, and a host of psychological symptoms, particularly if it is relocation to a setting such as a nursing home. Those most vulnerable to the relocation effect are, unfortunately, those most likely to be making the transition to institutions: physically frail older people who are moved involuntarily (Yawney & Slover, 1979).

**The Appropriate Resident.**    Because some of these very fragile older people are best suited to the nursing home environment, there is a seemingly contradictory finding that those for whom nursing home placement is most dangerous may be those who can benefit most from actually living in a home. Sherwood, Glassman, Sherwood, and Morris (1974) found that people whose life situation was judged poor enough so that institutionalization was deemed fully appropriate increased their life satisfaction after deciding on institutionalization. These elderly persons (those in poor health with few financial resources who lived alone) experienced the transition to a nursing home as a good thing, a welcome improvement over contending with the rigors of life in the community.

In addition to precarious life circumstances, personality may also affect how well suited one is to nursing home living. Unfortunately though, traits we would consider undesirable seem to predict good adjustment to this abnormal way of life. In the study of institutional adaptation mentioned in the previous section, the waiting-list subjects were followed during the process of entering and living in several high-quality, Chicago-area homes. After one year as residents, it was found, those who had declined the least in physical and behavioral functioning (or had improved) had a constellation of unpleasant personality traits. They tended to be highly aggressive and intrusive. They were likely to blame others rather than themselves. They were low in empathy and maintained a distrustful distance from other residents (Turner, Tobin, & Lieberman, 1972).

Reflection suggests that these findings should come as no surprise. Unpleasant behavior seems to best fit the exigencies of nursing home living. Aggression may be appropriate in places where resources available to residents are often so limited. Staying distant from others and inured to their suffering should be adaptive in these places where most people enter disabled and many soon die.

That being an aggressive and insensitive person may be helpful even in more limited ways in an institution is suggested by another study made at a different nursing home. At this high-quality facility, residents who benefited most from a special program to ameliorate excess disabilities tended to be highly domineering. They were bossy and likely to blame others rather than admit their own mistakes (Kleban, Brody, & Lawton, 1971).

Finally, at least one positive quality has been found to be associated with good adaptation to institutional living—the ability to explore and think about one's feelings. In the Chicago study, waiting-list subjects who had ranked high on a measure of experiencing (an introspective capacity) before entering a home were found to have adjusted better at the end of the first year than their less introspective peers (Gorney & Tobin, 1967). Evidently, having the capacity to explore one's feelings, at least before institutionalization, may enable a person to cope better with the stress of making this marked life change.

### Interventions

As a prelude to discussing some strategies to help older people in need of or at risk for institutionalization, we need to summarize what has been said so far. Although nursing homes may be appropriate for some older people, their negative aspects indicate it is best to be able to live outside. If a person must enter a home, the process of actually moving there may be traumatic. In addition, once in an institution, many residents spend an inordinate amount of time in useless, unproductive activity or no activity at all. These facts suggest that interventions be made at three points: preventing institutionalization from having to occur at all, easing the transition to a nursing home, and finally, encouraging as competent and productive living as possible in already-institutionalized people.

**Alternatives to Institutionalization.**    Nursing home placement often occurs at a time of maximum stress, when a person is ill and in a hospital and so is at his or her absolute physical worst. The decision to enter a home often has to be made suddenly, when a bed becomes available, leaving little time for reasoned inquiry or exploration of alternatives to institutionalization. In addition, our discussion of the social reasons for seeking long-term care suggests that sometimes institutionalization would not even need to be considered if a person had the needed community support. In fact, for the isolated older person living alone who may require only some services, the choice often continues to be between making do with too little help and being forced to accept too much—that is, entering a nursing home.

Data back up the impression that institutionalization is too widespread and too precipitous. Surveys reveal that many residents in nursing homes could function in less restrictive community environments (Barney, 1977). In addition, once admitted to long-term care, the person runs the risk of developing excess disabilities because the setting may be geared to providing more nursing services than he or she needs. In one survey, fully 47% of a random sample of residents were judged by experts as having been admitted to places offering the wrong level of care. Most of these elderly residents were felt to be overserved. Their physical problems simply did not warrant the level of nursing services provided at the place they had entered (Sherwood, 1975).

Several demonstration projects have shown that careful screening combined with the judicious use of community alternatives can prevent many older adults from being institutionalized. One project involved a team of professionals who evaluated the appropriateness of nursing home placement after a person in need had called a special triage number (Hodgson & Quinn, 1980). Through the use of home care, ambulatory services, and periodic evaluation, the team was able to prevent 25–30% of these callers at risk from entering long-term care.

The effectiveness of this program suggests the utility of psychological counseling at the time placement in a home is being considered. A counselor could work with the prospective resident's family, perhaps giving them encouragement for keeping the older person at home. He or she would provide valuable information about existing community services. The family and the older person could be encouraged to view discharge with this community help as a real future possibility even if it were eventually decided that entering an institution was indeed best.

Currently available community alternatives to nursing homes include the planned housing discussed in Chapter 3, which provides some services but still allows independent living. But because this housing is rarely available, the most promising avenue is to directly provide services enabling disabled older adults to stay in their own homes. Government-funded programs providing housekeeping and nursing help are one option. There are also more specialized services, such as the Friendly Visitor program or Meals on Wheels. Friendly Visitor volunteers call elderly persons on a regular basis or visit those in need of contact. In the Meals on Wheels program, volunteers deliver a noon meal to older persons who cannot prepare their own food and also, often, check on their medical condition. Other services that help impaired elderly people remain in the community include government funded transportation and telephone call-in services that offer reassurance and concrete advice to older callers in need.

Perhaps the most interesting innovations involve attempts not to help the older person directly but to ease the burden of those on whom the caretaking responsibility often falls—relatives struggling to care for disabled older people at home.

These services give caretakers a respite by relieving them of the need to be totally available on a full-time basis. They also give the frail older person needed medical attention and recreational and social services without the individual having to actually live in a nursing home.

*Geriatric day care* is one of the most interesting of these options. Catering to the older person who is somewhat disabled but usually not totally disoriented or bedridden, day care centers have been established in many communities, giving the older person a place to go during the day and offering a variety of services. Day care programs also usually offer transportation to the center and careful ongoing evaluation of the disabled person's needs. The older person usually spends many of his or her waking hours at the center, allowing caretakers time off for themselves.

One such program (reported in Weiler & Rathbone-McCuan, 1978), the Lexington Centers for Creative Living in Lexington, Kentucky, was conceived to fill the gap in the community between institutional services and home living. Its operation is funded by public and private sources, and it has an advisory board composed of community leaders interested in aging. The centers are open five days a week. Participants usually arrive at 9:00 and leave at 3:30, having been picked up by center-operated vans, some equipped for wheelchairs. The centers offer a variety of services, from psychological counseling to recreational opportunities to nursing care. Applicants are carefully screened, and the progress of participants is monitored regularly. One measure of the centers' success is that many people are able to eventually reduce the number of hours they need day care after attending the program.

Another option for helping caretakers cope with the frail elderly is to periodically hospitalize them on a planned basis, an arrangement in operation at a hospital in England since 1964 (Robertson, Griffiths, & Cosin, 1977). Like day care, this service carefully screens applicants for admission. Here, not only must a person be disabled, but his or her care must be straining the resources of family members who nevertheless want to keep the individual at home. This program involves the use of home health services plus three categories of hospital stay: periodic admission for 48 hours to the same ward at the hospital at about two-week intervals; longer admissions as needed to allow caretakers to go on vacations; and finally, admission whenever the patient has a pressing need for medical attention.

When caretakers who had a family member participating in this program were asked to evaluate it, almost all gave it high praise. Most said that without it they would not have been able to care for their relative at home. As these older people would otherwise, therefore, have been institutionalized full-time, the program was clearly cost-effective. It effectively deterred nursing home placement at a fraction of the cost.

**Alternatives within the Institution.**    The goal of this category of intervention is to help the person who has already decided to enter a nursing home—to ease the transition to institutional living and to combat physical and behavioral deterioration once placement occurs.

As mentioned, the research on relocation shock suggests this negative reaction is more likely to occur when a person is moved involuntarily. Although it is not possible to make what is often an involuntary move to a nursing home fully voluntary, staff members at one excellent institution, the Philadelphia Geriatric Center, have attempted a partial solution. Rather than following the common practice of leaving the older person out of discussions about nursing home placement, they try to include the individual as much as possible in the plans. They also try to give the future resident options regarding when the move will occur and where in the home he or she will be placed. Finally, they attempt to ease the shock of the move itself by encouraging advance visits to the facility (see Yawney & Slover, 1979).

In this institution (and others) a variety of programs are aimed at encouraging good mental and physical health once the person becomes a resident. A full range of recreational and rehabilitative activities is offered. There is group and individual psychotherapy. There are behavior modification programs to combat the development of excess disabilities. The physical environment is also planned with the impaired older person in mind: some buildings in the facility are, like the planned elderly housing discussed in Chapter 3, designed and decorated to encourage socialization, combat disorientation, and minimize the limitations imposed by sensory and motor disabilities.

A rare example of a program designed to deal with relocation shock and simultaneously enhance the psychological well-being of the already relocated was also developed at the Philadelphia Geriatric Center. A geriatric social worker there (Friedman, 1975) formed a resident welcoming committee composed of physically and mentally intact residents. The group's purpose was to support new residents and orient them to the home as well as giving those doing the welcoming a chance to assume a useful role. In addition, the committee members met each week to discuss their problems as volunteers as well as other aspects of life at the home. Although its effectiveness was not formally evaluated, the project did seem to help the new arrivals and the volunteer residents. Interestingly, its most rewarding aspect seemed to be the weekly group sessions. At these meetings the volunteers were able to come to terms with many of their own feelings about having been institutionalized. The group became close as these and other common experiences discussed increased members' sense of kinship with one another.

## Summary

Retirement is now expected for older workers, but there is a continuing controversy over its effects on the elderly. Some argue that retirement is detrimental, others that it is neutral or beneficial to the older person. Most people now retire before age 65; the average age is about 60. There has been a trend toward increased retirement at 65 and earlier over the past few decades.

An important influence on the decision to retire is the expectation of having adequate finances. Social Security is the primary source of retirement income, and many of the current system's provisions encourage people to leave work at 65 or before. Retirement is also encouraged by various other financial aids to the older person.

Another influence on retirement is employer and work-related pressures to leave the job. A recent congressional act has outlawed mandatory retirement policies for most workers under age 70. However, it is likely that age discrimination still often exists in the workplace, as evidenced by statistics that show older workers are less likely to be rehired after industry layoffs than the younger unemployed.

Ill health, in particular functional impairments, is another important reason workers retire. In fact, poor health was the primary reason most early-retiring males gave for leaving work in a recent nationwide study. Evidence suggests that these men, in general, were telling the truth about having physical problems. Some, however, may have overemphasized the extent of their physical disabilities to rationalize leaving work.

A person's work attitude is also important in the decision to retire—specifically, having negative feelings about one's job and positive ones about retirement. Interestingly, though, these two feelings are not related in themselves. Workers who say they like their jobs are just as favorable to the idea of retirement as those who say they dislike their jobs. General personality changes, specifically a decline in the importance placed on work, may make older men more able to accept the prospect of relinquishing their jobs at the standard retirement age.

The Cornell Study of Occupational Retirement was the first major source of data on how being retired affects the older person. This investigation and others have revealed that although retirement can often have sharply negative financial results, it has few negative consequences for physical health or morale. People seem to adapt very well to retirement, including housewives who must adjust to having a nonworking spouse at home.

Elderly people who are not happy in retirement include those who have money or health worries and possibly those whose previous interests are not compatible with the activities possible in this life stage. People seem to be able to predict accurately whether they will enjoy being retired.

To help those who may have problems with this major transition, preretirement programs attempt to orient older workers to retirement before it happens. A variety of educational and volunteer activities are also available to retirees.

Being widowed is a common event, particularly for older women. Most research on this stressful event either focuses on the period of mourning or examines the lifestyle of widows and widowers who have passed the period of acute bereavement. Several investigators have suggested that bereavement has certain characteristic symptoms and that mourning follows a predictable course. These experts believe, but have not proved, that if a person does not do what they call "grief work," he or she will have trouble recovering from a loved one's death.

Many factors may affect the intensity of bereavement or the difficulty of adapting to a spouse's death. The most frequently studied have been the age of the widowed person at the time the death occurred and whether the death was expected or sudden. The younger bereaved in general, and in particular those whose spouse's death is sudden, appear to have the most trouble recovering from this traumatic event. Older people seem to adjust better, and the mode of death seems irrelevant to their eventual recovery. In fact, for older women the lasting psycho-logical and physical consequences of being widowed are relatively few. Older men, however, have higher-than-expected death rates after being widowed, unless they remarry.

Two ambitious studies have revealed much about what it is like to live as a widow in an urban area today. Both surveys showed widows were extremely inde-pendent, rarely asking family and friends for help. Although most of those studied had been widowed for years, a large percentage still idealized their spouses and felt attached to the spouse's memory. Life was best for the most-educated widows who were able to adapt to their changed situation and worst for traditionally reared widows whose environment demanded new adaptations that could not be made. Many widows were living quite isolated lives.

This last finding suggests that services tailored to help widows could have been useful, although the women surveyed rarely reported receiving help from such infrequently available programs. One service providing a group where vulnerable widows had a chance to talk about their feelings did help these women adapt by the end of the first year of bereavement. Another, more extensive program in-volves a variety of counseling services, social activities, and other aids to the wid-owed.

Entering a nursing home, though a less common event for the older person than widowhood or retirement, is not as rare as the 5% estimate suggests. It may eventually happen to more than one-quarter of all people over 65. Numbers of institutional beds have rapidly increased, as has the cost of the system, particularly in the last two decades.

Long-term-care institutions vary in their admission requirements, the services they are certified as providing, and their mode of ownership, among many other things. They also vary in the quality of care, which may be measured by a home's amount of objective resources or by resident or staff morale and satisfaction. These two indexes themselves are often related, and both are functions of how affluent the residents are. Affluent residents get better care partly because they are more likely to have visitors who can monitor staff practices. Accordingly, it has been suggested that one way of raising nursing home quality would be to encourage institutions to open their doors more to the public. In the typical nurs-ing home, it has been found that residents spend most of their time sitting and doing nothing.

Residents of nursing homes are likely to be female, White, old-old, poor (at least eventually), and, most important, disabled. They are also disproportionately sin-gle, a fact that suggests the importance of a spouse or other caretaker in prevent-ing institutionalization. People usually enter institutions when they are not able to care for themselves in the community. Children often fight hard to keep parents from entering a nursing home and are often very involved with elderly parents.

Although many aspects of the nursing home environment itself encourage poor mental health, the high level of psychopathology found in institutional residents is often there before they arrive. It may be partly a consequence of making the decision to enter a nursing home. Also, the stress of the move can be problematic.

Elderly persons who are most appropriately placed in nursing homes are those who have the poorest life circumstances. Those who do best in this environment tend to be highly aggressive and insensitive.

Two interventions aimed at preventing institutionalization are geriatric day care, in which the older person spends the day at a center, and planned intermittent hospitalization, in which the person stays at a hospital as needed and at regular intervals. Institutions also have programs to ease relocation shock and encourage competence in residents. One program simultaneously serving these dual functions was a resident welcoming committee, in which long-term residents of the home participated in greeting and counseling new arrivals.

## Key Terms

*Mandatory and flexible retirement*            *Long-term care*
*Anticipatory socialization*            *Geriatric day care*
*Grief work*            *Planned intermittent hospitalization*

## Recommended Readings

Gelfand, D. E., & Olsen, J. K. **The aging network: Programs and services**. New York: Springer, 1979.
*Comprehensive picture of government and other programs for the elderly. Not difficult.*

Lopata, H. Z. **Widowhood in an American city**. Cambridge, Mass.: Schenkman, 1973.

Lopata, H. Z. **Women as widows: Support systems**. New York: Elsevier/North Holland, 1979.
*Two landmark studies of widows, described in detail. Also contain information on customs involving widows worldwide and an overview of widowhood in America. Not difficult.*

Parkes, C. M. **Bereavement: Studies of grief in adult life**. New York: International Universities Press, 1972.
*A moving, well-written book; comprehensive presentation of all pertinent research on bereavement, specifically the first year of mourning. Not difficult.*

Sherwood, S. (Ed.). **Long-term care**. Holliswood, N.Y.: Spectrum, 1975.
*An edited volume summarizing a wide array of topics relevant to long-term care. The chapter on psychosocial interventions within the institution is particularly good. Not difficult.*

Streib, G., & Schneider, C. J. **Retirement in American society: Impact and process**. Ithaca, N.Y.: Cornell University Press, 1971.
*The Cornell Study of Occupational Retirement, described in detail. Not difficult.*

# PART FIVE

# PSYCHOPATHOLOGY

# CHAPTER EIGHT

# Mental Disorders I: Description, Diagnosis, and Assessment

Mrs. Goldblum's husband began to notice a change in her behavior a few months after they moved from Philadelphia, where she had lived all her life, to their new home in Florida. His 76-year-old wife had always been a fastidious dresser and had kept an immaculate house. After their move she seemed gradually to take less interest in how she looked. In fact, one week he was shocked to see her wearing the same dirty dress three days in a row. Dinner or breakfast dishes were sometimes left uncleared, particularly if she was called away from the kitchen while she was cleaning. It was as if she simply forgot they were there.

He also noticed other changes in her personality. In Philadelphia, although she had been somewhat dependent on him, she had also been outgoing and very active. She had had a wide variety of friends, both old and new, and had been particularly close to her children and grandchildren. All this changed in Florida. She lost all interest in her family and had little desire to meet new people. Activities she used to love in Philadelphia, like playing bingo, dancing, and swimming, were plentiful at the retirement community, but she refused to participate in them. She just wanted to sit home and watch TV.

At first Mr. Goldblum was not too worried about his wife. In fact, he even liked it that she was staying home more. He was the one who had decided on the move over his wife's objections. He felt she just needed time to get over what he thought was her depression at the loss of her old friends and way of life. Although she had some problems sleeping and had lost weight, there was clearly nothing physically wrong with her. He had read that depression itself often caused these physical symptoms and also the disinterest in things and even the memory problems she seemed to be having.

He became alarmed, however, when one day a security officer at the nearby shopping center had to bring Mrs. Goldblum home. Apparently she had gone to pick up a few groceries and had left her wallet at the checkout counter. She had been found wandering in the parking lot, unable to remember her address or how to get home. This seemed impossible to Mr. Goldblum, as they lived only a few blocks away and she had never had any problem before with remembering anything so basic. After this upsetting incident, he became afraid to let her go out by herself for fear it might happen again; she, in turn, became completely housebound and dependent on him. Finally, at his wits' end, he decided to go to a clinic in Philadelphia his daughter had told them about that specialized in diagnosing cognitive and emotional problems in older people. He agreed to abide by any recommendations the clinic might make about how to deal with his wife's condition.

At the clinic, Mrs. Goldblum underwent several days of tests and interviews. She was thoroughly evaluated medically and given tests of brain function. The basic assessment team, however, consisted of mental health workers—a psychiatrist, a psychologist, and a social worker. The psychiatrist interviewed Mrs. Goldblum extensively, asking questions about her memory, her feelings about her husband, family, and friends, and her reaction to the move to Florida. He also asked her about what her life had been like in Philadelphia and even about events that had happened more than 50 years ago, before she had married. The social worker interviewed Mr. Goldblum about his perceptions and also phoned the Goldblum children who lived in the Philadelphia area to get their ideas: What was their view of their mother's condition? What might its cause be? What might be done to help?

Both the social worker and the psychiatrist concluded that although Mrs. Goldblum might have an incipient dementia, her main problem was depression. Her symptoms could be directly traced to having been uprooted from her home and forced to give up her friends and live far from her family. The social worker in particular, noticing how overprotective and at the same time domineering Mr. Goldblum was, felt the true cause of the problem was marital. Mr. Goldblum encouraged his wife's isolation. She was angry at him but was too intimidated to express it; her memory difficulty was a way of unconsciously getting back.

The psychologist, however, disagreed. He concluded that the psychological tests he had given Mrs. Goldblum clearly showed she had at least a moderate dementia. She had been unable to do most of the WAIS and had severe deficits in her ability to reason abstractly; she had an extremely poor memory and, in fact, had done so poorly on the standard tests that he had had to give her a special battery reserved for dementia patients. He did not deny that depression could have prevented her from doing as well as she might, but he held firm that she really did have an organic problem. Results from the CAT scan corroborated his findings; they showed a moderate to severe degree of cortical atrophy.

Before informing Mr. Goldblum of the results, the team met as a group to hash out their disagreements. They decided on a compromise diagnosis: dementia (probably senile) with a superimposed depression. They also considered the special circumstances associated with Mrs. Goldblum's problem—the move and her husband's overprotectiveness. They decided they would recommend that the couple move back to Philadelphia if at all possible. At the very least, they would suggest marital therapy and possibly a trial of antidepressant drugs for Mrs. Goldblum. It was also decided to tell Mr. Goldblum forthrightly that his wife might have an incurable organic condition but also to emphasize how her problem might be helped by environmental change, psychotherapy, and medication.

Certain ideas about mental disorders in the older person are common. Because old age is viewed so negatively, as purely a time of loss and stress, older people are thought to be more prone to have psychological problems than the young. They are expected to be depressed. Many are thought to be senile. Society sees old age as a time of difficulty—economic, physical, and just as frequently emotional.

As we saw in Chapter 6, however, for some people late life is a time of positive psychological growth. And as we noted in Chapter 7, the two major life events generally thought to engender late-life emotional difficulties—widowhood and retirement—do not commonly have this expected result. At least considered singly, these changes seem for the most part to cause surprisingly few long-term psychological problems.

We then need to begin by taking a second look at the assumption that psycho-pathology is normal in old age and by carefully examining the evidence. How common are mental disorders in the elderly? How does their frequency compare with that of other age groups? What types of problems are older people most likely to have? The answers to these questions come from what are called epidemiologic studies.

## Epidemiology of Late-Life Mental Disorders

*Epidemiology* is a branch of science dealing with understanding the frequency (prevalence) of diseases in the general population. Epidemiologists also study the distribution of illnesses—that is, who in the community is likely to suffer from the emotional or physical problems they are interested in.

### Purposes of Epidemiological Studies

These investigations help planners assess the need in a community for particular medical or health services (Kay & Bergmann, 1980). They can also give important insights into the causes of disorders. For example, having done surveys of the frequency of heart attacks in different countries, epidemiologists were among the first to implicate the role a high-fat diet might play in causing heart disease. They did this by detective work, determining that one thing differentiating the countries where people had an elevated rate of heart disease was higher consumption of saturated fats. Similar cross-national studies have been of great value in identifying factors that may engender other age-related diseases. For example, the connection noted earlier between exposure to noise and poor hearing was solidified by another epidemiological finding—that in primitive societies where low levels of noise are the norm, hearing difficulties are much less prevalent in later life.

### Problems in Measuring Psychological Disorders

Ideally, then, by measuring the varying rates of mental disorders among older people in different communities, we could not only assess the truth of the idea that the elderly are more disturbed but also get clues about what may actually cause emotional problems in late life. Unfortunately, accurately measuring the extent of psychological problems may not be as easy as diagnosing the presence of physical diseases. In the community surveys that may best reveal how common these difficulties are in an area, there is always a problem of getting all the respondents to agree to submit to interviewers asking them personal questions (see Kay & Bergmann, 1980). We might expect some of the very people most likely to have true psychological problems to refuse. Lower compliance, for instance, seems predictable in older adults who are paranoid or are frightened about their failing memory. (We might remember from Chapter 3 that epidemiologists have a parallel difficulty in accurately assessing the prevalence of impaired hearing in the elderly.)

The main reason these studies are not so accurate, though, stems from a larger problem in the mental health field as a whole: psychological diagnoses themselves are not highly reliable. It has been repeatedly shown that mental health professionals too often disagree on whether a given person should be diagnosed as having a mental disorder or what diagnostic category a patient fits into (Busse & Pfeiffer, 1977). To combat this problem, the American Psychiatric Association (1980) has recently developed a new diagnostic manual, the third edition of the *Diagnostic and Statistical Manual of Mental Disorders* (DSM-III), which spells out in detail the criteria to use when making a psychological diagnosis. In spite of the manual's extensive description of each category of problem, however, even skilled clinicians are still having trouble agreeing on how to classify patients at a highly acceptable level using the DSM-III system. The reliability of DSM-III diagnoses is still relatively low, probably because it is just too hard to apply written descriptions of symptoms to living human beings.

Because different researchers diagnose problems differently, prevalence studies of mental disorders in different communities cannot be easily compared. What looks like a low rate of emotional problems in a given area, for example, may really be an artifact, arising because the person studying the community has stricter-than-normal criteria for what he or she calls a problem (Kay & Bergmann, 1980). Community surveys, however, can give very general estimates of the prevalence of emotional problems that will allow us to make tentative statements about the extent of these disorders in the elderly and how it compares with their frequency in the young.

### Psychological Problems in Old Age

Although estimates vary, one classic survey of urban adults of all ages revealed that the prevalence of emotional disorders was quite high, roughly 25% (Srole, Langer, Michael, Opler, & Rennie, 1962). Estimates of the frequency of functional (nonorganic) psychological problems in older people are in the same range (see Allan & Brotman, 1981; Kay & Bergmann, 1980). Community surveys indicate that anywhere from 8% (Lowenthal, Berkman, & associates, 1967) to 30% (Kay, Beamish, & Roth, 1964) of older people suffer from what are called *functional psychological disorders.* Functional disorders are all those categories of emotional problems for which no established organic (physiological) cause has been found (see Table 8-1 for examples). In fact, older people appear even less susceptible to some of these problems than the young. The two most severe functional disorders, schizophrenia and manic-depressive psychosis, are less prevalent in the over-65 group than in young and middle adulthood (Kay & Bergmann, 1980). One reason is that these conditions less frequently develop for the first time in old age. In addition, there is some evidence that the severity of these disturbances lessens as a chronic sufferer gets older, so that by the age of 65+ fewer symptoms remain.

Problems having severe anxiety as their main symptom may also be less frequent in older people (Jarvik & Russell, 1979). Anxiety disorders in their various forms are very common in children and young adults and less common in old age. It may be that having a high level of anxiety predisposes a person to dying earlier

**TABLE 8-1.**   Common symptoms of some major functional psychological disorders and their prevalence in old age.

| *Disorder* | *Symptoms and Prevalence* |
|---|---|
| **Schizophrenia** | Bizarre delusions (irrational ideas) and/or auditory hallucinations (hearing voices), incoherence, illogical thinking, blunted affect (emotional tone). Prevalence decreases in old age. |
| **Manic-Depressive Psychosis** | Periods of highly elevated mood and activity alternating with periods of deep depression. In manic phase, marked increase in physical activity, sleeplessness, inflated self-esteem, racing thoughts, uncontrollable actions that may be reckless and self-destructive. In depressed phase, unhappy mood, guilt feelings, slowed thinking (see section on depression). Prevalence decreases in old age. |
| **Anxiety Disorders** | Symptoms of intense generalized anxiety or anxiety symptoms that occur in specific irrational situations (the latter are called phobias). Symptoms include motor tension, dizziness, sweating, heart pounding, irritability, and apprehensive brooding. Prevalence decreases in old age. |
| **Paranoid Disorders** | Systematized delusions of being persecuted; in paranoid schizophrenia may be accompanied by symptoms noted under "Schizophrenia." Prevalence increases in old age. |

(Jarvik & Russell, 1979); the data linking emotional stress to the development of physical illnesses (see Chapter 2) suggest this possibility. So people who survive to old age may be the less anxious members of the cohort. Alternatively, life may be less anxiety-provoking once a person is retired and one's children are grown. Or, best yet, people may really develop a kind of wisdom, a less stressed outlook on living, as they advance in years.

But even if less likely to suffer from anxiety disorders, older people do have their share of emotional problems. For example, as mentioned in Chapter 3, some may tend to develop paranoid reactions in response to impairments such as hearing loss. In addition, two disturbances in particular, depression and the dementias, affect older people to a greater extent than the young. In fact, the chronic intellectual disturbances called the dementias rarely begin much before late middle age. These most feared diseases of older adulthood are the conditions people are referring to when they say someone is senile or is suffering from hardening of the arteries.

The dementias and a type of acute brain disturbance called delirium affect primarily a person's intellect, and there are clearly established physical, or organic, bases for these problems. This is in contrast to functional psychological difficulties such as schizophrenia or anxiety disorders, which affect mainly the emotions rather than memory or IQ and for which no certain organic cause has yet been found. The sections below will first describe the most prevalent organic brain syndromes of old age—the two most common dementias and delirium. Then, because of its frequency in the elderly, we will look at the symptoms and possible causes of depression, the most important functional psychological disturbance of late life.

## The Dementias

### Symptoms

The term **dementia** actually refers to a group of chronic diseases that have basically similar symptoms. There is a progressive, often gradual decline in all intellectual functions. Problems are usually first seen in a person's memory for relatively recent events. The individual is able to remember important past events but has trouble remembering things that occurred within the last few days, hours, or even minutes. A person may forget, for example, that he or she has just made a phone call, gone shopping, or turned on the stove. Our clinical vignette illustrates some symptoms characteristic of an early-stage dementia—Mrs. Goldblum's tendency to forget which dress she had worn the previous day or that the dishes were left on the table after a meal.

Over time these problems get worse, and every aspect of the person's thinking becomes involved. Abstract reasoning becomes impossible. The person can no longer think through options when making decisions. Judgment becomes faulty. Individuals may act inappropriately, perhaps undressing in public or in other ways embarrassing themselves and others. They may behave recklessly and be unable to understand that they are endangering their life or health. Language becomes limited. Individuals may have difficulty naming objects and be unable to take a listener's point of view into account. They may be unable to adequately communicate their own thoughts.

Later, if the condition progresses to its final stage before death occurs, victims become disoriented to time, place, and person; that is, they have no idea of the date, where they are, or whom they are speaking to. Well-established memories are affected; individuals may forget basic facts about themselves, such as their name, date of birth, or birthplace. At this point, they may need full-time nursing care, as they are often unable to dress, feed themselves, or go to the toilet independently.

Finally, it is important to caution that not all people exhibit the symptoms of a dementia in this exact way. For example, some are able to perform basic tasks like dressing and going to the toilet in the presence of what otherwise look like extreme impairments of memory and reasoning. Others are less disabled in their memory and reasoning, for example, but need nursing care for these basic activities of daily living (Zarit, 1980).

### Prevalence

Epidemiologic studies in a variety of countries have revealed that about 5% to 8% of noninstitutionalized persons 65 and over are classified as having a moderate or severe dementia (Kay & Bergmann, 1980). Although these percentages are not large, they do mean that, numerically, there are many older people outside insti-

**BOX 8-1.   Caretakers of Dementia Victims in the Community: What Influences Their Feelings of Burden?**

As the statistics in the text reveal, many highly mentally impaired older people continue to live in the community. These disabled older people only rarely can participate in programs like day care or planned hospitalization that might lighten the load on those doing the caretaking, their families. In the absence of this institutionalized support, what makes the care of these difficult elderly easier? What influences make this care more burdensome? Zarit, Reever, and Bach-Peterson (1980) attempted to answer these questions.

Older people with senile dementia were tested for their level of impairment, and their primary caretakers were interviewed about the extent of their feelings of burden. The tests given to the dementia patients included measures of cognitive functioning as well as all-important indexes of functional disability. Most of the dementia sufferers tested were at least moderately disabled.

The degree of behavioral impairment the older person showed was *not* related to the feelings of burden reported by his or her primary caretaker. What did affect how difficult that care seemed was another factor—how often the dementia patient was visited by other members of the family. In other words, if the person doing the care felt supported and helped by other relatives of the impaired person, his or her job seemed easier. If the caretaker did not perceive others as being involved, the task seemed much more burdensome. So, surprisingly, it is not the problem itself that is overwhelming for a highly committed caretaker; it is the sense of being abandoned, left to deal with the problem all alone.

tutions who have marked problems dealing with the basics of daily living. In addition, the proportion of dementia patients in hospitals and nursing homes is much higher. Estimates of the prevalence of these illnesses in long-term-care facilities range as high as 70% (Blazer, 1980). Dementia is so common in nursing homes because this diagnosis, entailing as it does such functional disability, is often the actual reason for admission to long-term care.

The prevalence of dementia rises with age. For example, at least 20% of people over 80 living at home are estimated to suffer from this group of diseases (Kay, 1977). In view of the rising numbers of old-old, this increased frequency of dementia with advancing age causes public health specialists great concern. Some authorities suggest that the increase in late-life life expectancy (see Chapter 1) will mean dementia may be the number one health problem of the next century.

### Types of Dementia

To understand these threatening diseases, it is important first to stress again that several very different physical conditions may cause the same general pattern of progressive intellectual deterioration. Only one type of dementia, a relatively rare problem called normal-pressure hydrocephalus, is currently potentially curable (Marsden, 1978). The other, more prevalent dementias are not. The two most common types are called **senile dementia** (or **Alzheimer's disease** or **primary degenerative dementia**) and **multi-infarct dementia**. These conditions account for the vast majority of cases of dementia.

**Senile Dementia.**    Three names, *Alzheimer's disease, primary degenerative dementia,* and *senile dementia* are now used to refer to one disease having the same symptoms and physical basis. *Alzheimer's disease* was formerly the term used when the disorder began before age 65; senile dementia was the diagnosis when the symptoms occurred for the first time after age 65. Until recently, it was believed these were really two separate illnesses that could be distinguished by the rapidity of deterioration and the extent to which the illness ran in families. Alzheimer's disease—or dementia, Alzheimer's type—was supposed to occur before age 65, to progress more rapidly than senile dementia, and to lack any hereditary basis. It has come to seem likely that there is no reason for making this differentiation. Most experts currently agree that there is only one disease (Sloane, 1980). Unfortunately, however, the two old names are now used interchangeably to describe this unitary condition. Adding to the confusion, the framers of DSM-III have given the same problem the other name mentioned above—*primary degenerative dementia.*

About 50% of elderly people who suffer from dementia have this particular disease, making it the most prevalent chronic brain impairment of old age (Reisberg, 1981). The illness affects more women than men and seems to have a hereditary basis. It is more than four times as likely to strike a person if a member of his or her immediate family has been affected (Sloane, 1980).

The brains of these dementia victims show characteristic and widespread structural changes. Scattered throughout the cortex are a large number of filamentlike structures called **neurofibrillary tangles**. There are also abnormal bodies called **senile plaques**. There are other pathological anatomical changes. For example, often the brain has atrophied (shrunk) markedly, and there appear to be fewer interconnections between the existing intact neurons. The major result is that there simply are not enough normally functioning neurons in the higher centers of the brain responsible for intellect and memory to maintain adequate cognition. Enough of the person's brain is malfunctioning to cause the distressing symptoms of dementia. (Consult Reisberg, 1981, listed in the Recommended Readings, for an easily understood, more comprehensive description.)

Before these widespread abnormalities were discovered, dementia was sometimes thought to be the result of purely psychological factors. Some psychologists, looking at the problems the elderly faced, thought that older people developed memory and thinking impairments in an effort to shut out a hostile and unrewarding outside world. This belief was fueled by the common observation that dementias do often seem to begin or become worse, as in our clinical example, after environmental changes such as entering a nursing home or moving to a new city (see Sloane, 1980).

What looks like a dementia often temporarily appears after an older person experiences a change in his or her environment because the amount of new information that needs to be immediately assimilated creates a kind of sensory and memory overload. In addition, the stress of a change may cause or exacerbate intellectual impairments because of the disruptive impact of anxiety, whose negative effect on cognitive performance was discussed in Chapters 4 and 5. We can often see this in our own lives when on the first few days of a new job or after a move we feel overwhelmed by new stimuli and so seem incapable of remembering anything.

However, although senile dementia is often exacerbated by environmental change or other external factors, it does have a primarily organic basis. One classic study established this by autopsying the brains of elderly who had had memory losses of varying severity and no cognitive impairment. There was a good correlation between the number of senile plaques found and the intellectual abilities a person had evidenced near the time of death (Blessed, Tomlinson, & Roth, 1968; Roth, Tomlinson, & Blessed, 1966; Tomlinson, 1977).

The brains of people with senile dementia and normal older people do reveal observable differences. However, the differences are not in the presence or absence of abnormal brain structures themselves but in the extent of the pathological changes. In other words, people with dementia have more widespread damage but not qualitatively different brain changes (Kay, 1977; Terry & Wisniewski, 1977). Cognitively intact older people also have some senile plaques. They have neurofibrillary tangles and cortical atrophy as well. But these abnormalities are limited in number and are often confined to certain areas of the brain (Roth, 1980). In particular, they are not likely to be present in its outermost part, the neocortex. In people who have dementia the neocortex is involved, and the damage in general is much more marked and extensive (Reisberg, 1981).

The presence of some deteriorative changes in most elderly people may account for the fact that memory normally does show some decline in late life. In fact, these qualitative similarities between the brains of normal older adults and those of people with dementia also suggest that senile dementia is another chronic condition tied to normal aging (Kay, 1977). Although this idea is upsetting, then, it is likely that as all people age, they may tend to develop more and more degenerative changes, though at different rates. The relationship of abnormalities to advancing age is clearly shown in Figure 8-1. With age an increasingly greater proportion of subjects at autopsy manifest the physical signs characteristic of dementia. Unfortunately, then, were we to live to age 100 or more, many of us might develop this most dreaded condition.

**Multi-Infarct Dementia.**   The second most common dementia of old age, multi-infarct dementia, is caused by the death of a significant amount of brain tissue owing to many small infarcts, or strokes (Scheinberg, 1978). Because these strokes are in part precipitated by such potentially modifiable things as high blood pressure, there may be some ways of stemming the normal downhill course of this type of dementia by, for example, lowering blood pressure through diet and medi-

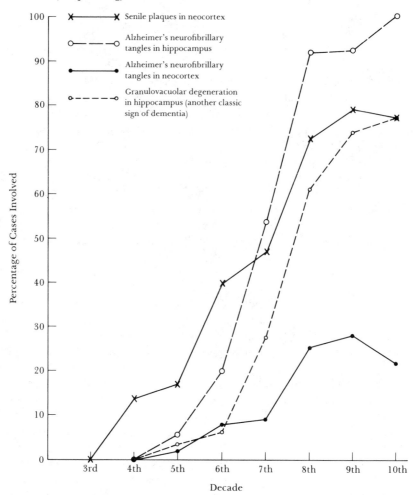

**FIGURE 8-1.**    Percentage of 219 routine hospital cases showing evidence of senile changes by decade of age. *(Source: Reprinted by permission from Figure 6, page 50 in* Aging and Dementia, *by W. Lynn Smith and Marcel Kinsbourne (Eds.). Copyright © 1977, Spectrum Publications, Inc., Jamaica, New York.)*

cation (Hachinski, Lassen, & Marshal, 1974; Scheinberg, 1978; Sloane, 1980). Normally, however, multi-infarct dementia usually gets progressively worse, just as senile dementia does, because these strokes tend to accumulate and affect progressively larger segments of the person's brain. They may not be important enough to cause severe damage individually, but in unison they can do tremendous harm.

Multi-infarct dementia used to be called arteriosclerotic dementia (*arteriosclerosis* is the medical term for what is commonly called "hardening of the arteries") because it was thought to be caused by atherosclerosis and arteriosclerosis, which stiffened and narrowed the walls of the arteries pumping blood to the brain

(Hachinski et al., 1974). These changes were thought to prevent enough blood from getting to the brain, thus impairing its functioning and so causing cognitive deterioration. It is now believed that the intellectual problems these older people suffer from are due mainly to strokes. In addition, this type of dementia is not as common as was once thought. Multi-infarct dementia was once viewed as the most prevalent chronic organic brain syndrome, but it is now believed to make up only about 15–20% of cases of dementia (Terry & Wisniewski, 1977). In another 25% or so of patients this condition plus evidence of senile dementia is found at autopsy (Reisberg, 1981).

Multi-infarct dementia affects more men than women. The two major dementias cannot be distinguished with certainty without autopsying the brain, but there are some external signs suggesting a person may have this condition. He or she may be sicker physically, suffering from other symptoms of impaired circulation; other, more classical signs of stroke may be present, such as specific motor or sensory problems; behavior may tend to get worse in steps rather than deteriorating gradually (Sloane, 1980). Because the number of strokes accumulates erratically, there is a corresponding random, stepwise decline in the adequacy of cognition. Figure 8-2 shows the pattern of deterioration in multi-infarct dementia and in senile dementia.

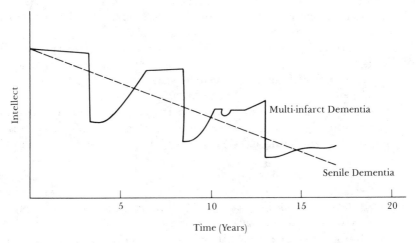

**FIGURE 8-2.** Course of intellectual deterioration in senile dementia and multi-infarct dementia. *(Source: Reprinted with permission of Macmillan Publishing Company, from* Brain Failure: An Introduction to Current Concepts of Senility, *by Barry Reisberg, M.D. Copyright © 1981 by Barry Reisberg, M.D.)*

### Personality Changes in Dementia

Even though changes in thinking are the hallmark of the dementias, the person affected by this group of diseases often also has concomitant emotional symptoms. These negative changes may result directly from loss of neurons in areas of the brain that control and modulate emotions (Reisberg, 1981). They also may have an indirect cause, resulting from awareness of one's failing powers and then struggling psychologically with this devastating perception.

Emotional responses may be unpredictable and show no consistent relation to how a person customarily behaved before the disease struck. Some older adults appear to understand their disability realistically; others appear ignorant that a problem exists. The person's behavior may be an exaggerated caricature of his or her former self or be totally foreign to it (Miller, 1977). The patient may become verbally or physically abusive or overly passive and compliant. There may even be no change in the person other than a cognitive one.

Two emotional concomitants of dementia, because of their frequency, deserve particular mention—denial and depression (Miller, 1977). Denial of one's dementia and the unhappy life circumstances it can lead to may take many forms. It may mean the person confabulates (makes up stories) to fill obvious gaps in memory. For example, instead of saying "I don't know" when a questioner asks "Where are you now?" a disoriented nursing home resident may reply "I am in a palace, and those women in white [the nurses] are my ladies-in-waiting." This response allows her to avoid the knowledge that she really has a memory problem and to shut out what may be for her an intolerable reality—living in an institution.

Less glaring manifestations of denial are quite common, as becomes clear in any visit to a nursing home. For instance, in a talk with a cognitively impaired institutionalized resident, it is not uncommon to hear him happily announce that his family has just visited and promises to take him home for good next week. Declining intellect helps make these delusions possible. The person who cannot remember what has really happened can more easily replace unhappy realities with acceptable, if unrealistic, memories and hopes.

Many dementias in their less severe stages are also accompanied by a depressive reaction, an understandably common response to the knowledge that one has memory problems. For example, even if Mrs. Goldblum's problem is really dementia, she also seems clearly depressed. We might surmise that in part her depression could be due to her awareness, even if not fully conscious, of having this most serious problem of late life.

Denial, depression, and other severe psychological reactions exacerbate the person's cognitive problems (Wang, 1977). Someone who is depressed or makes up a fantasy world to compensate for gaps in memory, for example, emotionally withdraws from the requirements of living in the outside world. Rather than grappling with cognitive challenges they can master, these individuals refuse to use even the intellectual reserves that are left. They have a form of excess disabilities, because they are capable of functioning at a much higher level intellectually than they actually do. This is one reason for the finding that although there is some relation between physical indexes of dementia, such as senile-plaque count, and behavioral evidence of impaired thinking, the correlation between these two measures is not nearly perfect (Wang & Busse, 1971). Psychological factors, such as withdrawal from external involvements, can greatly impair the person's thinking.

This may be true, for example, in our clinical vignette. We would expect that any beginning dementia Mrs. Goldblum has would only be exacerbated by her

**BOX 8-2.  Distinguishing Depression from Dementia:
A Diagnostic Problem**

Given the current state of our knowledge, the diagnostic label "dementia" is perhaps the most malignant one we have: the person's mind is going; his or her condition will get steadily worse. However, this dreaded label is sometimes applied inaccurately. Someone can have many dementialike symptoms and still not be suffering from dementia itself. In these cases, depression is often the culprit, as its signs can mimic those of an organic condition. Some depressed older people have memory problems, are unable to think clearly, and may even be incapable of caring for themselves (Folstein & McHugh, 1978; McAllister, 1983). These symptoms, so like those of dementia, are part of their emotional difficulties. Because depression is potentially curable, accurately making the often difficult diagnosis between true dementia and depression can mean the difference between a person's being ignored—usually consigned to a nursing home and forgotten—and being actively treated. Mrs. Goldblum's case illustrates the difficulty of making this differential diagnosis.

There is evidence that mental health workers in the United States may be too quick to assume dementia when an older person is really suffering from depression. A cross-national investigation of the frequency with which psychiatrists put patients into particular diagnostic categories revealed that American psychiatrists were more likely to classify a given older patient as demented than the British (Copeland, 1978). British psychiatrists, even when confronted with an older person experiencing classic symptoms of dementia, tended to look more closely for what these signs might also reflect, an underlying depression. As a consequence, the British used the diagnosis of depression more frequently and possibly more accurately and worked more actively to help their geriatric patients. This difference, which does not speak well for mental health professionals in the United States, may be changing somewhat as more people become sensitized to the fact that depressions can often mimic dementias.

refusing to go out by herself after her frightening experience at the shopping center. In fact, this clinical vignette illustrates the reason why, as noted in Chapter 3, a too difficult or too complex external environment may engender excess disabilities of any type. Negotiating an environment that is too incongruent with one's abilities may elicit an intolerable degree of anxiety, which may cause the person to retreat, abandoning any attempt to function at his or her potential. This very avoidance, in turn, results in the development of excess disabilities—that is, behaving as if one were more disabled than one actually is.

## Delirium

*Delirium,* or a delirious state, is a clouding of consciousness that occurs when a person suffers from a condition that causes an acute disturbance in brain functioning. A host of toxic substances, diseases, and even emotional upsets can precipitate the symptoms of delirium (see Table 8-2). Anyone, old or young, can become delirious. For example, an extremely high fever often causes delirium. Older people, however, because they are not as physiologically hardy as the young, are most likely to develop these symptoms of disturbed consciousness. Although delirium may clear up by itself, rapid diagnosis and treatment of the specific condition that is causing the delirium is often essential, because this underlying cause may be fatal.

**TABLE 8-2.**    Some causes of delirium in the elderly.

| | |
|---|---|
| **Medications** | Errors in self-administration; polypharmacy (taking a number of medications simultaneously); abuse of nonprescription drugs; side effects of drugs given appropriately; inappropriate drug dosage for the individual (older people may get toxic reactions from the normal "adult" dosage of a drug) |
| **Physical Problems** | Cardiac conditions, including heart attack; neurological problems such as tumors, encephalitis, stroke; metabolic disorders; pneumonia or any disease causing fever; constipation; heat stroke |
| **Environmental Changes or Stressors** | Death of spouse, move, hospitalization |
| **Poor Nutrition** | Inadequate vitamin or protein intake (older people are a group at risk for being malnourished) |
| **Surgery** | Aftereffects of anesthesia; surgical complications |
| **Accidents or Assaults** | Both may be more frequent in older people; physical and emotional effects may cause delirium |

### Symptoms

Unfortunately, some symptoms of delirium mimic dementia. A delirious person experiences memory loss, disorientation, and often an inability to care for himself or herself. In an older person who is expected to be "senile," the temptation to diagnose a delirium as dementia may be particularly strong. Delirious states, however, differ markedly in many ways from dementia.

In delirium there is a rapid disturbance in consciousness that may develop within a few hours or days. The delirious person has immediate problems with past as well as more recent memory. Visual hallucinations may be present. The person is likely to be totally lucid at times, with no signs of memory disturbance (Sloane, 1980). None of these symptoms is characteristic of dementia.

### Prevalence

Delirium is common among hospitalized older people because so many physical illnesses and medical interventions can precipitate these cognitive changes (Habot & Libow, 1980; see Table 8-2). For example, if a person is ill enough to be hospitalized, his or her treatment is likely to include the administration of drugs. Older people, being less physiologically sound, are much more likely to develop negative reactions to medications (see Kayne, 1978), and one side effect of drugs can be delirium.

Delirium itself is usually temporary. It either clears up spontaneously after treatment or ends in death if its cause is life-threatening and untreatable. In a few cases, however, delirium causes permanent brain damage and ends in dementia.

# Depression

Delirium and the dementias, as just mentioned, have two distinguishing features: they affect primarily intellect, and they have a clear organic cause. **Depression,** even though it can have associated with it problems in intellect, has mainly nonintellectual effects. Depressed people are at least potentially capable of doing very well on tests of memory and abstract thought, but their ideas about the world and their emotional reactions are abnormal. Depression also has no clearly visible anatomical basis, in contrast to the dementias.

## Symptoms

Someone who is **depressed** may have a great variety of physical and psychological complaints. Such a large, heterogeneous collection of symptoms is grouped under the diagnostic category of depression that no one person shows all or even most signs of the disorder (Becker, 1974). Depressions manifest themselves differently in different people, and depression in the older person may take a different form than in a younger adult (Gurland, 1976).

A leading investigator in the field (Beck, 1979) divides the clinical symptoms of depression into several major categories: emotional signs, changes in cognition, motivational signs, physical signs, and, in severe cases, delusions and hallucinations.

The symptoms that Beck lists under emotional signs are the most familiar to us. The depressed person may have crying spells, look glum, and be unable to feel any joyful emotion. Not everyone who is depressed, however, has these obvious mood changes. Depression, perhaps most commonly in the older person, may be what mental health clinicians call "masked." It may express itself only in the person's overfocusing, for example, on minor physical problems (Epstein, 1976). It takes careful observation to see that signs such as these really do signal a person is depressed.

Cognitive changes in depression include thoughts that one is worthless and useless, irrational guilt feelings, and ideas that the world is empty and has nothing positive to offer. In addition, the older depressed person may be convinced that he or she is getting senile or is terminally ill. These symptoms are called cognitive signs, because it is the depressed person's thoughts, or cognitions, about the self and the world that have become unrealistically skewed.

In severe cases a depressed person may lose contact with reality and have delusions (fixed irrational ideas) or hallucinations (visions or imaginary voices). Depressive delusions and hallucinations are likely to be severely self-blaming. For example, delusionally depressed people may have a conviction that they have committed horrible crimes or may hallucinate voices accusing them of heinous acts.

Depression often causes specific motivational changes—usually a strong desire to escape from the world or passively avoid it. The depressed person has trouble taking action. The person may be apathetic or, alternatively, indecisive and paralyzed with fear. He or she may be suicidal; in most depressions there is a clear indifference to whether one lives or dies. Mrs. Goldblum's depression, for example, seems characterized by a stance of passive avoidance. She neglects herself physically and avoids participating in the activities of her new community.

A wide variety of physical symptoms are also associated with depression. There may be disturbances of appetite—either indifference to food or compulsive overeating. There are problems with sleep, frequently sleeplessness or, less commonly, sleeping excessively. Digestion and elimination are also interfered with; nausea or constipation may occur. Fatigue, inability to concentrate, and slowed thinking are also characteristic.

Unfortunately for the mental health worker, who must make an accurate diagnosis, when depression in the older person involves mainly physical symptoms like slowed thinking, sleeplessness, and problems in eating and elimination, these signs are sometimes confused with normal aging (Epstein, 1976; Gurland, 1976). Older people normally need less sleep or may have minor difficulties with appetite or constipation. Treatable depressions may then be overlooked in the older person whose disease manifests itself only through physical symptoms.

### Prevalence

In adulthood symptoms of depression are fairly common. According to government figures, the prevalence of serious depression among adults in a given year is estimated to be rather high—as much as 15% of the population (Greist & Greist, 1979). Depression in people under 65 tends to strike women more often than men, but in the elderly it may affect both sexes equally (Gurland, 1976).

Studies of the frequency of depression in the elderly often show that a high proportion suffer from this disorder. Findings from the Duke Longitudinal Study—though, as we know, based on a select group not truly representative of community elderly—suggest the magnitude of the problem (Gianturco & Busse, 1978). In the Duke sample, 20–25% were diagnosed as depressed at a given round of testings. By the ninth or tenth evaluation, about 60% had been categorized as depressed at least once. In addition, depression in the Duke volunteers was likely to be chronic; the same people tended to be rated as depressed in successive testings.

### Types of Depression

Mental health workers often divide depression into two basic categories: **major** (also called psychotic or endogenous) **depression** and **minor** (also called neurotic or reactive) **depression.** It is commonly believed that these two types of depression are actually different illnesses, having different causes and outcomes and necessitating different treatments. However, it is increasingly being shown that in many cases making clear distinctions between categories is impossible. Many depressed people have some characteristics of both major and minor depressions simultaneously and so are difficult to fit into one or the other category. For this reason there is controversy over whether the practice of separating depression into two forms is really justifiable (Becker, 1974). However, those who treat depressed people are likely to still make this differentiation.

When a person is diagnosed as having a major depression, we expect him or her to have quite severe symptoms. The prognosis (expected outcome) of his or her problem is worse than with minor depression. The symptoms are likely to have appeared "out of the blue," without an external precipitant. The person is likely to show certain physical changes: loss of appetite, early morning awakening (the sufferer is able to get to sleep but wakes up spontaneously a few hours later), constipation, and slowed or speeded-up motor activity. The problem may run in the family. It is thought to be more responsive to medication than psychotherapy.

Because this type of depression may be partly hereditary, involves specific physical symptoms, has no apparent relation to environmental events, and seems most helped by medication, investigators have been led to think that it is endogenous— that is, it has a primarily internal, biochemical cause. It is generally believed that classic major depressions result from defects in brain chemistry.

In contrast, there is no evidence this is true of a person with minor depression. Here the symptoms clearly occur in reaction to events in the person's life, most often a loss, rejection, or other unpleasant occurrence. The condition, having an external precipitant, can often be cleared up by changing this depression-causing situation or modifying the person's response to it. For this reason psychotherapy, not medication, is the main treatment for this type of depression.

Depression can still usefully be considered as being more or less severe. However, firm distinctions between "major" and "minor" are not always or even often possible to make, because some major depressions have an external cause and can be helped by psychotherapy. In addition, some minor depressions appear to come on spontaneously, with no apparent external reason. In the older depressed person, the frequent combination of physical symptoms and clearly apparent situational causes may make the diagnosis even more difficult (Gurland, 1976). Depressions in old age often appear both minor and major simultaneously, with mixtures of both types of symptoms. For example, in our vignette, Mrs. Goldblum shows some physical signs characteristic of a major depression (loss of appetite, sleep disturbance), but her depression also seems minor in that it was precipitated by an external situation—the move.

### Causes

The spontaneous, seemingly internally generated quality of some depressions and the just as clear external reasons that seem to precipitate others have given rise to two lines of research on the cause of this frequent problem. Some studies and theories explore the psychology of depressive illness; others explore the biochemistry of depression.

**The Psychology of Depression.**   In the Duke Longitudinal Study, Gianturco and Busse (1978) examined the relation between changes in certain life situations and the onset of depression to see what events were most likely to precipitate the problem. Interestingly, depression was most closely tied to different life events for men and women. For women, a loss in finances was most likely to precede depression; for men, suddenly failing health was. To explain these provocative and unexpected findings, the researchers suggested an interesting possibility. Being in ill health may be more upsetting to men than women because they put a higher value on being strong and independent. When men get sick, the actual loss they are suffering is greater; it includes a loss not just of health but also of self-image.

Losses, particularly losses that are highly personally meaningful, have long been thought to be a primary precipitant of depression, whether in children, in young or middle-aged adults, or in the elderly (Lipton, 1976). As we know, retirement and widowhood are late-life losses that only sometimes cause depression. The type of loss that is thought to more commonly have this effect is losing one's health. For example, in one study the onset of an illness had preceded development of this condition in a full 18% of a group of depressed elderly (Roth & Kay, 1956). This association between physical illness and depression in old age has not been universally found (Palmore, Cleveland, Nowlin, Ramm, & Siegler, 1979). However, it seems reasonable that there is a relationship because being in ill health seems a type of stressful experience particularly prone to produce depression in people of any age.

Knowing that loss may produce depression, however, does not explain the psychological mechanism by which this occurs. For this we must turn to hypotheses, ideas offered by several writers who subscribe to the two very different world views about what causes emotional problems—behaviorism and psychoanalytic theory.

Behaviorists and psychoanalysts both have developed hypotheses about how loss causes a depression. They have varying interpretations about the mechanism that causes depressive symptoms to appear after a loss. These ideas about the genesis of depression have, as usual, been derived from observing younger people, but they are just as applicable to understanding depressions in old age.

Freud himself (1957) was the first to attempt to explain depression. He wanted to understand why the depressed person was often so guilt-ridden and self-blaming, sometimes feeling culpable for the most terrible crimes. He tied these symptoms to the loss of an ambivalently loved object or person and contrasted depression with the normal process of mourning. In mourning, he hypothesized, a person comes to terms with the loss of a loved person by identification. We saw an instance of this psychological mechanism in the last chapter's vignette. The bereaved person incorporates qualities of the lost loved one and his or her feelings about the individual; they become part of the survivor's own self-image. Normal mourning becomes depression, Freud reasoned, when the individual has unconscious negative feelings for the person one has lost. These negative feelings are then also turned inward, resulting in one's adopting toward oneself the unresolved angry feelings once reserved for the lost person. In Freud's view, then, the same negative feelings the depressed person had about the lost person have become part of his or her own self-image. This is why depressed people are so angry and critical toward themselves.

Freud's interpretation may apply to some old-age depressions but seems to be too limited in scope to cover all. Not all depressions appear as a consequence of loss of a person. As noted earlier, depression in the elderly often occurs, for example, after the onset of physical disease. It is difficult to see how Freud's analysis applies to these instances of old-age depression.

In fact, depressions in late life are more often characterized by apathy and a sense of helplessness and exhaustion (Cath, 1965; Gianturco & Busse, 1978) rather than the angry self-denigration Freud's theory was attempting to explain. In view of the symptoms so common to this condition in the older person—withdrawal, lack of interest in the outside world, slowed thinking and moving—some gerontologists (Cath, 1965) suggest another interpretation. Depression in old age is most often a consequence of feelings of helplessness and hopelessness in the face of unavoidable, quite real losses.

A similar general view of depression has been put forward by both a behaviorist and a psychoanalytic writer (see Becker, 1974, for review). For example, the psychoanalyst (Bibring, 1953) describes depression as occurring when losses shake a person's confidence in his or her ability to get gratification. These losses, he feels, also deprive the person of important external supports necessary to maintaining self-esteem. As a consequence a condition of "ego helplessness" occurs, and the person feels inadequate and incompetent. The symptoms of depression—apathy, withdrawal, low self-esteem—result from the person's feelings of helplessness.

This idea parallels that of the behaviorist (Seligman, 1975), who from his very different perspective has described helplessness as critical to the development of depression. This experimental psychologist's ideas about depression stem from an unlikely source—his research on a phenomenon called **learned helplessness** in laboratory animals. In a series of experiments he showed that dogs repeatedly exposed to inescapable electrical shocks eventually developed "depressive" symptoms. They became apathetic; they seemed sad; they appeared unable to think or move quickly. In addition, his fascinating finding was that when the animals were later put in a situation in which they could act to avoid the shocks, they were incapable of doing so. They had learned to be helpless, and this lesson interfered with any new learning and also perpetuated the depressive symptoms.

These experiments suggest that learned helplessness may form the basis for some old-age depressions in the following way: In the face of unavoidable losses or "shocks" such as becoming ill, the older person may lose faith in his or her ability to affect the environment. This sense of helplessness may directly lead to the cognitive, emotional, motivational, and even, to some extent, physical symptoms of the depressive syndrome. In addition, the feeling of being helpless itself may prevent the person from acting to compensate for losses and so restoring his or her sense of mastery. Like Seligman's experimental animals, the depressed older person may have learned inaction—that it is useless to try to affect the environment.

Using this analysis, we would predict that a person experiencing a series of inescapable negative events would be most prone to respond by developing the symptoms of a depression. In other words, "shocks" like widowhood or illness, if they occurred singly, would not necessarily be expected to engender long-term problems. However, if several befell a person within a short period, they would be more likely to cause difficulty.

There is evidence from the second Duke study that this is so. Palmore and associates (1979) examined the impact of five life events—subject's retirement, spouse's retirement, widowhood, departure of last child from home, and major illness—on the physical and psychosocial functioning of their middle-aged and elderly volunteers. As the learned helplessness model implies, when the researchers tested volunteers' morale (actually an index of depression), they found little or no long-term detrimental psychological effect of any of these events considered alone (one, last child leaving home, actually had a positive impact). However, if these events happened multiply, their cumulative influence was clearly negative. Volunteers who during the course of the study experienced several of these occurrences were adapting more poorly. Their morale, in particular (more so if they had few psychological or social resources), was likely to be low.

**The Biology of Depression.**    In contrast to these external explanations, other attempts to understand depression look internally, examining likely physiological causes. Here the major research focus has been on possible abnormalities in **neurotransmitters,** chemical substances that transmit impulses from neuron to neuron, as being responsible for some depressions. Currently, most biochemical research has been directed to the functioning of a particular class of neurotransmitters called **catecholamines.** A catecholamine called **norepinephrine,** in particular, has been implicated in depression.

Several lines of evidence point to low levels of norepinephrine as being responsible for depressive symptoms. Drugs known to decrease the amount of this chemical in the brain often produce depression. Drugs known to increase the amount of this substance in the brain have antidepressant effects; that is, they ameliorate or cure some existing depressions.

These findings have prompted what is called **the catecholamine hypothesis of depression.** According to this idea, depression-prone people have a biochemical defect—constitutionally low levels of brain catecholamines, particularly norepinephrine (see Greist & Greist, 1979). When a person's depressive symptoms seem to come out of the blue, the catecholamine hypothesis suggests this is due to a sudden decrease in brain catecholamines. The level of a chemical that destroys brain norepinephrine tends to be higher in the aged (Lipton, 1976). It is possible, but highly speculative, that this finding may relate in some way to the increased predisposition to becoming depressed among older people.

This idea about the genesis of depression is still speculative. Its veracity depends on indirect and circumstantial evidence. It seems likely, in fact, that even if some depressions are due mainly to a biochemical imbalance, their cause may be more complicated than just a deficiency of any one class of brain chemicals. As with the psychological interpretations described earlier, there also may be a variety of biochemical reasons for depression. A single physiological cause for the problem is unlikely to suffice (Greist & Greist, 1979).

### The Worst Consequence: Suicide

Most depressions do not end in suicide, but the reverse is true: most people who make serious suicide attempts are depressed. This is particularly so in old age. It is estimated that if we use a broad definition of depression, almost 100% of elderly suicides are preceded by depressive symptoms (Stenback, 1980). We would logically expect that since older people are more prone to developing depressions, they would also be more likely to attempt suicide than the young. Figure 8-3 shows this is clearly the case, but only for one group of elderly people—White males. The suicide rate rises fairly steadily with age in White men. By age 85 the rate for this group is more than triple that of any other.

There is no exact explanation why suicide is so high in this group of older men. Depression is just as prevalent in other elderly people as in White males. However, there are some speculations. One plausible suggestion is that some reversals of old age hit White males the hardest because they are so used to being at the top of the social ladder (Miller, 1979). Black males and White females may not be as bothered by losses that mean dependency and a diminution of status, in particular

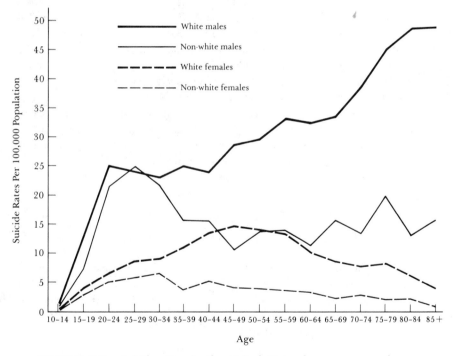

**FIGURE 8-3.** Suicide rates in the United States by age, sex, and race, 1974. *(Original Source: The National Center for Health Statistics. As it appears in Marv Miller, Suicide After Sixty: The Final Alternative, p. 4. Copyright © 1979 by Marv Miller.)*

being in poor health, because they are more used to a secondary place on the social scale. White males' need to accommodate to what are potentially more jarring reversals, plus the general predisposition men have to settle problems by action (Stenback, 1980), may partly account for their much higher suicide rate. This idea fits in with evidence that, particularly in the elderly, physical illness is often a contributing factor in suicide (Stenback, 1980).

Another important influence associated with old-age suicide may also disproportionately affect men—social isolation. Isolation from significant relationships is frequently mentioned in the analysis of causes of suicide in the elderly (Stenback, 1980). Men may be more prone to this problem in late life than women. At least, the current cohort of older men seem less likely to have many close relationships other than marriage, so they are much more vulnerable to being totally cut off from others by single losses like widowhood. This possibly more precarious position with regard to being isolated may also be a factor partly explaining their higher suicide rate (see also the section on widowhood in Chapter 7).

In addition, we need to understand something else about these statistics. They may be emphasizing to an unwarranted degree the differences in suicidal behavior between the sexes, because they reflect only the incidence of completed suicides, ones in which an obviously suicidal motive could be inferred. Men, more than women, make successful suicide attempts; and because they use more violent methods (shooting, jumping), their intentions are more often clear. Female suicides, because they tend to involve more passive methods (taking pills, for example), may more often be attributed to an accident rather than to a premeditated effort to end one's life (see Miller, 1979).

Finally, the figures leave out another fact about suicide specifically in the elderly. In contrast to the young, who are more likely to make a suicidal gesture to manipulate others or to get attention, suicide attempts by older people have a greater chance of being successful (see Shneidman and Farberow, 1961).

For this reason mental health workers are taught to treat suicide threats as particularly ominous in older people. In the isolated, ill, depressed older person who threatens to kill himself or herself, suicide is a real possibility.

## Assessment

The first step in dealing with depression, dementia, or any mental disorder is to determine that a problem exists and to understand it as completely as possible. This is the aim of ***the diagnostic evaluation,*** which is done in most mental health settings before any decisions are made about treatment. The actual diagnostic procedure may vary from place to place. However, our vignette illustrates how it is likely to take place, as well as the sometimes wide differences of opinion about what diagnosis a patient should have.

### Overview

During a mental health evaluation two things are done. The person is given a diagnostic label, and an attempt is made to understand the individual and all the parameters of his or her difficulty quickly but in as much depth as possible. Both giving the problem a diagnostic label and examining it in a more differentiated way are important to treating the disorder.

The practice of assigning diagnostic labels to a person is controversial. Some mental health workers, although they may think labels in the abstract are appropriate to use, dislike the particular diagnoses employed in the current classification system. Some believe that using diagnoses at all is a bad practice because they set up a self-fulfilling prophecy in which the person is labeled as "sick" and so tends to remain in and continue to act in that devalued role. Others go even further. They feel that the whole idea that a person who comes for treatment has a diagnosable problem is wrong. They see the situation, not the person, as pathological (see the next chapter's discussion of family therapy).

Nevertheless, in most mental health settings, DSM-III diagnoses are used. This practice has some advantages. The commonly used diagnostic labels convey a great deal of information in a few words to others in the field. They give a shorthand description of the person's symptoms, suggest possible causes of the problem, and give the mental health worker a sense of how the problem might be likely to progress. The diagnosis also implies some specifics about treatment—whether it is useful to pursue at all and what interventions might be successful.

We just saw how the labels "senile dementia" and "depression," for example, give very different information about causes, likely outcomes, symptoms, and effective treatment. A person labeled as having senile dementia is expected to behave differently than a depressed person. His or her problem has ominous implications that are absent in a diagnosis of depression. We also saw how difficult making the distinction between depression and dementia can be and how important it is not to diagnose dementia in a person who is depressed. The label a person receives, then, is both informative and crucial to his or her future. Accurate labeling is one primary purpose of a diagnostic assessment, even though in practice, as we saw in our clinical vignette, making an accurate diagnosis can be problematic.

The second goal of the person doing a diagnostic assessment is just as important to treatment—to understand the problem in a more detailed, specific way. The label by itself is too generalized to include important specifics about the person who has the diagnosis. For example, a person with "senile dementia" may be somewhat impaired or totally incapacitated. He or she may also be depressed or even have delusions. The family may be willing to keep the patient at home or insist on institutionalization. All these facts about the person and his or her problem are very relevant to the individual's care. The diagnostician, then, describes in depth the way the problem exists in the individual. He or she often also describes the patient's coping capacities, social milieu, and past behavior and suggests a treatment plan.

When an older person arrives for psychological care, the diagnostic procedure is likely to be identical in most respects to that used with a younger adult. However, it is increasingly being understood that often a complete physical examination is important in assessing the older adult. More often than for younger people, a physical problem may be causing what look like symptoms not just of dementia but of any functional disorder.

Apart from this medical assessment, the evaluation is done by a mental health worker—usually either a psychiatrist, a clinical psychologist, a psychiatric social worker, or, less frequently, a psychiatric nurse (see Table 8-3). Members of all four professions, when certified, are qualified to assess and treat psychological problems. This person, working alone or, as in our clinical vignette, as part of a diagnostic team in a hospital or clinic, may use one or more of the following general approaches to understanding older (or younger) patients: interviewing them or their relatives, observing their behavior, or giving them standard tests of personality and cognition. Only when the older person is too disabled physically to take certain tests or submit to certain interviews is the mental health worker likely to modify the evaluation approach to make it specifically geriatric (Lawton, Whelihan, & Belsky, 1980). And if specific questions such as the extent and severity of an existing dementia in an older person are being studied, special strategies are often required. In fact, an additional element of the diagnostic procedure used with older adults is often to test for the presence of dementia, even if the person appears to be suffering from a purely functional problem.

**TABLE 8-3.** The core mental health professions.

| *Title and Training* | *Special Additional Skills* |
|---|---|
| Psychiatrist, M.D., psychiatric residency (usually 3 years in mental health setting) | Administers drugs; diagnoses and treats medical problems; skilled in the diagnostic interview |
| Clinical psychologist, Ph.D. in psychology, clinical internship in mental health setting | Administers psychological tests; does research |
| Psychiatric social worker, B.A. or M.S.W., supervised field experience in mental health setting | Works with social agencies, families; knowledgeable about community services |
| Psychiatric nurse, R.N. in nursing plus specialized training in care and treatment of psychiatric patients (may also have M.A. or Ph.D.) | Gives physical care; can assess self-care abilities |

### The Diagnostic Question

The actual tests, interviews, or observations a mental health worker chooses to use are dictated by what is called the diagnostic question. The diagnostic question is simply the main problem that needs to be evaluated. For example, if the person arriving for help seems *clearly* to have no intellectual deficits but to be depressed, the diagnostician will focus mainly on understanding the manifestations and causes of the patient's depression. If the person's difficulty is likely to be dementia, the mental health worker will evaluate the person's cognitive capacities in more depth.

However, as we saw in our vignette, the person's disorder often cannot be clearly delineated in this way. This is why mental health assessments often cover a broad ground. The diagnostician or diagnostic team often makes a detailed evaluation of the person's strengths or weaknesses in many areas of life.

### Tests and Interviews Used

In many mental health settings the usual procedure is to have this far-ranging inquiry done by one person, any of the core mental health professionals whose training and special qualifications are listed in Table 8-3. Usually the person does an interview to obtain the following information:

1. What are the present problems? Has the person had these problems before?
2. Are there important precipitating events—a recent trauma such as death of a loved one, retirement, economic reversal, onset of physical illness?
3. What are the important events in the person's life history? Family circumstances? Immigration? Work experiences? Marriage? Children?
4. Is there a history of mental problems in the individual or his or her family?
5. What is the person's medical history? What medications is he or she taking? What illnesses are present?
6. What are the person's strengths? Previous coping strategies?
7. What is the person's mental and emotional status? Is he or she anxious or depressed? Are there memory problems? Difficulties in judgment? In the quality of thinking? In the person's ability for self-care?
8. What resources exist in the community to help the person—for example, senior centers, day care centers, social services?
9. How adequate is the person's social network? Who in the family and what friends might be counted on to help?
10. What type of intervention is appropriate for the person? Psychotherapy? Drug therapy? A change in the environment?

In some settings, however, and for some purposes, as in our vignette, a clinical team does the evaluation. In this case, the approach used by each member of the team is usually specific to his or her particular skills. The clinical psychologist will use selected psychological tests to assess the patient (some commonly used measures are listed in Table 8-4). The social worker will interview the family and gather information about community resources relevant to understanding the problem. The psychiatrist will interview the patient, using his or her training in skilled observation to understand the person in depth. If a psychiatric nurse is part of the assessment team, he or she may assess functional skills such as self-care capacities. Additional health professionals (physical therapist, neurologist, speech therapist) will be called in if needed.

**TABLE 8-4.** Psychological tests commonly used in clinical assessment.

| Title | Description |
|---|---|
| **Rorschach Inkblot Test** | Ten inkblots. Patient asked to say what each card looks like and why patient saw what he or she did. Psychologist usually uses complicated scoring system designed to reveal basic character structure and emotional conflicts, plus clinical judgment, in evaluating responses. |
| **Thematic Apperception Test (TAT)** | Twenty pictures. Patient asked to tell a story about each (or each of a selected group). Psychologist usually evaluates character and conflicts by looking at story content and structure without benefit of a specific scoring system (see also Chapter 6). |
| **Draw-A-Person Test (DAP)** | Patient asked to draw a human figure; then asked to draw someone of the other sex than the first figure. Psychologist evaluates personality by looking at various aspects of the drawing—for example, placement on the page, what body parts are emphasized. |
| **Bender Gestalt Test** | Nine cards, each showing a different geometric form. Patient asked to copy each form within limited time. Psychologist evaluates adequacy of the drawings to assess presence of brain damage as well as emotional problems. |
| **Minnesota Multiphasic Personality Inventory (MMPI)** | 550 objectively scored true/false test items. Each subscale assesses one of several types of functional mental disorders. |

*Note:* The WAIS, also commonly administered, is omitted because it was described in detail in Chapter 4.

### Assessment Strategies for Dementia

When the standard tests and evaluation strategy do not fit the older adult—for example, when a moderate or severe dementia is present—special techniques are required.

If the person to be tested for dementia has only a mild impairment, the psychologist is likely to assess cognitive capacities using the WAIS. However, if deficits are more pronounced, as in our clinical example, even this standard test will be too difficult. Scales have been developed specifically to test the cognitive abilities of severely impaired elderly people. The best-known of these measures, the Mental Status Examination, is described in Box 8-3.

In addition, for dementia in particular, special neuropsychological tests that measure in a more refined way damage to particular cognitive functions are often used. These measures need to be administered by a psychologist with special training in neuropsychology, the assessment and understanding of neurological problems. They give a more differentiated picture than the WAIS of an individual's particular intellectual deficits. The last behavioral index that is essential to understanding the older adult with dementia is the one that is so crucial to assess-

---

**BOX 8-3.    The Mental Status Examination**

In spite of marked differences in diagnostic strategy, there are some easy tests that almost every person involved in diagnosing dementia will have occasion to use. The classic among these measures is the Kahn-Goldfarb Mental Status Examination.

If any test can qualify as essential for diagnosing severe dementia, it is the scale below, the Kahn-Goldfarb Mental Status Questionnaire, used to assess low-functioning older adults. The test is so simple to give and easy to score that it can be administered by anyone with or without a background in psychological testing. It not only shows how severe the patient's disturbance is but also gives information about specific deficits in memory and orientation. Severity of impairment is rated by the number of questions answered wrong. The type of problem the person has is shown by the particular questions missed. This test or a similar variant is often used by itself, or it can be used in conjunction with other measures if a more detailed cognitive evaluation is needed.

| *Item* | *Measures* |
|---|---|
| 1. What is the name of this place? | Orientation |
| 2. Where is it located? | Orientation |
| 3. What is today's date? | Orientation |
| 4. What is the month now? | Orientation |
| 5. What is the year? | Orientation |
| 6. How old are you now? | Well-established memory |
| 7. When were you born (month)? | Well-established memory |
| 8. When were you born (year)? | Well-established memory |
| 9. Who is the president of the United States? | Well-established memory |
| 10. Who was the president before that? | Well-established memory |

*Additional Items Often Used for Recent Memory*
1. What is the time of day?
2. What were you doing before coming to this room?
3. What did you have for breakfast/lunch?
4. What is my [interviewer's] name?

---

ing adults with any severe physical impairment affecting independent living—a measure of functional capacities, such as the Katz ADL Scale (see Chapter 2).

Evaluation of dementia also usually includes specific medical measures. The person is likely to be given a CAT (computerized axial tomography) scan, which produces a computer-generated picture of the brain. The CAT scan, for example,

*Source: Scale adapted from "A Brief Objective Measure for the Determination of Mental Status of the Aged," by R. L. Kahn, A. I. Goldfarb, N. Pollack, and A. Peck. In *American Journal of Psychiatry*, 1960, 117, pp. 326–328. Copyright © 1960, the American Psychiatric Association. Reprinted by permission.

corroborated the psychologist's findings that Mrs. Goldblum had a dementia. Because the CAT scan is unable to confirm dementia except in severe cases, it is gradually being replaced by newer, more refined techniques of assessing brain structure and function.

Finally, the assessment of this problem in particular concerns the environment. The diagnostician needs to know how involved the person's family is. He or she will want to be aware of services in the community—nursing homes or options like day care for keeping the person at home. The diagnostician will also look carefully at the person's caretakers and the physical setting. Are excess disabilities being engendered? How might changes here improve the person's functioning?

### Recommendations

After the diagnostic evaluation for dementia or any functional disorder, a conference is usually held to discuss the findings and decide on treatment. As in our clinical example, there may be disagreements about various aspects of the person's condition and the best strategy for intervening. The final product is some consensus—specific recommendations for treatment based on a detailed understanding of the problem.

These recommendations may vary greatly. The team may advise the person to make a very radical life change, such as entering a nursing home. At the opposite extreme, the person may simply be told that his or her problem is so minimal it does not warrant treatment. In between is a broad array of other options, treatment strategies that will be examined in the next chapter in some depth. For example, in Mrs. Goldblum's case three major techniques for ameliorating emotional problems were suggested: environmental change, psychotherapy, and drug therapy. We will examine these approaches in the context of following what happens to Mrs. Goldblum after her assessment.

## Summary

Epidemiologic studies are surveys of the prevalence of illnesses in the general population. They are invaluable in determining the need for health care services and can give clues to the causes of diseases. In assessing mental health, however, the accuracy of many of these surveys is questionable, mainly because it is difficult to classify psychological disorders reliably.

Even though we cannot make refined estimates of the prevalence of psychological problems in different age groups, studies suggest that older people, contrary to myth, suffer from nonorganic psychological disorders no more frequently than the young. The elderly do disproportionately have certain types of problems. They are more likely to be depressed, somewhat more likely to develop paranoid reactions, and less likely to be schizophrenic, to be manic-depressive, or to have anxiety disorders than young and middle-aged adults. Organic brain syndromes are much more prevalent in the old than the young, particularly the collection of chronic organic conditions called the dementias.

The dementias are a group of chronic degenerative diseases involving a progressive deterioration of all intellectual functions, including memory, abstract reasoning, and judgment. Dementias get progressively more severe and in their final stages may affect the most basic skills—the ability to remember simple facts about oneself or one's life, to be oriented to the immediate environment, to take care of oneself physically. Dementia is very common in nursing homes. Only 5–8% of people over 65 living in the community have significant symptoms of dementia; however, this is a large number and the prevalence of dementia rises in successively older age groups, so that about 20% of noninstitutionalized people over 80 are thought to be affected. As the old-old increase in number, the public health problem posed by dementia should become increasingly acute.

The two most common types of dementia are senile dementia and multi-infarct dementia. In senile dementia, the most frequent type, intellectual impairment is caused by the presence of abnormal structures in the brain called senile plaques and neurofibrillary tangles and by other pathological brain changes. Anatomical studies reveal that the number of senile plaques correlates with the severity of intellectual impairment shown by demented patients, showing a clear physical basis for the disease. The pathological changes of dementia are present to a certain extent in the brains of cognitively intact older people, suggesting that senile dementia is on a continuum with normal aging.

Multi-infarct dementia is caused by many small strokes, which result in increasing amounts of brain damage. Symptoms are basically the same as in senile dementia, but deterioration in thinking may be more random, the patient may be sicker physically, and the condition may have a higher probability of being arrested (though not cured).

Dementias are often associated with unpredictable personality changes; in addition, denial and depression are prevalent reactions. Depression, in fact, by itself may appear to the outside observer as dementia, as its symptoms in the elderly may include cognitive impairment such as memory loss.

Delirium, the second major category of organic brain syndrome, is an acute disturbance in thinking that can be precipitated by a host of physical and emotional causes. Because delirium has some symptoms in common with dementia, it may be misdiagnosed as dementia in an older person. The consequences of this misdiagnosis may be fatal, as the underlying condition causing the delirium can be life-threatening. Delirium is particularly prevalent in hospitalized older people.

Depression, the most common functional psychological problem of old age, may express itself in cognitive, physical, motivational, and emotional signs. Some physical symptoms of depression are identical to somatic complaints that are relatively common in old age, making a differential diagnosis between depression and normal aging difficult. Depression is usually classified into two basic categories, major or minor, although there is controversy about the validity of this practice. Major depressions are thought to have an endogenous (physiological) cause; minor depressions appear to be brought on by painful events in the person's life.

Studies investigating psychological precursors of depression have tied depression to loss, in old age particularly loss of health. Classical Freudian theory attributes the genesis of depression to loss of an ambivalently loved person, but old-age depressions may often be more usefully viewed as reflections of a sense of helplessness in the face of losses that are highly personally meaningful. Depressive symptoms in humans may mimic the reactions of lower animals when exposed to a series of unavoidable shocks. The idea that it is a *series* of losses that is most likely to cause depression is corroborated by empirical findings. In the second Duke study a succession of closely spaced negative events like widowhood or illness was correlated with poor morale. Single changes did not have a long-term adverse impact.

Suicide is disproportionately prevalent in older White males. One reason may be that suicidal acts are associated with isolation, to which older males are most vulnerable. In addition, status reversals in late life may be more upsetting to White men because they are used to being at the top of the social hierarchy. However, these statistics reflect only the rate of completed obvious suicides. Female suicides are more likely to appear to be accidents, and females are more likely than males to attempt suicide unsuccessfully. Older people are also more serious when they threaten suicide than are young adults.

Researchers are investigating the possibility that major depressions are caused by low levels of brain catecholamines, particularly the chemical norepinephrine. However, it is almost certain that more than one physiological substance is involved in depression.

The first step in helping the person with psychological problems is to do a diagnostic assessment. Diagnostic assessments both label the problem that the person is suffering from and convey a description of it. Often the procedure and the measures used by mental health workers (psychiatrists, psychologists, psychiatric social workers, or psychiatric nurses) for diagnosing psychological problems do not differ much for older and younger adults. The diagnostician or diagnostic team tailors the evaluation to the question being asked. Usually, though, the diagnostic question is quite broad and is answered by doing a general clinical assessment that covers many aspects of the patient's behavior and life.

Often a single person does the assessment, using a general set of questions covering global aspects of the patient's functioning. Sometimes, though, the assessment is made by a clinical team, with a psychologist doing the psychological testing, a psychiatrist interviewing the patient, and a psychiatric social worker interviewing the family and contacting community resources; more rarely, a psychiatric nurse will also evaluate self-care skills. Assessment of dementia requires special tests, both behavioral and medical. After the evaluation, the case is usually discussed in a conference, where any diagnostic and therapeutic disagreements are worked out. Finally, a report is written that discusses the person's condition in depth and suggests possible avenues for amelioration.

## Key Terms

*Epidemiology*  
*Functional psychological disorders*  
*Dementia*  
*Senile dementia*

*Alzheimer's disease*  
*Primary degenerative dementia*  
*Neurofibrillary tangles*  
*Senile plaques*

*Multi-infarct dementia*

*Delirium*

*Depression*

*Major depression*

*Minor depression*

*Learned helplessness*

*Neurotransmitters*

*Norepinephrine*

*The catecholamine hypothesis of depression*

*The diagnostic evaluation*

*The Mental Status Examination*

## Recommended Readings

Beck, A. T. **Depression: Causes and treatment**. Philadelphia: University of Pennsylvania Press, 1979.

*Read particularly Part 1 of this comprehensive book for a detailed description of the symptoms, issues in classification, and course and prognosis of various types of depression. Not difficult.*

Birren, J. E., & Sloane, R. B. (Eds.). **Handbook of mental health and aging**. Englewood Cliffs, N.J.: Prentice-Hall, 1980.

*The most far-ranging and detailed of the edited collections surveying all aspects of mental health and aging. Among other topics, chapters cover epidemiology, diagnosis, assessment, and treatment of functional and organic mental disorders. Moderately to very difficult, depending on the chapter.*

Freud, S. Mourning and melancholia. In **Standard Edition** (Vol. 14). London: Hogarth Press, 1957.

*Freud's classic work on depression. Difficult.*

Reisberg, B. **Brain failure: An introduction to current concepts of senility**. New York: Free Press, 1981.

*Perhaps the clearest, most easily understood comprehensive discussion of causes, symptoms, and new approaches to treating the dementias that has been written to date. Highly recommended. Not difficult.*

Seligman, M. E. P. **Helplessness: On depression, development, and death**. San Francisco: W. H. Freeman, 1975.

*The theory of learned helplessness applied to depression as well as other phenomena such as anxiety, psychosomatic illnesses, and sudden death. Not difficult.*

# Mental Disorders II: Treatment

Because the Goldblums were a close-knit family, after the evaluation they met to discuss their options. The people at the center had urged Mr. and Mrs. Goldblum to move back to Philadelphia. The children thought this was good advice. After all, not only would their mother be in a familiar place among family and friends, but the center had been able to recommend a psychologist whose specialty was working with older people. They might not find someone with comparable qualifications in Florida.

Even though Mr. Goldblum had agreed to follow the center's recommendations, he objected to returning to Philadelphia. After all, he felt, they had so recently gone through the effort of one move, and it seemed too exhausting to undertake another. Besides, he thought he could easily find a geriatric psychotherapist in Florida, and his wife might improve if given some time in the new place. Mrs. Goldblum timidly suggested she would rather be living in Philadelphia, but her husband insisted they try just a few months more of living in Florida.

Unfortunately, things did not improve in Florida, and they ended up moving back. In Florida Mrs. Goldblum continued to get worse. She forgot things, was still frightened to go out by herself, and seemed lethargic and apathetic. In addition, their efforts to find psychological help failed. The therapists they did consult seemed to openly see Mrs. Goldblum as a hopeless case. In fact, one stated his opinion that no one over 65 could benefit from psychotherapy.

Luckily, the Goldblums easily sold their condominium in Florida, and their children found them an apartment in the pleasant Philadelphia suburb where they had lived most of their married life. They immediately got an appointment with the psychologist the center had recommended. Just in the first few days after moving back to Philadelphia, Mrs. Goldblum seemed to improve. When her children and old friends visited, she was full of energy, able to carry on a thoroughly intelligent conversation, and only somewhat abstracted when she tried to remember where she had put the coffee cups to serve her guests. However, she was clearly frightened of going out, even in this familiar neighborhood. When a good friend who lived a few blocks away asked her to visit, she gave the excuse that she was just too tired.

The psychologist saw Mr. and Mrs. Goldblum as a couple during the first few therapy sessions. Dr. Zaccarelli wanted, among other things, to see whether the marital relationship might be contributing to Mrs. Goldblum's problems. Like the social worker at the center, he observed that Mr. Goldblum seemed to assume his wife could do little for herself and constantly tried to take over for her. This was most obvious in Mr. Goldblum's practice of answering for his wife when the therapist asked her questions during the session.

After observing the situation, Dr. Zaccarelli decided on a two-pronged therapeutic strategy. He would try to change what he saw as a destructive marital pattern—Mr. Goldblum's tendency to see his wife as a patient and then to treat her like a child and prevent her from being more independent. The psychologist also decided to use desensitization to cure his patient of her phobia of leaving the house by herself, as he felt this difficulty was the main reason Mrs. Goldblum continued to be depressed. Having to stay home kept her from living a normal life and so naturally would make her apathetic and gloomy. Because he saw his patient as having a reactive depression, he did not recommend antidepressants. He knew that giving drugs to an older person was not a good idea unless they were absolutely needed.

As Dr. Zaccarelli had been trained in systems family therapy, his first step was to intervene actively to transform Mrs. Goldblum's role from that of patient to that of capable person. To do this, he immediately gave the Goldblums a home-work assignment. Even though his patient could not yet go outside by herself, she was to be completely in charge of certain household chores. These included or-dering groceries (by telephone) and doing the laundry (the building had ma-chines).

In addition, the psychologist made it clear to Mr. Goldblum that he considered Mrs. Goldblum capable of doing most things for herself, including taking charge of her treatment. So he asked Mr. Goldblum to sit in the waiting room during the sessions.

To help rid Mrs. Goldblum of her phobia, Dr. Zaccarelli instructed her to begin going out in easy steps. First, she was told to spend time in places where she was only slightly afraid of being alone, like the yard of her building. (As her fear was that she would forget how to get home, the psychologist told her to carry a card with her address whenever she left the house.) Then, gradually, she was to begin going farther from home as she gained more confidence. The psychologist knew that because the neighborhood was so familiar to his patient, she should have little problem remembering where she was even if her memory difficulties were in part organically based.

After a few months of therapy, Mrs. Goldblum was cured of her phobia. She could visit friends alone and do most chores by herself. She had a few shaky moments, but her anxiety always subsided when she realized she had her address written down. She kept the psychologist's number with her when she went out so she could call him in case of an emergency. Her depression too ended as a result of her phobia being gone.

Initially, when Mrs. Goldblum had begun therapy, she had been reluctant and somewhat put off. Not only was it embarrassing to admit she had mental prob-lems, but this doctor looked so young. She wondered how anyone that age could understand her problems or presume to advise her on how to live.

In the process of being in therapy, these negative feelings were totally re-versed. Mrs. Goldblum came to look forward eagerly to her sessions. She admired her therapist tremendously and felt he was an expert in many areas, but she also believed she had a lot to offer him. In fact, she felt that one of the things she could do for a person at his stage of life was to give him some understanding of what it was like to grow old—so, in addition to discussing how she was overcom-ing her phobia, she spent time during sessions telling Dr. Zaccarelli what the world had been like when she was growing up and teaching him some of the insights about living that she had acquired over the years.

Mr. Goldblum at first had some trouble with his wife's improvement, as it deprived him of his long-enjoyed position of taking care of her. He, in turn, began to get somewhat depressed. Dr. Zaccarelli was able to remedy this by seeing Mr. Goldblum for a few sessions and encouraging him to become active in the community, where he was known and had always been respected. They both continue to do well since their treatment ended.

Now that we know how prevalent psychological problems are in people over 65, we are in a position to see how adequately mental health professionals are dealing with these problems. We know from the last chapter that older people probably have just as high a rate of functional mental disorders as the young. In addition, they may have a problem younger people do not—dementia. We would therefore expect, if things were fair, that older people should be receiving a significant amount of treatment for mental health complaints.

## The Older Person and the Mental Health System

Unfortunately, this is not happening. People over 65, in proportion to their numbers, receive relatively little psychological care. They visit mental health clinics and private psychotherapists much less often than younger adults. They may arrive for help only in extreme situations, when a problem has reached crisis proportions. When they do come, they are likely to be referred to inpatient (residential) institutions, often those where the care is custodial rather than actively treatment-oriented. They are more likely to be given drugs instead of receiving psychotherapy. They may be discharged prematurely from treatment after a crisis has abated, without their problems being resolved (see Group for the Advancement of Psychiatry, 1970; Kahn, 1977b; Lowy, 1980; Pfeiffer, 1976).

There is a status hierarchy in the mental health system (see Table 9-1). Older people are concentrated at its lowest rungs. Although people over 65 form only 11% of the population, they account for about 30% of the residents of state and county mental hospitals (Pfeiffer, 1976). The care provided here is often what is called *custodial:* residents are merely housed, fed, and given medication. This is because these institutions are places of last resort in the mental health system. They usually serve chronic, severely disturbed, often impoverished patients whose prognosis is in most cases acknowledged as poor. The atmosphere of hopelessness that can pervade these institutions leads them to attract the least well-trained personnel.

As Table 9-1 shows, at the upper end of the mental health status hierarchy, the elderly are just as markedly underrepresented. It is estimated that, at most, 2% of all visits to private psychotherapists are made by people over 65 (U.S. Commission on Civil Rights, 1979). In addition, older people account for only about 4–5% of

**TABLE 9-1.**    Services provided and patients served in some types of mental health settings.

| Setting | Services[a] |
|---|---|
| **Inpatient** | |
| State or county mental hospital | Minimal treatment (psychotherapy) to chronic psychotic low-income patients |
| General hospital, psychiatric unit | More likely to provide active treatment to acutely psychotic patients |
| Private psychiatric hospital | More likely to provide active treatment to psychotic (acute and chronic) higher-income patients |
| **Outpatient** | |
| Community mental health center or other outpatient clinic | Active treatment to less disturbed low-income patients |
| Private therapist | Active treatment to less disturbed higher-income patients |

[a]There are many exceptions to these generalizations.

visits to mental health clinics (Redick & Taube, 1980). Private therapists and mental health clinics serve outpatients. Here treatment, particularly psychotherapy, is likely to be more vigorously attempted, because the people being served have less refractory, less chronic problems. Because their cure rate is so much greater, outpatients often benefit from receiving the best care by the best-trained mental health workers.

The philosophy of what is called "warehousing" severely disturbed people in large custodial care institutions came under fire in the late 1950s, and a reform movement got underway to release as many people as possible into the community. It became increasingly clear that large inpatient psychiatric facilities were, in the same way as nursing homes, often engendering excess disabilities. After a number of years of living in an institution, patients often became so used to being taken care of that they could not adapt to noninstitutional life, even if their original problem had abated. In addition, the newly discovered psychotropic drugs were so effective in curing many psychotic symptoms that for the first time many people even among the severely disturbed were capable of living in the community.

In 1963, in response to these facts, Congress passed the Community Mental Health Centers Act, which provided funds to shift patients from in- to outpatient settings. The act provided for establishment of a nationwide network of outpatient clinics, each serving the residents of a particular geographic region, called a catchment area. Residents could obtain help at their local clinic regardless of their ability to pay. All who needed outpatient care were to be offered treatment. In addition, the centers pledged to serve minority groups, including the elderly, in the same proportion as their numbers in the catchment area the clinic was mandated to serve (Sherwood & Mor, 1980; U.S. Commission on Civil Rights, 1979).

As we saw, however, because only about 4% of the people they treat are over

65, these centers are not fulfilling their commitment to serve older people. Were they doing this, they would be giving at least 11% of their services to older adults, their actual percentage in the population. Yet the policy of not warehousing patients in state and county mental hospitals is still being carried out. Older people are no longer being admitted in large numbers to these institutions (Redick & Taube, 1980). Since they are rarely being seen as outpatients and no longer being seen frequently in custodial inpatient facilities, we may ask what has happened to them.

### Where the Emotionally Disturbed Older Person Is Served

It is likely that many elderly people who are in some but not dire need are not being seen by mental health workers at all (Pfeiffer, 1976). Those in critical need of services who might have gone to state or county mental hospitals in the past are now often being warehoused in another type of inpatient facility. As you may have guessed, this new institution is the nursing home. Nursing homes have taken on the burden of caring for elderly people with severe psychological disabilities (Kahn, 1977b). It is estimated that they now house 75% or more of the psychologically disturbed elderly people who live in institutions (Sherwood & Mor, 1980).

From the point of view of giving adequate mental health care, nursing homes are just as malignant as the large psychiatric institutions they have replaced. Being institutions, they are just as likely to engender excess disabilities as the old psychiatric settings were. In addition, nursing homes, whose mission is not defined as serving people with emotional problems, are even less inclined to offer mental health services than the overcrowded state and county hospitals. However, as many as 80% of all long-term-care residents are estimated to have these very difficulties to a significant degree (Carver, 1974). So it seems clear that older people with psychological problems are often as neglected now as they once were. Several influences conspire to perpetuate this unfortunate reality.

### Why Older People Get Little Care

Our first temptation may be to blame the mental health profession itself for the current state of affairs. This, however, is only partly valid. Older people often do not get adequate services for another reason: they are less prone to go for treatment themselves.

**Barriers to Accepting Help.**   In contrast to young and middle-aged adults, who have grown up in an age that may encourage going for treatment and even frown on not doing so, people currently over 65 have lived most of their lives with the opposite idea, prevalent until recently: that a person who goes for psychological help is either crazy or too weak to handle his or her own problems. This onus is not felt by all of today's elderly. However, it seems safe to assume that a large proportion do believe, as Mrs. Goldblum did, that there is something shameful about admitting one needs treatment. It is just as logical that the same embarrassment may prevent some from visiting a mental health worker even when they legitimately need aid (Lazarus & Weinberg, 1980).

In addition, older people themselves are not immune from believing stereotypes about old age that would militate against their getting help: the presumption that a person over 65 is too old to change; the belief that being unhappy is normal at life's last stage. Unfortunately, these very stereotypes could have their greatest impact on the very group of elderly who might benefit from psychological services the most—those who are depressed. A depressed person might reasonably be particularly susceptible to these negative ideas because, as we saw in the last chapter, one hallmark of depression is just such a conviction of hopelessness about the possibility of change or happiness in life.

Older people with emotional problems do often visit at least one health care professional, however, their family doctor, and so this primary care physician ideally should be in a good position to overcome their biases (Lazarus & Weinberg, 1980). Family doctors might convince older adults that they could benefit from treatment and might make referrals for mental health services.

The primary care doctor is likely to be the stimulus and conduit by which a person does or does not get into the mental health services system, whether that person is old or young. In fact, it has been suggested that these physicians, even though they lack formal training in psychology, may actually be inadvertently providing much of the nation's mental health care (Kiesler, 1980). Some doctors are unable, and some are even unwilling, to refer their patients for psychological services. Sometimes they are unaware that the patient they see is really in need. Their reluctance to refer may be more pronounced when the patient is over 65, because added to it may be the conviction that all older people who are confused or agitated are likely to have dementia (Lazarus & Weinberg, 1980).

This belief, which suggests, possibly erroneously, that an older person is unlikely to benefit from seeing a mental health worker, was shown in the following study (Kucharski, White, & Schratz, 1979). A random sample of primary care physicians were mailed vignettes that described eight hypothetical patients, each with a different set of psychological symptoms. The descriptions sent to each doctor were identical except for the patients' ages. As expected, if the symptoms described were severe and so *could* have been due to dementia, there was a clear age difference in the tendency to refer. Then the doctors were likely to say they would suggest treatment only if the person was said to be under 65. Identical symptoms ascribed to an older person were less likely to be thought to warrant referral, even though they too might have been evidence of a functional problem.

**Barriers to Giving Help.**    We might argue, though, that this state of affairs is the fault of mental health professionals. They should educate older adults, primary care physicians, and the general public about the treatability of late-life psychological problems. They should make people aware that not all symptoms that look like dementia are dementia. Until recently, few mental health professionals have done so. One reason is not hard to guess. Psychoanalytic theory offers longstanding support for the same idea. In fact, in addition to its whole thrust being child-oriented (see Chapter 1), the original tenets of psychoanalysis specifically warn of the difficulty of treating older adults. Freud (1924) believed that even by the forties many people lacked the mental flexibility to undergo the type of radical personality change he advocated to cure psychological symptoms. Since many among those who provide psychological services subscribe to the traditional psychoanalytic approach, this dictum in itself is likely to have had a powerful inhibiting effect.

Moreover, the presumption that the elderly are untreatable rationalizes a tendency that may have fit in with the predisposition of some mental health workers: to avoid the close contact with an older adult that psychological treatment demands. We might hypothesize that for these professionals the prospect of dealing with an older person would evoke strong negative feelings: (1) fear of getting old oneself, (2) problems relating in an adult way because of anger at one's parents and other authorities, (3) inability to feel competent because the life experience of the older patient may seem more extensive and at the same time foreign (see Gotestam, 1980; Pfeiffer, 1976).

Finally, some providers of services at mental health clinics have put forth an additional reason to explain why they generally might not want to treat the elderly. They contend that the objective problems older people have, such as poor health, irreparable losses, and financial difficulties, will make the outcome of psychological treatment uncertain at best. Most older people, they argue, are more in need of concrete social services (like a homemaker or companion) than mental health interventions (U.S. Commission on Civil Rights, 1979).

Mental health clinicians, in contrast to those giving concrete services, attempt to change the responses of clients themselves. Rather than providing external help, they try to modify the maladaptive attitudes, self-defeating behavior, and upsetting feelings limiting the life of the person who has psychological problems. Contrary to the myths, there is no logical reason that someone over 65 should be any less responsive to these interventions than the young. In fact, a prominent psychiatrist who works with the elderly has actually implied an opposite argument (Pfeiffer, 1976). He contends that sometimes mental health services may be very effective precisely when an older person seems to have extremely limited external options. For example, he notes that psychotherapy may sometimes work well when an observer might think it would have the least impact: for a person who is isolated and has little opportunity to develop relationships outside the one with his or her therapist. In this case, Pfeiffer argues, the centrality of the therapeutic relationship can be life-sustaining, whether or not it is actually able to lead to the person's making many concrete changes in his or her life.

No one can win the argument that any intervention works or does not work without evaluating the evidence. This is why, in considering various treatments, we will be paying special attention to research demonstrating their effectiveness. When these investigations of effectiveness, or what are called ***outcome studies,*** are contradictory, I will resort to much less scientific criteria in judging their utility: my own subjective appraisal of whether and under what conditions a given treatment might benefit older adults.

There are mental health interventions specifically tailored for functional mental disorders and others used to help the patient with dementia. Looking first at the treatments for functional problems, we now consider the two major types—psychotherapy and chemotherapy (drug treatment).

## Psychotherapy

As is well known, the purpose of psychotherapy is to change a person's maladaptive behavior and mental problems by verbal means. A psychotherapist is someone who specializes in understanding and curing such problems. Although anyone can call himself or herself a psychotherapist, these mental health specialists usually have graduate training in psychotherapy. They are most likely to be trained in one of the core mental health professions listed in the last chapter.

Through talking to each other, the psychotherapist and the patient (or client) work to understand and eliminate the barriers that are preventing this person from living a full, productive, satisfying life. Psychotherapists vary greatly in the techniques they use to cure problems and in their basic understanding of what causes these difficulties. These different ideas are reflected by a diverse variety of schools of psychotherapy, of which only the most common will be discussed here. These approaches are the main ones used for people of all ages. Because interest in doing psychotherapy specifically with the elderly is so new, in one instance, in fact, our example of a not infrequently used treatment is of necessity taken from a case of a younger adult.

### *Psychoanalytic Psychotherapy*

Chapter 1 mentioned the basic principles of psychoanalytic theory: the idea that the experiences, events, and wishes of childhood are the key to understanding adult personality; the view that these wishes and experiences and other thoughts and memories in the unconscious are powerful determinants of all of a person's actions, both normal and pathological. These conceptions, plus the belief that the more able a person is to understand the content of these wishes and thoughts, the more psychologically healthy he or she will be, are the basis of ***psychoanalytic psychotherapy.***

**Description.** Psychoanalysts see functional psychological problems as the result of personality defects resulting from unfortunate childhood experiences. These experiences do not allow psychological development to proceed normally according to the pattern described in Chapter 1. Normally, feelings and fantasies in the id are subordinated, to a certain extent, as the child learns he or she must adapt to an external world (that is, develops an ego) and obey societal prescriptions of right and wrong (develops a superego). The problem, psychoanalysts believe, is that when a person's childhood is too depriving or too intensely gratifying, this normal development of an adequate ego (and superego) does not occur. Because id impulses have been too severely frustrated or not frustrated enough, they remain overly intense, and there is, in turn, a corresponding inadequacy in ego functioning.

According to this view, the symptoms of psychosis are the result of the most extreme impairment in ego development. The psychotic person's inappropriate behavior, irrational thinking, and disordered ways of perceiving the world are seen as manifestations of his or her id, which has totally overwhelmed the person's fragile ego to reign unchecked. In neurosis, the person's ego is reasoned to be strong enough to prevent this overt expression of id impulses. However, these impulses are still so intense that they must be expressed, though in an indirect form. The puzzling symptoms of neurotic people, which cause them so much unhappiness and which they realistically know are irrational (such as a compulsion to constantly wash one's hands or a fear of elevators), are viewed as disguised expressions of the id. It is these less severe disturbances that psychoanalytic therapy as devised by Freud was designed to treat.

The goal of **insight-oriented** psychoanalytic treatment is to enable the neurotic person to understand the content of the unconscious id impulses that are causing his or her symptoms. Therapist and patient agree that when these desires, wishes, and fantasies are fully revealed and understood, there will be no need to disguise them by maintaining a neurosis. The therapy, then, involves the neurotic person's attempting to uncover, or get insight into, these unconscious ideas and feelings, which stem from early childhood.

In contrast, the treatment usually recommended for psychotic and other more severely disturbed people is called **supportive.** The goal here is not necessarily to have patients understand their unconscious motivations but to help them solidify their more tenuous hold on reality. In this case, the therapist uses his or her understanding of the patient's dynamics—that is, the forces that motivate the patient—to do anything he or she can to make the ego stronger. In contrast to insight-oriented treatment, the therapist makes no effort to help the person gain an awareness of long-unconscious aspects of his or her personality.

Traditional insight-oriented psychoanalytic treatment involves a long-term commitment by the patient to explore diverse aspects of his or her personality, even when this exploration is painful and seems to have only the most remote connection to the problem that brought the individual to therapy. As part of what is called the therapeutic alliance, patient and therapist agree to collaborate on what is actually an unfocused examination of all aspects of the patient's current life and its roots in childhood experiences. In practice, often curing the actual symptoms that brought the person into therapy becomes secondary to the ultimate goal of treatment—to understand as much as one can about oneself. This, in fact, is the only purpose of psychoanalysis, the most intense form of psychoanalytically oriented treatment. Here the person attempts to understand all of his or her unconscious motivations; getting rid of the specific difficulty that may have brought the individual to the therapist is an incidental by-product of this goal.

Our brief description gives us a framework for understanding both how older adults are treated using this approach and, as we will see, some possible pitfalls in employing psychoanalytic techniques with the elderly. Although the literature on use of supportive or insight-oriented therapy with older people is sparse, there have been reports of both approaches being successfully applied in clinical situations.

**Insight-Oriented Therapy.**   One analyst (Meerloo, 1961) asserts that older people in particular can appreciate the connections between childhood experiences and adult behavior and so are uniquely suited for insight-oriented therapy. He relates a case history of an initially psychotic elderly man he successfully treated. In reading this account, notice the emphasis put on the transference (see Box 9-1), one's childhood, and the unconscious, all essentials of the psychoanalytic approach.

> A counselor [lawyer] develops an agitated melancholia after a gall bladder operation. He cannot sleep anymore and he cannot stop crying. . . . We started an analytically oriented form of psychotherapy. . . . He produced dreams at every session, which he started to interpret for himself without intervention. So uppermost were they now in his mind that some dreams pictured direct childhood memories . . . at a later period a fear of death came into the foreground . . . let me report one dream . . . [The patient reports] I was at the railroad station. . . . There was not much time. Will I be able to catch the train? The loudspeaker voice called the passengers to track 999. . . . I [the analyst] limited myself to letting the patient understand the general patterns [of the dream]. Track 999 was for him the last station of departure. He spontaneously interpreted the other part of the dream as his unwillingness to go. . . . In the meantime he had been able to go back to work [Meerloo, 1961, p. 175].

This example reveals the psychoanalytic perspective both on what causes psychological problems and on how they are cured. The lawyer's unconscious fear of death, which interpreting the dream makes conscious to him, is seen by the analyst as one reason that his patient's gall bladder operation resulted in his developing psychological problems. Learning about the true content of this fear and other aspects of his unconscious by analyzing his dreams allowed this lawyer, in the analyst's view, to be freed of his symptoms and to return to work.

**Supportive Therapy.**   Because in the treatment just described the patient gained insight into his unconscious, his therapy was very different from one employing a supportive approach. As mentioned earlier, in supportive therapy the unconscious is left unrevealed to the patient, but the therapist uses his or her understanding of the patient's unconscious to help strengthen the individual's fragile ego.

One psychiatrist developed an innovative treatment for severely regressed nursing home residents using a supportive approach (Goldfarb, 1953; Goldfarb & Turner, 1953). It was based on his analysis of his patients' underlying problem—their extreme dependency coupled with their need to feel more in control. Rather than helping them gain insight—that is, getting them to understand this need (which might have been impossible anyway, as many were cognitively impaired)—Goldfarb used the following strategy. He saw them briefly (about 15 minutes), relatively infrequently (less than once a week), and on a continuing basis. In the session he actively attempted to increase their sense of being in control by allowing them to feel they had somehow bested him or had him in their control. In other words, he arranged the situation so they felt they had triumphed over an authority figure, the doctor who was supposedly more powerful than they. His thought was that feeling this greater sense of power would help these nursing home residents function better.

---

**BOX 9-1.  Transference in the Older Person**

An extremely important concept central to psychoanalytic thinking about how therapy works is the concept of *transference.* Transference is a phenomenon thought to reliably occur as a natural consequence of being in treatment: the patient comes to view the therapist and the therapeutic relationship in a highly distorted way. The therapist is imbued with all sorts of unrealistic qualities, and the therapeutic relationship becomes overly important to the patient. These intense, highly charged feelings are called transference because they are thought to be carried over, or transferred, from a situation basic to the person's life—the relationship the patient had with his or her parents as a young child. It is felt that the patient, in the transference, recapitulates childhood experiences and projects onto the analyst all the feelings he or she had in early life for his or her parents.

In psychoanalytic theory transference is essential to the patient's recovery for several reasons. The emotional intensity of these strong feelings for the analyst is thought to enable the patient to continue to be motivated to undertake the often frustrating and painful task of understanding oneself. Transference also gives the patient essential information about his or her childhood feelings for parents and makes these emotions immediately relevant in the present. Through the transference, the patient relives these feelings and so understands them and becomes attuned to their continuing impact on his or her actions as an adult. In addition, the analyst, unlike the person's parents, serves as a good "mother" or "father" to the person, which allows the person to get over his or her negative childhood experiences.

Transference has always been viewed as the process of the patient's coming to view the therapist as a parent figure. Some gerontologists (Lazarus & Weinberg, 1980) question, though, whether in older patients, who are likely to have therapists years younger than themselves, this parental transference will always evolve. It may be that, rather than coming to view the therapist as a good parent, the older person may sometimes come to see the therapist as a good child. This unrealistic appraisal of the therapist as an ideal son or daughter may become even more likely if the older person feels neglected by his or her children or feels dependent and wants to regain a lost sense of competence.

This parent/child type of transference is evident in our clinical example. We might say, in fact, that Mrs. Goldblum's improvement occurred at least in part because she was able to regain her self-esteem by being able to view herself as a teacher—someone who could instruct her therapist about what it was like to get old.

**Evaluation.**  These two case examples do not prove that the psychoanalytic approach works with the bulk of older people. Even these particular patients might have improved just as much if given another therapy, a placebo, or no treatment at all. To complicate matters further, even if we were to do a controlled study and find the treatment to work, it might have been successful for reasons incidental to psychoanalytic theory itself—for example, the older person's being listened to or not directed in any way. In addition, we might imagine that making blanket statements about its effectiveness for all elderly would be limited by the very diversity of problems and ways of perceiving the treatment and the world that individuals might bring to therapy.

These are only a few probable reasons that some studies of the effectiveness of psychoanalytic treatment with the elderly report success and others do not (see Gotestam, 1980, for review). Contradictory results are endemic in the outcome literature in general. So, as suggested earlier, we are forced to look more to logic in judging the usefulness of this and other types of psychotherapy for the elderly. Knowing what we now know about the characteristics of the treatment, how likely are psychoanalytic techniques to be successful with the majority of today's older adults?

Unfortunately, of any type of treatment, insight-oriented psychoanalytic therapy seems to have least applicability for the cohort currently elderly. This speculation has nothing to do with Freud's idea that people over 65 are too rigid to profit from his approach. It has to do with the expectations today's older people are likely to bring to therapy and with the probable degree of comfort with which many of this cohort could comply with the requirements of particularly this treatment method.

To undergo insight-oriented therapy successfully, the patient must believe its basic assumptions—that there is an unconscious and that understanding the motives behind one's behavior is an important thing to do. In addition, the patient must accept the idea that emotional problems need to be cured indirectly, through understanding oneself in a general way. Although these ideas about the existence of an unconscious, the importance of self-knowledge, and the value of speculating on feelings are now part of the general cultural milieu, they were not while people currently elderly were growing up. An older patient's basic orientation, then, would be more likely to be incongruent with that of his or her psychoanalytically oriented therapist. This possibly incompatible world view might make it more difficult from the outset for the person to accept this type of therapy.

Being in this type of treatment may violate other ideas that are likely in the present cohort of older people—for example, that it is unacceptable to reveal all one's intimate feelings to another person and that a doctor is someone who tells a patient what to do to get better. In insight-oriented treatment, the therapist remains relatively quiet while the patient brings up material relevant to his or her cure. The patient is responsible not only for directing the conversation but also for talking honestly and forthrightly on all topics and about all feelings. The difficulties of undertaking these unusual and unaccustomed activities, plus the time and money commitment the therapy demands, may make it seem too distant and difficult to fit the needs of many older people.

For these and related reasons, when even prominent psychoanalytically oriented therapists have written review articles on psychotherapy with the elderly, they usually conclude by saying that most older people will respond best to a particular type of supportive, rather than insight-oriented, approach. One has written that psychoanalytically oriented therapists working with older adults should be highly active (Pfeiffer, 1976). They should have their patients talk about more down-to-earth, current concerns than is common in insight-oriented therapy; they should be unusually attuned to the difficulties older people might have in revealing all their thoughts and feelings.

For many succeeding cohorts of elderly, too, it is unlikely that the traditional psychoanalytic approach will be often used—but for a very different reason than its lack of applicability to old age. Traditional psychoanalytic techniques are increasingly less popular among today's young adult patients and therapists alike. In short, this treatment strategy may in itself be a cohort phenomenon—one specific to the group of adults currently middle-class and middle-aged.

### Behavior Therapy

Psychoanalytically oriented therapists, as we just saw, use supportive therapy when patients are too disturbed to engage in the process of examining their inner feelings and motives. However, at the very minimum, this therapy can be used only when the patient is able to talk to the therapist. In addition, psychoanalytic treatment is used just for functional mental disorders or for physical illnesses that have a clear psychological component. As was apparent in almost every earlier chapter, the treatment techniques called behavior therapy and behavior modification have the advantage of wider applicability. Behavioral approaches are used to help people become more independent in general, by eliminating excess disabilities. They are also used to change behavior that may be problematic but is not defined as being a psychological disturbance, such as poor memory, incontinence, or Type A responses.

**Description.**   This wider area of application is due to the different theoretical framework of behaviorism. To recapitulate the discussion in Chapter 1, behaviorists believe all responses are learned in very simple ways, acquired directly by the process of classical or operant conditioning or indirectly by observation. Emotional problems are not a discrete entity, separate from other categories of learned behavior. Functional disorders are responses that have been acquired in the same ways as any other form of learned behavior. The only problem is in their content: the individual learning this type of response unfortunately learned the wrong thing. Somehow reinforcements were set up in such a way that they favored the person's acquiring what is really problematic behavior. The behavior therapist sees his or her job as rearranging these reinforcement contingencies so that the person will now learn more adaptive responses. This is done by extinguishing the old, disturbed behavior and reinforcing new, healthy responses. When therapist and patient work together to accomplish this relearning, the treatment is called **behavior therapy**. When the process involves the therapist's rearranging reinforcements without collaboration by the patient (actually, behaviorists always say "client"), the approach is called **behavior modification**.

So far in this book, we have seen diverse applications of this simple strategy to

treat a variety of problems not given diagnostic labels. Now we will examine behavioral approaches designed to treat two disorders that do have labels—phobias
and depression. Each of these two treatments was selected from among the wide
variety of behavior therapy techniques for a different reason. The first, called
**systematic desensitization,** is one of the most widely used behavioral approaches
and is the therapy of choice for the treatment of phobias. Desensitization was used
in our clinical vignette.

The second technique, a treatment for depression, is important as an example
of the new **cognitive behavior** orientation in practice. As noted in Chapter 1, this
general approach is rapidly becoming the most predominant one among
behaviorists. In contrast to traditional behavior therapy, which is confined to modifying overt responses, cognitive behavior therapists consider ideas, or cognitions,
to be just as important in the genesis and treatment of psychological problems as
visible, externally measurable responses. Rather than working just with actions,
they try to change the content of the patient's faulty cognitions because they
believe these thoughts or ideas are crucially important to a person's becoming and
staying emotionally disturbed (Mahoney, 1977).

**Systematic Desensitization.**    The widely used technique of systematic desensitization, a variation of which was used in Mrs. Goldblum's case, is designed to
cure not just phobias but other emotional responses like anger and disgust that
occur in inappropriate situations and prevent the person suffering from them
from fully enjoying life. Phobias, however, are the most common of these negative
emotional reactions. A phobia is an intense, irrational fear of a particular person,
situation, or object. The phobic person knows this fear is unreasonable but cannot
avoid feeling overwhelming anxiety at even the thought of being in close proximity to the situation that arouses the phobic response.

Phobias, being a type of anxiety disorder, may, as noted earlier, be less frequent
among the elderly than the young; however, that does not mean they are rare or
absent in people over 65. They may be present simultaneously when a person's
primary diagnosis is another functional problem, as in our clinical vignette; or
they may exist on their own. They may be relatively benign, limited to a single
rarely encountered object, such as snakes. Alternatively, they may involve many
situations or be attached to as basic an activity as, in our vignette, going outside.
In phobias of the latter kind, involving an immediately salient, all-encompassing
situation, the problem is severely incapacitating. The person's life is severely cur-
tailed by the phobia.

Behaviorists view phobias as developing because of inappropriate classical conditioning. As described in our example of the older adult afraid of the bath (see
Chapter 1), a neutral situation comes to arouse fear by virtue of having been
associated with an inherently anxiety-provoking one. This can also be seen in our
clinical vignette. Mrs. Goldblum's experience of memory loss would be viewed by
the behaviorist as an unconditioned stimulus evoking intense anxiety. Because this
anxiety-provoking event occurred concurrently with being out alone, fear became

conditioned to the initially neutral event being out alone. Being out alone, then, became a conditioned stimulus for intense anxiety.

Our clinical vignette also illustrates a second crucial characteristic of a phobia, its resistance to extinction. After her traumatic experience, the idea of leaving the house by herself was so anxiety-provoking that Mrs. Goldblum never went out alone. This inability to encounter the feared situation after the event that precipitated the phobia is common among phobic people. However, it only serves to perpetuate the symptom. Because the person does not come in contact with the frightening situation, he or she is never able to learn the fear is inappropriate. Put more technically, extinction cannot occur because there is no exposure to the conditioned stimulus in the absence of its being connected to the unconditioned one. For extinction to take place, the person would have to expose himself or herself to the newly feared conditioned stimulus repeatedly without its being paired with the inherently anxiety-provoking one.

Systematic desensitization attempts to remedy this problem. Its purpose is to make the anxiety manageable enough so that the person will be able to approach and stay in the phobic situation long enough for extinction to occur. To reduce the phobic person's fear from an intolerable level to a manageable one, the behavior therapist usually does two things: (1) the therapist trains the person in relaxation techniques, and (2) he or she has the person approach the situation in graded steps (see Wolpe, 1973). At each step in encountering the phobic situation, the person is taught to perform the relaxation response, which is incompatible with fear.

In relaxation training, the usual first step in desensitization, the therapist teaches the person to relax, using the type of instructions mentioned in Chapter 2. The therapist usually tapes these soothing instructions, telling the client to practice relaxation daily by using the tape. After mastering the art of being relaxed under non-anxiety-provoking conditions, the client is ready for the second step in the procedure: to gradually approach the phobic situation.

To encounter the situation in manageable steps, therapist and client first work together to construct what is called a fear hierarchy, a list of phobia-related situations that vary in their capacity to produce a full-blown fear response. The therapist usually asks the client to arrange these situations on a scale from 1 to 100, with the least anxiety-provoking situation at the low end of the scale. Using our vignette as an example, for Mrs. Goldblum, the situation "going out alone in the yard of my building" would be relatively low on her fear hierarchy. High on her hierarchy, for example, might be the situation "being alone in a strange city far from home."

The purpose of constructing the fear hierarchy is so the phobic person can then follow it step by step. As in our clinical example, situations at the low end of the scale are often easily confronted, as they elicit some tension but not an intolerable amount. When these low-level tension-producing situations are encountered without the person's fear being reinforced, the limited anxiety attached to them can extinguish. This extinction is believed to generalize to the more feared stimuli, making them, in turn, somewhat less anxiety-provoking than they initially were.

The high-intensity feared situations now are thought to evoke a tolerable level of anxiety. They can then be confronted and the fear attached to them extinguished. Finally, when the item that is uppermost on the person's hierarchy is approached and the by now limited anxiety generated by it is extinguished, the person is cured of the phobia.

Relaxation is often but, as our case example shows, not invariably used as part of desensitization. When it is employed, the behavior therapist instructs the client to relax when he or she confronts each item on the hierarchy. It is thought that this response, because it is incompatible with being anxious, facilitates the extinction of fear in the phobic situation.

Desensitization can be done either in fantasy or, as in our case history, *in vivo* (in the real world). When desensitization is carried out in fantasy, the procedure is the same as when the phobic situation is approached directly, except that the client is asked only to imagine each item on his or her fear scale. As in *in vivo* desensitization, the therapist has the patient proceed gradually up the scale, pairing the relaxation response with each feared scene.

**Cognitive Behavior Therapy for Depression.**   The idea behind *cognitive behavior therapy for depression* is that the depressed person's unrealistically negative cognitions are central to his or her becoming and staying depressed. These faulty cognitions are seen as responsible for all the other signs of the disorder described in Chapter 8—the depressed individual's sad mood, the inability to do anything, even the person's physical symptoms. Because of this premise, the therapy focuses on getting the patient to become aware of and then to learn to control and modify his or her depression-generating thoughts (see Beck, 1973, 1974; Rush, Khatami, & Beck, 1975).

As the first step in the treatment, the therapist and patient work together to identify the specific content of the depression-causing cognitions and the situations that are likely to set them off. Usually, these negative thoughts are thought to have an automatic and involuntary quality that is outside the person's awareness. The person will know that after a certain type of experience he or she gets depressed, even though logically the event should not have this effect. What happens, in the cognitive behavior therapist's view, is that the experience sets off highly unpleasant automatic thoughts that the person is not focally aware of, which then cause a full-blown depression.

Depression-generating cognitions are believed to have certain basic attributes. They often magnify the negative significance of what may objectively be only slightly unpleasant events. They usually involve "overgeneralization": the person reaches some globally catastrophic conclusion based on a single negative experience. They may selectively abstract an unwarranted unhappy implication from a quite benign happening. They may arbitrarily infer something negative from a really neutral situation.

Once the person has identified these thoughts and the situations that evoke them, he or she is taught to monitor the cognitions, to become attuned to their unrealistic quality, and eventually to control them. Clients learn to say to themselves, for example, when one of these thoughts arises, "I'm exaggerating" or "I'm taking this out of context" or "I'm jumping to conclusions." The therapist encourages this active effort at self-control by continually challenging the person to explain the logic behind each thought. The therapist may, for example, ask the client to argue rationally for the validity of a negative cognition or to check out the truth of a depression-generating belief in the real world. The hope is that eventually the person will be able to view these unrealistic thoughts objectively and so then more easily neutralize them by substituting appropriate cognitions.

Here is a report of the therapy in operation with a middle-aged man:

> A 53 year old white male engineer's initial depressive episode 15 years ago necessitated several months' absence from work. Following medication and psychotherapy he was asymptomatic up to four years ago—[since then] his symptoms were only partially relieved with various treatments.
>
> When the patient started cognitive-behavioral therapy he showed moderate psychomotor retardation. He was anxious, sad, fearful and pessimistic. He was self-deprecating and self-reproachful without any interest in life. He reported decreased appetite, early morning awakening, lack of sexual interest and worries about his physical health. . . . Treatment, terminated after 5 months, consisted of 20 sessions. He was evaluated 12 months after the conclusion of therapy.
>
> Therapist and patient set an initial goal of his becoming physically active. [To do this, he made a list that] included raking leaves, having dinner and assisting his wife in apartment sales. His cognitive distortions were identified by comparing his assessment of each activity with that of his wife.
>
> In comparing his wife's resume of his past experiences he became aware that he had 1) undervalued his past by failing to mention any previous accomplishments, 2) regarded himself as far more responsible for his "failures" than she did and 3) concluded that he was worthless since he had not succeeded in attaining certain goals in the past. When the two accounts were contrasted he could discern many of his cognitive distortions. In subsequent sessions his wife continued to serve as an "objectifier."
>
> In mid-therapy the patient compiled a list of new attitudes that he had acquired since initiating therapy. These included:
>
> . . . I am starting at a lower level of functioning at my job, but it will improve if I persist. . . . I can't achieve everything at once. . . . My expectations from my job and life should be scaled down to a realistic level. . . . He was instructed to reread the list daily for several weeks even though he already knew the content. . . . As the patient gradually became less depressed, he returned to his job for the first time in two years. He undertook new activities . . . as he continued the log [Rush et al., 1975, pp. 400–401].*

This example illustrates the basic format of the therapy. First the unrealistic thoughts are identified, then their illogical basis is continually pointed out, and finally the person is taught to remember the new, better cognitions. The new, more adaptive thoughts are solidified and cemented in by having the person repeatedly practice them.

*From "Cognitive and Behavior Therapy in Chronic Depression," by A. J. Rush, M. Khatami, and A. T. Beck. In *Behavior Therapy*, 1975, *6*, pp. 400–414. Copyright 1975 by the Association for the Advancement of Behavior Therapy. Reprinted by permission.

**Evaluation.** Certain attributes of behavior therapy common to both the treatments just described and to all other behavioral interventions suggest that this approach might be suited to many older people. The behavior therapist's focus is problem-oriented. The therapist works directly to change the person's symptoms, rather than treating a hypothetical unconscious cause. In addition, the behavior therapist acts more like a traditional doctor than the analyst. The therapist is the expert, telling clients what is wrong with them and giving them specific prescriptions for how to cure their problems. Finally, behavior therapy does not require that the patient tell all of his or her private thoughts to the therapist. Instead, the patient needs only to reveal things connected to his or her problem and to be honest about whether he or she has been able to accomplish the therapist's directives.

All these characteristics suggest that behavior therapy may be more compatible with the world view of the typical older person today. However, to date there is no empirical research specifically testing the value of desensitization or cognitive behavior therapy for older adults. There are case reports attesting to the fact that desensitization works with the elderly (Cautela, 1969), but there is also a negative statement about its usefulness. One author (Zarit, 1980) observes that older people may have more trouble constructing desensitization hierarchies than the young. Also, we have no reports of cognitive therapy being used with older depressed people, even though we can easily imagine that this treatment might be fruitfully applied to treat at least some depressions in old age.

### Group Therapy

Group approaches for treating psychological problems became popular during World War II as a solution to the large numbers of people needing psychological services and the scarcity of professionals trained to serve them. Since that time these methods have become increasingly popular. Groups now have widely diverse aims and goals that are not limited to helping emotionally disturbed people. There are, for instance, encounter groups, designed for growth and, at least in theory, limited to healthy people. In an encounter group, members interact honestly and openly and discuss highly personal concerns. This intense emotional experience is expected to enhance their sensitivity to how they affect others and deepen their understanding of how others feel. Groups have also been set up to help people deal with specific problems. Previous chapters have described, for example, the use of group strategies to modify Type A behavior, overcome memory problems, change sexual attitudes, encourage reminiscence, and deal with the major life transitions of retirement, widowhood, and living in a nursing home. Groups for older people may not be focused on problems but may have as their sole aim promoting social contact, sharing information, or engaging in recreational activities (Zarit, 1980).

**Description.** In contrast to all the groups just enumerated, psychotherapy groups are unique because they are designed to help people with emotional problems deal with and resolve these difficulties.

To understand their potential to help older adults suffering specifically from these disorders, we first need a sense of what the group method in itself may offer people of any age. In a classic text on group psychotherapy, Yalom (1975) posits a series of curative influences that underlie the operation of psychotherapy groups. He asserts that these influences are common to all successful groups regardless of what seem to be marked differences among them. Psychotherapy groups may vary radically in many aspects of their surface appearance—in their members, in the setting, in the frequency with which they meet, in their theoretical orientation. Despite these and other differences, Yalom says, the things that help group members change through having this type of experience are likely to be the same.

Two major advantages of groups are that they facilitate interpersonal learning and that they allow their members to develop socializing techniques. These benefits occur because the group offers a unique forum for each member to learn how others see his or her strengths and weaknesses and the impact of his or her actions. Honest responses from other group members teach the participants what they are doing wrong and how to relate in better ways.

Groups also cause positive change because they can offer mutual support to members, provide a sense of the universality of their problems, and instill hope based on observing others. Groups offer support because, with many others behind them, individual participants have the comfort of knowing they are not struggling with their problems alone. They promote hope and a sense of "universality" because participants often encounter other members with similar problems who may be coping more successfully. This makes a person's own difficulties seem less unique, problematic, and insurmountable. Related to these benefits is another hypothetical curative influence of groups: they promote modeling. By observing how others in the group deal with similar problems, the person can learn new strategies for dealing with his or her own difficulties.

Among still other influences, Yalom notes that, in contrast to individual therapy, groups allow each member to be "altruistic"—that is, to give support and help to other group members. We might expect this last benefit of group psychotherapy to be particularly useful for building self-esteem in an older person who may feel useless because he or she no longer has the chance to give to others.

All these possible benefits (some of which may also occur in individual treatment) suggest the potential value of using group psychotherapy for the elderly. In fact, as with other group methods, group therapy has been used relatively often with older adults (Zarit, 1980). Psychotherapy groups have been formed to help a diverse variety of older people, from those who have relatively minimal problems to those who are quite severely impaired. The range of elderly who have profited from this technique is illustrated clearly by the following two case examples.

A group composed of rather severely disturbed institutionalized elderly was set up in a nursing home, meeting weekly (Saul & Saul, 1974). Some members were depressed and asocial; some were diagnosed as having dementia. All could follow a conversation and showed some social awareness but were impaired enough initially to be considered hopeless by some of the staff. The leader (an activity worker) took an active role with the group and encouraged members to openly explore their feelings and concerns.

After six months some positive changes were noticed in the participants. For example, one handicapped man, initially angry, withdrawn, and seemingly se-verely cognitively impaired, came to life in the group. Eventually his psychological functioning improved so much that he was moved to another floor housing more intact residents. A woman with an initial diagnosis of senile dementia was able to actually leave the home and move to a facility permitting more independent liv-ing. Her improvement too was partly attributed to the group sessions.

In contrast, a group serving relatively highly functioning elderly was just as successful using a quite different approach (Butler & Lewis, 1973). Several age-integrated psychotherapy groups were established whose members ranged from age 15 to above 80. The aim was both to promote personality change and to counteract age segregation. It was felt that different generations could be enor-mously helpful to one another as they shared difficult experiences characteristic of different life stages.

Members of the groups, though upset and having problems, were not psychotic or intellectually impaired. They met weekly over a long period. The length of a person's attendance averaged about two years. Older members had unique con-tributions to make, which, in turn, helped them by enhancing their sense of self-worth. They brought their wisdom and breadth of experience of the life cycle to benefit the group. (See also the section on reminiscence, Chapter 6.) And they served as models of growing older to younger participants.

**Evaluation.**   Like all outcome research, studies evaluating the success of group therapy with the elderly have yielded contradictory results (Gotestam, 1980). So once again we must turn to conjecture to assess the potential value of this type of treatment.

Groups seem to have great promise for helping lonely, isolated elderly people who can particularly benefit from the unique curative effects just described. How-ever, as in psychoanalytic treatment, some older adults may not get all that they might out of groups. In group therapy a person is supposed to discuss personal problems openly. Being this revealing may be even more difficult for many of today's elderly to do in a group of peers than it is with an individual therapist. In fact, one author (Altolz, 1978) suggests that in her experience older people are slower to become comfortable in groups and are much more likely to shy away from discussing the personal issues appropriate to this type of treatment than are younger adults.

Other cautions about the use of this type of therapy with older people apply to the operation of groups with people of any age: they can intensify an older adult's isolation if he or she is rejected or criticized by fellow group members (Hartford, 1980). Groups should also not be billed as being for discussion of objective topics when their covert aim is to provide psychotherapy. It has been suggested that this latter problem may be especially frequent in work with older people because of the diversity of types of groups used with the aged. For example, in senior centers groups are often set up for socialization. Sometimes they have a hidden agenda for providing psychotherapy even if their members have no need of or desire for such treatment (Zarit, 1980).

### Marital and Family Therapy

In marital and family therapy a therapist usually sees the members of a couple or family together regularly. This procedure evolved in response to the common observation that as one member of a couple or family began to improve in individual treatment, a peculiar phenomenon often occurred. Either the patient's spouse or another family member developed emotional problems, or the family somehow sabotaged the treatment so that the patient once again became disturbed. In other words, it was found that the problems an individual had were actually localized in the family rather than being specific to the person. It was a disturbed family or couple that seemed to need treatment, not a disturbed individual (Glick & Kessler, 1980; Satir, 1967).

**Description.**   Family and couple therapy is based on the idea that patterns of individual psychopathology are really a function of pathological relationships between people and that only by addressing these disturbed relationships can an individual's problems be cured. There are diverse schools within family therapy (for example, psychoanalytically oriented family therapy or behavioral family treatment). However, all therapists who do this form of treatment agree on this basic premise. In addition, many couple and family therapists now subscribe to a new method of viewing and treating couples and families called ***the structural or systems approach*** (see Haley, 1971). This orientation, radically different from either behaviorism or psychoanalysis, evolved in reaction to orthodox ways of viewing psychiatric problems. One impetus for its development was the often poor cure rate of traditional, particularly psychoanalytic, treatment methods.

As described earlier, psychoanalysts see problems as localized in the person and due to unfortunate childhood experiences. Systems family therapists believe the opposite. They see psychological symptoms as caused by the person's current situation and believe it is the situation that is pathological, not the individual. In this view disturbed behavior is an adaptive, appropriate response to a pathological present environment.

This perspective dictates a very different treatment. Because the systems family therapist views having insight into one's childhood as irrelevant to changing emotional problems, he or she does not focus on the person's past or the person's fantasies. As in our clinical vignette, the therapist attempts to intervene actively to change the disturbed family interactions that are keeping the person a patient, using any of a variety of techniques. In our vignette the therapist tried to change Mr. Goldblum's tendency to overprotect his wife by redefining her as a capable person. He felt that engineering this change in the pattern of the Goldblums' marital interaction would lead to a marked improvement in his patient's symptoms. In addition, he gave the Goldblums "homework"—a set of instructions to follow between sessions—to repair their faulty communication pattern.

Another interesting technique a structural family therapist may use is called "prescribing the symptom." The therapist directs the family or patient to do the very thing that bothers them on a regular basis at home. The family that cannot stop arguing will be told they must have a fight every evening; the patient who is worried about her uncontrollable anxiety attacks will be told she must have an anxiety attack on demand. The idea is that when the symptom becomes compulsory, it loses its involuntary aspect. It can then be more easily brought under conscious control and given up.

The following is an example of a family approach developed specifically for the elderly—an interesting technique combining elements of insight-oriented and systems family therapy. First the family interactions are actively restructured by separating the patient from his family. Once out of his home, the person usually improves, as we would expect if we took the view that the pathological situation is causing the patient's problems. At this point the family is able to engage in insight-oriented family therapy. In the second phase of the treatment, the family meets together to gain an understanding of their mutually destructive ways of interacting. They learn in phase two of the therapy to substitute more positive actions and emotions for their formerly maladaptive ones.

> Mr. H. aged 82 was tall, good looking, and appeared younger than his age. His wife, 20 years his junior, was an attractive woman whom people often mistook for his daughter. Two years before admission, Mr. H. gave up his factory job. His wife operated a beauty shop and provided for both. Shortly before admission Mr. H. stopped helping his wife with housework which had become one of his chores after retirement. The couple was in constant conflict. Mrs. H. could not stand her husband's aging. He acted out by becoming more regressed and childish. . . . Without telling his wife, he manipulated his married daughters to help him with his housework. He tried to get his daughters to side with him against his demanding wife. By admitting Mr. H. to the day hospital we accomplished phase 1. There was no reason for the daughters to sneak into the house to help their father with his chores and he no longer annoyed his wife at her work. He was able to develop a more positive and less destructive role for himself in the family. . . . Although hostile towards each other, husband and wife communicated well and took sole responsibility for their behavior. Phase 2 was achieved. Mr. H. reestablished his own self-respect in the family. We also helped the family to accept the father and husband in a new role. . . . Mr. H. was discharged, improved from the hospital [Grauer, Betts, & Birnbom, 1973, p. 24].*

**Evaluation.**   Marital or family therapy seems particularly suited to some situations that may cause problems between an aging couple or within a family with aging parents—for example, adapting to role shifts usually occurring at the end of the life cycle. One of these changed situations, when one member of a couple or family becomes ill, was illustrated in our clinical vignette.

Because a spouse's illness is almost certain to cause changes in the way a husband and wife are used to relating, it can create problems between them. Retirement is another example of a life event involving a changed role that may cause

---

*From "Welfare Emotions and Family Therapy in Geriatrics," by H. Grauer, D. Betts, and F. Birnbom. In *Journal of the American Geriatrics Society*, 1973, *21,* p. 24. Copyright 1973 by the American Geriatrics Society. Reprinted by permission.

problems in some marriages. When these events do lead to difficulty between a couple, marital therapy seems to be the logical treatment.

A related situation seems ideally suited for family therapy—when children must cope with an ill or disabled parent or parents. This common occurrence often evokes problems between parent and child as they have to adapt to what may be a complete role reversal (Lazarus & Weinberg, 1980). A parent's illness, in turn, can easily create conflicts among the caretaking children as they struggle with the burden of dealing with a dependent parent. For example, in one study poor health in a parent was correlated with the tendency of a family to have generally poor relationships (Johnson & Bursk, 1977). Family therapy seems logically to be the treatment of choice for these and other problems that have a significant impact on the family as a whole.

---

**BOX 9-2.   Group Therapy for Children of Elderly Parents**

The difficulty of coping with a newly dependent mother or father is becoming an almost predictable stress for middle-aged children as the chances of a parent's surviving to an advanced age become greater and greater.

Apart from sometimes having to make the painful choice of putting a mother or father in a nursing home, middle-aged children dealing with older disabled parents have more general problematic considerations and concerns. They must somehow decide how involved they should be, how much they should press siblings to share in caretaking tasks, and how they should structure their lives to balance their own needs with the needs of the elderly person. Making these decisions is tailor-made for evoking negative feelings: guilt arising from a sense that one is not doing enough, resentment at having to shoulder an unaccustomed burden, anger at siblings who may not be perceived as doing their fair share. Although family therapy, as suggested in the text, does seem ideal for dealing with problems that may arise in this situation, the following example illustrates the usefulness of another technique—group therapy with others dealing with the same life event.

Small groups of middle-aged children having trouble coping with elderly parents met for eight weekly sessions (Hausman, 1979). The problems discussed were those just mentioned as well as others that being in this circumstance evoked—for example, fear of one's own aging; difficulty dealing with one's parent in a mature, adult way.

Although the effectiveness of these groups was not compared with that of another form of treatment or no treatment, the members did report that the groups were helpful. They said they learned a good deal from the sessions about what would be best for their parents—for example, to respect the older person's need for independence—and about what kinds of parent/child relationships do and do not work. Most important, they also benefited from a general curative influence of groups: they learned they were not alone in having problems.

# Chemotherapy

An important goal has always been to develop a pill to cure emotional disorders. In the 1950s this aim was partially realized by the synthesis of a series of drugs that were effective in ameliorating and in some instances eliminating many symptoms of functional psychological problems. Drugs that specifically affect emotional functioning are called ***psychotropic*** ("changing the psyche") agents. They work neurologically to alter feelings, thought processes, behavior, and even physical symptoms characteristic of a variety of functional mental disorders.

There are three major types of psychotropic medicines: ***Antipsychotic drugs*** act to combat the symptoms of schizophrenia. ***Antidepressant drugs*** ameliorate the symptoms of major depressions. ***Antianxiety drugs*** calm the patient suffering from a variety of anxiety disorders. In addition, lithium carbonate, a substance that is a salt rather than a complex chemical, is particularly effective for manic states and is used in the treatment of manic-depressive psychosis.

Psychotropic drugs, in particular the antianxiety agent Valium, are among the most frequently prescribed medicines in the United States. Older people, in addition to taking more drugs than the young, are more frequent users of this class of medication. It is thought that 1 in 3 persons over 60 uses psychotropic medicines in a given year (Walker & Brodie, 1980). Some surveys of nursing homes, where the incidence of psychological problems is high, show that as many as 75% of residents have some type of mood-altering medication prescribed for them at a given time (Baldessarini, 1977). In view of these figures, it is important to examine the benefits and drawbacks of these drugs.

## *Antipsychotic Drugs*

Antipsychotic medications have revolutionized the treatment of schizophrenia. These drugs are largely responsible for enabling patients to be discharged from psychiatric institutions with the advent of the reform movement described earlier. These drugs often have dramatic effects on the most extreme schizophrenic symptoms. They do more than just tranquilize; they clear up the delusions, hallucinations, and other bizarre symptoms of schizophrenia (Baldessarini, 1977). Anyone who works on an inpatient psychiatric unit cannot fail to be impressed by their power. Within hours after being given one of these drugs, an incoherent, wildly psychotic patient can be transformed into someone who can be reasoned with, talked to, and eventually discharged, perhaps to live a relatively normal life outside the hospital.

Antipsychotic drugs, however, are not panaceas. They do not cure all the problems schizophrenics have. They work only to a limited extent with some people and not at all with others. They have side effects, most of which are merely annoying but others can be serious, permanent, and in rare cases fatal. They actually do not cure the basic schizophrenia but only suppress symptoms while the person is on the drug. Because of the inconvenience of taking pills every day and because of annoying side effects, many schizophrenic patients decide to go off their medication; this decision often leads to relapse, another psychotic episode, and readmission to the hospital.

Even though, as noted in Chapter 8, there may be proportionately fewer people over 65 who suffer from schizophrenia, antipsychotic medicines are prescribed in relative abundance for older people. This is particularly true in long-term-care facilities (Baldessarini, 1977). In many of these instances the drug is given appropriately even if the person's primary problem is not schizophrenia. Dementia patients, for example, may develop delusions and hallucinations in addition to their cognitive problems. These symptoms may be helped by antipsychotic drugs, even though the person suffering from dementia is not truly schizophrenic. In addition, to treat paranoid reactions, which are more prevalent in older people, antipsychotic drugs may often be appropriately tried (Baldessarini, 1977).

Unfortunately, though, as occurs not just for the elderly but for deprived institutionalized groups of any age, these drugs are sometimes prescribed to sedate patients who do not need them. They may be used to quiet someone who is merely agitated, demanding, or annoying but not psychotic. For example, in one survey of elderly at 12 Veterans Administration hospitals, 23% of the patients found to be receiving psychotropic drugs had no diagnosis of mental disorder. For these and other patients surveyed, the most common mood-altering drugs given were antipsychotic medicines (reported in Walker & Brodie, 1980).

It is easy to imagine, in view of what we know about long-term-care facilities, that the temptation to use these drugs could be strong. Particularly in a resource-poor home, lack of services may mean there is realistically no opportunity to do anything for a demanding patient other than sedating him or her. Also, homes rarely employ more than one consulting psychiatrist. Because they do not have the time to get to know residents well, these often overworked doctors are more likely to dispense medicines inappropriately. This practice is particularly risky for older people because they are more likely to develop toxic reactions to medicines. For this reason, the careless use of antipsychotic drugs with older adults is not just unwarranted but may often be detrimental to health.

### Antidepressant Drugs

Antidepressant drugs, too, are frequently prescribed for the elderly because of their high incidence of depression. As Table 9-2 shows, there are two main categories of antidepressant drugs: the tricyclic antidepressants and the MAO (monoamine oxidase) inhibitors. Of these types, the former are much more frequently used for all age groups and are almost invariably the drugs of choice for older people. The person taking an MAO inhibitor must scrupulously avoid certain common foods and beverages that contain a chemical called tyramine. The patient must also be careful to avoid certain common medications. If a person forgets and ingests any of these substances while taking an MAO inhibitor, a life-threatening hypertensive crisis (an episode of very high blood pressure) may develop. This means that the drugs cannot be prescribed when an individual has memory problems (Karasu & Murkofsky, 1976)—the very difficulties that are often a symptom of depression in late life. For this reason, and because the drugs cannot be used when someone has high blood pressure, the MAO inhibitors are rarely recommended for older people (Blumenthal, 1980; Janowsky, Davis, & El-Yousef, 1974).

**TABLE 9-2.**　A partial list of psychotropic drugs.

| Major Classes and Chemical Types | Trade Names |
| --- | --- |
| **Antipsychotic Drugs** | |
| Phenothiazines | Thorazine, Mellaril, Prolixin, Stelazine, Trilafon |
| Thioxanthenes | Taractan, Navane |
| Butyrophenones | Haldol |
| **Antidepressant Drugs** | |
| Tricyclics | Elavil, Sinequan, Tofranil |
| MAO inhibitors | Marplan, Nardil, Parnate |
| **Antianxiety Drugs** | |
| Benzodiazepines | Librium, Valium, Dalmane, Tranxene, Serax |
| Barbiturates | Nembutal, Seconal |
| Antihistamines | Benadryl, Atarax, Vistaril |
| Propanediols | Miltown, Tybatran |

Like the antipsychotic drugs, antidepressants can work wonders for some people, particularly those whose depressions are most refractory to psychotherapy. These medicines work best when a person has classic symptoms of a major depression (see Chapter 8). They work less well or not at all with atypical and minor depressions. They also take from one to three weeks to begin to act and so may discourage some people from taking them for the required time. They have side effects that may be unpleasant and discourage their appropriate use. Negative side effects tend to be more pronounced and more frequent among older users (Baldessarini, 1977).

### Antianxiety Drugs

Antianxiety drugs are probably the most widely used and also the most subject to abuse of any class of psychotropic medicines. These drugs (see Table 9-2) are also called minor tranquilizers, because they are used for less severe emotional disorders in which the individual suffers from anxiety but is not psychotic or severely depressed. They calm, sedate, and relax the anxious person. Some help combat insomnia and so are prescribed as sleeping pills. In general, these drugs have been shown to be effective with older people as well as the young (Stotsky, 1975).

Despite their popularity, in recent years the use of these medicines on an ongoing basis to treat simple anxiety has been severely, and justly, criticized because of the potential for abuse. In the older person, the drugs can be prescribed inappropriately to combat symptoms that may be relatively normal as one ages, such as some lessening of the number of hours needed for sleep. The problem with using this class of drugs with the elderly in particular is not just that toxic effects may more frequently occur but also that the desired effect of the medicine may itself create difficulties. Antianxiety drugs often make the person drowsy as part of calming his or her anxiety. This sedative effect may increase the risk of the older person's falling. And as we know from our earlier discussion of osteoporosis, falls are more dangerous in late life. Sedation will also exacerbate any cognitive problems an older person may have, by decreasing mental alertness. For these reasons, the consensus is that this class of medicines, too, should be used more cautiously and more rarely with the elderly (Pfeiffer, 1978).

### Psychotropic Drugs and the Older Person

In general, although there is great variability among older people, the elderly tolerate psychotropic drugs less well than younger adults. This means that a dose of these medicines that would be well within the range a younger person could handle is more likely to be excessive for people in their seventies or eighties (Baldessarini, 1977; Janowsky et al., 1974). Because the older person metabolizes and excretes medicines less efficiently, they remain in the body longer. In addition, some common side effects of psychotropic drugs can exacerbate physical difficulties more likely in late life. For example, the tricyclic antidepressants are used only with caution in the elderly because older people are more prone to have cardiac problems. These drugs can cause heartbeat irregularities (Baldessarini, 1977) and so precipitate a heart attack in the susceptible person.

Toxic effects from psychotropic drugs include delirium as well as a variety of more specific reactions, such as that mentioned above (see also the discussion of sexuality in Chapter 6). Most negative side effects are not life-threatening, but they can be annoying. The potential for a given medicine's having untoward effects increases if the person is concurrently taking other drugs, as is common in old age (Blazer, Federspiel, Ray, & Schaffner, 1983; Janowsky et al., 1974). Medications are likely to interact, often in unknown ways, with the psychotropic drug. The incidence of negative reactions in the elderly is also higher because cognitive, emotional, and even vision problems may result in the drug not being taken as prescribed (Gollub, 1978).

All these cautions suggest that in older people psychotropic medications should be prescribed more sparingly and in lower doses. Their use should also be carefully supervised (Karasu & Murkofsky, 1976). A major aim of a relatively new area of inquiry called **geriatric psychopharmacology** is to determine what some guidelines for this proper use might be. As in other areas relating to physical functioning, here too we are just beginning to understand what is normal and appropriate in late life (Maddox, 1974). What psychotropic drugs in what doses should be most effective for the typical and not so typical older person with psychological problems?

## Treatments for Dementia

Methods of treating dementia comprise the same two categories as those used to treat functional psychological problems: (1) attempts to improve a patient's thinking using nonbiological means, either by talking to the person or by restructuring his or her external environment, and (2) efforts to treat the illnesses physically, either by the use of drugs or by other medical measures designed to directly alter brain function.

### Environmental Treatments

The outside world can be restructured in a variety of ways to help a person with dementia. For example, any of the interventions suggested in Chapter 3 to help maximize physical independence and minimize sensory problems are likely to have the benefit of improving cognitive functioning. The treatments described next, however, in contrast to the more general strategies mentioned earlier, have been developed specifically to improve cognition alone. They were devised for use in institutions but also can be easily adapted for use with older people in the community.

The philosophy of these interventions is similar to that underlying any attempt to ameliorate excess disabilities. The nursing home patient with dementia is thought to be functioning at a lower level than possible. It is believed that the resident will perform at a higher level if the environment maximizes his or her potential. In this case it is assumed that the patient will improve intellectually if the quality of external input received about the environment is increased.

**Reality Orientation.**   Reality orientation is not a single technique but a set of related strategies designed to be used with severely confused patients (Brook, Degun, & Mather, 1975; Kohut, Kohut, & Fleishman, 1979; Taulbee, 1978). These interventions are based on the premise that disorientation can be lessened by increasing the amount of accurate exposure that patients get to basic facts about themselves and their external situation.

A reality orientation program often requires the total commitment of a nursing home's staff. Its basic outline is likely to take the following form: First, a concerted effort is made never to listen to delusional talk without informing the person about reality. For example, if a disoriented resident speaks about being in a palace or hotel, the staff will unfailingly tell the patient his or her true whereabouts. In addition, staff members will instruct the person's family and other visitors to correct the resident's misperceptions rather than playing along with the delusions.

The staff also repetitively goes over external reality with confused residents. They are told such things about their environment as whom they are talking to, where they are, and the date. These instructions occur on an ongoing basis, as part of staff members' normal interaction with residents during the day. In addition, the home may provide weekly or biweekly reality orientation groups or classes that give residents the same input in a more structured way.

What follows might be a typical staff member's approach to a resident in a nursing home practicing reality orientation. The italicized words are the cues that orient the person to his surroundings:

"Good *morning, Mr. Y.* How are you today? [Wait for reply.] It's a beautiful *fall day* and it's such a clear, crisp *morning*. Are you ready for *breakfast?* [Wait for reply.]

Here's your *breakfast* tray. It's 8 o'clock in the *morning* and your *breakfast* is here. These *pancakes* look delicious, Mr. *Y*" [Adapted from Kohut et al., 1979, p. 68].

In these sentences, the staff member tries to convey to the individual the basics of what is going on. He is reminded of the time of day, his name, the season, the weather, and what he is expected to do (eat breakfast). When a nursing home undertakes a reality orientation program, all interactions with patients are expected to follow this general format.

A program also often includes the simultaneous use of environmental props designed to increase orientation. The most commonly used of these are large calendars and clocks and what is called a reality orientation board (see Figure 9-1). Prominently displayed throughout the nursing home, these physical signs of reality serve as constant reminders to disoriented patients.

---

TODAY IS WEDNESDAY

THE DATE IS JUNE 29, 1983

THE WEATHER IS SUNNY

THE NEXT HOLIDAY IS INDEPENDENCE DAY

THE NEXT MEAL IS LUNCH

TOMORROW IS THURSDAY

---

**FIGURE 9-1.**    The reality orientation board.

In addition, a loudspeaker at the home may announce facts about the external world, such as the time and date, at intervals during the day. Patients may be encouraged to personalize their rooms—for example, to keep pictures of their family and familiar objects by their beds. As simple an object as a mirror may be used as a reality orientation tool. Here the idea is that it too anchors residents in reality by reminding them of something basic about themselves: how they look.

**Remotivation Therapy.**    Remotivation therapy is a group approach used with patients who are not as impaired as those who need reality orientation but still might benefit from being more attuned to the external world (Birkett & Boltuch, 1973; Weiner, Brok, & Snadowsky, 1978). A trained leader conducts sessions in which a small group of patients meet regularly to discuss different objective topics, such as current events, sports, or movies. In contrast to group therapy, whose goal is to have group members understand their own and the other participant's problems and feelings, remotivation groups are designed specifically to enhance the older person's awareness of external reality. In addition, as other groups do, they promote socialization among relatively withdrawn older people.

Remotivation groups involve a planned discussion that includes five specific steps, or objectives. The discussion is led in such a way that all five are undertaken in sequence during a particular session. The first step, called "creating a climate of acceptance," is accomplished within the first few minutes of the meeting. The leader shows the group members he or she appreciates them by welcoming them and complimenting them on the way they look, for example. The leader then goes on to step two, "using objective ideas as a bridge to the real world." This step involves guiding the discussion gently to the primary topic of the meeting by asking the group members related questions or reading related material, such as poetry. In the next step, "sharing the world we live in," the leader involves the group in the actual topic of the session by showing slides or pictures or asking pertinent questions. In step four, "appreciating the work of the world," the leader guides the discussion so that group members will comment on the topic's personal significance in their lives. At the end of the session, the leader undertakes the last objective, "creating a climate of appreciation." Here the leader lets each member of the group know he or she is glad of that person's contributions. The leader also asks each individual to comment on what he or she got out of the group.

**Evaluation.**   Of the two treatments just described, reality orientation has been more frequently used. In fact, some elements of the procedure, such as the reality orientation board, now probably appear in many, if not most, nursing homes. However, this technique has been attacked for its basic premise—the idea that somehow just knowing basic facts about oneself and the external world is necessarily going to improve the regressed dementia patient's life (Zarit, 1980). Moreover, as is true of other treatments, studies evaluating whether reality orientation has any effect at all have had contradictory results.

One investigation, however, which showed that the procedure might lead to some cognitive improvement in patients, gave some clues about what conditions might be important for its success. In this study (Brook et al., 1975), one group of dementia patients were taken out of their normal surroundings and placed by themselves in a highly stimulating reality orientation room containing newspapers, a reality orientation board, and interesting objects. Another group were placed in the same room but this time with a therapist who discussed the objects with the residents and pointed out the items on the reality orientation board. Only the second group improved. This result suggests that interpersonal stimulation is important to the effectiveness of reality orientation; mere exposure to external reminders of reality does not work. In addition, the researchers found that the therapist-led approach was effective in improving cognition only when the patient was not too severely impaired to begin with. This means that a second condition for the technique's effectiveness is good patient selection. The person employing reality orientation should deal with only moderately demented older people.

There are no studies evaluating which type of patients might benefit most from remotivation therapy. However, one investigation (Birkett & Boltuch, 1973) did show that this approach seemed to help older patients in a psychiatric hospital; unfortunately, though, remotivation therapy was not statistically superior to the treatment it was being compared with, traditional group psychotherapy. So the utility of remotivation's underlying rationale or carefully planned sequence of steps remains unproved.

### Biological Treatments

**Description.**   The primary approach to treating dementia biologically is eminently logical. Researchers try to determine what substances the patient is lacking that could relate to his or her problems and then attempt to remedy these deficiencies using drugs, diet, or other physical treatments. For example, in both senile dementia and multi-infarct dementia brain blood flow and oxygen levels are decreased. In senile dementia, brain levels of a neurotransmitter called acetylcholine are strikingly low (Davies & Maloney, 1976). Investigators, reasoning that these deficiencies might be causing or exacerbating dementias, have focused on ameliorating these specific deficits. As described below, they have tried to increase the amount of blood getting to the brain by using drugs called **vasodilators.** They have attempted to increase the amount of cerebral oxygen by having patients inhale high concentrations of oxygen. Finally, they have given dementia sufferers dietary supplements of a substance that is a precursor to acetylcholine, to try to stimulate its production in the brain.

Drugs called vasodilators enlarge the diameter of blood vessels by relaxing the muscle lining their walls and so increase blood flow through these vessels. These drugs have been used particularly for patients with multi-infarct dementia, because it is reasoned that the small strokes causing this condition are due to blood vessels' having become blocked. It is believed that vasodilators may help prevent this blockage from occurring as well as increase the blood supply to brain areas that may be malfunctioning because of lack of adequate blood circulation (Sathananthan & Gershon, 1975).

A treatment called hyperbaric oxygen therapy has also been used, mainly for multi-infarct dementia patients, to increase the amount of oxygen getting to the brain. The patient inhales pure oxygen at regular intervals in the hope that the cerebral concentration of this substance essential to brain functioning will be increased and cognitive processes will improve (Thompson, 1975).

Finally, a chemical called choline has been given to senile dementia patients with the aim of stimulating acetylcholine production. Because choline is the material from which the brain makes acetylcholine, it was thought that ingestion of large quantities of choline might increase the individual's synthesis of this neurotransmitter (Boyd, Graham-White, Blackwood, Glen, & McQueen, 1977; Perry, Perry, & Tomlinson, 1977).

**Evaluation.**   Although patients given these treatments have sometimes been reported to improve in mood, alertness, or sociability, none of the methods has been able to improve thinking (Eisdorfer & Stotsky, 1977; Hicks, Funkenstein, Da-

---

**BOX 9-3.   Gerovital, the Wonder Drug**

In the late 1950s some exciting news came from Rumania. Dr. Anna Aslan, who operated a clinic there for people suffering from disorders of old age, reported on the use of a miracle drug that appeared to have remarkable properties. Not only could it cure the symptoms of dementia, but, Dr. Aslan claimed, it could also reverse many other signs of aging. Her drug improved vision, smoothed wrinkles, restored agility, and generally overcame most detrimental signs of senescence. Dr. Aslan named the astounding discovery Gerovital.

Unfortunately, though, Dr. Aslan had neglected to do something crucial. She had never done double-blind studies to see whether her drug was really effective. Her enthusiastic reports of the drug's efficacy were based on her own subjective impression that, after leaving her institution, patients were better; there were no experimental studies of whether the medicine worked.

Sadly, when these controlled studies were finally done by other investigators, Gerovital, like other antidementia drugs, may have improved patients' mood but had no other beneficial effects. The initial reports of Gerovital's effectiveness could be attributed to Dr. Aslan's patients' receiving good care at the clinic and to her overenthusiastic expectations, transmitted to her elderly subjects, about having found an antiaging pill (Jarvik & Milne, 1975).

---

vis, & Dysken, 1980). The complexity of deciding why existing biological interventions do not work is illustrated by some hypotheses offered to explain the uselessness of just the first-described type of substance, the vasodilators: (1) The drugs may be ineffective because insufficient cerebral blood flow may not cause multi-infarct dementia. (2) They may not work because they may dilate only healthy blood vessels, not, as is needed, diseased or partly blocked ones. (3) Even if blood circulation is increased to areas of the brain served by these diseased vessels, the drugs may not work because already damaged areas will not be able to make use of it (Sathananthan & Gershon, 1975). These possibilities suggest how little we know about why these interventions failed and what might be done to have others succeed—and how far we may still be from finding a biological substance that can cure dementia once it has developed.

## Summary

Older people do not receive their fair share of mental health services. They are overrepresented in custodial inpatient facilities and underrepresented in outpatient settings, where active treatment (psychotherapy) is likely to occur. Furthermore, now that state and county mental hospitals are accepting fewer patients, severely mentally impaired elderly people are likely to be sent to nursing homes. As nursing homes usually offer minimal mental health care, this means that many disturbed older people in need are not getting psychological help.

Older people, primary care physicians, and the mental health establishment are responsible for this state of affairs. The elderly are reluctant to go for treatment, having grown up in an era that stigmatized getting this help. Primary care physicians, because they may be more prone to assume the older person with certain symptoms has dementia, are less likely to refer an elderly patient to a psychotherapist. Some mental health workers, sharing this prejudice, are unwilling to treat older people. In spite of these ideas, there is no evidence that people over 65 are less able than the young to profit from mental health interventions.

Mental health interventions include psychotherapy and biologically oriented treatment methods. In psychotherapy, a trained person attempts to change disturbed behavior by psychological means. There are many schools of psychotherapy, which differ in their assumptions about what causes psychological problems and how these difficulties can best be treated.

Psychoanalytic psychotherapy may be either insight-oriented or supportive. In insight-oriented psychoanalytic treatment a less severely disturbed patient tries to gain insight into his or her unconscious motivations. In supportive psychoanalytically oriented therapy a more severely disturbed patient is helped to function in the real world by a therapist who attempts to strengthen the individual's fragile ego. This cohort of older people may be less suited to traditional insight-oriented therapy because it demands things they may find too foreign or too difficult to comply with; these include speaking without getting much input from the therapist, making a long-term commitment to treatment, and revealing personal matters. For this reason, a more directive, supportive form of this therapy may work best with today's elderly.

Behavior therapy is based on the premise that mental disorders are learned behavior subject to the same laws of learning as any other type of behavior. The behavior therapist uses knowledge of the principles of learning to extinguish disturbed behavior and build more positive responses in the client. Desensitization is an important behavior therapy technique and the most used behavioral treatment for phobias. It involves teaching the phobic person relaxation techniques and then having the individual gradually approach and stay in the phobic situation until the anxiety extinguishes. Usually, at each step in encountering the phobic situation, the person undergoing desensitization employs the relaxation response. Cognitive therapy for depression is based on the premise that the depressed person's problem is caused by unrealistic cognitions. Patient and therapist actively work to eliminate these ideas and substitute more appropriate thoughts in their place. Both these treatments (as well as behavior therapy in general) seem well suited to helping older people, but there have been no controlled studies to date demonstrating their effectiveness with the elderly.

Group psychotherapy is used relatively often with older people and may logically have many benefits. The curative influences of groups may include a chance to develop social skills and learn about the impact of one's behavior; a chance to be helpful to others in the group; a chance to understand that one's problems are not unique and to use others dealing with similar problems as models; and a feeling of being supported by the group. This form of therapy has been reported to be helpful to diverse groups of elderly, but it also has some limitations. Studies evaluating the success of therapy groups with older populations have yielded mixed results.

In marital and family therapy a couple or family usually attend sessions together. The idea is that pathological relationships are responsible for psychological problems and that the therapist should attempt to change these relationships. In addition, the family therapist who believes in the structural, or systems, approach feels that the disturbance a particular family member shows is often an adaptive response to a disturbed family environment rather than a sign of individual pathology. For that reason, the therapist tries to intervene actively to change the unhealthy family environment and shift the family's definition of a single member as disturbed. Marital and family therapy seems well suited to dealing with problems that may arise between an aging couple or within a family with aged parents. However, once again there have been only clinical reports of the effectiveness of this treatment for the elderly.

The three categories of psychotropic drugs used to treat functional psychological problems are antipsychotic drugs, antidepressants, and antianxiety medications. Antipsychotic drugs can be extremely helpful in ameliorating schizophrenic or schizophreniclike symptoms; however, they are not always effective, have side effects, and should never be prescribed just to tranquilize agitated or demanding older people. Antidepressants are effective particularly in ameliorating major depressions, but they too have their limitations with the elderly. The class of antidepressants called the MAO inhibitors can rarely be safely prescribed for older depressed people. Antianxiety drugs are helpful in calming anxiety and sometimes inducing sleep, but they too can be dangerous for the older person, in part because of their very sedating properties. In general, psychotropic drugs should be used more cautiously and in lower doses with older people because the elderly are more likely to develop toxic reactions to medications.

Environmental and biological treatments for dementia have not been very effective in enhancing cognitive functioning. Reality orientation and remotivation therapy are the two major environmental approaches. In reality orientation, severely impaired institutionalized patients are stimulated to become oriented to their environment by being constantly reminded of reality by the institutional staff and surrounding objects. In remotivation therapy, less disoriented elderly participate in group discussions designed to enhance contact with the outside world. Reality orientation may be somewhat helpful with moderately demented patients who are stimulated by another person to become oriented. In contrast, none of the biological treatments devised to cure dementia has had any effect on improving cognition. These strategies have included the use of drugs to dilate blood vessels, dietary supplements to stimulate acetylcholine production, and the administration of oxygen.

## Key Terms

*Custodial care*
*Inpatient versus outpatient care*
*Outcome studies*
*Psychoanalytic therapy*

*Insight-oriented psychoanalytic treatment*
*Supportive psychoanalytic treatment*
*Transference*
*Behavior therapy*

| | |
|---|---|
| *Behavior modification* | *Antipsychotic drugs* |
| *Systematic desensitization* | *Antidepressant drugs* |
| *Cognitive behavior therapy for depression* | *Antianxiety drugs* |
| *Group therapy* | *Geriatric psychopharmacology* |
| *Marital and family therapy* | *Reality orientation* |
| *Structural or systems family therapy* | *Remotivation therapy* |
| *Chemotherapy* | *Vasodilators* |
| *Psychotropic drugs* | |

## Recommended Readings

Baldessarini, R. J. **Chemotherapy in psychiatry**. Cambridge, Mass.: Harvard University Press, 1977.
*Comprehensive discussion of psychotropic drugs, their uses, and their side effects. Includes section on geriatric psychopharmacology. Moderately difficult.*

Gershon, S., & Raskin, A. G. (Eds.). *Aging*. Vol. 2: **Genesis and treatment of psychological disorders in the elderly**. New York: Raven Press, 1975.
*Collection of articles on brain changes in dementias and the varying biological attempts at cure. One article reviews psychotropic-drug effectiveness with the elderly. Difficult.*

Haley, J. Family therapy: A radical change. In J. Haley (Ed.), **Changing families: A family therapy reader**. New York: Grune & Stratton, 1971.
*Article explaining the philosophy behind structural family therapy. (The book contains a collection of articles describing different family therapy approaches.) Not difficult.*

Kahn, R. L. The mental health system and the future aged. In S. H. Zarit (Ed.), **Readings in aging and death: Contemporary perspectives**. New York: Harper & Row, 1977.
*Discusses the past and present place of the elderly in the mental health system and offers some optimistic projections for their future place. Not difficult.*

Weiner, M. B., Brok, A. J., & Snadowsky, A. M. **Working with the aged: Practical approaches in the institution and community**. Englewood Cliffs, N.J.: Prentice-Hall, 1978.
*Excellent on environmental treatments for dementia, particularly for the institutionalized aged. Very simple and readable.*

Wolpe, J. **The practice of behavior therapy** (2nd ed.). Elmsford, N.Y.: Pergamon Press, 1973.
*The originator of systematic desensitization describes this procedure in detail as well as some other behavior therapy techniques. Not difficult.*

Yalom, I. D. **The theory and practice of group psychotherapy** (2nd ed.). New York: Basic Books, 1975.
*Each chapter of this widely used text discusses a different curative influence of groups. Not difficult.*

Zarit, S. H. **Aging and mental disorders: Psychological approaches to assessment and treatment**. New York: Free Press, 1980.
*Intelligent, thoughtful, comprehensive book critically reviewing the literature on evaluation and psychotherapy of older people with psychological problems and giving a wealth of specific treatment techniques from the author's clinical experience. Mandatory reading for those interested in doing psychotherapy with the elderly. Moderately difficult.*

# DEATH AND DYING

# At the End of Life

By age 81, when Mrs. Morgan learned she had inoperable cancer, she was already a veteran at dealing with death. There was the crucial life experience, almost 20 years before, of caring for her husband during his lingering illness. Mr. Morgan had been a childhood diabetic and had his first stroke at age 45; his wife was credited by everyone with keeping him alive a good ten years longer than anyone would have believed. Then, only four years ago, there was her younger sister's mercifully short six-month bout with cancer. Once again she received praise from everyone when she moved in to take over the housework and nursing duties that helped her only sibling to avoid what she dreaded most—spending her last days in a hospital or nursing home. And there was that surprisingly frequent dull ache that still remained from the remote past, the memory of her firstborn deprived of life at age 1 by a flu epidemic in 1923.

So now it was finally her turn to join them. Miraculously, when she accidentally overheard the doctor saying soberly to her daughter "The cancer has metastasized to the liver," there was a sense of acceptance and even calm. This was amazing because she had always been terrified of death. There was her lifelong scrupulous avoidance of airplanes, one that had denied her many an enjoyable vacation; her intense weeklong anxiety before every scheduled checkup at the doctor's; her silly quirk about taking the service road rather than hazard the greater danger of highway driving. All these death phobias were a family joke. Even she had to laugh because they were so incongruous with her other qualities. Here was a woman so fearless, so inherently competent, so full of joy at experiencing and confronting almost any other challenge of life.

Perhaps this was the reason, she thought, that now, at the real possibility, she was not afraid to die. After all, she had few regrets about having missed out on living. Unlike her sister, who had never married, she had had those precious years with a worried-over, argued-with, and always adored husband. There were her children and grandchildren, the unashamed center of her world. True, it might have been nice to have lived at a time when it was expected for women to have a career. She had been told she was a born manager and would have been excellent in business. All in all, though, her past had been rich and full. Besides, she had to admit to a more mundane reason for her surprising courage: even with this unquestionably terminal diagnosis, she knew, someone of her age could live a long time.

As she also was well aware, however, cancer is a debilitating disease. So, though not fearing the actual end, she did fear dying: the wearying, intractable pain she remembered so well from nursing her sister; even worse, the dependency, the need to have help with the most personal and intimate bodily acts. Like her sister, she dreaded the idea of dying among strangers in a hospital. She still regretted having allowed her husband to spend his last days hooked up to machines—a decision prompted by her doctor's argument that the intensive care unit would prolong his life. If the truth be known, she wanted to die at home among her familiar surroundings, the precious reminders of her past. Living the extra few days medical science might permit paled in importance compared with that.

But she could not afford a private nurse, and it was out of the question to have her relatives take on the burden of her care. She knew very well the toll that caring for a dying loved one could exact. She also remembered her anger, combined with reluctant understanding, at the response of her very own family to the terminal illnesses of her sister and husband. Particularly toward the end, they were hesitant to visit. They wanted to be there and yet at the same time wanted to avoid it. They could not bear witnessing the pain of the last days, suffering they knew could not be assuaged. They were also terrified of being present at the moment of death. In many ways, then, it was better to have people more acquainted with and so less frightened by dying to help her in those final days. At the same time, these caretakers should be humanitarian, concerned with her psychological as well as physical needs.

As with the rest of her life, then, Mrs. Morgan set about competently arranging her own death. Being widely read, she had heard about the growing hospice movement. She knew that the atmosphere at hospices epitomized what she required: a staff psychologically sensitive and yet skilled at minimizing physical pain; an environment with unlimited visiting hours and many of the amenities of home. She also knew she would not have to worry too much about her family if she spent her last illness in the hospice. Counseling was provided to bereaved relatives, and practical help was offered in making the funeral arrangements. She felt real relief and a new sense of security when she discovered, applied to, and was accepted at a hospice about 50 miles from her town. Still, this implied nothing about needing the services of the program in the near future. After all, she fully expected to live an independent life for many more years.

On any list of central human concerns, death, the inevitable end of old age, would rank high. However, despite unanimity about its importance to the living, this topic was only recently discovered by behavioral scientists. As late as the mid-1950s, the psychological literature contained almost nothing on death (Kastenbaum & Costa, 1977). It was only in the last decade that the psychology of death arrived.

Death not just arrived but became the new popular area for psychological study in the 1970s. It was suddenly the focus of heavily attended courses and numerous research projects; it even became an activist cause. As we will see, this intense interest in death, particularly the elevation of dying into a well-scrutinized art, has been a mixed blessing. At the very least, though, it suggests what we expected all along: the end of life is an important concern not just for the elderly but for all of us.

A first major area of psychological inquiry has been to examine the contours of this concern or preoccupation in itself. A second has been to look carefully at a major aspect of death that is amenable to human control—the psychological conditions under which people die. Because death transcends old age, so has research in this interesting area (see Kastenbaum & Costa, 1977, for a general review). However, this being a book about older adults, we will pay particular attention to studies examining the end of life at the end of the life span.

## Preoccupations with Death

### *The Thought*

The elderly, as was true in our vignette, often have extensive personal experience dealing with the deaths of loved ones, and such deaths are temporally close to their own. We would therefore naturally assume that older adults think a good deal about this topic—more, at least, than the young. The accuracy of this idea has been tested in the same way as with reminiscence, by simply asking people of various ages.

In one study (Cameron, Stewart, & Biber, 1973) 4420 persons aged 8 to 99 were interrupted and asked to tell or write what they had been thinking about within the past five minutes. They were also asked whether the idea of death had crossed their mind in passing and to categorize their mood as happy, sad, or neutral. To see whether death preoccupations varied in different situations or at different times, respondents were approached during all daylight hours and in a variety of places (for example, in school or at home).

The researchers found no variation by time or place in the frequency of death thoughts. Also, somewhat surprisingly, subjects reported having these ideas in conjunction with a variety of moods. There were sex and age differences but only in the percentage of subjects reporting that the idea of death had crossed their minds. Women had these momentary thoughts more frequently than men; early adolescents, young adults, and the elderly more often than other age groups. Finally, although death as a focal concern was reported only 3–4% of the time, it fleetingly occurred to subjects of all ages with astonishing frequency during this short period. A full 17% of the men and 23% of the women said the thought had occurred at least once during the five minutes.

It may be that the procedure of specifically asking about death thoughts caused some subjects to report them even in their absence. In addition, this investigation is limited because it did not inquire into the actual content of these concerns. So the elderly may in fact think more about their own death than do people of other ages. Despite these cautions, though, this research does question the truth of the prevailing prejudice. Everyone seems to be concerned with death—the elderly no more than anyone else.

One finding is particularly puzzling, however—that death preoccupations, either fleeting or focal, were equally associated with positive and negative moods. We would expect this idea to be a most unpleasant focus of a person's thoughts. In fact, in another investigation also exploring the perceptions of different age groups (Kogan & Wallach, 1961), there was shared agreement on "death" as the most aversive of a wide range of concepts. This research also showed something

else of importance about age differences: even though death was negatively evaluated by everyone, the elderly rated it more positively than the young.

### The Fear

The finding of less aversion toward death as a general topic fits in with the fact
that only a small proportion of elderly people admit to fearing their own death; at
least this was so of the Duke volunteers. During interviews, when they were asked
the simple question "Are you afraid to die?" only 10% of the sample said yes.
Another 55% of the responses showed ambivalence; for instance, a subject might
say "No, but I want to live as long as possible" or "No, but I don't want to be sick
or dependent for a long time." The remaining large group answered with an un-
equivocal no (Jeffers & Verwoerdt, 1977).

This lack of fear could have been predicted from Erikson's theory. In Erikson's
view, as we know, a person's central task in old age is to accept this very outcome,
the fact that he or she is going to die; so the Duke results may be a kind of
validation of the Eriksonian perspective. Actually, Erikson would imagine a wide
difference of feeling in this very area among individual older adults, depending on
whether they had reached the developmental pinnacle of integrity. In fact, Mrs.
Morgan's lack of fear might be explained by her so clearly having reached this
psychological milestone.

Mrs. Morgan's own explanation for her surprising sense of calm, having lived a
full life, may help account for the Duke findings. Death should be much more
threatening to younger people because they have more to lose. It robs them of a
long future and the chance to fulfill their plans and goals. In old age the end of life
does not equal this deprivation. Because older adults have had their fair chance to
achieve and experience, they should be relatively unafraid of death.

As was also apparent in our clinical example, however, we might be justified in
being suspicious of this brave talk. The Duke sample was composed of elderly
people in good health and therefore far from the prospect of really confronting
their imminent demise. As one volunteer perceptively put it, "No, I'm not afraid
to die—it seems to be a perfectly normal process. But you never know how you
will feel when it comes to a showdown. I might get panicky" (Jeffers & Verwoerdt,
1977, p. 148).

And as with that other taboo topic, sexuality (or, as illustrated in Chapter 2,
even admitting one is ill), expressing fear of death may not be easy for a proud
older person in the presence of someone else. This means the study's face-to-face
interviews may be the poorest format for eliciting real feelings in this far from
neutral area.

Then there is an even more problematic general complication. It may be
equally difficult to admit these feelings to oneself. A person who blandly denies he
or she is afraid of death may really be too anxious to approach the subject. If we
assume, as many philosophers and psychologists do, that death is a main source of
anxiety for all of us, then the absence of overt fear might even mean its opposite:
it could be a sign of the most intense inner turmoil.

**BOX 10-1.   Fantasies about Death**

Fear or its opposite is just one continuum along which perceptions about death can vary. We might expect that ideas about this unavoidable certainty would have a host of meanings to older people, personal nuances that it may be possible to capture in a more differentiated way. In one Duke study, researchers (Jeffers & Verwoerdt, 1977) were able to reveal these rich and variegated perceptions by using a sentence-completion test. They asked elderly subjects to complete the following items: (1) "When a man dies . . . ," (2) "Death is . . . ," and (3) "I feel when I die. . . ."

The responses could be categorized as having five dominant themes. Some respondents pictured death simply as the cessation or continuation of life. They produced sentences such as "one ceases to exist" or "my spirit and soul will carry on." Others viewed death in interpersonal terms; for them it meant either a reunion with loved ones who had already died or a separation from those still living. Death might be seen as a reward for a life well lived or, more rarely, as a punishment for transgressions. Several subjects' sentences reflected uncertainty or curiosity, a sense of anticipation. Finally, infrequently death was viewed as the enemy, the cruel disruptor of life or the bearer of pain.

The emotions subjects expressed were congruent with these ideas. Those who saw death as a happy reunion said they welcomed the prospect; those who viewed it as the enemy reacted to it with fear.

So it is difficult to know the true extent of death anxiety in the elderly. There is little social desirability in admitting to this fear. Besides, from the psychoanalytic point of view a superficial yes or no is a totally inadequate indication of a person's real concern. This was graphically demonstrated when three different measures of death anxiety were given to a group of adults. The tests varied on a continuum from tapping conscious fear to progressively less conscious levels of awareness (Feifel & Branscomb, 1973). Each measure elicited a different degree of anxiety. When asked directly, most subjects denied fearing death. When instructed to fantasize about it, they produced imagery that showed mainly ambivalence. On the final index, a word-association test, their answers betrayed frank fear. As psychoanalysts might suspect, at this deepest, least conscious level, the elderly were as fearful as anyone else. This was not the case on tests eliciting more surface anxiety. In sum, people may be more apprehensive about death than they admit, particularly older adults.

This study also highlights the difficulty in interpreting findings on death anxiety: different ways of measuring the concept are likely to uncover different degrees of fear. But despite this important methodological problem, death anxiety has been a popular focus of research. In particular, psychologists have attempted to determine for whom and under what conditions this core anxiety is most acute (see Pollack, 1979–80, for a general review).

### Factors Affecting Death Anxiety

For the elderly, our vignette and chapter discussion suggest some clues to what these conditions might be. The first has to do with psychological health: people who have achieved the ultimate in late-life adjustment, integrity, should be less afraid to die. Another relates to the situation: individuals for whom death is imminent may be more anxious about its prospect. A final possibility follows from our general speculation about why the elderly view death more positively than the young: older adults who are more interested in the future should, like young people generally, fear death more.

Studies (Rhudick & Dibner, 1961) do show that low death anxiety goes along with good psychological adjustment. In the one investigation specifically exploring the relation of death anxiety to the Eriksonian concept of ego integrity, however (Nehrke, Bellucci, & Gabriel, 1977–78), the results were disappointing. Here, measures of ego integrity and death anxiety were administered to three diverse groups: elderly persons living in their own homes, public housing occupants, and residents of nursing homes.

Because this study was one of the very few empirical tests of Erikson's theory, the researchers initially had the difficult task of deciding how to operationalize the amorphous concept of ego integrity. They chose two particular scales. One, a measure called "locus of control," tapped the extent to which a person saw his or her own actions, rather than fate or uncontrollable outside forces, as responsible for what happens in life. The other was a measure of morale. These tests were given to the subjects, along with two death-anxiety scales, because being satisfied with life and having a sense of one's own responsibility in living seemed the dual hallmarks of the Eriksonian ideal.

Unfortunately, it was only among one sample, the residents of public housing, that the expected relationship between ego integrity and low death anxiety emerged. This is an important piece of evidence calling into question the validity of Erikson's last life stage. Actually, the opposing results for the two other groups are compatible with another just as reasonable interpretation. People to whom personal mastery and responsibility are important have the most to fear from death, as it means the ultimate in lack of control. People who are happiest in life should be the ones made most anxious by the possibility of relinquishing living.

But this idea suggests that the opposite of our original hypothesis about imminent death might be true. Elderly people who are near death—for instance, Mrs. Morgan's sister during her last days—are likely to be in pain and consequently far from enjoying life. In fact, the physical suffering that a debilitating fatal illness causes may be viewed as nature's kind way of helping us accept and even embrace the idea that our life will end. So, at least using painful illness as our indicator of proximity, closeness to death should really equal less anxiety.

This proposition fits in with clinical observations of the elderly. Rarely, psychologists note (Kastenbaum & Aisenberg, 1972), do possibly imminently terminal elderly patients seem to overtly fear death. However, if we look at the category of patient described in our vignette, one in whom an ultimately fatal disease has merely been diagnosed, a quite different picture emerges.

One important purpose of the previously described study, using measures of both conscious and unconscious anxiety, was to see whether closeness to death, using the index of life-threatening illness, was associated with less fear. The researchers compared a group of patients with likely fatal diseases with samples of physically healthier adults. On no level of awareness were there any differences at all. Their result was echoed in another study that specifically examined ill and healthy elderly persons (Devins, 1979). Here too the groups showed identical degrees of fear.

One might have predicted both these findings simply from reading our vignette. As our clinical example suggests, having a terminal diagnosis need not mean a person psychologically feels close to death. Perhaps, then, it is only our last possibility that truly captures this subjective conviction of proximity: no longer being interested in the future.

In fact, the degree to which a person looks forward to a future does relate to the extent of verbalized, or surface, death fear. Elderly persons who have many goals and plans report being more anxious about death (Bascue & Lawrence, 1977). But this implies that death anxiety is not just an undesirable emotion. Its absence can even mean something quite negative, that an individual no longer looks forward to life. The idea that no feeling about this most stressful event should be seen as inherently good or bad seems important in approaching our next area of inquiry: the psychological responses of people who are dying.

## Dying

### *The Patient's Responses*

The best-known belief about dying patients emphasizes uniformity. Individuals progress through fixed stages in reacting to the knowledge that they are terminally ill. Other ideas about psychological responses are more fluid, stressing the importance of individual differences and the impact of previous personality in determining reactions.

**Stages of Dying: Description and Critique.**   The now famous stage theory of dying was the fruit of a pioneering effort to talk with fatally ill patients about their disease and impending death. Twenty years ago at a major teaching hospital, a psychiatrist, Dr. Elisabeth Kübler-Ross, took this then unheard-of step. She was convinced that, in the process of attending to physical needs, health care providers were isolating the dying person emotionally—a neglect she planned to remedy by reaching out in a direct way.

As part of an ongoing seminar, she got permission to interview dying patients. The hospital staff was resistant and hostile to the very thought. Her subjects, however, had a different response. Many were relieved to talk openly about their condition for the first time; they had been denied the chance before. To the surprise of the hospital personnel, many knew their "true" diagnosis even though a great effort had usually been made to conceal this knowledge. Dr. Kübler-Ross published her discovery that open communication was often important to the dying in a 1969 book, *On Death and Dying.* This simple insight alone has led to a revolution in the way the fatally ill are approached.

The main purpose of *On Death and Dying,* however, was to describe a five-stage sequence that the interviews suggested predictably occurred when a patient became aware he or she was terminally ill. The individual's first response was denial, the conviction that a mistake had been made. Denial was usually accompanied by frantic activity—the search for another doctor or a disconfirming set of laboratory tests. Soon, though, reality had to sink in, and so denial would give way to another response. This second reaction was anger.

In the anger stage, the individual would lash out and generally bemoan the injustice of fate, railing at anyone in the immediate environment. Family and doctors were seen as uncaring and insensitive; the idea that the person, not someone else less deserving, was dying was the object of his or her rage. Eventually this reaction too would yield to a much more placid one, bargaining.

The essence of the bargaining stage was the entreaty for more time, the promise to be good if death could simply be put off until after that always present next important event. Kübler-Ross illustrated this response with a particularly poignant case example of a woman who begged God just to let her live long enough to attend the marriage of her oldest son.

> The day preceding the wedding she left the hospital as an elegant lady. Nobody would have believed her real condition. She . . . looked radiant. I wondered what her reaction would be when the time was up for which she had bargained. . . . I will never forget the moment she returned to the hospital. She looked tired and some-what exhausted and before I could say hello—said, "Now don't forget I have another son" [1969, p. 83].

When this reaction could not continue, it was replaced by a deep sadness, the fourth stage, depression. Then, usually just before death, depression was replaced by the fifth and final response, acceptance. In this last stage the patient, by now quite weak, was neither upset nor angry. He or she calmly awaited death and even felt a sense of anxious expectation at its prospect.

The preceding stages were never envisioned as a straitjacket, a procrustean bed for the ideal in how to die. Unfortunately, however, the theory has been uncritically applied in just this way. Patients have been labeled as pathological if their responses did not fit into the five-stage sequence. Attempts have even been made to hurry a person from stage to stage. The very perspective that this so human process may be neatly encapsulated into stages is dangerous for another reason. It can justify our distancing ourselves from the individual and negating the validity of his or her concerns. Rather than encouraging the understanding, for instance, that depression in a person facing death is a justified response that should be empathized with, the theory inadvertently allows us to view it clinically as a phase. An individual's legitimate complaints at caretakers are now too easily passed off as invalid, mere signs of the anger stage. So, as with bereavement, this ground-breaking effort to look at the emotions of dying patients has been both good and bad. It brought attention to a neglected area, but it soon was inappropriately elevated into a universal truth.

Actually, as in our vignette, although people do appear to experience different emotions in reacting to possibly impending death, there is little evidence that these feelings encompass discrete stages. Moreover, patients do not progress in a fixed way from one feeling to another (Dubois, 1980; Kastenbaum, 1981).

The study demonstrating this was one of the few that put the stage theory to empirical test. Metzger (1979–80) devised a scale composed of statements tailored to fit each stage and then administered it several times to two couples. In each case the woman was suffering from potentially fatal breast cancer and had been aware of her condition for some time. Husbands and wives were separately asked which items seemed to best apply to the patient's feelings currently and at four points since her initial diagnosis. The times chosen were specific to each couple, ones the investigator, knowing the person's history, felt would be likely in each case to reflect a different stage.

Contrary to the theory, hope was the most common emotion described at each time. This quite positive feeling may have been particular to the couples chosen. The sample (two cases) was small and in some ways unrepresentative, as the women may not have been terminally ill. In addition, not being longitudinal, the data may not be accurate; it is easy to inadvertently distort when asked to recall even more factual information from the past. However, a continuing feeling of hope does seem a psychologically reasonable response. Our vignette shows how this most human emotion may be present even in the face of an unequivocally terminal diagnosis.

Our clinical example also suggests another problem with the stage idea. Unlike what the theory assumes, even when confronted with the reality of certain death, a person may not decide once and for all that he or she is soon to die. Other observers have often noticed there is a variable understanding of this most unpalatable fact. The patient may cycle between awareness and denial at different times (Shneidman, 1976). Even more interesting, denial and an accurate appreciation of impending death can simultaneously coexist. A psychiatrist (Weisman, 1976) uses the descriptive phrase **middle knowledge** to illustrate this psychological state, one he has observed often in his work with dying patients. He sees middle knowledge as most likely to become apparent at serious transition points during a terminal illness, as when the patient undergoes a setback or notices others equivocating about the possibility of his or her recovery. In Weisman's words, middle knowledge

> is marked by unpredictable shifts in the margin between what is observed and inferred. Patients seem to know and want to know, yet they often talk as if they did not know and did not want to be reminded of what they have been told. Many patients rebuke their doctors for not having warned them about complications in treatment or the course of an illness even though the doctors may have been scrupulous about keeping them informed. These instances of seeming denial are usually examples of middle knowledge [p. 459].

Mrs. Morgan's response fits better into this category than into the stage assumption of all-or-none awareness. Her behavior seemed predicated on a clear understanding of her diagnosis, yet she was convinced she would not need the hospice program for a long time. In addition, her emotions and actions had no relation to the sequence predicted by the stage theory. But this lack of fit seems reasonable. Given what we know about the importance of individual differences in other areas of life, it makes sense that people face this final crisis of living in a far from patterned way.

**Personality: A Crucial Determinant.**    An appreciation of the importance of individual variability does not imply that no predictability occurs. Our earlier discussion of personality continuity suggests that at least one general pattern should be evident: a person's approach to this last life event should be compatible with his or her style of handling stressful events before. This too was apparent in our vignette; Mrs. Morgan assertively dealt with her own illness in the same way as she had competently taken over for her husband and sister during theirs.

Continuity was also demonstrated in an empirical study of how a large group of terminal cancer patients adapted to their disease. Hinton (1975) gained information about patients' previous personalities by asking their spouses and related this information to patients', nurses', and spouses' assessments of patients' current psychological state. People who were described as having coped well in the past were currently rated as less depressed, irritable, or withdrawn. Those pictured as directly facing problems earlier in life were more likely to show an appreciation that their illness was fatal. Once again, this study was not longitudinal, so we do not know whether evaluations of the patient's past personality were biased by the way a respondent perceived his or her spouse acting in the present. With this caution in mind, though, it does seem reasonable, on the basis of psychoanalytic theory and what we know about overall personality stability, that some consistency would be evident here too.

However, as we also would expect from our earlier discussion of personality (see Chapter 6), in this study too, continuity did not universally occur. More neurotic, less stable people seemed to cope with their illness as well as anyone else. They were neither more depressed nor more anxious than others rated as well adjusted, and they were no more likely to deny the fact of impending death. Actually, their surprisingly good adaptation paralleled Mrs. Morgan's, in view of her previous lifelong fear of death. But this finding raises a final consideration about dying: Is there a "best" way of reacting to being fatally ill?

Interestingly, from the perspective of survival, there may be. Weisman and Worden (1975) found that personality was correlated with longevity among a group of cancer patients. Those who lived longer than expected tended to maintain good, responsive relationships with others, especially in the terminal phase of their disease. In interesting commonality with the findings on survival after entering a nursing home, these long-lived patients were also more assertive. One reason for their longevity, then, may be identical to that explaining the longer survival of aggressive residents in institutions. In a situation of limited resources, patients who demand the most get the better care that prolongs their lives. It is important now to understand whether a situation of limited resources is an apt description of the environment those who are dying actually face.

---

**BOX 10-2.    Observations at Murray Manor**

It makes sense that people to whom death is probably totally foreign, such as the young, should shun the terminally ill out of fear. However, we might expect more acceptance from the old. The elderly, particularly the old-old, are likely to have firsthand exposure with death; their own closeness to dying might cause empathy and so result in less distaste for those near death.

But this optimistic prediction does not appear to hold true. One set of field observations at a nursing home called Murray Manor (Gubrium, 1975) revealed that residents were far from willing to encounter their neighbors who were dying.

The home was set up so that some floors functioned as a hospital, areas where residents were sent after a medical emergency. These sections were well-known and were ones the healthier occupants took care to avoid. The observer noted that when forced to traverse one of these floors, residents were visibly apprehensive. They carefully scrutinized the area first to be sure it was free from signs of dying; only then did they proceed quickly to their destination. Moreover, their visits to friends on the hospital floors were brief and infrequent. That residents seemed as averse as anyone else to encountering impending death is epitomized by a statement recorded when by chance a "near death" patient entered the dining room of the more intact: "I'd rather be dead than that way. How can anyone eat with that around?" (p. 205).

---

### Caretakers' Responses

The vignette illustrates the likely reaction we have when visiting a dying person, even one we may love—fear coupled with the desire to get away. Not only is it difficult to see someone weak and in physical pain, but there is the terror associated with the chance of actually witnessing the moment of death. This instinctive desire to avoid is typical. It characterizes the responses of both people asked to think about terminal illness in the abstract (Epley & McCaghy, 1977–78) and those who are actually visiting possibly dying relatives in an intensive care unit (Sherizen & Paul, 1977–78). However, we might hope for a different response from those whose work involves daily dealings with death. How do the primary caretakers of the dying, health care personnel, respond? This question has been studied using two very different methods—through questionnaires or interviews and through direct observations of how hospital staff members care for terminally ill patients.

**Assessments through Questionnaires.**    The more indirect questionnaire method has produced some contrasting results, ones epitomized by two surveys of practicing physicians done only a few years apart. The first (Caldwell & Mishara, 1972) demonstrated the fear and avoidance long viewed as typical. When 73 doctors were asked to fill out a questionnaire about how they treated dying patients, only 13 complied. Most refused when the nature of the topic was revealed.

However, the somewhat more recent study (Rea, Greenspoon, & Spilka, 1975) had a radically different outcome. Here, of the 174 physicians approached, only 11 refused. Here also participants seemed deeply affected by the area being explored. Not only did they willingly answer the items on the questionnaire, but they often elaborated by extensive remarks on the positions taken. The investigators were touched by the deep humanity and concern for the terminally ill that clearly shone through—empathy illustrated, for instance, by a response from a pathologist who mentioned that he "often felt like crying after a day of doing diagnostic sections in connection with surgery. 'It upsets me to think of the devastating effect my diagnosis will have on the patients and families' " (p. 300).

A closer, more psychoanalytic look at these superficially incompatible studies shows a common underlying theme. Doctors are not calloused but deeply affected by the plight of the fatally ill. Avoidance and its direct opposite are but two ways of handling the intense feeling this topic evokes.

However, from the patient's point of view, the contrasting expressions of involvement do make a difference. Avoidance and active concern translate into very different patient care. To determine whether either mode predominates, researchers have turned to a second approach—naturalistic observations of how hospital personnel actually treat the terminally ill.

**Assessments through Direct Observation.**   A classic study of how dying patients are treated used this naturalistic method. Two sociologists (Glaser & Strauss, 1968) entered several hospitals and observed the daily actions of personnel on different wards over several months. Their framework for understanding this behavior was fascinating. The process of caring for the dying was viewed by the investigators merely as another type of work; it was important to understand how that job was organized.

The staff's work did seem structured in a definite, though not explicitly spelled out, way: it was organized according to the course the illness was likely to take. Based on the person's diagnosis and physical state at admission, an expectation was set up concerning how his or her pattern of dying would be likely to proceed. This projected temporal schedule implicitly determined the treatment. The actual pattern and tempo the fatal disease followed, these acute observers called by a descriptive name—the individual's *dying trajectory.*

Glaser and Strauss identified and labeled a variety of dying trajectories. For example, a common one found on emergency wards was "the expected swift death." A patient would arrive whose death was imminent, perhaps from an accident or heart attack, and who had no chance of surviving. Another frequent pattern was "expected lingering while dying." This, for instance, was common for progressive, slowly fatal chronic diseases, such as cancer. A trajectory called "entry-reentry" might also characterize some cancer patients. These individuals, in the course of their lingering illness, would return home several times between hospital stays. Or the pattern here might be "suspended sentence," a return home for an unknown length of time terminated by death.

Trajectories often changed during the course of a person's stay. For instance, what was initially defined as "expected swift death" might later become "lingering while dying" or even "expected to recover." An admission trajectory of "expected to recover" might also unexpectedly turn into its opposite if the person's condition suddenly deteriorated.

These shifts, though, particularly when abrupt and not planned for, were likely to severely impair the smooth functioning of the work. Care set up according to a different schedule had to change quickly. The impact, as shown here, could be negative even when the change was for the better:

> One patient who was expected to die within four hours had no money, but needed a special machine in order to last longer. A private hospital at which he had been a frequent paying patient for thirty years agreed to receive him as a charity patient. He did not die immediately but started to linger indefinitely, even to the point where there was some hope he might live. The money problem, however, created much concern among both family members and the hospital administrators. Paradoxically, the doctor continually had to reassure both parties that the patient (who lived for six weeks) would soon die; that is to try to change their expectations back to "certain to die on time" [1968, pp. 11–12].

Another, more common trajectory had the same paradoxical effect, one in which the patient vacillated between "certain to die on time" and "lingering." In this problematic pattern the family would be called in for a last look at the dying man and then, unexpectedly, he would begin to recover. Family and nurses could go through this cycle repeatedly. The physician and chaplain might also be involved. Here too staff members were usually relieved when at last they could say for certain that the end was really near. (Of course, the hospital personnel were not always callously wishing for death. The opposite trajectory, a patient expected to recover who then died, was just as or even more upsetting.)

Miscalculated trajectories such as these not only upset the staff but also injured the patient. For instance, if an individual was "vacillating" or lingering too long, personnel, in their frustration, might get annoyed at the dying person. They could become less responsive, give less adequate care, and so possibly hasten death. Another type of occasional mismatch had the same effect: assigning a person to a service unsuited to his or her trajectory. For instance, if, as sometimes happened, a patient needing constant care was put on a ward where only periodic checks were provided, he or she might die between observations.

The hospital's whole mode of operation clearly suggested to the observers that the facility was predestined to ignore the dying person's emotional needs. As just demonstrated, the goal was smooth, efficient work, doing the best job in a technical sense. This orientation, combined with the built-in frustration of human dying being inherently unpredictable, set up an obviously malignant situation, one militating against the likelihood of humane, psychologically sensitive care.

So the framework of dying trajectories forcefully brought home the fact that care of the dying needed much improvement. A second set of observations, this time several years later at another traditional health care setting, the nursing home, only reinforced the identical idea. Here the basic approach was similar. Two sociologists (Watson & Maxwell, 1977) spent six weeks observing interactions in a nursing home in an attempt to get a first-hand picture of how the dying (and ill) were being treated. Their interesting method for ascertaining how the staff worked was more empirical than that of the other investigators. They looked for evidence in the physical proximity of nurses to residents at varying distances from death and in the spatial arrangement of the ward itself.

To get the first type of data, maps were drawn of the floor areas where residents lived. The map of each floor was then subdivided into rectangles of approximately equal size. The location of the nursing station was noted, and then observers noted two additional things: where the most disabled (or most ill) residents were and where the nurses were likely to be.

An hour-long period was selected each day for the six weeks, and each entry by a nurse or other worker into a particular area was listed. Residents were also observed, and their concentration in different areas of the floor was noted in a similar way.

The results for the nurses are shown in Figure 10-1. In the area housing severely disabled residents, the highest-status personnel, the R.N.s, spent considerably more time in the nursing station than their counterparts did in the section housing the less impaired. The results for the residents, though not shown, are somewhat compatible. The disabled or very ill rarely appeared near the nursing station but usually were found in the region of the resident bedrooms. By comparison, the relatively healthy (or distant from death) patients appeared relatively often in all subareas of their region, including those nearest the nursing station.

To get their second type of data, the researchers chose a ward housing the most disabled residents and looked at the location of the sleeping quarters of those who were closest to death. They divided the floor into subareas and used scores on the mental status exam as their index of nearness to death. They predicted that residents with the lowest scores would be housed in the dormitory area, as far away as possible from the nursing station and medical service offices, where contact with staff was most likely (see Figure 10-2).

Residents in the dormitory area did in fact have lower mental status scores, and they were indeed much more likely to be near death. On the floor as a whole, 20 (45%) of the residents died within a 15-month period, and of those deaths 18 (90%) occurred among residents in the dormitory.

Taken together, these two types of information about proximity seemed to the researchers to converge in making an identical point: people furthest from death get the most attention; those who are disabled or dying are relatively avoided by hospital personnel.

Fortunately, though, this negative conclusion needs to be qualified in part. The data may not really reveal what the investigators say. For instance, the R.N.'s job in the area housing the disabled may require more report writing and so more time in the nursing station than if the nurse were dealing with a less impaired group. Residents near death might be found most frequently in their rooms for a much more mundane reason than staff neglect—their illness itself and the resulting lack of mobility. Even the results on dormitory placement do not necessarily show those near death are suffering from neglect. A more direct, more accurate way of assessing this question would be to look at the actual time staff spent with the dormitory group.

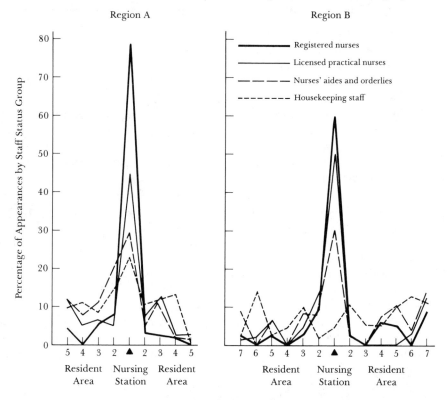

Region A                                    Region B

**FIGURE 10-1.**   Variations in appearances of direct-care staff in nursing-station areas in the regions of extremely disabled patients (A) and nondisabled patients (B). *(Source: From* Human Aging and Dying: A Study in Sociocultural Gerontology, *by W. H. Watson and R. J. Maxwell. Copyright © 1977 by St. Martin's Press. Reprinted by permission of the publisher. Original source: Maxwell, R. J., Bader, J. E., and Watson, W. H. Territory and Self in a Geriatric Setting,* The Gerontologist, *1972, 12, 413–417.)*

| 5 | 4 | 3 | 2 | 0 | 2 | 3 | 4 | 5 |
|---|---|---|---|---|---|---|---|---|
| | Dormitory Area | | | RN Station | | | Bedrooms and Medical Service Offices | |

**FIGURE 10-2.**   Map of the floor division of the research ward. *(Source: From* Human Aging and Dying: A Study in Sociocultural Gerontology, *by W. H. Watson and R. J. Maxwell. Copyright © 1977 by St. Martin's Press. Reprinted by permission of the publisher. Original source: Maxwell, R. J., Bader, J. E., and Watson, W. H. Territory and Self in a Geriatric Setting,* The Gerontologist, *1972, 12, 413–417.)*

## BOX 10-3.   The Social Loss of the Aged Dying

As is only reasonable, hospital personnel may have very different reactions to deaths that occur in patients of different types. Death in a geriatric patient is expected. The person has no future to contribute; he or she has lived a fair share of time. Death in a child is much more upsetting. A child who dies is being robbed of all he or she has: the potential to flower, develop, and be a fulfilled, contributing adult. Death in a young or middle-aged adult is often most tragic. This individual is in his or her prime. The loss will be keenly felt by others. The person is at the height of his or her powers, often the focal center on which a family depends.

As part of the observation of dying trajectories, Glaser (1966) coined the term *social loss* to account for these discrepancies. When someone of high social loss (such as a younger adult) died, the nursing staff could be devastated. When death occurred in a very old person, it was sometimes even an occasion for an emotion of a different kind.

The researcher noted that, generally, patients on geriatric wards of the hospital were given much less time and attention. Their care was more perfunctory; the staff was not as involved. These patients were often viewed as socially dead even while biologically alive. Their biological death, then, might even be viewed with positive feelings, as a social gain. No longer would funds, caretaking time, and other resources be devoted to one whose living seemed already to have long been done.

Several factors appeared to cause a revaluation of this age hierarchy regarding death. If the older patient was a highly educated professional (for example, a professor or lawyer) and had continued to practice his or her profession until becoming terminally ill, the death might be viewed as more of a loss. If the patient was socially prominent or the family was clearly upset and highly involved, the nurses might develop more concern at his or her demise. Personality traits and the length of hospitalization could also affect the response. The longer a patient was on the ward, the more likely staff members would be to develop an attachment, particularly if the person was pleasant, cooperative, and charming; and the more prone they would then be to feel sorry or regretful when death finally arrived.

But naturalistic observations such as these have had a powerful effect. Particularly the earlier study of the operation of hospitals was important in fueling a now national movement to humanize the way people die.

## Interventions

The effort to make terminal care more humane encompasses two distinct avenues for change—modifying the system and helping the person through psychotherapy.

### Changing the System

**Hospice Care.**  The most radical change in traditional hospital care of the dying is the development of a completely new alternative—the hospice. A true hospice is an organization providing both inpatient and home care for terminally ill patients and aid to their families (Cohen, 1979). The word *hospice,* however, can also refer to any program set up specifically to minister to the needs of the dying. The institutional component of the hospice alternative was described in our vignette.

As implied in our clinical example, hospice care is for people with lingering, painful, terminal illnesses—in particular, cancer. The hospice philosophy is very different from the aim of hospitals, producing the best cure: it is to provide the most sensitive care. To accomplish their quite special goal, staff members are skilled in techniques to minimize physical discomfort (Pear, 1983). They are also trained in providing a supportive psychological environment, one that assures both patient and family of not being abandoned in the face of approaching death (Cohen, 1979). Here is a description of their work in action, an account of how the first secular American hospice, the New Haven–Branford Hospice, came to be and how it operates (Rossman, 1977).

The initial catalyst for the New Haven hospice was the presence at Yale in the mid-1960s of two leaders in the then beginning effort to change terminal care: Dr. Kübler-Ross, the author of *On Death and Dying*, and Dr. Cecily Saunders, the physician organizer of St. Christopher's, a world-famous English hospice. Their seminars on what was wrong with traditional medical care of the dying stimulated some among the Yale community to explore the feasibility of developing an alternative in the New Haven area. A primary member of the group was the chaplain at Yale–New Haven Hospital, who took a year leave from his job in order to go to England to study the fledgling hospice movement there. Working from his observations, the group planned an American hospice based on the British model.

The group faced a continuing struggle to avoid having the proposed New Haven hospice labeled as just another hospital. They also had problems gaining support because their program was really an implicit criticism of how the current system handled terminal care. However, funds and support were found, and the New Haven Hospice was incorporated in the early 1970s. The main job then was to set it up in the best way possible.

In observing the British programs, the Americans noted that a crucial element for success was hiring the right staff. What was needed was a quite special person: one who was competent, compassionate, and not afraid to take on a completely new, professionally unsanctioned, and emotionally arduous job. There were particular obstacles in recruiting M.D.s. The hospice concept required giving up the primary goal of medicine—cure. Many young doctors who might have been interested initially were warned by colleagues and teachers at the medical school that they would lose patients and prestige by becoming identified as a death specialist. Then there was the problem of finding personnel with the expertise to do the training, one eventually solved for the physicians by hiring a doctor from St. Christopher's Hospice to direct the program.

Another difficulty involved reconciling the desire of the idealistic staff to do away with the traditional hospital hierarchy and the practical realization that smooth functioning of the hospice necessitated some chain of command. There were also problems in finding a site for the inpatient facility. Residents living near each proposed location opposed the building because they imagined the dying housed there wandering about the neighborhood spreading disease and gloom. At the same time, though, there was growing community and institutional enthusiasm for the idea. Finally, a six-acre tract of farmland was purchased and an architectural plan approved that gave priority to the needs of patients and families.

The result is the 44-bed hospice, a structure whose design emphasizes the joy of life even when housing those facing imminent death. As patients enter the facility, they first approach transition spaces that prepare them psychologically and relieve anxiety. Visitors entering the building also see no sign of death. The staff dining room and a day care center for the children of employees are what is visible. The rooms themselves have the same theme. Each has greenhouse windows full of flowering plants. Furnishings are homey, halls warmly lit and spacious. Every convenience is provided for patients and families. The feeling is that this is a home.

The perspective about pain control is quite different from that usually taught in American medical schools. Eliminating or reducing discomfort is the primary aim of treatment. Doctors try to prevent the pain before it recurs, decrease the anxious anticipation and memory surrounding it, but still keep the patient as alert and independent as possible. Also in contrast to the traditional approach, the psychological contribution to pain is dealt with. Staff members try to shift the focus of the ill person as much as possible from preoccupation with his or her discomfort. They emphasize pleasurable activities within the institution, and they train families to avoid expressions of anxiety and fear that might intensify the actual pain experience itself. The effect can be pronounced.

> One woman for example was in great misery because she wanted to live to see a grandchild about to be born, but knew it to be impossible. The controlling of her pain, however, made it possible for her to recover enough strength to knit a gift for the child she would never see, thus helping brighten her last days. Another hospice patient had been lying all of the time in a fetal position with a hot water bottle clutched to his chest, staring into space, moaning in his private hell which he said was compounded by pain that was like fire . . . but when the hospice team showed him they could control his pain he became a different person, able to live rather than vegetate during his last days [Rossman, 1977, p. 126].

**Home Care.**   Although hospices such as this one in New Haven are becoming more widely available, they still can serve only a fraction of those who might be helped. In addition, for many facing death, placement in a house of dying may not be psychologically or even realistically sound. Denial and hope of survival are important emotions in the terminally ill. Sometimes these emotions are accurate. We all have heard of people whose death was imminent living for years or decades more. However, there is an alternative to the institutional component of the hospice program that may eliminate these problems— dying at home. In a recent survey (cited in Hine, 1979–80) a home death was preferred by the vast majority of people. It was favored four to one over spending one's last days in a hospital.

There are impediments to this more natural way of dying, however, ones that make hospital deaths much easier from the point of view of relatives. Without special help, such as that offered as part of the hospice alternative, families simply do not have the ability to give the proper care. One family devised from its own experience with a home death a list of services that might be offered so others could choose this option too (Hine, 1979–80): Moral support and professional aid should be available from doctors, nurses, and morticians. Special equipment and medical supplies are often needed so the person's bedroom can serve as a hospital room. Nurses will have to teach the family how to give injections and how to care for the person physically. Finally, health care personnel also need to instruct relatives in what to look for as the illness progresses, particularly in the cues that signal imminent death.

This set of requirements (currently available only where hospice programs exist) and our vignette amply show that caring for a person with a lingering, fatal illness is a physically and emotionally draining task. So it is likely that because hospitals are set up to provide terminal care, most people will continue to spend their last days there. Efforts therefore need to be made to help hospitals (and nursing homes) become more responsive to the dying patient's needs. Standards of psychologically responsive care should be developed, and staff should be specifically trained.

**Humanizing Hospital Care.**    As a prelude to devising specific standards for a given institution, some general guiding principles have been offered, propositions that evolved from the discussions of an international task force concerned with terminal care (Kastenbaum, 1976). First, as not just patients but also family, staff, and the general community all have legitimate interests, the actual guidelines should take each group's needs into account. This approach will obviate what is currently a common pretense—that everything being done is for the patient alone. Honest communication will be improved, and in the long run the individual will be getting better care. Next, to combat the current impersonal delivery of services, the patient's own values, preferences, and outlook must be an explicit determinant of the treatment. Lastly, this same individually tailored approach should also apply to the institution or health care setting in a particular community. Standards devised should be consonant with the fundamental needs, attitudes, and ethical principles of the particular population that the facility is set up to serve.

Our earlier discussion of dying trajectories amply demonstrates that even these explicit humanitarian guidelines are not enough. They must be combined with specific staff education, training in giving psychologically sensitive care. Being at the top of the status hierarchy, doctors are a good group on which to focus this effort. Ideally, training might be offered in medical school, before a physician has learned to operate in just the physical care mode.

Although such training is still quite new, increasing numbers of medical schools currently do offer at least some education in the psychology of death and dying

(Davis & Jessen, 1980–81). But a 1975 poll revealed that fewer than half offered an elective course of this type (Liston, 1975).

In one unusual variation of the traditional classroom experience (Davis & Jessen, 1980–81), medical students are assigned to follow members of the clergy who work with the dying and their families. In addition to attending a regular seminar, students who take this elective course are required to spend one full night (from 5:30 P.M. to 8:00 A.M.) "on call" with the chaplain at a community hospital. They then write an essay about what they have learned.

The on-call chaplain visits the emergency room and the intensive care and coronary care units, consulting with staff and ministering to families and to patients who are either seriously ill or dying. The chaplain is also paged during the night when his or her services are needed. The student who accompanies the chaplain on all these rounds is encouraged to discuss ethical, psychological, and other issues that arise in the course of this intensive experiential introduction to death and dying. One student's moving account illustrates the personal effect that the resulting insight into the psychology of death may have.

> It was perhaps most meaningful that we ended our night with a cesarean section and a live healthy baby! Once again however life was taken for granted and really not much attention was given to it. Procedure was high priority . . . . Doctors examine noses, anuses—in essence every projection or hole in the human body—and yet the very thing that holds these examined parts together—life—is not examined seemingly or fully . . . . It seemed ironic to end our "death" call with a birth—maybe we peeked into the meaning of death [1980–81, p. 163].

Obviously, in this instance the "on call" night had an immediate emotional impact. However, we still do not know whether a limited course on the psychology of dying can really produce a lasting change. A one-session exposure to death from a humanistic perspective can so easily be eclipsed by the other technical-care-oriented experiences of medical school.

To determine whether psychologically oriented death education has lasting value, Dickinson and Pearson (1980–81) polled recent graduates to find out whether reported attitudes toward dying patients related to these young physicians' having taken a course on death during their training. There were differences in attitudes depending on the amount of formal instruction. The 20% of the physicians who had taken an entire course on death and dying were less likely to rigidly think it essential that every patient be told of the diagnosis. They were also more likely to report being comfortable with dying patients. It may be that these differences were due to initial self-selection, the more psychologically attuned students having decided to take what was an optional course. However, the other alternative is just as possible: death education helps.

### Helping the Individual through Psychotherapy

Reasons for mental health workers to avoid the dying mirror those for shunning older adults. Here, too, treatment is not a good investment. The individual being helped has no future to enjoy the fruits of therapy. Here, too, dealing with the patient may evoke some powerful negative emotions. In this case close contact with a terminally ill person seems tailor-made to bring up unwelcome thoughts of the therapist's own mortality. As the psychology of death has gained in popularity, however, so has interest in using psychological interventions to help people undergoing this final life crisis (see McKitrick, 1981–82). Among others, psychoanalytic and behavioral approaches have been used.

A psychoanalyst (Eissler, 1955) was one of the first to develop a strategy for doing psychotherapy with the dying. Working from his Freudian framework, he spelled out two different supportive techniques that should be employed, depending on whether the patient denies or acknowledges his or her condition. In the first instance, the therapist should give support through empathic displays of sorrow and pity but not convey a sense of despair. In addition, rather than enabling the patient to confront the reality of being terminally ill, the therapist should help the patient maintain his or her fantasy. In the interest of bolstering courage and psychic energy, the therapist should reinforce denial, conveying a belief that the dying person will survive.

If the ill individual understands he or she is dying, however, the task of treatment involves less dissembling. Now the therapist should try as much as possible to demonstrate to the person that he or she is not alone. This is done by open attempts at identification, efforts focused on enabling the ill individual to view the therapist as a companion to ease the loneliness of the journey from life.

Psychoanalytically oriented psychotherapy such as the preceding is the most common approach used in treating the dying. Behavioral techniques have been much more rarely tried. The authors of the hypothetical operant strategy outlined below (Rebok & Hoyer, 1979–80) note some reasons why. There is an aversion to applying an approach so seemingly mechanical for such a deeply human problem. On the surface it seems as if here dying were being viewed as a deviant behavior to be remedied. However, behavior therapy need not be incompatible with humanistic goals. In this case a treatment is outlined that may help the person feel less fearful in the face of death.

Given the complaint of overpowering death anxiety, the patient's first job would be to clearly define the crux of the fear. The patient would be asked what is most troubling about impending death. If, as an example, it was fear of being out of control, then modifying this anxiety in particular would be the main focus of the therapeutic work.

The individual would be instructed to keep a daily log of when the response occurred. He or she also might be asked to rate the intensity of fear in different situations. Careful attention would be paid to specific antecedent events eliciting the response. For instance, patients might observe that their anxiety was aroused when the medical staff did not keep them informed of their treatment or when doctors and nurses began to look hopeless or equivocated about the facts of the disease. Then the intervention would be tailored to remedy these occurrences. The patient might learn to directly change the staff behavior; the feasibility of home or hospice treatment might be explored; or the patient might learn to reward himself or herself for thinking more positive thoughts, such as "I am really the one in control."

The authors of this plan stress that any intervention must be employed judiciously and with caution, as often no treatment may be best. They also emphasize that standard operant principles must be used flexibly with this quite special group. For instance, rather than blindly applying behavioral strategies, the therapist may need to spend a good deal of time listening to and empathizing with the ill person. Given these cautions, though, it is interesting that in this last event of aging, as in so many others, a simple behavioral approach may produce results.

## Summary

Though neglected until quite recently, the psychological study of death and dying became a popular topic in the last decade. Research has been focused in two major areas: (1) the prevalence of death preoccupations (particularly death anxiety) and the factors affecting this fear and (2) the study of people who are dying.

Contrary to the common assumption, the elderly are not more preoccupied with death than other age groups. People of all ages think about this topic surprisingly frequently. Older people do differ, though, in that they view death more positively than younger adults.

Only a small percentage of elderly people, when asked directly, say they fear death. Erikson's theory would predict this, as in his view "integrity," the ideal outcome of the last developmental stage in life, involves accepting the prospect of death. Moreover, logically, older adults should fear death less, as it is not robbing them of a full life. However, the elderly may really have a good deal of underlying death anxiety, fear not manifested by answers to direct questions. For instance, in one study using measures of both conscious and unconscious processes, on the deepest level, death anxiety was quite pervasive among people of all ages, and the elderly were as fearful as anyone else.

For older adults we might predict three influences would be related to the intensity of death fear: having reached the stage of "integrity," being temporally close to death, and being invested in the future. However, there is no evidence of a relation between death fear and either the Eriksonian ideal of integrity or proximity (indexed by terminal illness). Only the last hypothetical variable, interest in the future, does relate to death anxiety. Elderly persons who have more goals and plans fear death more; this finding suggests that anxiety (or any other emotion) about this crucial life event should not be viewed as inherently negative.

The best-known belief about dying patients is that they progress through a series of stages in reacting to the knowledge that their illness is terminal. The stage theory grew out of clinical interviews done 20 years ago, the first effort to actually talk to patients about their feelings in this taboo area. The five stages are denial, anger, bargaining, depression, and finally (usually just before death), acceptance.

Unfortunately, the stage theory has often been inappropriately elevated into a prescription for the right way to die. In fact, the idea that there are universal stages of dying is not accurate. In an empirical test of the theory, hope was the most common emotion manifested during the course of life-threatening illness. And contrary to what the stage conceptualization assumes, people may not decide once and for all they are dying. They may cycle at different times between aware- ness and denial and sometimes simultaneously appear to know and not know the facts about their condition. This latter psychological state has been called middle knowledge.

Although there is no progression through predictable stages, there is another kind of pattern in response to impending death. To some extent, but not univer- sally, a person's adaptation is consonant with his or her previous personality style. The way an individual reacts, in turn, is correlated with survival. Cancer patients who maintain good relations with others and are assertive in expressing their needs during their illness tend to live longer than would be expected statistically.

Most people tend to avoid the dying. Questionnaires and direct observation have been used to find out whether this same tendency is characteristic of health care personnel. Avoidance and direct expressions of anxiety and intense concern, each the result of a different questionnaire study of physicians, converge in illus- trating a high level of emotional involvement. However, these two contrasting types of behavior mean very different patient care.

Unfortunately, naturalistic observations of actual behavior in medical settings point to distancing, or avoidance, as the predominant style of response. In one compelling set of observations, the concept of dying trajectories was used as an organizing framework for understanding how the job of caring for the terminally ill was carried out. By *dying trajectory* the investigators meant the temporal course the fatal illness took. When an individual's dying trajectory did not fit staff expec- tations, the work was made more difficult. The paradox then was that actually positive events, such as improvement in a patient who was expected to die, could evoke frustration and anger because they disrupted the smooth operation of the work. Another set of observations in a nursing home had a similar theme. High- status personnel tended to avoid patients near death, and these quite ill residents had beds as far as possible from areas housing staff. In both studies the conclusion is that the dying are not being given psychologically sensitive care.

Observations such as the preceding have led to a national movement to provide better terminal care. The most radical alternative to traditional hospital treatment is the hospice, a place and program devoted to caring for the dying. The focus is on pain control and providing the most supportive psychological environment for the ill person to spend his or her last days. The hospice program typically contains both an institutional and a home-care component. Home care of the dying, though preferred by many, requires special help to families who decide to take on this demanding commitment. Other possibilities involve modifying hospitals them- selves, developing standards of humane care, and educating staff to be psychologi- cally sensitive. This latter approach has been pursued for medical students by means of courses on death and dying, instruction that may have lasting effects. A final increasingly popular avenue is psychotherapy. Both special psychoanalytic and behavioral strategies have been proposed for treating the terminally ill.

## Key Terms

*Middle knowledge*
*Dying trajectory*
*Hospice*

## Recommended Readings

Glaser, B., & Strauss, A. L. *A time for dying*. Chicago: Aldine, 1968.
  *Dying trajectories and the observational approach explained. Very interesting and well written. Not difficult.*
Kastenbaum, R., & Costa, P. T. Psychological perspectives on death. *Annual review of psychology*, 1977, *28,* 225–249.
  *General review of existing psychological research on death. Read if you want an overview of death research in every age group. Moderately difficult.*
Kübler-Ross, E. *On death and dying*. New York: Macmillan, 1969.
  *The most widely known book on death and dying. The five stages illustrated with many clinical examples. Not difficult.*

# References

Abrahams, J. P., & Birren, J. E. Reaction time as a function of age and behavioral predisposition to coronary heart disease. *Journal of Gerontology*, 1973, *28*, 471–478.

Adams, G. *Essentials of geriatric medicine*. New York: Oxford University Press, 1977.

Aldrich, C. K., & Mendkoff, E. Relocation of the aged and disabled: A mortality study. *Journal of the American Geriatrics Society*, 1963, *11*, 185–194.

Allan, C., & Brotman, H. *Chartbook on aging in America*. Washington, D.C.: 1981 White House Conference on Aging, 1981.

Allison, P., & Stewart, J. Productivity differences among scientists: Evidence for accumulative advantage. *American Sociological Review*, 1974, *39*, 596–606.

Alpert, R., & Haber, R. N. Anxiety in academic achievement situations. *Journal of Abnormal and Social Psychology*, 1966, *61*, 207–215.

Altolz, J. A. S. Group psychotherapy with the elderly. In I. M. Burnside (Ed.), *Working with the elderly: Group process and techniques*. North Scituate, Mass.: Duxbury Press, 1978.

American Psychiatric Association. *Diagnostic and statistical manual of mental disorders* (3rd ed.). Washington, D.C.: American Psychiatric Association, 1980.

Anderson, B., & Palmore, E. Longitudinal evaluation of ocular function. In E. Palmore (Ed.), *Normal aging II*. Durham, N.C.: Duke University Press, 1974.

Andres, R. The normality of aging: The Baltimore Longitudinal Study. Pub. No. (NIH) 79-1410. *National Institute on Aging Science Writer Seminar Series*. Department of Health, Education and Welfare (U.S. Public Health Service), 1979.

Arenberg, D. Comments on the processes that account for memory declines with age. In L. W. Poon, J. L. Fozard, L. S. Cermak, D. Arenberg, & L. W. Thompson (Eds.), *New directions in memory and aging*. Hillsdale, N.J.: Erlbaum, 1980.

Atchley, R. C. Retirement and leisure participation: Continuity or crisis? *Gerontologist*, 1971, *11*, 13–17.

Atchley, R. C. Issues in retirement research. *Gerontologist*, 1979, *19*, 44–54.

Baldessarini, R. J. *Chemotherapy in psychiatry*. Cambridge, Mass.: Harvard University Press, 1977.

Ball, J. F. Widow's grief: The impact of age and mode of death. *Omega*, 1976–77, *7*, 307–333.

Baltes, P. B., Cornelius, S. W., Spiro, A., Nesselroade, J. R., & Willis, S. L. Integration versus differentiation of fluid/crystalized intelligence in old age. *Developmental Psychology*, 1980, *16*, 625–635.

Baltes, P. B., & Labouvie, G. V. Adult development of intellectual performance: Description, explanation and modification. In C. Eisdorfer & M. P. Lawton (Eds.), *The psychology of adult development and aging*. Washington, D.C.: American Psychological Association, 1973.

Baltes, P. B., Reese, H. W., & Lipsett, L. P. Life-span developmental psychology. *Annual review of psychology*, 1980, *31*, 65–110.

Baltes, P. B., & Schaie, K. W. The myth of the twilight years. *Psychology Today*, March 1974, pp. 35–40.

Baltes, P. B., & Schaie, K. W. On the plasticity of intelligence in adulthood and old age: Where Horn and Donaldson fail. *American Psychologist*, 1976, *31*, 720–725.

Baltes, P. B., & Willis, S. L. Toward psychological theories of aging and development. In J. E. Birren & K. W. Schaie (Eds.), *Handbook of the psychology of aging*. New York: Van Nostrand Reinhold, 1977.

Barney, J. L. Community presence as a key to quality of life in nursing homes. *American Journal of Public Health*, 1974, *64*, 265–268.

Barney, J. L. The prerogative of choice in long-term care. *Gerontologist*, 1977, *17*, 309–314.

Bascue, L. O., & Lawrence, R. E. A study of subjective time and death anxiety in the elderly. *Omega*, 1977, *8*, 81–90.

Beck, A. T. *The diagnosis and management of depression*. Philadelphia: University of Pennsylvania Press, 1973.

Beck, A. T. The development of depression: A cognitive model. In R. J. Friedman & M. N. Katz (Eds.), *The psychology of depression: Contemporary theory and research*. Washington, D.C.: V. H. Winston, 1974.

Beck, A. T. *Depression: Causes and treatment* (7th ed.). Philadelphia: University of Pennsylvania Press, 1979.

Becker, J. *Depression: Theory and research*. Washington, D.C.: V. H. Winston, 1974.

Benet, S. Why they live to be 100 or even older in Abkhasia. In S. H. Zarit (Ed.), *Readings in aging and death: Contemporary perspectives*. New York: Harper & Row, 1977.

Bennett, R., & Eckman, J. Attitudes towards aging: A critical examination of recent literature and implications for future research. In C. Eisdorfer & M. P. Lawton (Eds.), *The psychology of adult development and aging*. Washington, D.C.: American Psychological Association, 1973.

Berezin, M. Psychodynamic considerations of aging and the aged: An overview. *American Journal of Psychiatry*, 1972, *128*, 1483–1491.

Bersoff, D. N. Silk purses into sow's ears; The decline of psychological testing and a suggestion for its redemption. *American Psychologist*, 1973, *28*, 892–899.

Bibring, E. The mechanism of depression. In P. Greenacre (Ed.), *Affective disorders*. New York: International Universities Press, 1953.

Birkett, D. P., & Boltuch, B. Remotivation therapy. *Journal of the American Geriatrics Society*, 1973, *21*, 368–371.

Birkhill, W. R., & Schaie, K. W. The effect of differential reinforcement of cautiousness in intellectual performance among the elderly. *Journal of Gerontology*, 1975, *30*, 578–583.

Birren, J. E. A summary: Prospects and problems of research on the longitudinal development of man's intellectual capacities throughout life. In L. F. Jarvik, C. Eisdorfer, & J. E. Blum (Eds.), *Intellectual functioning in adults*. New York: Springer, 1973.

Birren, J. E. Translations in gerontology—from lab to life, psychophysiology and speed of response. *American Psychologist*, 1974, *29*, 808–815.

Birren, J. E., Butler, R. N., Greenhouse, S. W., Sokoloff, L., & Yarrow, M. R. *Human aging: A biological and behavioral study*. Washington, D.C.: U.S. Public Health Service, 1963.

Birren, J. E., Casperson, R. C., & Botwinick, J. Age changes in pupil size. *Journal of Gerontology*, 1950, *5*, 216–221.

Birren, J. E., & Renner, V. J. Research on the psychology of aging: Principles and experimentation. In J. E. Birren & K. W. Schaie (Eds.), *Handbook of the psychology of aging*. New York: Van Nostrand Reinhold, 1977.

Blazer, D. The epidemiology of mental illness in late life. In E. W. Busse & D. G. Blazer (Eds.), *Handbook of geriatric psychiatry*. New York: Van Nostrand Reinhold, 1980.

Blazer, D., Federspiel, C. F., Ray, W. A., & Schaffner, W. The risk of anticholinergic toxicity in the elderly: A study of prescribing practices in two populations. *Journal of Gerontology*, 1983, *38*, 31–35.

Blazer, D., & Williams, C. D. Epidemiology of dysphoria and depression in an elderly population. *American Journal of Psychiatry*, 1980, *137*, 439–444.

Blessed, G., Tomlinson, B. E., & Roth, M. The association between quantitative measures of dementia and of senile changes in the cerebral grey matter of elderly subjects. *British Journal of Psychiatry*, 1968, *114*, 797–811.

Bloch, A., Maeder, J., & Haissly, J. Sexual problems after myocardial infarction. *American Heart Journal*, 1975, *90*, 536–537.

Block, M. R., Davidson, J. L., & Grambs, J. D. *Women over forty: Visions and realities.* New York: Springer, 1981.

Blum, J. E., Clark, E. T., & Jarvik, L. F. The New York State Psychiatric Institute study of aging twins. In L. F. Jarvik, C. Eisdorfer, & J. E. Blum (Eds.), *Intellectual functioning in adults.* New York: Springer, 1973.

Blumenthal, M. Depressive illness in old age: Getting behind the mask. *Geriatrics,* April 1980, pp. 34-43.

Bonner, C. D. *Homberger and Bonner's medical care and rehabilitation of the aged and chronically ill* (3rd ed.). Boston: Little, Brown, 1974.

Botwinick, J. Cautiousness in advanced age. *Journal of Gerontology,* 1966, *21,* 347-353.

Botwinick, J. *Cognitive processes in maturity and old age.* New York: Springer, 1967.

Botwinick, J. Intellectual abilities. In J. E. Birren & K. W. Schaie (Eds.), *Handbook of the psychology of aging.* New York: Van Nostrand Reinhold, 1977.

Botwinick, J. *Aging and behavior* (2nd ed.). New York: Springer, 1978.

Botwinick, J., & Birren, J. E. Mental abilities and psychomotor responses in healthy aged men. In J. E. Birren, R. N. Butler, S. W. Greenhouse, L. Sokoloff, & M. R. Yarrow (Eds.), *Human aging: A biological and behavioral study.* Washington, D.C.: U. S. Public Health Service, 1963.

Botwinick, J., & Storandt, M. Cardiovascular status, depressive affect and other factors in reaction time. *Journal of Gerontology,* 1974, *29,* 543-548.

Botwinick, J., & Thompson, L. W. Age difference in reaction time: An artifact? *Gerontologist,* 1968, *8,* 25-28.

Boyd, W. D., Graham-White, J., Blackwood, G., Glen, I., & McQueen, J. Clinical effects of choline in Alzheimer senile dementia. *Lancet,* 1977, *3,* 711.

Boylin, W., Gordon, S. K., & Nehrke, M. F. Reminiscing and ego integrity in institutionalized elderly males. *Gerontologist,* 1976, *16,* 118-124.

Bozian, M. W., & Clark, H. M. Counteracting sensory changes in the aging. *American Journal of Nursing,* 1980, *80,* 473-476.

Brash, D. E., & Hart, R. W. Molecular biology of aging. In J. A. Behnke, C. E. Finch, & G. B. Moment (Eds.), *The biology of aging.* New York: Plenum, 1978.

Broderick, C. Sexuality and aging: An overview. In R. L. Solnick (Ed.), *Sexuality and aging.* Los Angeles: University of Southern California Press, 1978.

Brody, E. M. A million procrustean beds. *Gerontologist,* 1973, *13,* 430-435.

Brody, E. M. *Long-term care of older people.* New York: Human Sciences Press, 1977.

Brody, J. E. Emotions found to influence nearly every human ailment. *New York Times,* May 24, 1983, p. C1.

Brook, P., Degun, G., & Mather, M. Reality orientation, a therapy for psychogeriatric patients: A controlled study. *British Journal of Psychiatry,* 1975, *127,* 42-45.

Bultena, G. L., & Powers, E. A. Denial of aging: Age identification and reference group orientations. *Journal of Gerontology,* 1978, *33,* 748-754.

Busse, E. W. A physiological, psychological and sociological study of aging. In E. Palmore (Ed.), *Normal aging.* Durham, N.C.: Duke University Press, 1970.

Busse, E. W. Theories of aging. In E. W. Busse & E. Pfeiffer (Eds.), *Behavior and adaptation in late life* (2nd ed.). Boston: Little, Brown, 1977.

Busse, E. W., & Blazer, D. The theories and processes of aging. In E. W. Busse & D. Blazer (Eds.), *Handbook of geriatric psychiatry.* New York: Van Nostrand Reinhold, 1980.

Busse, E. W., & Pfeiffer, E. Functional psychiatric disorders in old age. In E. W. Busse & E. Pfeiffer (Eds.), *Behavior and adaptation in late life* (2nd ed.). Boston: Little, Brown, 1977.

Butler, R. N. Successful aging and the role of the life review. *Journal of the American Geriatrics Society,* 1974, *22,* 529-535.

Butler, R. N. Research programs of the National Institute on Aging. *Public Health Reports,* 1977, *92,* 3-8.

Butler, R. N. Thoughts on geriatric medicine. Pub. No. (NIH) 78-1406. *National Institute on Aging Science Writer Seminar Series.* Department of Health, Education and Welfare (U.S. Public Health Service), 1978.

Butler, R. N. Ageism: A foreword. *Journal of Social Issues,* 1980, *36*(2), 8-11.

Butler, R. N., & Lewis, M. I. *Aging and mental health.* St. Louis: Mosby, 1973.

Bynum, J. E., Cooper, B. L., & Acuff, F. G. Retirement reorientation: Senior adult education. *Journal of Gerontology,* 1978, *33,* 253-261.

Caldwell, D., & Mishara, B. L. Research on attitudes of medical doctors toward the dying patient: A methodological problem. *Omega*, 1972, *3*, 341–346.

Cameron, P. The generation gap: Time orientation. *Gerontologist*, 1972, *12*, 117–119.

Cameron, P., Stewart, L., & Biber, H. Consciousness of death across the life-span. *Journal of Gerontology*, 1973, *28*, 92–95.

Canestrari, R. E. Paced and self-paced learning in young and elderly adults. *Journal of Gerontology*, 1963, *18*, 165–168.

Carp, F. M. Some components of disengagement. *Journal of Gerontology*, 1968, *23*, 382–386.

Carver, E. J. Geropsychiatric treatment: Where, why, how. In W. E. Fann & G. L. Maddox (Eds.), *Drug issues in geropsychiatry.* Baltimore: Williams and Wilkins, 1974.

Cath, S. H. Some dynamics of middle and later years: A study in depletion and restitution. In M. A. Berezin & S. H. Cath (Eds.), *Geriatric psychiatry: Grief, loss and emotional disorders in the aging process.* New York: International Universities Press, 1965.

Cath, S. H. The orchestration of disengagement. In A. Monk (Ed.), *The age of aging: A reader in social gerontology.* Buffalo, N.Y.: Prometheus Press, 1979.

Cautela, J. R. A classical conditioning approach to the development and modification of behavior in the aged. *Gerontologist*, 1969, *9*, 109–113.

Charles, D. C. Explaining intelligence in adulthood: The role of the life history. *Gerontologist*, 1973, *13*, 483–487.

Christenson, C. V., & Gagnon, J. H. Sexual behavior in a group of older women. *Journal of Gerontology*, 1965, *20*, 351–356.

Clayton, P. J. The sequelae and nonsequelae of conjugal bereavement. *American Journal of Psychiatry*, 1979, *136*, 1530–1534.

Clayton, P. J., Halikas, J. A., Maurice, W. L., & Robins, E. Anticipatory grief and widowhood. *British Journal of Psychiatry*, 1973, *122*, 47–51.

Cleveland, W. P., & Gianturco, D. T. Remarriage probability after widowhood: A retrospective method. *Journal of Gerontology*, 1976, *31*, 99–103.

Cockerham, W. C., Sharp, K., & Wilcox, J. A. Aging and perceived health status. *Journal of Gerontology*, 1983, *38*, 349–355.

Cohen, K. P. *Hospice: Prescription for terminal care.* Germantown, Md.: Aspen Systems Corp., 1979.

Cohn, R. M. Age and the satisfactions from work. *Journal of Gerontology*, 1979, *34*, 264–272.

Colavita, F. *Sensory changes in the elderly.* Springfield, Ill.: Charles C Thomas, 1978.

Cole, S. Age and scientific performance. *American Journal of Sociology*, 1979, *84*, 958–977.

Coleman, P. G. Measuring reminiscence characteristics from conversation as adaptive features of old age. *International Journal of Aging and Human Development*, 1974, *5*, 281–294.

Comfort, A. A biologist laments and exhorts. In L. F. Jarvik (Ed.), *Aging into the 21st century.* New York: Gardner Press, 1978.

Comfort, A. *The biology of senescence* (3rd ed.). New York: Elsevier/North Holland, 1979.

Comfort, A. Sexuality in later life. In J. E. Birren & R. B. Sloane (Eds.), *Handbook of mental health and aging.* Englewood Cliffs, N.J.: Prentice-Hall, 1980.

Cooper, A. F., & Curry, A. R. The pathology of deafness in the paranoid and affective psychoses of later life. *Journal of Psychosomatic Research*, 1976, *20*, 97–105.

Copeland, J. R. M. Evaluation of diagnostic methods: An international comparison. In A. D. Issacs & F. Post (Eds.), *Studies in geriatric psychiatry.* New York: Wiley, 1978.

Corby, N., & Solnick, R. L. Psychosocial and physiological influences on sexuality in the older adult. In J. E. Birren & R. B. Sloane (Eds.), *Handbook of mental health and aging.* Englewood Cliffs, N.J.: Prentice-Hall, 1980.

Corso, J. F. Auditory perception and communication. In J. E. Birren & K. W. Schaie (Eds.), *Handbook of the psychology of aging.* New York: Van Nostrand Reinhold, 1977.

Costa, P. T., McCrae, R. R., & Norris, A. H. Personal adjustment to aging: Longitudinal prediction from neuroticism and extraversion. *Journal of Gerontology*, 1981, *36*, 78–85.

Craik, F. I. M. Age differences in human memory. In J. E. Birren & K. W. Schaie (Eds.), *Handbook of the psychology of aging.* New York: Van Nostrand Reinhold, 1977.

Cumming, E., & Henry, W. E. *Growing old.* New York: Basic Books, 1961.

Dangott, L., & Nallia, M. Stereotyping the role of oldness limits the growth potential. *Humanitas*, 1977, *13*, 39–52.

Davidson, P. O., & Davidson, S. M. *Behavioral medicine: Changing health lifestyles.* New York: Brunner/Mazel, 1980.

Davidson, S. M., & Marmor, T. R. *The cost of living longer.* Lexington, Mass.: Heath, 1980.

Davies, P., & Maloney, A. Selective loss of central cholinergic neurons in Alzheimer's disease. *Lancet*, 1976, *2*, 1403.

Davis, G., & Jessen, A. An experiment in death education in the medical curriculum: Medical students and clergy "on call" together. *Omega*, 1980-81, *11*, 157-166.

de Beauvoir, S. *The coming of age*. New York: Putnam, 1972.

Dembroski, T. (Ed.). *Proceedings of the Forum on Coronary Prone Behavior*. Pub. No. (NIH) 78-1451. Washington, D.C.: Department of Health, Education and Welfare, 1977.

Dennerstein, L., Wood, C., & Burrows, G. D. Sexual response following hysterectomy and oophorectomy. *Obstetrics and Gynecology*, 1977, *49*, 92-96.

Dennis, W. *Age and Achievement:* A critique. *Journal of Gerontology*, 1956, *11*, 331-333.

Dennis, W. The age decrement in outstanding scientific contributions: Fact or artifact. *American Psychologist*, 1958, *13*, 457-460.

Dennis, W. Creative productivity between the ages of 20 and 80 years. *Journal of Gerontology*, 1966, *21*, 1-8.

Devins, G. M. Death anxiety and voluntary passive euthanasia: Influences of proximity to death and experiences with death in important other persons. *Journal of Consulting and Clinical Psychology*, 1979, *47*, 301-309.

Dickinson, G. E., & Pearson, A. A. Death education and physicians' attitudes toward dying patients. *Omega*, 1980-81, *11*, 167-174.

Doppelt, J. E., & Wallace, W. L. Standardization of the Wechsler Adult Intelligence Scale for older persons. *Journal of Abnormal and Social Psychology*, 1955, *51*, 312-330.

Dubois, P. M. *The hospice way of death*. New York: Human Sciences Press, 1980.

Ebersole, P. P. Establishing reminiscing groups. In I. M. Burnside (Ed.), *Working with the elderly: Group process and techniques*. North Scituate, Mass.: Duxbury Press, 1978.

Eichorn, G. L. Aging: Genetics and the environment. Pub. No. (NIH) 79-1450. *National Institute on Aging Science Writer Seminar Series*. Department of Health, Education and Welfare (U.S. Public Health Service), 1979.

Eisdorfer, C. Developmental level and sensory impairment in the aged. In E. Palmore (Ed.), *Normal aging*. Durham, N.C.: Duke University Press, 1970. (a)

Eisdorfer, C. Rorschach rigidity and sensory decrement in a senescent population. In E. Palmore (Ed.), *Normal aging*. Durham, N.C.: Duke University Press, 1970. (b)

Eisdorfer, C. Stress, disease and cognitive change in the aged. In C. Eisdorfer & R. O. Friedel, *Cognitive and emotional disturbance in the elderly*. Chicago: Yearbook Medical Publishers, 1977.

Eisdorfer, C., & Stotsky, B. A. Intervention, treatment and rehabilitation of psychiatric disorders. In J. E. Birren & K. W. Schaie (Eds.), *Handbook of the psychology of aging*. New York: Van Nostrand Reinhold, 1977.

Eisdorfer, C., & Wilkie, F. Intellectual changes with advancing age. In L. F. Jarvik, C. Eisdorfer, & J. E. Blum (Eds.), *Intellectual functioning in adults*. New York: Springer, 1973.

Eissler, K. R. *The psychiatrist and the dying patient*. New York: International Universities Press, 1955.

Ekerdt, D. J., Bosse, R., & LoCastro, J. S. Claims that retirement improves health. *Journal of Gerontology*, 1983, *38*, 231-236.

Engen, T. Taste and smell. In J. E. Birren & K. W. Schaie (Eds.), *Handbook of the psychology of aging*. New York: Van Nostrand Reinhold, 1977.

Epley, R. J., & McCaghy, C. H. The stigma of dying: Attitudes toward the terminally ill. *Omega*, 1977-78, *8*, 379-393.

Epstein, L. J. Depression in the elderly. *Journal of Gerontology*, 1976, *31*, 278-282.

Erikson, E. H. *Childhood and society* (2nd ed.). New York: Norton, 1963.

Erikson, R. C. Problems in the clinical assessment of memory. *Experimental Aging Research*, 1978, *4*, 255-272.

Erikson, R. C., Poon, L. W., & Walsh-Sweeney, L. Clinical memory testing of the elderly. In L. W. Poon, J. L. Fozard, L. S. Cermak, D. Arenberg, & L. W. Thompson (Eds.), *New directions in memory and aging*. Hillsdale, N.J.: Erlbaum, 1980.

Feifel, H., & Branscomb, A. B. Who's afraid of death? *Journal of Abnormal Psychology*, 1973, *81*, 282-288.

Ferraro, K. F. The health consequences of relocation among the aged in the community. *Journal of Gerontology*, 1983, *38*, 90-96.

Fillenbaum, G. G. The working retired. *Journal of Gerontology*, 1971, *26*, 82-89. (a)

Fillenbaum, G. G. On the relation between attitude to work and attitude to retirement. *Journal of Gerontology*, 1971, *26*, 244-248. (b)

Folstein, M. F., & McHugh, P. R. Dementia syndrome of depression. In R. Katzman, R. D. Terry, & K. L. Bick (Eds.), *Aging.* Vol. 7: *Alzheimer's disease, senile dementia and related disorders.* New York: Raven Press, 1978.

Foner, A., & Schwab, K. *Aging and retirement.* Monterey, Calif.: Brooks/Cole, 1981.

Fozard, J. L, & Popkin, S. J. Optimizing adult development: Ends and means of an applied psychology of aging. *American Psychologist,* 1978, *33,* 975–989.

Fozard, J. L., Wolf, E., Bell, B., McFarland, R. A., & Podolsky, S. Visual perception and communication. In J. E. Birren & K. W. Schaie (Eds.), *Handbook of the psychology of aging.* New York: Van Nostrand Reinhold, 1977.

Freud, S. Mourning and melancholia. *Standard edition* (Vol. 14). London: Hogarth Press, 1957.

Freud, S. On psychotherapy. *Collected papers* (Vol. 1). London: Hogarth Press, 1924.

Friedman, M., & Rosenman, R. H. *Type A behavior and your heart.* Greenwich, Conn.: Fawcett, 1974.

Friedman, S. The resident welcoming committee: Institutionalized elderly in volunteer services to their peers. *Gerontologist,* 1975, *15,* 362–367.

Furry, C. A., & Baltes, P. B. The effect of age differences in ability extraneous performance variables on the assessment of intelligence in children, adults and the elderly. *Journal of Gerontology,* 1973, *28,* 73–80.

Gambria, L. M. Daydreaming about the past: The time setting of spontaneous thought intrusions. *Gerontologist,* 1977, *17,* 35–38.

Gambria, L. M. Sex differences in daydreaming and related mental activity from the late teens to the early nineties. *International Journal of Aging and Human Development,* 1979–80, *10,* 1–34.

Gardner, E. F., & Monge, R. H. Adult age differences in cognitive abilities and educational background. *Experimental Aging Research,* 1977, *3,* 337–383.

Gelfand, D. E., & Olsen, J. K. *The aging network: Programs and services.* New York: Springer, 1979.

George, L. K. The impact of personality and social status factors upon levels of activity and psychological well being. *Journal of Gerontology,* 1978, *33,* 840–847.

George, L. K., & Maddox, G. L. Subjective adaptation to loss of the work role: A longitudinal study. *Journal of Gerontology,* 1977, *32,* 456–462.

Gianturco, D. T., & Busse, E. W. Psychiatric problems encountered during a long-term study of normal aging volunteers. In A. D. Issacs & F. Post (Eds.), *Studies in geriatric psychiatry.* New York: Wiley, 1978.

Glamser, F. D. Determinants of a positive attitude towards retirement. *Journal of Gerontology,* 1976, *31,* 104–107.

Glamser, F. D. The impact of pre-retirement programs on the retirement experience. *Journal of Gerontology,* 1981, *36,* 244–250.

Glamser, F. D., & DeJong, G. F. The efficacy of pre-retirement preparation programs for industrial workers. *Journal of Gerontology,* 1975, *30,* 595–600.

Glaser, B. The social loss of aged dying patients. *Gerontologist,* 1966, *6,* 77–80.

Glaser, B., & Strauss, A. L. *A time for dying.* Chicago: Aldine, 1968.

Glick, I. D., & Kessler, D. R. *Marital and family therapy* (2nd ed.). New York: Grune & Stratton, 1980.

Goldfarb, A. I. Recommendations for psychiatric care in a home for the aged. *Journal of Gerontology,* 1953, *8,* 343–347.

Goldfarb, A. I., & Turner, H. Psychotherapy of aged persons. *American Journal of Psychiatry,* 1953, *109,* 916–921.

Gollub, J. Psychoactive drug misuse among the elderly: A review of prevention and treatment programs. In R. C. Kayne (Ed.), *Drugs and the elderly.* Los Angeles: University of Southern California Press, 1978.

Gorney, J. E., & Tobin, S. S. Experiencing among the aged. Paper presented at 20th annual meeting of Gerontological Society, St. Petersburg, Fla., November 8–11, 1967.

Gotestam, K. G. Behavioral and dynamic psychotherapy with the elderly. In J. E. Birren & R. B. Sloane (Eds.), *Handbook of mental health and aging.* Englewood Cliffs, N.J.: Prentice-Hall, 1980.

Gottesman, L. E. Nursing home performance as related to resident traits, ownership, size and source of payment. *American Journal of Public Health,* 1974, *64,* 269–276.

Gottesman, L. E., & Bourestam, N. C. Why nursing homes do what they do. *Gerontologist,* 1974, *14,* 501–506.

Gottesman, L., & Brody, E. Psychosocial intervention programs within the institutional setting. In S. Sherwood (Ed.), *Long-term care.* Holliswood, N.Y.: Spectrum, 1975.

Granick, S., & Friedman, A. S. Educational experience and the maintenance of intellectual functioning by the aged: An overview. In L. F. Jarvik, C. Eisdorfer, & J. E. Blum (Eds.), *Intellectual functioning in adults.* New York: Springer, 1973.

Granick, S., Kleban, M. H., & Weiss, A. D. Relationships between hearing loss and cognition in normally hearing aged persons. *Journal of Gerontology*, 1976, *31*, 434–440.

Grauer, H., Betts, D., & Birnbom, F. Welfare emotions and family therapy in geriatrics. *Journal of the American Geriatrics Society*, 1973, *21*, 21–24.

Greenblatt, M. The grieving spouse. *American Journal of Psychiatry*, 1978, *135*, 43–47.

Greist, J. H., & Greist, T. H. *Antidepressant treatment: The essentials.* Baltimore: Williams and Wilkins, 1979.

Grosicki, J. P. Effect of operant conditioning on modification of incontinence in neuropsychiatric geriatric patients. *Nursing Research*, 1968, *17*, 304–311.

Group for the Advancement of Psychiatry. *Towards a public policy on mental health care of the elderly.* Report No. 79. New York: Group for the Advancement of Psychiatry Publications Office, 1970.

Grzegorczyk, P. B., Jones, S. W., & Mistretta, C. M. Age related differences in salt taste acuity. *Journal of Gerontology*, 1979, *34*, 834–840.

Gubrium, J. F. *Living and dying at Murray Manor.* New York: St. Martin's Press, 1975.

Gurland, B. J. The comparative frequency of depression in various adult age groups. *Journal of Gerontology*, 1976, *31*, 283–292.

Gutmann, D. L. An exploration of ego configurations in middle and later life. In B. L. Neugarten & associates (Eds.), *Personality in middle and late life.* New York: Atherton, 1964.

Gutmann, D. L. *The country of old men: Cultural studies in the psychology of later life.* Ann Arbor: Institute of Gerontology, University of Michigan–Wayne State University, 1969.

Gutmann, D. L. The cross-cultural perspective: Notes towards a comparative psychology of aging. In J. E. Birren & K. W. Schaie (Eds.), *Handbook of the psychology of aging.* New York: Van Nostrand Reinhold, 1977.

Habot, B., & Libow, L. S. The interrelationship of mental and physical status and its assessment in the older adult: Mind-body interaction. In J. E. Birren & R. B. Sloane (Eds.), *Handbook of mental health and aging.* Englewood Cliffs, N.J.: Prentice-Hall, 1980.

Hachinski, V. C., Lassen, N. A., & Marshal, J. Multi-infarct dementia. *Lancet*, 1974, *2*, 207–209.

Haley, J. Family therapy: A radical change. In J. Haley (Ed.), *Changing families: A family therapy reader.* New York: Grune & Stratton, 1971.

Hall, D. A. *The ageing of connective tissue.* London: Academic Press, 1976.

Han, S. S., & Geha-Mitzel, M. Coping with sensory losses in aging. In J. M. Ordy & K. R. Brizzee (Eds.), *Aging.* Vol. 10: *Sensory systems and communication in the elderly.* New York: Raven Press, 1979.

Harkins, S. W., Chapman, C. R., & Eisdorfer, C. Memory loss and response bias in senescence. *Journal of Gerontology*, 1979, *34*, 66–72.

Harris, L., & associates. *Aging in the eighties: America in transition.* Washington, D.C.: National Council on the Aging, 1981.

Hartford, M. E. The use of group methods for work with the aged. In J. E. Birren & R. B. Sloane (Eds.), *Handbook of mental health and aging.* Englewood Cliffs, N.J.: Prentice-Hall, 1980.

Hartley, J. T., Harker, J. O., & Walsh, D. A. Contemporary issues and new directions in adult development of learning and memory. In L. Poon (Ed.), *Aging in the 1980's: Psychological issues.* Washington, D.C.: American Psychological Association, 1980.

Hausman, C. P. Short term counseling groups for people with elderly parents. *Gerontologist*, 1979, *19*, 102–107.

Havighurst, R. J., & Glasser, R. An exploratory study of reminiscence. *Journal of Gerontology*, 1972, *27*, 245–253.

Havighurst, R. J., McDonald, W. J., Maeulen, L., & Mazel, J. Male social scientists: Lives after sixty. *Gerontologist*, 1979, *19*, 55–60.

Hayflick, L. The cell biology of human aging. *New England Journal of Medicine*, 1976, *295*, 1302–1308.

Haynes, S. G., McMichael, A. J., & Tyroler, H. A. Survival after early and normal retirement. *Journal of Gerontology*, 1978, *33*, 269–278.

Helsing, K. J., Szklo, M., & Comstock, G. W. Factors associated with mortality after widowhood. *American Journal of Public Health*, 1981, *71*, 802–809.

Heyman, D. K., & Gianturco, D. T. Long-term adaptation by the elderly to bereavement. *Journal of Gerontology*, 1973, *28*, 359–362.

Heyman, D. K., & Jeffers, F. C. Effect of time lapse on consistency of self-health and medical evaluations of elderly persons. *Journal of Gerontology*, 1963, *18*, 160–164.

Hickey, T. *Aging and health.* Monterey, Calif.: Brooks/Cole, 1980.

Hicks, L. H., & Birren, J. E. Aging, brain damage, and psychomotor slowing. *Psychological Bulletin*, 1970, *74*, 377–396.

Hicks, R., Funkenstein, H. H., Davis, J. M., & Dysken, M. W. Geriatric psychopharmacology. In J. E. Birren & R. B. Sloane (Eds.), *Handbook of mental health and aging*. Englewood Cliffs, N.J.: Prentice-Hall, 1980.

Hine, V. H. Dying at home: Can families cope? *Omega*, 1979–80, *10*, 175–187.

Hinton, J. The influence of previous personality on reactions to having terminal cancer. *Omega*, 1975, *6*, 95–111.

Hodgson, J. H., & Quinn, J. L. The impact of the triage health care delivery system upon client morale, independent living and the cost of care. *Gerontologist*, 1980, *20*, 364–371.

Holmes, M. B., & Holmes, D. *Handbook of human services for older persons*. New York: Human Sciences Press, 1979.

Holmes, T. H., & Rahe, R. H. The Social Readjustment Rating Scale. *Journal of Psychosomatic Research*, 1967, *11*, 213–218.

Horn, J. L. Organization of data on life-span development of human abilities. In L. R. Goulet & P. B. Baltes (Eds.), *Life-span developmental psychology: Research and theory*. New York: Academic Press, 1970.

Horn, J. L. Psychometric studies of aging and intelligence. In S. Gershon & A. Raskin (Eds.), *Aging*. Vol. 2: *Genesis and treatment of psychologic disorders in the elderly*. New York: Raven Press, 1975.

Horn, J. L., & Donaldson, G. On the myth of intellectual decline in adulthood. *American Psychologist*, 1976, *31*, 701–719.

Horn, J. L., & Donaldson, G. Faith is not enough: A response to the Baltes-Schaie claim that intelligence does not wane. *American Psychologist*, 1977, *32*, 369–373.

Hoyer, W. J. Application of operant techniques to the modification of elderly behavior. *Gerontologist*, 1973, *13*, 18–22.

Hoyer, W. J., Labouvie, G. V., & Baltes, P. B. Modification of response speed deficits and intellectual performance in the elderly. *Human Development*, 1973, *16*, 233–242.

Hulicka, I. M. Age differences in retention as a function of interference. *Journal of Gerontology*, 1967, *22*, 180–184.

Hulicka, I. M., & Grossman, J. L. Age group comparisons for the use of mediators in paired associate learning. *Journal of Gerontology*, 1967, *22*, 46–51.

Hultsch, D. F. Learning to learn in adulthood. *Journal of Gerontology*, 1974, *29*, 302–308.

Huttman, E. D. *Housing and social services for the elderly: Social policy trends*. New York: Praeger, 1977.

Introduction: The age of the aging, congregate living. *Progressive Architecture*, August 1981.

Ireland, L. M., & Bond, K. Retirees of the 1970's. In C. S. Kart & B. Manard (Eds.), *Aging in America: Readings in social gerontology*. Sherman Oaks, Calif.: Alfred, 1976.

Jacobs, S., & Ostfeld, A. An epidemiological review of the mortality of bereavement. *Psychosomatic Medicine*, 1977, *39*, 344–357.

Janowsky, D., Davis, J. M., & El-Yousef, M. K. Side effects associated with psychotropic drugs. In W. E. Fann & G. L. Maddox (Eds.), *Drug issues in geropsychiatry*. Baltimore: Williams and Wilkins, 1974.

Janson, P., & Ryder, L. K. Crime and the elderly: The relationship between risk and fear. *Gerontologist*, 1983, *23*, 207–212.

Jantz, R. K., Seefeldt, C., Galper, A., & Serock, K. *Children's attitudes towards the elderly: Final Report*. College Park: University of Maryland, 1976.

Jarvik, L. F. Discussion: Patterns of intellectual functioning in the later years. In L. F. Jarvik, C. Eisdorfer, & J. E. Blum (Eds.), *Intellectual functioning in adults*. New York: Springer, 1973.

Jarvik, L. F. The aging central nervous system: Clinical aspects. In H. Brody, D. Harman, & J. M. Ordy (Eds.), *Aging*. Vol. 1: *Clinical, morphologic and neurochemical aspects in the aging central nervous system*. New York: Raven Press, 1975.

Jarvik, L. F., & Falik, A. Intellectual stability and survival in the aged. *Journal of Gerontology*, 1963, *18*, 173–176.

Jarvik, L. F., & Milne, J. F. Gerovital-H3: A review of the literature. In S. Gershon & A. Raskin (Eds.), *Aging*. Vol. 2: *Genesis and treatment of psychologic disorders in the elderly*. New York: Raven Press, 1975.

Jarvik, L. F., & Russell, D. Anxiety, aging and the third emergency reaction. *Journal of Gerontology*, 1979, *34*, 197–200.

Jeffers, F. C., & Verwoerdt, A. How the old face death. In E. W. Busse & E. Pfeiffer (Eds.), *Behavior and adaptation in late life* (2nd ed.). Boston: Little, Brown, 1977.

Johnson, E. S., & Bursk, B. J. Relationships between the elderly and their adult children. *Gerontologist*, 1977, *17*, 90–96.

Kahana, E. A congruence model of person-environment interaction. In P. G. Windley & G. Ernst (Eds.), *Theory development in environment and aging*. Washington, D.C.: Gerontological Society, 1975.

Kahn, R. L. Excess disabilities in the aged. In S. H. Zarit (ed.), *Readings in aging and death: Contemporary perspectives*. New York: Harper & Row, 1977. (a)

Kahn, R. L. The mental health system and the future aged. In S. H. Zarit (Ed.), *Readings in aging and death: Contemporary perspectives*. New York: Harper & Row, 1977. (b)

Kahn, R. L., Goldfarb, A. I., Pollack, M., & Peck, A. Brief objective measures for the determination of mental status of the aged. *American Journal of Psychiatry*, 1960, *117*, 326–328.

Kahn, R. L., & Miller, N. E. Adaptational factors in memory function in the aged. *Experimental Aging Research*, 1978, *4*, 273–289.

Kahn, R. L., Zarit, S. H., Hilbert, N. M., & Niederehe, G. Memory complaint and impairment in the aged; the effect of depression and altered brain function. *Archives of General Psychiatry*, 1975, *32*, 1569–1573.

Kane, R. L., Solomon, D. H., Beck, J. C., Keeler, E., & Kane, R. A. *Geriatrics in the United States: Manpower projections and training considerations*. Lexington, Mass.: Heath, 1981.

Karasu, T. B., & Murkofsky, C. M. Psychopharmacology of the elderly. In L. Bellack & T. B. Karasu (Eds.), *Geriatric psychiatry: A handbook for psychiatrists and primary care physicians*. New York: Grune & Stratton, 1976.

Kart, C. S., & Manard, B. B. Quality of care in old age institutions. *Gerontologist*, 1976, *16*, 250–256.

Kart, C. S., Metress, E. S., & Metress, J. F. *Aging and health: Biologic and social perspectives*. Menlo Park, Calif.: Addison-Wesley, 1978.

Kastenbaum, R. Toward standards of care for the terminally ill, part III: A few guiding principles. *Omega*, 1976, *7*, 191–193.

Kastenbaum, R. *Death, society, and human experience* (2nd ed.). St. Louis: Mosby, 1981.

Kastenbaum, R., & Aisenberg, R. *The psychology of death*. New York: Springer, 1972.

Kastenbaum, R., & Candy, S. E. The 4% fallacy: A methodological and empirical critique of extended care facility population statistics. *International Journal of Aging and Human Development*, 1973, *4*, 15–21.

Kastenbaum, R., & Costa, P. T. Psychological perspectives on death. *Annual review of psychology*, 1977, *28*, 225–249.

Katz, S., Ford, A. B., Moskowitz, R. W., Jackson, B. A., & Jaffee, M. W. Studies of illness in the aged: The index of ADL—a standardized measure of biological and psychosocial function. *Journal of the American Medical Association*, 1963, *185*, 914–919.

Kay, D. W. K. The epidemiology and identification of brain deficit in the elderly. In C. Eisdorfer & R. O. Friedel (Eds.), *Cognitive and emotional disturbance in the elderly*. Chicago: Yearbook Medical Publishers, 1977.

Kay, D. W. K., Beamish, P., & Roth, M. Old age mental disorders in Newcastle-upon-Tyne: Part 1. A study of prevalence. *British Journal of Psychiatry*, 1964, *110*, 146–158.

Kay, D. W. K., & Bergmann, K. Epidemiology of mental disorders among the aged in the community. In J. E. Birren & R. B. Sloane (Eds.), *Handbook of mental health and aging*. Englewood Cliffs, N.J.: Prentice-Hall, 1980.

Kayne, R. (Ed.). *Drugs and the elderly*. Los Angeles: University of Southern California Press, 1978.

Keating, N. C., & Cole, P. What do I do with him 24 hours a day? Changes in the housewife role after retirement. *Gerontologist*, 1980, *20*, 84–89.

Kiesler, C. A. Mental health policy as a field of inquiry for psychology. *American Psychologist*, 1980, *35*, 1066–1080.

Kimmel, D. C., Price, K. F., & Walker, J. W. Retirement choice and retirement satisfaction. *Journal of Gerontology*, 1978, *33*, 575–585.

Kitson, G. C., Lopata, H. Z., Holmes, W. M., & Meyering, S. M. Divorcees and widows: Similarities and differences. *American Journal of Orthopsychiatry*, 1980, *50*, 291–301.

Kleban, M. H., Brody, E. M., & Lawton, M. P. Personality traits in the mentally-impaired aged and their relationship to improvements in current functioning. *Gerontologist*, 1971, *11*, 134–140.

Kogan, N., & Wallach, M. A. Age changes in values and attitudes. *Journal of Gerontology*, 1961, *16*, 272–280.

Kohn, R. R. *Principles of mammalian aging* (2nd ed.). Englewood Cliffs, N.J.: Prentice-Hall, 1978.

Kohut, S. J., Kohut, J. J., & Fleishman, J. J. *Reality orientation for the elderly*. Oradell, N.J.: Medical Economics Co., 1979.

Kosberg, J. I. Differences in proprietary institutions caring for affluent and non-affluent elderly. *Gerontologist*, 1973, *13*, 299–304.

Kosberg, J. I. Making institutions accountable: Research and policy issues. *Gerontologist*, 1974, *14*, 510–516.

Kovar, M. G. Health of the elderly and use of health services. *Public Health Reports*, 1977, *92*, 9–19.

Kübler-Ross, E. *On death and dying.* New York: Macmillan, 1969.

Kucharski, L. T., White, R. M., & Schratz, M. Age bias, referral for psychological assistance and the private physician. *Journal of Gerontology*, 1979, *34*, 423–428.

Labouvie, G. V. Implications of geropsychological theories for intervention: The challenge for the 70's. *Gerontologist*, 1973, *13*, 10–14.

Labouvie-Vief, G., & Gonda, J. N. Cognitive strategy training and intellectual performance in the elderly. *Journal of Gerontology*, 1976, *31*, 327–332.

Labouvie-Vief, G., Hoyer, W. J., Baltes, N. N., & Baltes, P. B. Operant analysis of intellectual behavior in old age. *Human Development*, 1974, *17*, 259–273.

Langer, E., Rodin, J., Beck, P., Weinman, C., & Spitzer, L. Environmental determinants of memory improvement in late adulthood. *Journal of Personality and Social Psychology*, 1979, *37*, 2003–2013.

Larson, R. Thirty years of research on the subjective well being of older Americans. *Journal of Gerontology*, 1978, *33*, 109–125.

LaRue, A., Bank, L., Jarvik, L., & Hetland, M. Health in old age: How do physicians' ratings and self-ratings compare? *Journal of Gerontology*, 1979, *34*, 687–691.

Lawton, M. P. Assessment, integration, and environments for the elderly. *Gerontologist*, 1970, *10*, 38–46.

Lawton, M. P. *Planning and managing housing for the elderly.* New York: Wiley, 1975.

Lawton, M. P. Environmental change: The older person as initiator and responder. In N. Datan & N. Lohmann (Eds.), *Transitions of aging.* New York: Academic Press, 1980.

Lawton, M. P., Greenbaum, M., & Liebowitz, B. The lifespan of housing environments for the aging. *Gerontologist*, 1980, *20*, 56–64.

Lawton, M. P., Whelihan, W. I., & Belsky, J. K. Personality tests and their uses with older adults. In J. E. Birren & R. B. Sloane (Eds.), *Handbook of mental health and aging.* Englewood Cliffs, N.J.: Prentice-Hall, 1980.

Lazarus, L. W., & Weinberg, J. Treatment in the ambulatory care setting. In E. W. Busse & D. G. Blazer (Eds.), *Handbook of geriatric psychiatry.* New York: Van Nostrand Reinhold, 1980.

Leaf, A. Getting old. *Scientific American*, 1973, *229*, 44–53.

Lehman, H. C. *Age and achievement.* Philadelphia: American Philosophical Society, 1953.

Lehman, H. C. The age decrement in outstanding scientific creativity. *American Psychologist*, 1960, *15*, 128–134.

Lemon, B. W., Bengston, V. L., & Peterson, J. A. An exploration of the activity theory of aging: Activity types and life satisfaction among in-movers to a retirement community. *Journal of Gerontology*, 1972, *27*, 511–523.

Leon, G. R., Gillum, B., Gillum, R., & Gouze, M. Personality stability and change over a 30-year period—middle age to old age. *Journal of Consulting and Clinical Psychology*, 1979, *47*, 517–524.

Lewis, C. N. Reminiscing and self-concept in old age. *Journal of Gerontology*, 1971, *26*, 240–243.

Lewis, M. I., & Butler, R. N. Life review therapy. *Geriatrics*, November 1974, pp. 165–173.

Lindemann, E. Symptomatology and management of acute grief. *American Journal of Psychiatry*, 1944, *101*, 141–148.

Lindsley, O. R. Geriatric behavioral prosthetics. In R. Kastenbaum (Ed.), *New thoughts on old age.* New York: Springer, 1964.

Lipton, M. A. Age differentiation in depression: Biochemical aspects. *Journal of Gerontology*, 1976, *31*, 293–299.

Liston, E. H. Education on death and dying: A neglected area in the medical curriculum. *Omega*, 1975, *6*, 193–198.

Lopata, H. Z. *Widowhood in an American city.* Cambridge, Mass.: Schenkman, 1973.

Lopata, H. Z. The absence of community resources in support systems of urban widows. *Family Coordinator*, 1978, *27*, 383–388. (a)

Lopata, H. Z. Contributions of extended families to the support systems of metropolitan area widows: Limitations of the modified kin network. *Journal of Marriage and the Family*, 1978, *40*, 355–364. (b)

Lopata, H. Z. *Women as widows: Support systems.* New York: Elsevier/North Holland, 1979.

Lowenthal, M. F., Berkman, P. L., & associates. *Aging and mental disorder in San Francisco: A social psychiatric study.* San Francisco: Jossey-Bass, 1967.

Lowenthal, M. F., Thurnher, M., Chiriboga, D., & associates. *Four stages of life: A comparative study of women and men facing transitions.* San Francisco: Jossey-Bass, 1975.

Lowy, L. Mental health services in the community. In J. E. Birren & R. B. Sloane (Eds.), *Handbook of mental health and aging.* Englewood Cliffs, N.J.: Prentice-Hall, 1980.

Maas, H. S., & Kuypers, J. A. *From thirty to seventy: A forty-year study of adult life styles and personality.* San Francisco: Jossey-Bass, 1975.

MacDonald, M. L., & Butler, A. K. Reversal of helplessness: Producing walking behavior in nursing home wheelchair residents using behavior modification procedures. *Journal of Gerontology,* 1974, *29,* 97–101.

Maddox, G. L. Drugs, physicians, and patients. In W. E. Fann & G. L. Maddox (Eds.), *Drug issues in geropsychiatry.* Baltimore: Williams and Wilkins, 1974.

Maddox, G. L. (conf. chairman). *Assessment and evaluation strategies in aging: People, populations and programs.* Durham, N.C.: Duke University Center for the Study of Aging and Human Development, 1978.

Maddox, G. L., & Douglass, E. B. Self-assessment of health: A longitudinal study of elderly subjects. *Journal of Health and Social Behavior,* 1973, *14,* 87–93.

Maddox, G. L., & Douglass, E. B. Aging and individual differences: A longitudinal analysis of social, psychological and physiological indicators. *Journal of Gerontology,* 1974, *29,* 555–563.

Mahoney, M. J. Reflections on the cognitive-learning trend in psychotherapy. *American Psychologist,* 1977, *32,* 5–13.

Manard, B. B., Kart, C. S., & Van Gils, D. W. L. *Old age institutions.* Lexington, Mass.: Heath, 1975.

Marsden, C. D. The diagnosis of dementia. In A. D. Issacs & F. Post (Eds.), *Studies in geriatric psychiatry.* New York: Wiley, 1978.

Marx, J. L. Aging research (I): Cellular theories of senescence. *Science,* 1974, *186,* 1105–1107. (a)

Marx, J. L. Aging research (II): Pacemakers for aging? *Science,* 1974, *186,* 1196–1197. (b)

Masters, W. H., & Johnson, V. E. *Human sexual response.* Boston: Little, Brown, 1966.

Mattoon, M. A. *Jungian psychology in perspective.* New York: Free Press, 1981.

Maurer, J. F., & Rupp, R. R. *Hearing and aging.* New York: Grune & Stratton, 1979.

Maxwell, R. J., Bader, J. E., & Watson, W. H. Territory and self in a geriatric setting. *Gerontologist,* 1972, *12,* 413–417.

Mazess, R. B., & Forman, S. H. Longevity and age exaggeration in Vilcabamba, Ecuador. *Journal of Gerontology,* 1979, *34,* 94–98.

McAllister, T. W. Overview: Pseudodementia. *American Journal of Psychiatry,* 1983, *140,* 528–533.

McClannahan, L. E. Therapeutic and prosthetic living environments for nursing home residents. *Gerontologist,* 1973, *13,* 424–429.

McClelland, D. C. Testing for competence rather than for "intelligence." *American Psychologist,* 1973, *28,* 1–14.

McCourt, W. F., Barnett, R. D., Brennan, J., & Becker, A. We help each other: Primary prevention for the widowed. *American Journal of Psychiatry,* 1976, *133,* 98–100.

McFarland, R. A., Tune, G. S., & Welford, A. T. On the driving of automobiles by older people. *Journal of Gerontology,* 1964, *19,* 190–197.

McKitrick, D. Counseling dying clients. *Omega,* 1981–82, *12,* 165–187.

McMahon, A. W., & Rhudick, P. J. Reminiscing in the aged: An adaptational response. In S. Levin & R. J. Kahana (Eds.), *Psychodynamic studies on aging: Creativity, reminiscing, and dying.* New York: International Universities Press, 1967.

Medvedev, Z. A. Caucasus and Altay longevity: A biological or social problem? *Gerontologist,* 1974, *14,* 381–387.

Meerloo, J. A. Geriatric psychotherapy. *Acta Psychotherapeutica,* 1961, *9,* 169–182.

Metzger, A. M. A Q-methodological study of the Kübler-Ross stage theory. *Omega,* 1979–80, *10,* 291–301.

Miller, E. *Abnormal ageing: The psychology of senile and pre-senile dementia.* London: Wiley, 1977.

Miller, M. *Suicide after sixty: The final alternative.* New York: Springer, 1979.

Milne, J. S. Prevalence of incontinence in the elderly age groups. In F. L. Willington (Ed.), *Incontinence in the elderly.* London: Academic Press, 1976.

Monea, H. E. The experiential approach in learning about sexuality in the aged. In R. L. Solnick (Ed.), *Sexuality and aging.* Los Angeles: University of Southern California Press. 1978.

Nehrke, M. F., Bellucci, G., & Gabriel, S. J. Death anxiety, locus of control and life satisfaction in the elderly: Toward a definition of ego-integrity. *Omega,* 1977–78, *8,* 359–368.

Neugarten, B. L. Summary and implications. In B. L. Neugarten & associates (Eds.), *Personality in middle and late life.* New York: Atherton, 1964.

Neugarten, B. L. Personality and aging. In J. E. Birren & K. W. Schaie (Eds.), *Handbook of the psychology of aging.* New York: Van Nostrand Reinhold, 1977.

Neugarten, B. L., & associates (Eds.). *Personality in middle and late life.* New York: Atherton, 1964.

Neugarten, B. L., & Gutmann, D. L. Age-sex roles and personality in middle age: A thematic apperception study. In B. L. Neugarten & associates (Eds.), *Personality in middle and late life.* New York: Atherton, 1964.

Neugarten, B. L., Havighurst, R. J., & Tobin, S. S. Personality and patterns of aging. In B. L. Neugarten (Ed.), *Middle age and aging: A reader in social psychology.* Chicago: University of Chicago Press, 1968.

Neugarten, B. L., Wood, V., Kraines, R. J., & Loomis, B. Women's attitudes towards the menopause. In B. L. Neugarten (Ed.), *Middle age and aging: A reader in social psychology.* Chicago: University of Chicago Press, 1968.

Newman, G., & Nichols, C. R. Sexual activities and attitudes in older persons. *Journal of the American Medical Association,* 1960, *173,* 33–35.

Ordy, J. M., & Brizzee, K. R. Functional and structural age differences in the visual system of man and nonhuman primate models. In J. M. Ordy & K. R. Brizzee (Eds.), *Aging.* Vol. 10: *Sensory systems and communication in the elderly.* New York: Raven Press, 1979.

Ordy, J. M., Brizzee, K. R., Beavers, T., & Medart, P. Age differences in the functional and structural organization of the auditory system in man. In J. M. Ordy & K. R. Brizzee (Eds.), *Aging.* Vol. 10: *Sensory systems and communication in the elderly.* New York: Raven Press, 1979.

Ostfeld, A. M. Conference summary. In A. M. Ostfeld & C. P. Donnelly (Eds.), *Epidemiology of aging.* Pub. No. (NIH) 75-711. 1975.

Oyer, H. J., Kapur, Y. P., & Deal, L. V. Hearing disorders in the aging: Effects upon communication. In H. J. Oyer & E. J. Oyer (Eds.), *Aging and communication.* Baltimore: University Park Press, 1976.

Palmore, E. The effects of aging on activities and attitudes. *Gerontologist,* 1968, *8,* 259–263.

Palmore, E. (Ed.). *Normal aging.* Durham, N.C.: Duke University Press, 1970.

Palmore, E. Attitudes toward aging as shown by humor. *Gerontologist,* 1971, *11,* 181–186. (a)

Palmore, E. The promise and problems of longevity studies. In E. Palmore & F. C. Jeffers (Eds.), *Prediction of the lifespan.* Lexington, Mass.: Heath, 1971. (b)

Palmore, E. (Ed.). *Normal aging II.* Durham, N.C.: Duke University Press, 1974.

Palmore, E. Compulsory versus flexible retirement: Issues and facts. In S. H. Zarit (Ed.), *Readings in aging and death: Contemporary perspectives.* New York: Harper & Row, 1977.

Palmore, E., & Cleveland, W. P. Aging, terminal decline, and terminal drop. *Journal of Gerontology,* 1976, *31,* 76–81.

Palmore, E., Cleveland, W. P., Nowlin, J. B., Ramm, D., & Siegler, I. C. Stress and adaptation in later life. *Journal of Gerontology,* 1979, *34,* 841–851.

Parkes, C. M. *Bereavement: Studies of grief in adult life.* New York: International Universities Press, 1972.

Pear, R. Nation's hospice movement worries about its own life. *New York Times,* May 15, 1983, p. E8.

Perry, E. K., Perry, R. H., & Tomlinson, B. E. Dietary lecithin supplements in dementia of Alzheimer type? *Lancet,* 1977, *2,* 242–243.

Pfeiffer, E. Psychotherapy with elderly patients. In L. Bellack & T. B. Karasu (Eds.), *Geriatric psychiatry: A handbook for psychiatrists and primary care physicians.* New York: Grune & Stratton, 1976.

Pfeiffer, E. Use of drugs which influence behavior in the elderly: Promises, pitfalls and perspectives. In R. C. Kayne (Ed.), *Drugs and the elderly.* Los Angeles: University of Southern California Press, 1978.

Pfeiffer, E., & Davis, G. C. Determinants of sexual behavior in middle and old age. *Journal of the American Geriatrics Society,* 1972, *20,* 151–158.

Pfeiffer, E., Verwoerdt, A., & Davis, G. C. Sexual behavior in middle life. *American Journal of Psychiatry,* 1972, *128,* 1262–1267.

Pfeiffer, E., Verwoerdt, A., & Wang, H. S. Sexual behavior in aged men and women 1: Observations on 254 community volunteers. *Archives of General Psychiatry,* 1968, *19,* 753–758.

Pickett, J. M., Bergman, M., & Levitt, H. Aging and speech understanding. In J. M. Ordy & K. R. Brizzee (Eds.), *Aging.* Vol. 10: *Sensory systems and communication in the elderly.* New York: Raven Press, 1979.

Planek, T. W., & Fowler, R. C. Traffic accident problems and exposure characteristics of the aging driver. *Journal of Gerontology,* 1971, *26,* 224–230.

Plemons, J. K., Willis, S. L., & Baltes, P. B. Modifiability of fluid intelligence in aging: A short term longitudinal training approach. *Journal of Gerontology*, 1978, *33*, 224–231.

Pollack, J. M. Correlates of death anxiety: A review of empirical studies. *Omega*, 1979–80, *10*, 97–121.

Pollack, R. H., & Atkeson, B. M. A lifespan approach to perceptual development. In P. B. Baltes (Ed.), *Life–span development and behavior; Volume 1*. New York: Academic Press, 1978.

Pollman, A. W. Early retirement: A comparison of poor health to other retirement factors. *Journal of Gerontology*, 1971, *26*, 41–45.

Poon, L. W., Fozard, J. L., Cermak, L. S., Arenberg, D., & Thompson, L. (Eds.). *New directions in memory and aging*. Hillsdale, N.J.: Erlbaum, 1980.

Poon, L. W., Fozard, J. L., & Treat, N. J. From clinical and research findings on memory to intervention programs. *Experimental Aging Research*, 1978, *4*, 235–253.

Poon, L. W., Walsh-Sweeney, L., & Fozard, J. L. Memory skill training for the elderly: Salient issues on the use of imagery mnemonics. In L. W. Poon, J. L. Fozard, L. S. Cermak, D. Arenberg, & L. W. Thompson (Eds.), *New directions in memory and aging*. Hillsdale, N.J.: Erlbaum, 1980.

Potash, M., & Jones, B. Aging and decision criteria for the detection of tones in noise. *Journal of Gerontology*, 1977, *32*, 436–440.

Prentis, R. S. White collar working women's perception of retirement. *Gerontologist*, 1980, *20*, 90–95.

Proppe, H. Housing for the retired and the aged in Southern California: An architectural commentary. *Gerontology*, 1968, *8*, 176–179.

Rahe, R. H. Life change and subsequent illness reports. In E. K. Gunderson & R. H. Rahe (Eds.), *Life stress and illness*. Springfield, Ill.: Charles C Thomas, 1974.

Raphael, B. Preventative intervention with the recently bereaved. *Archives of General Psychiatry*, 1977, *34*, 1450–1454.

Rea, M. P., Greenspoon, S., & Spilka, B. Physicians and the terminal patient: Some selected attitudes and behavior. *Omega*, 1975, *6*, 291–302.

Rebok, G. W., & Hoyer, W. J. The functional context of elderly behavior. *Gerontologist*, 1977, *17*, 27–34.

Rebok, G. W., & Hoyer, W. J. Clients nearing death: Behavioral treatment perspectives. *Omega*, 1979–80, *10*, 191–201.

Redick, R. W., & Taube, C. A. Demography and mental health care of the aged. In J. E. Birren & R. B. Sloane (Eds.), *Handbook of mental health and aging*. Englewood Cliffs, N.J.: Prentice-Hall, 1980.

Reif, H., & Strauss, A. The impact of rapid discovery upon the scientist's career. *Social Problems*, 1965, *12*, 299–311.

Reisberg, B. *Brain failure: An introduction to current concepts of senility*. New York: Free Press, 1981.

Rhudick, P. J., & Dibner, A. S. Age, personality, and health correlates of death concerns in normal aged individuals. *Journal of Gerontology*, 1961, *16*, 44–49.

Riegel, K. F. History of psychological gerontology. In J. E. Birren & K. W. Schaie (Eds.), *Handbook of the psychology of aging*. New York: Van Nostrand Reinhold, 1977.

Riegel, K. F., & Riegel, R. M. Development, drop and death. *Developmental Psychology*, 1972, *6*, 306–319.

Riegel, K. F., Riegel, R. M., & Meyer, G. A study of the dropout rates in longitudinal research on aging and the prediction of death. *Journal of Personality and Social Psychology*, 1967, *5*, 342–348.

Riley, M., & Foner, A. *Aging and society*. Vol. 1: *An inventory of research findings*. New York: Russell Sage Foundation, 1968.

Robertson, D., Griffiths, R. A., & Cosin, L. Z. A community based continuing care program for the elderly disabled. *Journal of Gerontology*, 1977, *32*, 334–339.

Rodin, J., & Langer, E. Aging labels: The decline of control and the fall of self-esteem. *Journal of Social Issues*, 1980, *36*(2), 12–29.

Rose, C. L., & Bell, B. *Predicting longevity: Methodology and critique*. Lexington, Mass.: Heath, 1971.

Rosen, J. L., & Neugarten, B. L. Ego functions in the middle and later years: A thematic apperception study. In B. L. Neugarten & associates (Eds.). *Personality in middle and late life*. New York: Atherton, 1964.

Rosenthal, R. *The hearing loss handbook*. New York: Schocken Books, 1978.

Roskies, E. Considerations in developing a treatment program for the coronory-prone (Type A) behavior pattern. In P. O. Davidson & S. M. Davidson (Eds.), *Behavioral medicine: Changing health lifestyles*. New York: Brunner/Mazel, 1980.

Rossman, I. Anatomic and body composition changes with aging. In C. E. Finch & L. Hayflick (Eds.), *Handbook of the biology of aging*. New York: Van Nostrand Reinhold, 1977.

Rossman, I. Clinical assessment in geriatrics. In G. L. Maddox (conf. chairman), *Assessment and evaluation strategies in aging: People, populations and programs.* Durham, N.C.: Duke University Center for the Study of Aging and Human Development, 1978.

Rossman, P. *Hospice.* New York: Fawcett Columbine, 1977.

Roth, M. Aging of the brain and dementia: An overview. In L. Amaducci, A. N. Davison, & P. Antuono (Eds.), *Aging.* Vol. 13: *Aging of the brain and dementia.* New York: Raven Press, 1980.

Roth, M., & Kay, D. W. K. Affective disorder arising in the senium II: Physical disability as an aetiological factor. *Journal of Mental Science,* 1956, *102,* 141-150.

Roth, M., Tomlinson, B. E., & Blessed, G. Correlation between scores for dementia and counts of "senile plaques" in cerebral grey matter of elderly subjects. *Nature,* 1966, *209,* 109-110.

Rush, A. J., Khatami, M., & Beck, A. T. Cognitive and behavior therapy in chronic depression. *Behavior Therapy,* 1975, *6,* 398-404.

Salthouse, T. A. Age and memory: Strategies for localizing the loss. In L. W. Poon, J. L. Fozard, L. S. Cermak, D. Arenberg, & L. Thompson (Eds.), *New Directions in memory and aging.* Hillsdale, N.J.: Erlbaum, 1980.

Sathananthan, G. L., & Gershon, S. Cerebral vasodilators: A review. In S. Gershon & A. Raskin (Eds.), *Aging.* Vol. 2: *Genesis and treatment of psychologic disorders in the elderly.* New York: Raven Press, 1975.

Satir, V. M. *Conjoint family therapy: A guide to theory and technique* (Rev. ed.). Palo Alto, Calif.: Science and Behavior Books, 1967.

Saul, S. R., & Saul, S. Group psychotherapy in a proprietary nursing home. *Gerontologist,* 1974, *14,* 446-450.

Saxon, S. V. & Etten, M. J. *Physical change and aging: A guide for the helping professions.* New York: Tiresias Press, 1978.

Schaie, K. W. A general model for the study of developmental problems. *Psychological Bulletin,* 1965, *64,* 92-107.

Schaie, K. W. Translations in gerontology—from lab to life: Intellectual functioning. *American Psychologist,* 1974, *29,* 802-807.

Schaie, K. W. Toward a stage theory of adult cognitive development. *International Journal of Aging and Human Development,* 1977-78, *8,* 129-138.

Schaie, K. W. External validity in the assessment of intellectual development in adulthood. *Journal of Gerontology,* 1978, *33,* 695-701.

Schaie, K. W. Intelligence and problem solving. In J. E. Birren & R. B. Sloane (Eds.), *Handbook of mental health and aging.* Englewood Cliffs, N.J.: Prentice-Hall, 1980.

Schaie, K. W., & Baltes, P. B. Some faith helps to see the forest: A final comment on the Horn and Donaldson myth of the Baltes-Schaie position on adult intelligence. *American Psychologist,* 1977, *32,* 1118-1120.

Scheidt, B. J., & Schaie, K. W. A taxonomy of situations for an elderly population: Generating situational criteria. *Journal of Gerontology,* 1978, *33,* 848-857.

Scheinberg, P. Multi-infarct dementia. In R. Katzman, R. D. Terry, & K. Bick (Eds.), *Aging.* Vol. 7: *Alzheimer's disease: Senile dementia and related disorders.* New York: Raven Press, 1978.

Schiffman, S. Food recognition by the elderly. *Journal of Gerontology,* 1977, *32,* 586-592.

Schiffman, S. Changes in taste and smell with age: Psychophysical aspects. In J. M. Ordy & K. R. Brizzee (Eds.), *Aging.* Vol. 10: *Sensory systems and communication in the elderly.* New York: Raven Press, 1979.

Schiffman, S., & Pasternak, M. Decreased discrimination of food odors in the elderly. *Journal of Gerontology,* 1979, *34,* 73-79.

Schow, R. L., Christensen, J. M., Hutchinson, J. M., & Nerbonne, M. A. *Communication disorders of the aged: A guide for health professionals.* Baltimore: University Park Press, 1978.

Schwartz, A. N. Planning micro-environments for the aged. In D. S. Woodruff & J. E. Birren (Eds.), *Aging: Scientific perspectives & social issues.* New York: D. Van Nostrand, 1975.

Schwartz, G. E., & Weiss, S. M. What is behavioral medicine? *Psychosomatic Medicine,* 1977, *39,* 377-381.

Seligman, M. E. P. *Helplessness: On depression, development, and death.* San Francisco: W. H. Freeman, 1975.

Selmanowitz, V. J., Rizer, R. L., & Orentreich, N. Aging of the skin and its appendages. In C. E. Finch & L. Hayflick (Eds.), *Handbook of the biology of aging.* New York: Van Nostrand Reinhold, 1977.

Shanas, E. *The health of older people: A social survey.* Cambridge, Mass.: Harvard University Press, 1962.

Shanas, E. Health status of older people: Cross-national implications. *American Journal of Public Health*, 1974, *64*, 261–264.

Shanas, E. Social myth as hypothesis: The case of the family relations of old people. *Gerontologist*, 1979, *19*, 3–9. (a)

Shanas, E. The family as a social support system in old age. *Gerontologist*, 1979, *19*, 169–174. (b)

Shanas, E., & Maddox, G. L. Aging, health and the organization of health resources. In R. H. Binstock & E. Shanas (Eds.), *Handbook of aging and the social sciences*. New York: Van Nostrand Reinhold, 1976.

Sheppard, H. L. Work and retirement. In E. Shanas & R. H. Binstock (Eds.), *Handbook of aging and the social sciences*. New York: Van Nostrand Reinhold, 1976.

Sherizen, S., & Paul, L. Dying in a hospital intensive care unit: The social significance for the family of the patient. *Omega*, 1977–78, *8*, 29–40.

Sherwood, S. Long-term care: Issues, perspectives and directions. In S. Sherwood (Ed.), *Long-term care*. Holliswood, N.Y.: Spectrum, 1975.

Sherwood, S., Glassman, J., Sherwood, C., & Morris, J. N. Preinstitutionalization factors as predictors of adjustment to a long-term care facility. *International Journal of Aging and Human Development*, 1974, *5*, 95–105.

Sherwood, S., & Mor, V. Mental health institutions and the elderly. In J. E. Birren & R. B. Sloane (Eds.), *Handbook of mental health and aging*. Englewood Cliffs, N.J.: Prentice-Hall, 1980.

Shin, K. E., & Putnam, R. H. Age and academic-professional honors. *Journal of Gerontology*, 1982, *37*, 220–227.

Shneidman, E. S. Death work and stages of dying. In E. Shneidman (Ed.), *Death: Current perspectives*. Palo Alto, Calif.: Mayfield, 1976.

Shneidman, E. S., & Farberow, N. L. Statistical comparisons between attempted and committed suicides. In N. L. Farberow & E. S. Shneidman (Eds.), *The cry for help*. New York: McGraw-Hill, 1961.

Shock, N. W. Biological theories of aging. In J. E. Birren & K. W. Schaie (Eds.), *Handbook of the psychology of aging*. New York: Van Nostrand Reinhold, 1977.

Siegler, I. C. The terminal drop hypothesis, fact or artifact. *Experimental Aging Research*, 1975, *1*, 169–185.

Silverstone, B., & Wynter, L. The effects of introducing a heterosexual living space. *Gerontologist*, 1975, *15*, 83–87.

Simonton, D. K. Age and literary creativity; A cross-cultural and transhistorical survey. *Journal of Cross-Cultural Psychology*, 1975, *6*, 259–277. (a)

Simonton, D. K. The sociocultural context of individual creativity: A transhistorical time series analysis. *Journal of Personality and Social Psychology*, 1975, *32*, 1119–1133. (b)

Simonton, D. K. Creative productivity, age and stress: A biographical time series analysis of 10 classical composers. *Journal of Personality and Social Psychology*, 1977, *35*, 791–804 (a)

Simonton, D. K. Eminence, creativity and geographic marginality: A recursive structural equation model. *Journal of Personality and Social Psychology*, 1977, *35*, 805–816. (b)

Slater, P. E. Prolegomena to a psychoanalytic theory of aging and death. In R. Kastenbaum (Ed.), *New thoughts on old age*. New York: Springer, 1964.

Sloane, R. B. Organic brain syndrome. In J. E. Birren & R. B. Sloane (Eds.), *Handbook of mental health and aging*. Englewood Cliffs, N.J.: Prentice-Hall, 1980.

Smith, A. D. Aging and interference with memory. *Journal of Gerontology*, 1975, *30*, 319–325.

Smith, A. D. Age differences in encoding, storage and retrieval. In L. W. Poon, J. L. Fozard, L. S. Cermak, D. Arenberg, & L. Thompson (Eds.), *New directions in memory and aging*. Hillsdale, N.J.: Erlbaum, 1980.

Snyder, L. H., Pyrek, J., & Smith, K. C. Vision and mental function of the elderly. *Gerontologist*, 1976, *16*, 491–495.

Solnick, R. L. Sexual responsiveness, age, and change: facts and potential. In R. L. Solnick (Ed.), *Sexuality and aging*. Los Angeles: University of Southern California Press, 1978.

Solomon, K., & Vickers, R. Attitudes of health workers towards old people. *Journal of the American Geriatrics Society*, 1979, *27*, 186–191.

Spirduso, W. W. Reaction and movement time as a function of age and physical activity level. *Journal of Gerontology*, 1975, *30*, 435–440.

Spirduso, W. W. Physical fitness, aging and psychomotor speed: A review. *Journal of Gerontology*, 1980, *35*, 850–865.

Srole, L., Langner, T. S., Michael, S. T., Opler, M. K., & Rennie, T. A. C. *Mental health in the metropolis: The midtown Manhattan study.* Vol. 1. New York: McGraw-Hill, 1962.

Stenback, A. Depression and suicidal behavior in old age. In J. E. Birren & R. B. Sloane (Eds.), *Handbook of mental health and aging.* Englewood Cliffs, N.J.: Prentice-Hall, 1980.

Stotsky, B. A. Psychoactive drugs for geriatric patients with psychiatric disorders. In S. Gershon & A. Raskin (Eds.), *Aging.* Vol. 2: *Genesis and treatment of psychologic disorders in the elderly.* New York: Raven Press, 1975.

Strehler, B. L. *Time, cells, and aging.* New York: Academic Press, 1962.

Streib, G., & Schneider, C. J. *Retirement in American society: Impact and process.* Ithaca, N.Y.: Cornell University Press, 1971.

Sutherland, S. S. The psychology of incontinence. In F. L. Willington (Ed.), *Incontinence in the elderly.* London: Academic Press, 1976.

Sward, K. Age and mental ability in superior men. *American Journal of Psychology,* 1945, *58,* 443–479.

Tallmer, M., & Kutner, B. Disengagement and the stresses of aging. *Journal of Gerontology,* 1969, *24,* 70–75.

Taulbee, L. R. Reality orientation: A therapeutic group activity for elderly persons. In I. M. Burnside (Ed.), *Working with the elderly: Group process and techniques.* North Scituate, Mass.: Duxbury Press, 1978.

Terry, R. D., & Wisniewski, H. Structural aspects of aging of the brain. In C. Eisdorfer & R. O. Friedal (Eds.), *Cognitive and emotional disturbance in the elderly.* Chicago: Yearbook Medical Publishers, 1977.

Thomas, P. D., Hunt, W. C., Garry, P. J., Hood, R. B., Goodwin, J. M., & Goodwin, J. S. Hearing acuity in a healthy elderly population: Effects on emotional, cognitive, and social status. *Journal of Gerontology,* 1983, *38,* 321–325.

Thompson, G. B. Work vs. leisure roles: An investigation of morale among employed and retired men. *Journal of Gerontology,* 1973, *28,* 339–344.

Thompson, L. W. Effects of hyperbaric oxygen on behavioral functioning in elderly persons with intellectual impairment. In S. Gershon & A. Raskin (Eds.), *Aging.* Vol. 2: *Genesis and treatment of psychologic disorders in the elderly.* New York: Raven Press, 1975.

Thompson, L. W., Eisdorfer, C., & Estes, E. H. Cardiovascular disease and behavioral changes in the elderly. In E. Palmore (Ed.), *Normal aging.* Durham, N.C.: Duke University Press, 1970.

Tibbitts, C. Can we invalidate negative stereotypes of aging? *Gerontologist,* 1979, *19,* 10–20.

Tissue, T. Another look at self-rated health among the elderly. *Journal of Gerontology,* 1972, *27,* 91–94.

Tobin, J. D. Normal aging—the inevitability syndrome. In S. H. Zarit (Ed.), *Readings in aging and death: Contemporary perspectives.* New York: Harper & Row, 1977.

Tobin, J. D., & Andres, R. Diabetes and aging. Pub. No. (NIH) 79-1408. *National Institute on Aging Science Writer Seminar Series.* Department of Health, Education and Welfare (U.S. Public Health Service), 1979.

Tobin, S. S. How nursing homes vary. *Gerontologist,* 1974, *14,* 516–519.

Tobin, S. S. Institutionalization of the aged. In N. Datan & N. Lohmann (Eds.), *Transitions of aging.* New York: Academic Press, 1980.

Tomlinson, B. E. Morphological changes and dementia in old age. In W. L. Smith & M. Kinsbourne (Eds.), *Aging and dementia.* Jamaica, N.Y.: Spectrum, 1977.

Treas, J. Family support systems for the aged: Some social and demographic considerations. *Gerontologist,* 1977, *17,* 486–491.

Treas, J., & Van Hilst, A. Marriage and remarriage rates among older Americans. *Gerontologist,* 1976, *16,* 132–136.

Treat, N. J., Poon, L. W., Fozard, J. L., & Popkin, S. J. Toward applying cognitive skill training to memory problems. *Experimental Aging Research,* 1978, *4,* 305–319.

Treat, N. J., & Reese, H. W. Age, pacing, and imagery in paired-associate learning. *Developmental Psychology,* 1976, *12,* 119–124.

Turner, B. F., Tobin, S. S., & Lieberman, M. A. Personality traits as predictors of institutional adaptation among the aged. *Journal of Gerontology,* 1972, *27,* 61–68.

U.S. Commission on Civil Rights. *The Age Discrimination Study: A report of the United States Commission on Civil Rights.* Part II. Washington, D.C.: U.S. Government Printing Office, 1979.

U.S. Congress. Senate Special Committee on Aging, Subcommittee on Long-Term Care. *Nursing home care in the United States: Failure in public policy.* (Series of papers.) Washington, D.C.: U.S. Government Printing Office, 1974–1976.

Vaughan, W. J., Schmitz, P., & Fatt, I. The human lens—a model system for the study of aging. In J. M. Ordy & K. R. Brizzee (Eds.), *Aging*. Vol. 10: *Sensory systems and communication in the elderly*. New York: Raven Press, 1979.

Verwoerdt, A., Pfeiffer, E., & Wang, H. S. Sexual behavior in senescence: II. Patterns of sexual activity and interest. *Geriatrics*, February 1969, pp. 137–154.

Vincente, L., Wiley, J., & Carrington, A. The risk of institutionalization before death. *Gerontologist*, 1979, *19*, 361–367.

Walford, R. L. *The immunologic theory of aging*. Baltimore: Williams and Wilkins, 1969.

Walker, J. I., & Brodie, K. H. Neuropharmacology of aging. In E. W. Busse & D. G. Blazer (Eds.), *Handbook of geriatric psychiatry*. New York: Van Nostrand Reinhold, 1980.

Wang, H. S. Dementia of old age. In W. L. Smith & M. Kinsbourne (Eds.), *Aging and dementia*. Jamaica, N.Y.: Spectrum, 1977.

Wang, H. S., & Busse, E. W. Dementia in old age. In C. E. Wells (Ed.), *Dementia*. Philadelphia: F. A. Davis, 1971.

Wasow, M., & Loeb, M. B. Sexuality in nursing homes. In R. L. Solnick (Ed.), *Sexuality and aging*. Los Angeles: University of Southern California Press, 1978.

Watson, W. H., & Maxwell, R. J. *Human aging and dying*. New York: St. Martin's Press, 1977.

Wechsler, D. *Manual for the Wechsler Adult Intelligence Scale*. New York: Psychological Corporation, 1955.

Wechsler, D. *WAIS-R Manual*. New York: Psychological Corporation, 1981.

Weg, R. B. The physiology of sexuality in aging. In R. L. Solnick (Ed.), *Sexuality and aging*. Los Angeles: University of Southern California Press, 1978.

Weiler, P. G., & Rathbone-McCuan, E. *Adult day care: Community work with the elderly*. New York: Springer, 1978.

Weiner, M. B., Brok, A. J., & Snadowsky, A. M. *Working with the aged: Practical approaches in the institution and community*. Englewood Cliffs, N.J.: Prentice-Hall, 1978.

Weisman, A. D. Denial and middle knowledge. In E. Shneidman (Ed.), *Death: Current perspectives*. Palo Alto, Calif: Mayfield, 1976.

Weisman, A. D., & Worden, J. W. Psychosocial analysis of cancer deaths. *Omega*, 1975, *6*, 61–75.

Welford, A. T. Age and skill: Motor, intellectual and social. In A. T. Welford (Ed.), *Interdisciplinary topics in gerontology (4) Decision making and age*. Basel: Karger, 1969.

Welford, A. T. Motor performance. In J. E. Birren & K. W. Schaie (Eds.), *Handbook of the psychology of aging*, New York: Van Nostrand Reinhold, 1977.

Whitbourne, S. K. Test anxiety in elderly and young adults. *International Journal of Aging and Human Development*, 1976, *7*, 201–210.

Wilkie, F. L., & Eisdorfer, C. Systemic disease and behavioral correlates. In L. F. Jarvik, C. Eisdorfer, & J. E. Blum (Eds.), *Intellectual functioning in adults*. New York: Springer, 1973.

Willington, F. L. Introduction. In F. L. Willington (Ed.), *Incontinence in the elderly*. London: Academic Press, 1976.

Willis, S. L., & Baltes, P. B. Intelligence in adulthood and aging: Contemporary issues. In L. Poon (Ed.), *Aging in the 1980's*. Washington, D.C.: American Psychological Association, 1980.

Withers, W. Some irrational beliefs about retirement in the United States. In A. Monk (Ed.), *The age of aging: A reader in social gerontology*. Buffalo, N.Y.: Prometheus Press, 1979.

Wolpe, J. *The practice of behavior therapy* (2nd ed.). Elmsford, N.Y.: Pergamon Press, 1973.

Woodruff, D. S., & Walsh, D. A. Research in adult learning: The individual. *Gerontologist*, 1975, *15*, 424–430.

Yalom, I. D. *The theory and practice of group psychotherapy* (2nd ed.). New York: Basic Books, 1975.

Yawney, B. A., & Slover, D. L. Relocation of the elderly. In A. Monk (Ed.), *The age of aging: A reader in social gerontology*. Buffalo, N.Y.: Prometheus Press, 1979.

York, J. L., & Calsyn, R. J. Family involvement in nursing homes. *Gerontologist*, 1977, *17*, 500–505.

Zarit, S. H. *Aging and mental disorders: Psychological approaches to assessment and treatment*. New York: Free Press, 1980.

Zarit, S. H., Cole, K. D., & Guider, R. L. Memory training strategies and subjective complaints of memory in the aged. *Gerontologist*, 1981, *21*, 158–164.

Zarit, S. H., Reever, K. E., & Bach-Peterson, J. Relatives of the impaired elderly: Correlates of feelings of burden. *Gerontologist*, 1980, *20*, 649–655.

Zuckerman, H., & Merton, R. K. Age, aging and age structure in science. In M. Riley, M. Johnson, & A. Foner (Eds.), *Aging and society*. Vol. 3: *A sociology of age stratification*. New York: Russell Sage Foundation, 1972.

# Name Index

# Subject Index